Road Biking™
Utah

A Guide to the State's Best Bike Rides

Wayne D. Cottrell

FALCONGUIDES

GUILFORD, CONNECTICUT
HELENA, MONTANA
AN IMPRINT OF GLOBE PEQUOT PRESS

To my wife, Ann; and son, Tyler, who was still too young to ride a bicycle as of publication. To the memory of my mother, Barbara, who, among countless other things, purchased my first bicycle. To the memory of Richard Barnum-Reece, director of many Utah races, who was eager to review a draft of this project. And to the memory of Alan Butler, Bill Corliss, and Terry McGinnis, men who added to the passion and excitement of Utah cycling.

To buy books in quantity for corporate use or incentives, call **(800) 962–0973** or e-mail **premiums@GlobePequot.com**.

FALCONGUIDES®

FalconGuides is an imprint of Globe Pequot Press.
Falcon, FalconGuides, and Outfit Your Mind are registered trademarks and Road Biking is a trademark of Morris Book Publishing, LLC.

Photos by Wayne D. Cottrell unless otherwise indicated.
Maps by Trailhead Graphics Inc. © Morris Book Publishing, LLC
Layout: Kevin Mak
Project editor: John Burbidge

Library of Congress Cataloging-in-Publication Data
Cottrell, Wayne D.
  Road biking Utah : a guide to the state's best bike rides / Wayne Cottrell.
      p. cm. – (FalconGuides)
  Includes bibliographical references and index.
  ISBN 978-0-7627-3962-2
  1. Bicycle touring–Utah–Guidebooks. 2. Cycling–Utah–Guidebooks. 3. Utah–Guidebooks. I.
Title.
  GV1045.5.U8C68 2010
  796.6'409792–dc22
                                        2010002387

Printed in the United States of America
10 9 8 7 6 5 4 3 2 1

Contents

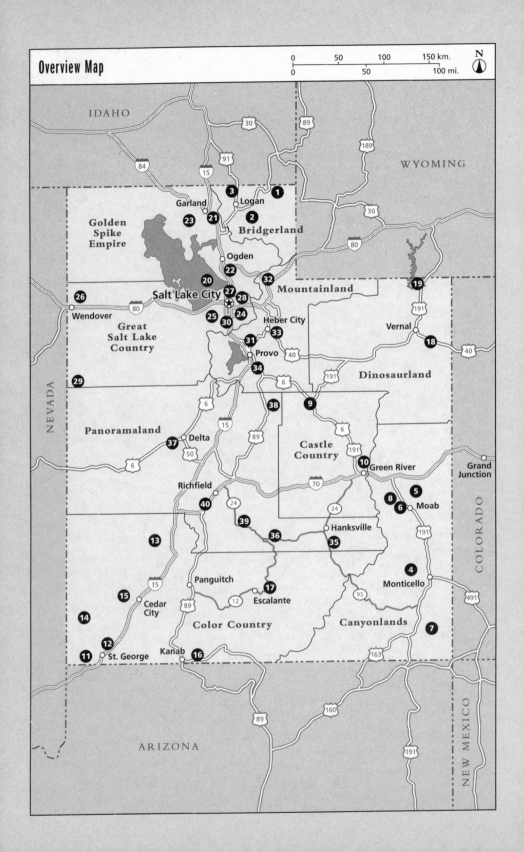

Overview Map

0   50   100   150 km.
0   50   100 mi.

N

IDAHO

WYOMING

30

89

91

84

15

189

3   Logan

1

Garland

23   21   2

Bridgerland

80

Golden
Spike
Empire

Ogden

22

32   Mountainland

19

26   20

Salt Lake City   27   28

191

Wendover   80   25   24   Heber City   Vernal

30   31   33   18

29   34   Provo   40   Dinosaurland   40

6

Great
Salt Lake
Country

6   38   9   191

Panoramaland   15   89   Castle
Country   191

37   Delta   6   191   Green River   Grand
Junction

50   40   10

Richfield   70

8   5

24   6   Moab

40   39   24   191

13   36   Hanksville   95   4   Monticello

35   491

Panguitch   17   7

15   12   Escalante

15   Cedar
City   89   Color Country   Canyonlands   163

14   12

11   St. George   Kanab   16   89   160

NEVADA

COLORADO

NEW MEXICO

ARIZONA

Preface

Utah's "modern era" began in 1847, with the arrival of the first Mormon pioneers from points east. Prior to that year, Utah had been frequented by trappers, fur traders, prospectors, and explorers. Prior to that, and continuing today, Utah was the home of several Native American cultures. Utah, now with a growing population of 2.74 million (2008 estimate), became the forty-fifth state in 1896. Utah's introduction to statehood came after about fifty years of turmoil involving conflicts between Native Americans, members of the Mormon church, and the U.S. government. During that period, the east and west branches of the transcontinental railroad were connected near Promontory Point, forever altering America's transportation system. Also during that period, pioneer settlers, overwhelmingly members of the Mormon church, established communities throughout the state. With the twentieth century came preservation, and the setting aside of Utah's precious nature and scenery in seven national forests, five national parks, six national monuments, two national recreation areas, wilderness areas, wildlife management areas, primitive areas, and other protected regions. The twentieth century also saw Utah's largest cities, along the Wasatch Front, become large and cosmopolitan. Today, it is estimated that over 85 percent of Utah's population lives within 60 miles of Salt Lake City. The twenty-first century introduced Salt Lake City and Utah to the world with the staging of the 2002 Winter Olympic Games. A total of seventy-seven nations—at the time, the most ever in a Winter Olympics—competed in seventy-eight snow and ice events, also the most ever at the time.

Because I lived in the Wasatch Front region for over eleven years, my urban fervor and sheer familiarity had nearly all of the *Road Biking Utah* rides starting and ending near Salt Lake City. But with some reading and exploration, I realized that nearly 200 of Utah's incorporated towns and cities are not in the Wasatch Front, thanks to the enterprising pioneers who dispersed into the Utah territory after arriving in Salt Lake City, under Brigham Young's direction. Most of the cities and towns are small, barely a portion of a percent of Utah's overall population. Some of them are gateways to Utah's major park- and forestlands, such as Escalante, Moab, Torrey, and Vernal. As for the others, unless one has business dealings or a connection to the local heritage, the need to visit is not readily apparent. These communities reveal, however, a wealth of history, festivals, picturesque settings, historic buildings, and even legends, not to mention an abundance of local recreational opportunities. One of the objectives of *Road Biking Utah* is to introduce the arches, basins, canyons, deserts, flats, lakes, mountains, ridges, and rivers of an expansive Utah to a wide cycling audience. *Road Biking Utah* should be informative to anyone, ranging from the native Utah cyclist to an out-of-state visitor eager to do a destination ride.

Road Biking Utah was primarily an individual effort, but I could not have completed the book without the help of my wife, Ann, who endured numerous long scouting trips. She can be credited for a significant proportion of the photos. She also, along with other family members, offered useful encouragement along the way.

Introduction

Road biking Utah? Popular lore might have one believe that Utah is saturated with unpaved trails and slickrock, making the entire state a mecca for mountain biking. All of this is true, but the road biking in Utah is excellent as well. There are thousands of miles of paved roads! Ask any of Utah's road biking prodigies, all of whom groomed their skills on the highways and back roads of this most mountainous state: Marty Jemison (USA Pro road race champion in 1999), Steve Johnson (CEO of USA Cycling), Levi Leipheimer (three-time Tour of California champion; USA Pro road race champion and Tour de France podium finisher in 2007), Jeff Louder (stage winner, Cascade, High Uintas, Redlands, and other classics), and David Zabriskie (only American to win stages in all three of the "grand tours": Giro d'Italia, Vuelta d'Espana, and Tour de France), not to mention the countless age-groupers who have succeeded in national championship races. The Tour of Utah, an annual, high-level professional stage race inaugurated in 2006, confirms it—yes, there is road biking in Utah.

The main objective of *Road Biking Utah* was coverage. I wanted to cover the entire state, despite the fact that about 85 percent of Utah lives within a narrow, 120-mile band stretching from Brigham City on the north to Santaquin on the south. After some serious head-scratching, a ride distribution scheme based on U.S. Geological Survey 30 x 60 minute quadrangles (quads) was developed. These quads conveniently divide Utah—the thirteenth-largest state in the United States—into forty-seven sec-

Riding out of the saddle on the east side of Bear Lake.

1

tors, although not all of them have paved roads. Suitable coverage was achieved by trying to locate at least one ride in each of the quads. The rides include popular recreational routes, other routes that are familiar to Utah's cycling subpopulation, and a few out-of-the-way routes that even Utah's most avid cyclists may not know.

Loops and Canyons

Loops or canyons? Closed circle or out-and-back routes? The ideal ride, according to FalconGuides, is a loop. Utah's mountainous terrain precludes opportunities for loops in many areas, however. This is partially because of Utah's ruggedness, wherein difficult terrain prohibits the construction of through roads. This is also partially because only 0.7 percent of Utah is urbanized; the other 99.3 percent of the state is rural. Paved roads do not necessarily crisscross these areas, given the low demand for roads. Were the book restricted to loops, then many of Utah's dramatic and gorgeous canyons would be excluded from consideration. This would not be acceptable. That said, about 25 percent of the book's rides are loops; the rest are out-and-back routes that typically penetrate a canyon.

Riding in Traffic

A national survey of pedestrian and cyclist attitudes and behaviors was conducted in 2002. One of the findings was that 79 percent of all cyclists primarily use roads, as opposed to sidewalks, bike paths, or trails, for their riding. Part of this is by default: If there were more paths (Class I bike facilities), then the percentage of cyclists sharing roads with motorists would be smaller. Utah does not have an extensive bike path network, but the roads are generally well-kept and suitable for cycling. Most of the rural roads do not have striped shoulders, but are wide enough—and lightly traveled enough—for a rider to feel comfortable near the edge of the pavement. In the urban areas, most of the city streets and highways have shoulders. Nonetheless, *Road Biking Utah* avoids heavily trafficked roads that are not particularly appealing for cycling. Always be alert when riding in traffic, even on lightly trafficked roads. Stay to the right, exercising caution on blind curves and crests. Control your speed on twisting descents, and avoid crossing the centerline. Use hand signals when turning, and wear bright, colorful clothing. Wear an ANSI-approved helmet, and equip your bicycle with lights if you plan to or might be riding at night.

Another finding of the 2002 survey was that the mean distance of travel of the typical bicycle trip was 3.9 miles. Only 7.3 percent of all trips were longer than 10 miles. None of the *Road Biking Utah* rides are shorter than 10 miles, implying that the routes serve a particular class of cyclist. If you are a "short trips" cyclist, then be sure that you are properly conditioned and equipped to complete a *Road Biking Utah* ride. That said, most cyclists find that long trips on a bicycle are quite doable, provided that the bicycle is a proper fit, the saddle is comfortable, and the body is reasonably conditioned. So, if you have never ridden a bicycle more than 10 miles, do not be discouraged by the *Road Biking Utah* ride lengths.

Rules of the Road

Utah did not have a bicycle helmet use law as of this writing, but it does have a "3-foot" rule. That is, a driver is required to leave a 3-foot buffer between his or her vehicle and a bicycle while passing. In Utah, as elsewhere, bicyclists are required to follow the same "rules of the road" as motorists.

How to Use This Guide

Road Biking Utah is divided into nine sections. Each chapter represents a different region of Utah, as defined by the Utah Travel Council. Bridgerland includes Cache and Rich Counties in extreme northern Utah. Among Bridgerland's superlatives are the 1,500-year-old Jardine Juniper (oldest juniper tree in the Rocky Mountains) and Peter Sinks, site of the coldest temperature ever recorded in Utah (-69 degrees F). Canyonlands includes Grand and San Juan Counties in the extreme southeastern corner of Utah. This region boasts five of Utah's most well-known national parks and monuments (Arches, Canyonlands, Hovenweep, Natural Bridges, and Rainbow Canyon), as well as a portion of the most popular Native American park in the United States, Monument Valley. Castle Country covers Carbon and Emery Counties in central Utah. This region is known for its coal mining and for the San Rafael Desert badlands, where outlaws such as Butch Cassidy used to evade capture.

Color Country is a huge region located in southwestern Utah. Beaver, Garfield, Iron, Kane, and Washington Counties are all part of Color Country. Five more of Utah's most popular national parks and monuments are located here: Bryce Canyon, Cedar Breaks, Glen Canyon, Grand Staircase-Escalante, and Zion. Several state parks that are nearly as glorious as their national counterparts are here, too, including Coral Pink Sand Dunes, Kodachrome Basin, and Snow Canyon. Dinosaurland, in the extreme northeastern corner of Utah, includes Daggett, Duchesne, and Uintah Counties. Paleontologist Earl Douglass began combing this region in the early 1900s for prehistoric mammal bones and stumbled upon one of the greatest prehistoric reptile (dinosaur) bone collections ever found. Also, the petroleum deposits in this region are vast and untapped. The Golden Spike Empire occupies northwestern Utah. The transcontinental railroad was completed in this region in 1869, with the driving of the golden spike (more than one was actually driven) to connect eastbound and westbound railroad tracks. This act reduced the transcontinental travel time from six months to six days, forever transforming the United States.

Great Salt Lake Country includes Salt Lake and Tooele Counties. About 40 percent of Utah's population lives in this region. Utah's largest (and capital) city, Salt Lake City, is in this region, as is the state's feature attraction, the Great Salt Lake. This saltwater behemoth is the largest lake west of the Mississippi River, the largest salt lake in the Western Hemisphere, and the fourth-largest terminal lake (no outlet) in the world. Mountainland occupies Summit, Utah, and Wasatch Counties in north-central Utah. The state's highest mountain, King's Peak (13,528 feet), is in this region. Most of the 2002 Winter Olympic Games events were held at venues in this region, including alpine skiing, biathlon, bobsledding, cross-country skiing, freestyle skiing, luge, ski jumping, snowboarding, and tobogganing. Panoramaland, in west-central Utah, covers Juab, Millard, Piute, Sanpete, Sevier, and Wayne Counties. This is a region of contrasts, from the magnificent rock formations of Capitol Reef, to the lofty tri-peak of Mount Nebo, to the spacious and arid Great Basin Desert.

Each region is described in greater detail in the chapters. From two to seven rides are included in each. To find a ride, consult the Utah map located with the table of contents. Rides are grouped into four categories: rambles, cruises, challenges, and classics.

Rambles are the easiest and shortest rides, accessible to almost all cyclists. Rambles range in length from 10 to 35 miles. The shortest rides may have some hills, while the longer rides may be almost entirely flat. These rides should take no more than a few hours to complete.

Cruises are intermediate in difficulty and distance. The distances range from 15 to 50 miles, depending on the amount of climbing. The longest cruises may take the better part of a day to complete, although fit and speedy cyclists will need no more

Well downstream of the Desolation Canyon rapids, the Green River meanders peacefully.

than a few hours. None of the cruises in this book offer an intermediate spot to spend the night, so be prepared to complete these rides in one day.

Challenges are difficult and are intended for cyclists in good condition. All of these include climbing that may be long, steep, or both. The distances range from 30 to 60 miles. While many of the cruises include climbing that some may consider challenging, the challenges penetrate Utah's mountains and higher elevations, where the rider must do some serious climbing. Some of the roads on these routes may be closed during the winter. Challenges will take several hours even for the fittest cyclists. An overnight stay may not be necessary for these rides, since most of them conclude with a downhill return to the finish.

Classics are long and epic, and are suitable for cyclists looking for priceless memories of Utah's most spectacular scenery. The distances range from 60 to 110 miles, and the rides usually include some climbing (although not necessarily as strenuous as the challenges). A cyclist in competitive condition can complete these routes in four to seven hours. Recreational and touring riders may want to split these rides over two days, although overnight accommodations may be rustic (i.e., camping).

Utah's altitude ranges from about 2,200 feet in the far southwestern corner of the state to over 13,000 feet in the Uinta Mountains in northeastern Utah. Except for the St. George environs, most of Utah is at 4,000 feet or higher, making most of the state susceptible to snowfall. Areas higher than 7,000 feet tend to get "accumulating" snow; that is, snow that does not melt until a springtime thaw. Roads that ascend higher than this altitude may be impassable during the winter. Plan ahead and check road conditions, as well as the weather forecast, during the winter season (November 1—March 31). Also, be aware that the temperature drops about 3 degrees F for every 1,000 feet of climbing.

Each ride is provided with three forms of description. Any one, two, or three of these forms can be used to understand a route. The first is a map. Each map shows the route's setting, starting point, road and highway names, turn locations, and distance markers. The second is Miles and Directions. Each M and D section provides a line-by-line list of mileage markers and important points along the ride, such as road names, turns, changes in gradient, traffic controls, railroad crossings, and cattle guards. The third is a written description of the ride. For riders looking for a little more detail than can be provided on a map or list of milepoints, the written description provides a discussion of what the rider can expect to see and experience while bicycling the route. Most rides can probably be understood and completed using just the map and the M and D, but the written descriptions add some color and background information to the routes.

Highway and Street Names

A significant proportion of the *Road Biking Utah* rides use numbered state and U.S. highways. The nomenclature for a state highway is "SR," which stands for "State

Route," followed by the number. Similarly, the nomenclature for a U.S. highway is "US," followed by the number. Neither of these are necessarily what the rider will see on a street sign. For example, many street signs will read STATE HIGHWAY followed by the number, or just HIGHWAY followed by the number. In a few odd cases, a sign will read STATE HIGHWAY with no number. Some old street signs, still in use, will indicate a state highway number that has been discontinued (such as Highway 129 in the Milford Flat area; see Escalante Desert Ramble).

In many rural areas in Utah, and frequently within parks and forests, street signs simply do not exist. As an alternative, destination signs such as TO LAKE or TO CAMP-GROUND are occasionally provided. Where applicable, this type of signing is indicated in the discussion and route log.

Road Biking Utah rides intentionally avoid freeways, although one has a short segment on a freeway shoulder (Emigration Trail Classic), and several rides cross freeways (via grade-separated overpasses or underpasses). Interstate freeway nomenclature is an "I" followed by the system number, such as I-15 or I-80.

Road Surface Conditions and Shoulders

Unless otherwise noted, the riding surface (i.e., pavement) is in good condition. There are three condition categories: good, fair, and poor. Good condition is not necessarily excellent but is generally devoid of potholes, cracks, and other cycling hazards. Fair condition typically means rough, such as a chip seal surface or a road with some cracking or other form of deterioration. Poor condition can mean that the road is strewn with potholes, has gravel encroachment, or is spalling (i.e., the asphalt is wearing away to reveal the underlying aggregate, or rocks). Particularly poor roads have been avoided. It should be noted that road conditions can change over time; for example, a road improvement project can quickly boost a road's condition from fair to good. Similarly, a road surface's condition can deteriorate after a harsh winter with numerous freeze-thaw cycles.

Also, unless otherwise noted, the roads have shoulders that are adequate for cycling. Many of the rural roads do not have striped shoulders but are wide enough to accommodate low volumes of traffic and bicycles. Most state highways have roadside striping, although in some cases the shoulder width varies. *Road Biking Utah* avoids highways with consistently narrow shoulders and heavy traffic. Always stay to the right, wear bright clothing, signal as needed, and keep ears and eyes open to approaching motor vehicles. Be especially alert to vehicles pulling wide trailers. In many cases, the driver is not fully aware of "where" his or her trailer is relative to the shoulder. You, however, should be keenly aware.

Cattle Guards

Eighteen of the forty *Road Biking Utah* rides feature one or more cattle guards. They serve as barriers to livestock, particularly in open ranges. While the guards are generally effective in deterring cattle crossings, they present an uncomfortably bumpy surface to cyclists. The best strategy is to simply ride straight across; the vibrations can be minimized if the tires are aligned with the narrow longitudinal rails on top. If possible, stand on the pedals to reduce saddle pressure. Be particularly cautious in wet conditions, as a guard can become slippery.

How to Use the Maps

Each map shows the given cycling route and starting–ending point against a backdrop of important roads, geographical features, communities, and landmarks. The maps include a limited amount of information, by intention, to emphasize the given route. Selected mile markers, along with the direction of travel, are included on each map. For out-and-back rides, the mile markers generally pertain to the outbound direction of travel. The total length of the ride is listed adjacent the starting–ending point. Each map provides all of the graphical information needed to navigate a *Road Biking Utah* route. Note that the scale of each map may be different. If the rider is in need of more detailed map information, then the list of maps provided after each ride description should be consulted.

Rides at a Glance

(Listed by category and distance)

Rambles

14 miles	City Creek Canyon Ramble, ride 27
17 miles	Bear River Valley Ramble, ride 21
20 miles	Bonneville Salt Flats Ramble, ride 26
20 miles	Coal Country Ramble, ride 9
21 miles	Heber Valley Ramble, ride 33
21 miles	Green River Ramble, ride 10
23 miles	Delta-Sevier River Ramble, ride 37
24 miles	Escalante Valley Ramble, ride 14
24 miles	Ibapah Valley Ramble, ride 29
25 miles	Echo Canyon Ramble, ride 32
27 miles	Jordan River Ramble, ride 30
30 miles	Escalante Desert Ramble, ride 13
33 miles	Colorado River Ramble, ride 6

Cruises

15 miles	Bingham Canyon Cruise, ride 25
26 miles	Hobble Creek Canyon Cruise, ride 34
33 miles	Blacksmith Fork Canyon Cruise, ride 2
37 miles	East Layton Cruise, ride 22
38 miles	Capitol Reef Country Cruise, ride 36
40 miles	Cache Valley North Cruise, ride 3
45 miles	Fremont Indian Country Cruise, ride 40
46 miles	Arches Cruise, ride 5
47 miles	Antelope Island Cruise, ride 20
48 miles	Dinosaur Country Cruise, ride 18
51 miles	Johnson Canyon Cruise, ride 16
51 miles	Islands in the Sky Cruise, ride 8
51 miles	Bear Lake Cruise, ride 1

Challenges

Classics

Map Legend

Limited Access Freeway	══════════⟨80⟩══════════
U.S. Highway / Featured U.S. Highway	═══⟨89⟩═══ / ═══⟨89⟩═══
State Highway / Featured State Highway	───⟨101⟩─── / ───⟨101⟩───
County or Local Road / Featured Road	──CR 2414── / ──CR 2414──
Bike Route / Featured Bike Trail	▪▪▪▪▪▪▪▪▪ / ▪▪▪▪▪▪▪▪▪

Dirt Road/Trail	- - - - -	Visitor Center	❷
Railroad	─┼─┼─┼─	Headquarters	👫
Lake/River/ Major River	⬭	Campground	⛺
River/Creek	∿	Point of Interest/ Structure	▪
Marsh/Swamp	≈	Mountain/Peak	▲
Sand	∴	Parking	🅿
Waterfall	⩘	City/Town	○
Spring	⸱	Bridge	⦵
National Park/Forest/ Monument/WMA	▭	Viewpoint/ Overlook	◪
Other Boundary	─·─·─	Marina	⚙
State Line	──·──··	Airport	✛
Trailhead (Start)	➓	Ski Area	⛷
Mileage Marker	17.1◆──	University/College	🎓
Small Park	⚐	Direction Arrow	→

Bridgerland

B ridgerland combines Cache and Rich Counties in the extreme, upper northern corner of Utah. Idaho is immediately to the north, and Wyoming is immediately to the east. The population of the region was 114,821 in 2008, 98 percent of which lives in Cache County; it is Utah's fourth most populous region. It is named in honor of Jim Bridger, the legendary mountain man, trapper, scout, and guide. Jim Bridger traveled throughout the Rocky Mountains and the surrounding areas between 1820 and 1840, from Colorado to Canada, and is reputed to have been the first white man to see the Great Salt Lake. He never really settled in Bridgerland, but he regularly rendezvoused there with other mountain men, exchanging furs and tall tales. He also traded with the native Shoshone. Today, 83 percent of Bridgerland's population is concentrated in a relatively narrow strip of ten cities along the US 91 highway corridor in Cache County. Logan, the seat of Cache County, is the center of activity. The remainder of the population resides in valley, lakeside, and mountainside towns and settlements scattered about some 2,200 square miles. The most common gateway to Bridgerland from points south is Sardine Canyon, along US 89/US 91. The canyon can close during winter storms.

Bridgerland is set in the northern extremes of the Middle Rocky Mountains Province, a region bound by the Wasatch Range on the west and the Uinta Mountains on the southeast. The province is characterized by dramatic alpine scenery, interspersed with troughs and valleys carved by rivers of ice that formed during glacial eras of the past. Earthquakes along the Wasatch Fault have played a role in sending some of the mountain faces—particularly the Wellsville Mountains, which form a portion of the western border of Bridgerland—shooting toward the heavens with dizzyingly steep inclines. Ancient Lake Bonneville used to occupy Bridgerland's valleys, where most of the region's current population lives today. The lake receded some time ago into the Great Salt Lake, leaving behind Bear Lake, in Rich County, and a still-visible shoreline along the foothills. Cache and Rich Counties are separated by the Bear River Range. Most of this area is in the Wasatch-Cache National Forest. US 89 is the only highway through the range, via Logan Canyon; it is about 45 miles from Logan, the seat of Cache County, to Garden City, gateway to Rich County and Bear Lake. Average temperatures in the Cache Valley range from 15 degrees F to 34 degrees F in December and January to 52 degrees F to 89 degrees F in July and August.

Cache County is home to Utah State University (870 faculty and 23,000 students in 2006), the American West Heritage Center (a living history farm and the Festival of the American West), Hardware Ranch (sleigh rides and herds of elk in the winter), Sherwood Hills Resort (hiking, horseback riding, and golf on the slopes of the Wellsville Mountains), the Daughters of Utah Pioneers Cache Museum, Ellen Eccles Theatre (the annual Utah Festival Opera), a striking Mormon temple and tabernacle (in Logan), and cheese. In fact, Cache County is one of the nation's largest producers of Swiss cheese. The centerpiece of sparsely populated Rich County is Bear Lake, making this area home to beaches, boating, diving, fishing, hiking, snowmobiling (in the winter), waterskiing, and raspberries. One of Bridgerland's great contrasts is the agricultural abundance of Cache County and the relatively infertile Rich County. Hay and raspberries are the only crops that truly thrive in Rich County. The valley floor in Cache County is at 4,525 feet elevation, while Bear Lake is at 5,917 feet. The high altitudes, combined with the northern latitude, keep Bridgerland cooler than the rest of Utah. Outdoor cycling is not a favored activity during the winter, and even late autumn and early spring can be wintry at times. If you are eager to get out on Bridgerland's roads during these times of the year, be sure to check road conditions first, as well as the weather forecast. It may also be prudent to check on air quality, as inversions can occur in Cache County during the winter. (An inversion occurs when air temperature increases with altitude, such that cold air underlies warm air. In industrialized areas, air pollutants can get trapped in such systems for days, particularly when there is little wind, making breathing difficult for those with respiratory problems and for those trying to push the pace on a bicycle.) Three Bridgerland rides are described on the following pages, including two in Cache County and one in Rich County.

1 Bear Lake Cruise

The Bear Lake Cruise is a 51-mile lap of Bear Lake; the preferred direction is clockwise, such that the rider remains on the lake side of the road. The ride uses US 89 and SR 30 on the western side of the lake, and Eastshore Road (in Idaho) and Cisco Road (in Utah) on the eastern side. Contrary to what many maps indicate, all of the roads on the east side of the lake are paved. The lap around the lake is relatively flat, except for a few rolling hills along the northerly stretches of the east side. The elevation ranges from 5,927 feet along North Beach to 6,040 feet adjacent Indian Creek, on the east side of the lake. Pavement is smooth on the west and south sides of the lake, and fair on the north and east sides of the lake.

Start: Garden City Park, 450 South Bear Lake Boulevard, Garden City, 0.5 mile south of the junction between US 89 and SR 30.
Length: 51.1 miles (loop).
Terrain: Mostly flat, with a few rolling hills along the northern half of the east side of the lake. Minimum and maximum elevations: 5,927 to 6,040 feet.
Traffic and hazards: US 89 and SR 30 (west side of the lake): 2,000 vehicles per day in 2005. Eastshore Road and North Cisco and East Cisco Drives (east side of the lake): 100 vehicles per day. Seasonal traffic volumes can be higher along SR 30 between Laketown and Garden City; the short Lakeside Bicycle Path, also referred to as "The Bear Trail," is a parallel alternative to the highway. The rider should use the path during periods of heavy traffic. The path extends from Harbor Village Resort to Ideal Beach Resort, a distance of 4.2 miles.

Getting there: Most drivers will arrive at the lake from the southwest, via US 89. From I-15 north, exit toward Logan via US 89/US 91. Traverse Sardine Canyon to enter the Cache Valley. The highway heads directly into the heart of Logan. After making a right turn at 400 North to continue on US 89, head northeast into Logan Canyon. It is about 40 miles to the lake from here. The Logan Canyon drive ascends to the Bear Lake Summit (elevation 7,800 feet) before making a twisting descent to Bear Lake. The lake is also accessible from the southeast via SR 16 and SR 30, and from the north via US 89 (from Idaho).

The Ride

Bear Lake—the so-called Caribbean of the Rockies—straddles the Utah–Idaho border in the extreme northern corner of Utah. The freshwater lake, shaped like a long, skinny oval, is 112 square miles in area, 22 miles long, and 6 to 8 miles wide. It is not Utah's largest lake (that would be the Great Salt Lake), nor even Utah's largest freshwater lake (that would be Utah Lake), but is arguably the most scenic. The clear turquoise-hued waters are striking, especially in changing lighting conditions. The colors are created by natural limestone and calcium carbonates suspended in the water.

As described by Joseph Rich, an early settler after whom Bear Lake's county is named, "Only men with plenty of hair on 'em are tough enough to stand the climate of Bear Lake, but what a country! Streams full of fish; the most beautiful lake on earth…" As for the climate, do not be dissuaded by Mr. Rich's comment. Granted, it is not a place for year-round water sports, or even outdoor cycling, but there is plenty of bird watching, boating, fishing, sailing, and riding to be had. Pay no heed to reports of the "Bear Lake Monster," an alleged 90-foot creature shaped like a huge brown snake that supposedly inhabits the lake. The locals are, perhaps, just trying to scare cyclists like you away from this pristine region. (Actually, the rumor was started by Joseph Rich himself to draw attention to the area.)

While the lake roads will generally be clear (of snow) year-round, getting to the lake from the southwest, along US 89 through Logan Canyon, may be a challenge during and following winter storms. As for bears, according to history, the region once "swarmed" with grizzly and black bears, hence the name. Before the Endangered Species Act became law in 1973, local sheep ranchers were killing an average of one bear a day. But the Act has failed to repopulate the area with these large mammals, so today bear sightings are as rare as the Bear Lake Monster.

The ride begins at Garden City Park, a small park located on the east side of SR 30, in Garden City, 0.5 mile south of the junction with US 89. Garden City is a small town, but it's the largest town on this ride. The population was 460 in 2008, with summer homes, lake views, beaches, an annual raspberry season, and the popular Raspberry Days Festival (in August). Average daily traffic volumes are about 2,000 on the west side of the lake, and no more than 100(!) on the east side.

Approximately half of the ride is in Idaho, in appropriately named Bear Lake County. North of Garden City, you will pass through the settlements of Lakota (Utah) and Fish Haven (Idaho). There are plenty of lake views, and it can be windy at times. When you reach St. Charles (Idaho, population 128 in 2008), you are at the northern edge of the lake. The Gutzon Borglum (aka Borgholm) Monument (sculptor of the presidential faces at Black Hills, South Dakota) is on the left at mile 11.8. Turn right onto North Beach Road at mile 13.5.

As you ride along the northern edge of the lake, you will notice the dike. The structure is there to divert the Bear River into the lake. (This allows upriver locals to use the lake as a reservoir; unfortunately, the introduction of the new waters has led to the extinction of several of the lake's endemic species.) On your left is the Bear Lake National Wildlife Refuge, followed by Mud Lake; on your right is Idaho North Beach State Park.

The road makes a short climb, then bends right, toward the south. The east side of the lake is very quiet, with no towns, only a few small subdivisions, beaches, and lakeside campsites. This portion of the course features nearly constant scenic views of the lake. At the southern end of the lake, the road bends to the left, away from the lake, preparing for entry into Laketown (population 191 in 2008). Rendezvous Beach, with more than 1 mile of sandy beaches, campgrounds, and picnic spots, is adjacent.

The Mountain Man Rendezvous is held here every September, with cooking, story-telling, and shootin' competitions. Turn right onto SR 30 in Laketown for the return trip to Garden City, on the west side of the lake. Besides the four towns and settlements through which the ride passes, you will observe a "new type" of community as you circumnavigate the lake: private resort developments that capitalize on the lake's vivid scenery and recreational opportunities. Evidence of this is clear in Pickleville, about halfway between Laketown and Garden City on SR 30. (On the plus side, the Pickleville Playhouse features musical-comedy performances during the summer.) Continue north on SR 30 to Garden City. Look for Garden City Park as you near Garden City's "center."

For a post-ride cooldown activity, the Garden City Boardwalk extends from the eastern edge of the park, through a wetland, to the beach. The Bear Lake Road Race, featuring a lap of the lake followed by a short climb into the adjacent foothills (to make the race a little harder), is generally held every May.

Miles and Directions

0.0 From Garden City Park in Garden City, turn right onto SR 30 (Bear Lake Boulevard) and head north.

0.5 At the junction of SR 30 and US 89, continue straight. You're now on US 89.

1.8 Bear Lake Marina, one of three entries to Bear Lake State Park.

4.6 Enter Bear Lake County, Idaho. This is now the Oregon Trail Scenic Byway.

7.0 Enter Fish Haven. Fish Haven General Store is adjacent.

11.8 Enter St. Charles; Gutzon Borglum Monument is on the left. Minnetonka Market is on the right.

13.1 Cross Big St. Charles Creek. Fish ladder is nearby.

13.5 Turn right onto North Beach Road. Bear Cave convenience store is on the corner.

18.4 North Beach, second of three entries to Bear Lake State Park.

19.0 Restrooms on the right.

19.4 Restrooms on the right.

20.4 Short climb, followed by a right turn onto Eastshore Road. Begin rolling terrain.

24.2 East Shore development on the right; the first of a series of east shore subdivisions.

25.4 Road surface changes to chip seal (a bit rougher than asphalt).

25.9 Cattle guard.

28.2 Cattle guard; enter Rich County, Utah. Now on Cisco Road.

31.7 Cisco Beach; restrooms.

37.5 Restrooms on the right.

40.6 Road curves left; veer away from lake—now on the fringes of Laketown.

41.1 Cattle guard.

41.6 Stop; turn right onto SR 30. Mini-mart on the corner.

43.4 Rendezvous Beach, third of three access points to Bear Lake State Park.

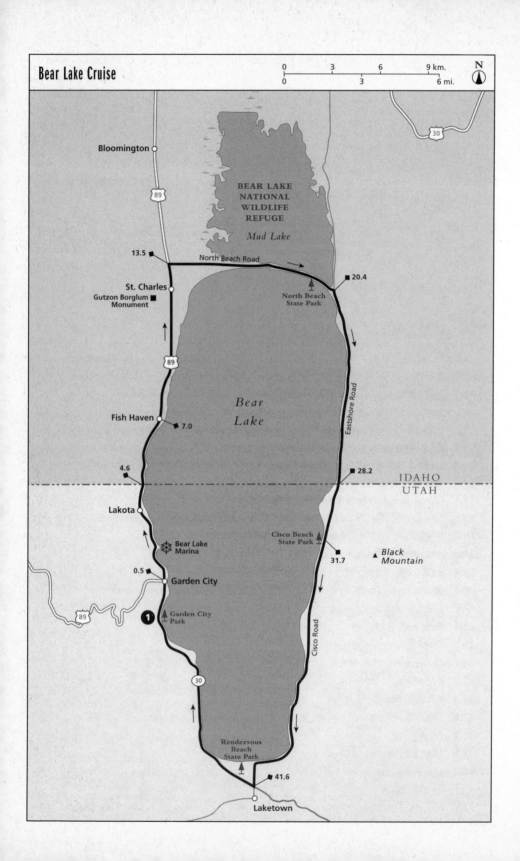

44.4 Rest area on the right; vending machines and restrooms.

48.2 Enter Garden City; now on Bear Lake Boulevard.

48.3 Bike path begins on the right; use path if highway traffic is heavy.

48.8 Pickleville Playhouse is on the left.

51.1 End of ride; turn right to enter Garden City Park.

Local Information

Bear Lake Convention and Visitors Bureau: www.bearlake.org. This Web site has information on the accommodations and restaurants listed below.

Bear Lake Chamber of Commerce: www.bearklakechamber.com.

Town of Garden City official Web site: www.gardencityut.us.

Rich County official Web site: www.richcountyut.org.

Bear Lake State Park Information: www.utah.com/stateparks/bear_lake.htm.

Restaurants

Bear Lake Motor Lodge Restaurant and Motel: 50 South Bear Lake Boulevard (SR 30), Garden City; (435) 946-3271.

Bear Lake West Restaurant: 155 North Highway 89, Fish Haven, Idaho; (208) 945-2222; www.bearlakewest.com/restaurant_info.php.

Harbor Village Inn and Restaurant: Harbor Village Resort, 785 North Bear Lake Boulevard, Garden City; (435) 946-3448 or (800) 324-6840.

LaBeau's Drive-In: 69 North Bear Lake Boulevard, Garden City; (435) 946-8821.

Accommodations

Bear Lake Motor Lodge: 50 South Bear Lake Boulevard (SR 30), Garden City; (435) 946-3271. Has a restaurant.

Blue Water Beach Resort: 2126 South Bear Lake Boulevard (SR 30); (435) 946-3333 or (800) 756-0795. Camping as well.

Canyon Cove Inn: 315 West Logan Highway (US 89), Garden City; (435) 946-3565.

Harbor Village Resort: 785 North Bear Lake Boulevard (US 89); (435) 946-3448 or (800) 324-6840.

Ideal Beach Resort: 2176 South Bear Lake Boulevard (SR 30); (435) 946-8519; http://idealbeach.net.

Bear Lake KOA Campground: 485 North Bear Lake Boulevard, Garden City; (435) 946-3454; www.bearlakecampgrounds.com. Open May through October. (Bicycle rentals available!)

Bear Lake State Park: Several primitive sites and day-use areas located along the east shore of the lake (First Point, Second Point, South Eden, Cisco Beach, Rainbow Cove, and North Eden) and at Rendezvous Beach (178 sites); (435) 946-3343; www.utah.com/stateparks/bear_lake.htm.

Maps

DeLorme: Utah Atlas & Gazetteer: Page 13 B5.

Benchmark: Utah Road & Recreation Atlas: Page 38 B2.

2 Blacksmith Fork Canyon Cruise

The Blacksmith Fork Canyon Cruise is a 32.6-mile out-and-back, gradual ascent and descent of Blacksmith Fork Canyon. The climb is never particularly steep, making this ride a "cruise" rather than a "challenge." Elevations range from 4,558 feet at the Blacksmith Fork River crossing at the mouth of the canyon to 5,587 feet at Hardware Ranch. The canyon is quite scenic as it penetrates the Wasatch-Cache National Forest, especially during the spring when the wildflowers are in bloom.

Start: East Park, Main Street and 700 East, in Hyrum.
Length: 32.6 miles (out-and-back).
Terrain: Gradual uphill, with a few "mini-rollers" to the turnaround, followed by a gradual descent to the finish. Minimum and maximum elevations: 4,558 to 5,587 feet.
Traffic and hazards: SR 101: 2,730 vehicles per day immediately east of SR 165 in 2005; 1,505 vehicles per day along the lower slopes of Blacksmith Fork Canyon; 610 vehicles per day at Hardware Ranch.

Getting there: From US 89/US 91, head east on SR 101, entering Hyrum. Turn right onto 400 West, followed by a left onto Main Street to stay on SR 101. East Park is located just west of the intersection between SR 101 and SR 165, at 700 East. Cache Valley Transit's Cache Valley Commuter South runs between Hyrum and central Logan, via a circuitous route, every forty-five to ninety minutes.

The Ride

Blacksmith Fork Creek originates in the Monte Cristo Mountains, a range with peaks cresting at over 9,000 feet in southeastern Cache County. The creek courses through Blacksmith Fork Canyon in the southeast corner of Cache Valley, eventually draining into the Logan River. The "blacksmith" reference may have been to some blacksmithing equipment that Jedediah Smith and his trapper buddies cached in the canyon, to which they had to return to retrieve. Alternatively, the "blacksmith" may have been Andrew Anderson, a local. The canyon penetrates the Bear River Range, the mountains that form the imposing eastern edge of Cache Valley. Most of the canyon is in the Wasatch-Cache National Forest. The Utah Division of Wildlife Resources has also incorporated the canyon into the Hardware Ranch Wildlife Management Area, thereby preserving the canyon's abundant natural and enhanced resources. One of these is Hardware Ranch, an entertaining and informative center that offers sleigh rides and snowmobile rentals in the winter, and a cafe and displays year-round (and wagon rides when there is no snow). There are also the prospects of viewing elk and their offspring during spring calving season.

Ornithologists appreciate the views of turkey vultures in the summer, bald eagles in the winter, and golden eagles year-round. The trained bird-eye might also notice species such as yellow warblers, warbling vireos, American dippers, hermit thrushes, orange-crowned warblers, black-throated gray warblers, American kestrels, American

There is great riding by the lush riverside greenery in Blacksmith Fork Canyon.
ANN COTTRELL

white pelicans, barn swallows, violet-green swallows, western tanagers, broad-tailed hummingbirds, yellow-rumped warblers, song sparrows, red-breasted nuthatches, fox sparrows, blue grouse, and winter wrens. The canyon is popular and is accessible via a paved road that extends eastward from the city of Hyrum to the terminus at Hardware Ranch. From this point, there are trails that continue for some distance into the backcountry, to connect with other canyons and trails.

The mouth of Blacksmith Fork Canyon is entered from the city of Hyrum, the limits of which actually snake up the canyon for some distance. Hyrum was named for the brother of Joseph Smith, the famous LDS prophet. Hyrum, 8 miles south of Logan, had a population of 7,636 in 2008, fourth-largest in Cache County. The city's primary employer is E.A. Miller, Inc., a meat-packing plant that is one of the largest in the United States. Hyrum grew rapidly during the 1990s but retains a "country town" feel. The city claims the 450-acre Hyrum Reservoir and the coincident Hyrum State Park, and Elite Hall (which has one of the few remaining spring-loaded dance floors—should there not be more of these?). The reservoir is fed by the Little Bear River and is a popular site for water sports, fishing, sunbathing, and camping. The reservoir freezes during the winter, making it a fine spot for ice fishing, skating, and iceboating. City residents have spectacular views of the Wellsville Mountains toward the west and the Bear River Range toward the east. Although nearly every municipality in Utah has a Fourth of July celebration, Hyrum offers Star Spangled Week, with a parade, rodeo, and fireworks.

The entire length of Blacksmith Fork Canyon is traversed as part of the MS 150, an annual cycling event (each June) that raises money for multiple sclerosis research. Turn left onto Main Street (SR 101) upon exiting East Park and start heading east, toward the Bear River Range. Cross 800 East (SR 165) and continue eastward on SR 101. Although this ride is, in general, an ascent followed by a descent, a 6 percent downhill comes at mile 1.1. Notice the cozy enclave of homes to your left as you make the descent. Enter the Hardware Ranch Wildlife Management Area at mile 1.8, then cross the Blacksmith Fork River (also referred to as Blacksmith Fork Creek) at mile 1.9. From this point, the creek parallels the road for the entire length of the canyon. Enter Wasatch-Cache National Forest at mile 2.2. The canyon narrows here as the road starts to wind amidst the steep walls. Towering overhead are stratified rocks from the Devonian era. The Leatham Formation is the topmost layer; Beirdneau sandstone and Hyrum dolomite are among the underlying layers. As you ascend the canyon, rock formations from other, earlier eras become prominent, including Silurian- and Cambrian-era quartzite and dolomite. There are frequent clearings after traveling up the canyon for several miles. These become more frequent as the canyon walls open, providing excellent locales for parks, camping, picnics, and fishing.

The Hyrum City Hydroelectric Power Plant and Hyrum City Park are on the right at mile 8.5. The park is a popular rest stop in the MS 150. Fishing spots begin to appear on the right beyond the park, including a picturesque pond, a wetlands area (where anglers wear tall wading boots), and the ever-present Blacksmith Fork Creek. The road—which is actually a state highway (SR 101)—continues to wind up the canyon. Cross Rock Creek, a Blacksmith Fork tributary, at mile 14.7. The canyon opens up to reveal a meadow. The Monte Cristo Range looms on the horizon. Stay left at the Y in the road at mile 15.8, entering the Hardware Ranch area. Note the historical buildings. The highway and the pavement end at mile 16.3. The Hardware Ranch Visitors Center is on an overlook to the right. Restrooms and information are available inside. There is also an outhouse at the adjacent trailhead. Once you have absorbed the splendor (and taken care of business), turn around here to begin the descent.

Note the savannah on the right. The information display discusses the indigenous elk, including their prehistoric ancestors (who, unlike today's elk, had sharp teeth!). The descent, similar to the ascent, is not steep and will require pedaling. Exit the Hardware Ranch area at mile 16.6; cross Rock Creek at mile 17.9. Blacksmith Fork Creek is on the left; from the vantage point of the descent, the creek's meandering path is quite evident. At certain points, the bends in the creek create postcard scenes. Take time for a long peek at these; also, look for the variety of birdlife (see above list). Note that the creek actually rushes, particularly during the late spring and early summer months. A wetlands area, beckoning anglers, is on the left at mile 22.3.

A.J. Peterson and Hyrum City Parks appear on the right and left at miles 24.0 and 24.1, respectively. Hyrum's hydroelectric power plant is also on the left here. Pioneer Campground is on the left at mile 24.3, and Shenoah Picnic Site is on the left at mile 24.5. The canyon narrows around mile 26.3, once again revealing the steep, craggy formations that you observed while ascending. Leave Wasatch–Cache National Forest at mile 30.4 and cross the Blacksmith Fork River at mile 30.6. Exit the canyon, beginning a short 6 percent climb at mile 31.0. Crest the climb at mile 31.5 and return to "civilization," as the homes of Hyrum start to appear on the left. Cross 800 East (SR 165) at mile 32.4. At 700 East (mile 32.6), turn right to enter East Park and complete the ride.

Miles and Directions

0.0 Start at East Park, Main Street and 700 East in Hyrum. Exit and turn left onto Main Street (SR 101).

0.1 Go straight at the traffic signal at 800 East (SR 165).

1.1 Begin 6 percent descent.

1.7 Descent ends.

1.8 Enter Hardware Ranch Wildlife Management Area.

1.9 Cross Blacksmith Fork River.

2.1 Begin gradual ascent.

2.2 Enter Wasatch-Cache National Forest. Canyon narrows.

7.4 Keep straight at Left Hand Fork access road.

8.0 Shenoah Picnic Site (restrooms) is on the right.

8.2 Pioneer Campground is on the right.

8.5 Hyrum City Park and hydroelectric power plant are on the right.

8.6 A.J. Peterson Park is on the left.

9.0 Canyon opens. Small lake and wetlands area are on the right.

14.7 Rock Creek crossing (tributary of Blacksmith Fork Creek). Large meadow area (both sides).

15.8 Stay left at Y in road. Enter Hardware Ranch area.

16.3 End of SR 101, end of pavement. Turn around here (visitor center on overlook to the right).

16.6 Hardware Ranch buildings. Gradual, winding descent beyond here.

17.9 Rock Creek.

22.3 Wetlands area on the left.

23.5 Small pond (popular fishing spot) on the left.

24.0 A.J. Peterson Park on the right.

24.1 Hyrum City Park (and power plant) on the left (port-a-potties).

24.3 Pioneer Campground on the left.

24.5 Shenoah Picnic Site on the left.

25.1 Left Hand Fork access road on the right (continue descent).

30.4 Leave Wasatch-Cache National Forest.

30.6 Cross Blacksmith Fork River.

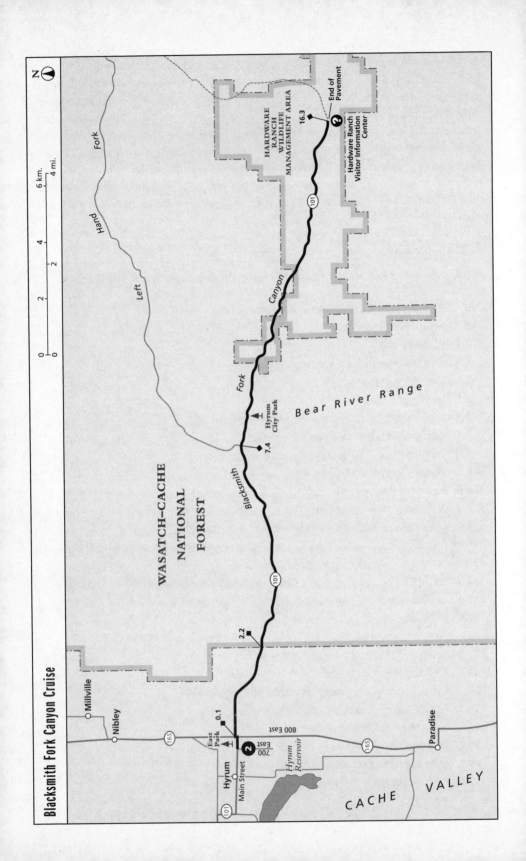

Blacksmith Fork Canyon Cruise

N

6 km.
4 mi.

HARDWARE RANCH WILDLIFE MANAGEMENT AREA

End of Pavement

16.3

Hardware Ranch Visitor Information Center

101

Canyon

Hand Fork

Left Fork

Fork

Hyrum City Park

7.4

Bear River Range

WASATCH–CACHE NATIONAL FOREST

Blacksmith

101

2.2

Millville

Nibley

165

0.1

East Park

2

700 East

800 East

Hyrum

Main Street

Hyrum Reservoir

101

165

Paradise

CACHE VALLEY

31.0 Begin 6 percent climb.

31.5 Crest of climb; now on the fringes of Hyrum (residences on the left).

32.4 Traffic signal at 800 East (SR 165).

32.6 End of ride; turn right to enter East Park.

Local Information

Hardware Ranch Wildlife Management Area information: http://wildlife.utah.gov/hardware ranch/visit.php.

City of Hyrum official Web site: www.hyrumcity .com.

Restaurants

Arctic Circle/Barros Tacos: 110 North 800 East, Hyrum; (435) 245-4966.

Pizza Plus: 70 North 800 East, Hyrum; (435) 245-7587.

Accommodations

Hyrum Lake State Park: Located in Blacksmith Fork Canyon; (435) 735-6168; www.utah .com/stateparks/hyrum_lake.htm.

Maps

DeLorme: Utah Atlas & Gazetteer: Page 12 D3.

Benchmark: Utah Road & Recreation Atlas: Page 37 E9.

Rand McNally: Salt Lake City & Vicinity Including Logan, Ogden, and Provo: Pages 48–49 AW57.

3 Cache Valley North Cruise

The Cache Valley North Cruise is arguably the "perfect" cycling loop because of its format: a ride that uses lightly trafficked roads that pass through small settlements, almost at evenly spaced intervals, with a few changes in terrain but no major climbs. The ride starts in Smithfield and visits Amalga, Newton, Clarkston, Trenton, Lewiston, and Richmond in northern Cache County. The elevation varies from 4,413 feet across Clay Slough, between Amalga and Newton on SR 218, to 4,882 feet south of Clarkston on SR 142. The preferred route direction is clockwise so that most of the turns will be to the right.

Start: Richard V. Hansen Baseball Park, Smithfield, on SR 218 (100 North), near 400 West, 0.7 mile west of US 91.

Length: 40.3 miles (loop).

Terrain: Flat, false flats, and gradual upgrades and descents; one steep descent and one short climb. Minimum and maximum elevations: 4,413 to 4,882 feet.

Traffic and hazards: SR 218: 3,500 vehicles per day in Smithfield and 1,400 vehicles per day in Amalga in 2004. SR 23: 1,500 vehicles per day in Newton. SR 142: 700 vehicles per day in Clarkston and 1,500 vehicles per day in Trenton. SR 61: 3,000 vehicles per day in Lewiston. US 91: 11,500 vehicles per day in Richmond and 13,500 vehicles per day in Smithfield. Cyclists should be especially alert when traveling along US 91 in Smithfield, as this is where the heaviest traffic volumes are found on this route. Watch out for turning vehicles.

Getting there: From Logan, head north on US 91 (Main Street in Logan). Continue for 7 miles, through North Logan and Hyde Park, to Smithfield. Turn left at the traffic signal (100 North) and travel west for 0.7 mile to the Richard V. Hansen Baseball Park. Turn left to enter the parking area. Or take the Cache Valley Commuter North (Cache Valley Transit District) from the transit center at 500 North and Main Street in Logan. There is no fare, and the travel time to Smithfield (alight at 200 West and 100 North) is about twenty minutes.

The Ride

Cache Valley is about 60 miles long and 15 miles wide. Bands of the Northwestern Shoshone occupied the valley before white settlers moved in. During the early nineteenth century, Jim Bridger and other "mountain men" stashed their furs here, regularly returning to rendezvous and check on their "cache." The fertile land makes the Cache Valley one of Utah's most productive agricultural regions. The dairies here are also highly productive, with cheese topping the list of foods. Cycling is popular in Cache County, and you are bound to see other riders on this route. One of my colleagues has referred to Cache County as "cycling mad." The Cache Valley North Cruise takes in some cycling-friendly roads in the northern part of the county. These roads are used annually for cycling events, including the two-day MS 150, a metric century for women (Little Red "Riding" Hood), and a road race, starting in Newton, which periodically serves as the state championship. The Richmond-to-Smithfield portion of the ride traverses the same route as Lotoja (albeit in the opposite direction), an annual 203-mile event that is the longest one-day bicycle race in the United States.

The ride begins in Smithfield (population 9,535 in 2008; Cache County's second-largest city), some 7 miles north of Logan, on the northern fringes of the urbanized area. The city is named in honor of John Glover Smith, the area's first Mormon bishop. Head west from Richard V. Hansen Baseball Park on SR 218. You will pass through Amalga (population 480, named for the Amalgamated Sugar Company, a sugar beet processor) and Newton (population 803; the name is a shortened form of New Town). In Newton, SR 218 becomes SR 23, then SR 142. The latter highway bends right and heads north to Clarkston (population 754, named for Israel Justus Clark, an interpreter of Native American languages who settled here), then right again in Clarkston to head east to Trenton. The Martin Harris Pageant, a musical re-creation of pioneer and Mormon history, is held each August in Clarkston. The town also reenacts the Pony Express each June, although the actual route passed nowhere near here.

After a surprisingly steep descent, and after crossing SR 23, enter Trenton (population 510, named after Trenton, New Jersey—true). Once east of Trenton, get off the highway by turning left to head north on 1600 West. This road will take you into Lewiston (population 2,030, named after William H. Lewis, the local ward's first Mormon bishop), a sprawling city that stretches to the Idaho border. Turn right and head east on SR 61, into the center of Lewiston. Turn right onto Main Street (there are a mini-mart and vending machines on the corner, as well as a park) and head south to 1600 South, where you will turn left to continue heading east. The road bends right, then left, descending to cross the Cub River (allegedly named by Brigham Young; as implied, it is a tributary of the Bear River), then climbing, until eventually intersecting with US 91. Turn right—this is a major highway, but the daily volume of 11,500 vehicles is fairly low for a highway with four lanes. Plus, there is a wide shoulder. Enter Richmond (population 2,364; conflicting accounts on the origin of the name)—note the Pepperidge Farm (yummy!) factory on the right. Richmond is home to Casco (Fat Boy ice cream sandwiches and Casco ice cream bars—you surely deserve one of these if you complete this course) and Sego Milk (evaporated milk). Richmond is also home to a large number of Holstein cows—the annual Black and White Days, held in May, are a celebration of…the cow. Continue through Richmond on US 91; enter Smithfield some 4 miles to the south. Turn right at the signal to return to SR 218. Look for the Richard V. Hansen Baseball Park on the left, less than 1 mile after making the turn. The park is named in honor of Richard Hansen, the longtime coach of the Smithfield Blue Sox, a semipro baseball team that has won several state championships. Parking may be tight at game time.

A cyclist enters Trenton in northern Cache Valley.

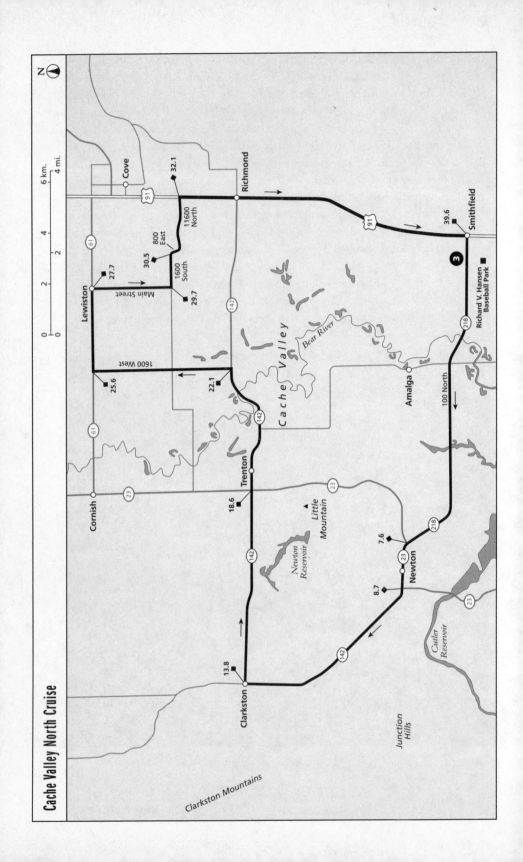

Cache Valley North Cruise

Miles and Directions

0.0 From Richard V. Hansen Baseball Park, 100 North and 500 West in Smithfield, head west (100 North).

2.5 Road bends left; now on 6200 North (still on SR 218).

5.2 Begin upgrade.

6.0 Railroad crossing (one track).

7.0 Crest, after a steep 0.3-mile segment.

7.6 SR 218 ends; now on SR 23 (7100 North).

7.7 Enter Newton; now on Main Street (still on SR 23).

8.1 Bep's Country Market and Newton town park are on the left.

8.7 Now on SR 142.

8.9 Road bends right, now on 8200 West (still on SR 142); begin climb.

10.9 Crest, followed by rolling terrain.

11.7 Road curves right, then descends, then curves right; now on 8600 West (SR 142).

13.3 Enter Clarkston; now on 200 East (SR 142).

13.8 Turn right onto Center Street—still on SR 142.

14.4 Leave Clarkston; now on 10400 North (SR 142).

15.8 Road bends right then left; now on 10200 North (SR 142).

17.5 Begin steep descent.

18.6 At the bottom of the descent, come to intersection with 4800 West (SR 23). Enter Trenton; now on Main Street (SR 142).

18.9 Railroad crossing (two tracks).

19.2 Vending machines on the left.

19.5 Road begins a series of curves to the right and left—enjoy the local odor.

22.1 Turn left onto 1600 West.

22.4 Enter Lewiston.

23.6 Go straight at the stop sign at 1600 South.

25.6 At the stop sign, turn right onto Center Street (SR 61). Mini-mart on the corner.

27.7 Turn right onto Main Street. Theurer's Market, mini-mart, and park are at the intersection.

29.7 At the stop sign, turn left onto 1600 South.

30.5 Road bends right—now on 800 East—then left to cross the Cub River; begin climb.

31.2 Cub River Sports Complex on the left.

32.0 Railroad crossing (one track).

32.1 At the stop sign, turn right onto 900 East (US 91). Four-lane highway with a shoulder.

32.3 Enter Richmond; Pepperidge Farm factory on the right.

33.4 Maverik (mini-mart) and city park on the right. Also Big J Burgers and Taco Maker.

34.5 Leave Richmond.

38.6 Enter Smithfield.

39.6 At the traffic signal, turn right onto 100 North (SR 218). McDonald's and mini-mart near this corner.

40.1 Railroad crossing (two tracks).

40.3 End of ride at 500 West; turn left into Richard V. Hansen Baseball Park.

Local Information

City of Lewiston Web site: www.lewiston-ut
.org.
City of Richmond Web site: http://richmond-
utah.com
City of Smithfield Web site: www.smithfield
city.org.

Restaurants

Callaway's: 54 North Main Street, Smithfield;
(435) 563-9179.
Eddie's: 695 South Main Street, Smithfield;
(435) 563-6565.
L.D.'s Café & Video: 39 West Main Street, Richmond; (435) 258-5135.

Accommodations

Clint's Bed and Breakfast: 165 North State
Street, Richmond; (435) 258-3768.

Maps

DeLorme: Utah Atlas & Gazetteer: Page 12
B3.
Benchmark: Utah Road & Recreation Atlas:
Page 37 C9.
*Rand McNally: Salt Lake City & Vicinity
Including Logan, Ogden, and Provo:* Pages
7–9, 13–17, 22–24; W56 on page 24.

Canyonlands

The Canyonlands encompass Grand and San Juan Counties in extreme southeastern Utah. With just 24,644 people in 2008, in 11,414 square miles, this is Utah's least populated region. The Green and Colorado Rivers border the region on the west; Colorado is directly to the east, and Arizona is to the south. Canyonlands is "a seemingly infinite high desert of rock, with spectacular formations and rugged gorges that have been carved over the centuries by the Colorado and Green Rivers" (Laine and Laine 2004). The landscape is of "sheer-walled majesty and otherworldly desolation that challenges one's capacity for wonder" (Campbell et al 2002). "Intricate mazes of canyons, delicate arches, and massive rock monoliths make this region like no other" (McRae and Jewell 2004). The descriptions are not propaganda—the words are all true. I was awestruck, dumbstruck, and mesmerized on my first visit to Canyonlands, and each trip produces new, startling discoveries. Can the Canyonlands be seen from a road bicycle? Yes and no—on a road bike, the rider is restricted to what can be seen from the roads in this area, which is only marvelous and spectacular. There is much more to be seen from the backways and trails that penetrate the canyons, mesas, and peaks, of course, but paved roads are plentiful. In the words of Edward Abbey, one must walk or even crawl to truly experience the power and energy of the Canyonlands. The routes in this section avoid long roads that have no looping connections, such as those that penetrate the Needles and Maze Districts of Canyonlands National Park, as well as those for which there is no definitive starting point. Road bike rides in these areas would be epic for their distance and scenery. Whatever route you choose, be prepared for the remoteness of these areas; that is, bring plenty of fluids, along with bike repair equipment.

Half of Canyonlands' population lives in the communities of Blanding, Bluff, Castle Valley, Moab, Monticello, and Green River, the latter of which straddles the border between Canyonlands and Castle Country. Moab—the "Heart of the Canyonlands"— is the largest city in the region, with 5,121 residents in 2008. A visit to Moab during the peak summer months (May to September), however, can find over four times that many people within the city. The Navajo Nation sprawls over a large area in the so-called Four Corners region (where Utah, Arizona, Colorado, and New Mexico all meet at a point). The Navajo Nation covers all of San Juan County south of the San Juan River. Bluff and Mexican Hat border the Nation, and the towns of Aneth, Gouldings, and Montezuma Creek are entirely inside Navajo borders. Portions of the Canyonlands are preserved in two national parks (Arches and Canyonlands), a national recreation area (Glen Canyon), three national monuments (Hovenweep,

Natural Bridges, and Rainbow Bridge), a national forest (Manti-La Sal), two primitive areas (Dark Canyon and Grand Gulch), three state parks (Dead Horse Point, Edge of the Cedars, and Goosenecks), a state historical monument (Newspaper Rock), numerous recreation areas (Canyon Rims, Dewey Bridge, Fisher Towers, Sand Flats, and others), and three Native American reservations (Navajo, Uintah and Ouray, and Ute Mountain). Scenic drives are abundant. The five courses in this chapter visit several of these magnificent areas, traveling on some of the scenic roads.

4 Abajo Mountains Challenge

The Abajo Mountains Challenge is a 43.2-mile loop that begins with a long mountain climb and descent and concludes with a series of rolling hills and long, false flats. With the exception of a few city streets in Monticello, the entire ride is on national forest roads and state highways; thus, the pavement is generally smooth. The elevation varies from 5,991 feet near Church Rock, well north of Monticello, to 8,843 feet high in the Abajos—be prepared for some thin air. Also, be aware of the potential for wintry weather between November and March.

Start: Veterans Memorial Park, 100 North and 1st East, Monticello.
Length: 43.2 miles (loop).
Terrain: Mountainous, followed by rolling hills and false flats. Minimum and maximum eleva- tions: 5,991 to 8,843 feet.
Traffic and hazards: SR 211: 365 vehicles per day west of US 191 in 2005. US 191: 3,265 vehicles per day in Monticello.

Getting there: From I-70 and Moab, head south on US 191 to Monticello (about 55 miles south of Moab).

The Ride

The Abajo Mountains tower to 11,362 feet in a cluster located to the west of Monticello in southeastern Utah. Abajo means "below," apparently named by early Spanish explorers who climbed the La Sal Mountains, located to the northeast, and viewed the Abajos from their lofty vantage point. The Abajos are also referred to as the "Blues," or "Blue Mountains," because of their dark, somber appearance from a distance. The Abajos are an exemplary "island" range—that is, a small mountain range, or laccolith, that was most likely formed by small igneous (volcanic) intrusions that lifted and domed overlying layers. The range is contained within the largest unit of the Manti-La Sal National Forest. The Abajos beckon; although the ride is arduous, the scenery and descents are very worthwhile. The town of Monticello, elevation 7,066 feet, is nestled against the eastern slopes of the Abajos. With a population of 2,018 in 2008, Monticello is one of a handful of towns in Utah having an elevation of over 7,000 feet. The average annual snowfall is 60 inches.

Five pioneer Mormon families moved north to Monticello from Bluff in 1887, attracted to the cool climate (great for raising cattle and sheep). Disputes over water rights and grazing lands made the town a hostile place during the early years of Mormon settlement. Stories were that cowboys would ride through town, shooting out windows, in an attempt to scare off the homesteaders. Order eventually came to the town by 1910, the year of its incorporation. Monticello hosts the annual Blue Mountain Bike Chase, a 25-mile cross-country race held in the Abajos. The town also hosts one of the oldest multi-sport events in the United States: the Blue Mountains to Canyonlands Triathlon, a 42-mile point-to-point cross-country ski, road bike, and road run that starts in the Abajos each March.

Start at Veterans Memorial Park in Monticello (100 North, east of Main Street). Turn left onto Main Street (SR 191) and head south. Turn right at 200 South and head west, toward the mountains. The road jogs left then right, becoming Abajo Drive. A steady 6-mile climb, intermittently steep, begins at mile 1.1. Enter Manti-La Sal National Forest at mile 2.6; you are now on North Creek Road (although some sources continue to refer to this as Abajo Drive). Note the change in the treescape around mile 4.0, as you enter an alpine environment. The trees get taller, and the "green" becomes more intense. Dalton Springs and Buckboard Campgrounds appear on the left at miles 5.3 and 6.8, respectively. You may feel the urge to reach out and touch the clouds; keep climbing. The gradient finally eases at mile 7.3. Although the alpine environment is evident, you may still see some barren areas. This is because locations that face toward the north tend to have thicker levels of vegetation than other locations. Monticello Lake and a restroom are on the right at mile 8.2. A view of the surrounding, rugged Canyonlands landscape can be seen starting at mile 9.4.

Stay on the main road, which becomes Hart's Draw Road, at mile 10.5. The descent begins in earnest here. There is a convenient scenic view pullout at mile 12.7; if you want to take time to enjoy the view, it may be wise to pull over here, rather than risking a look-around while descending. The ridge in the foreground is Peters Point. The La Sal Mountains are to the far north, and the San Juan Mountains are to the far east. Beyond the pullout, the road continues on a steep, winding descent. It passes through an open range, so watch for cattle. The road levels at mile 15.0; from here the course features rolling hills and false flats, with moderate climbs and descents. Leave Manti-La Sal National Forest at mile 16.3. Note the gradual change in landscape from alpine to high desert.

Turn right onto SR 211, the Indian Creek Scenic Byway, at mile 19.0. Signs beckon you to turn left, as this byway continues to Newspaper Rock and the Canyonlands National Park's Needles District. This would make for a very long ride, however. An automobile trip to the Needles District is highly recommended.

Head east on SR 211. Watch for weeds encroaching upon the shoulder. The highway heads downhill gradually to mile 21.5, followed by a gradual climb. Note the flood crossing at mile 23.3. Starting at mile 23.8, there are five cattle guards in the next 5 miles. The highway crests at mile 24.4, revealing a grand, sweeping vista of large rocks, mesas, canyons, and mountains on the horizon. SR 211 ends at mile 28.7, at the junction with US 191. As you approach the junction, George Rock is on the right, Sugar Loaf Rock is on the left, and Church Rock is directly ahead. Each of these is a solitary mound or column of Entrada sandstone. The most interesting is Church Rock, which resembles a small church building, and which may have actually been used for church services at one time.

Turn right and head south on US 191 as it passes through a corridor of foothills dotted with green trees and shrubs. The highway climbs gradually, then more steeply,

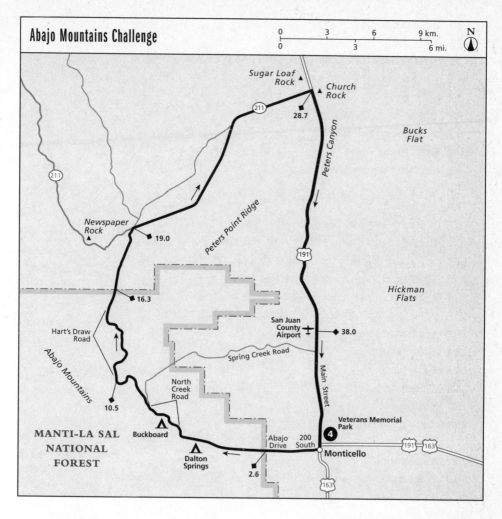

Sugar Loaf Rock ▲

▲ Church Rock

■ 28.7

Peters Canyon

Bucks Flat

211

Newspaper Rock ▲

Peters Point Ridge

■ 19.0

191

Hickman Flats

■ 16.3

Hart's Draw Road

San Juan County Airport ✚

◆ 38.0

Spring Creek Road

Abajo Mountains

North Creek Road

Main Street

■ 10.5

Veterans Memorial Park

MANTI-LA SAL NATIONAL FOREST

Buckboard ⛺

⛺ Dalton Springs

Abajo Drive

200 South

④

191 163

Monticello

■ 2.6

163

from mile 32.4. Roughlock RV Park is on the left at mile 35.4. Once the highway crests, at mile 36.7, the landscape opens up to reveal fertile grazing grounds. After traversing a few rollers and false flats, including a ride past the San Juan County Municipal Airport (the runway parallels the highway), enter Monticello from the north at mile 42.1. You are now on Monticello's Main Street. Turn left at 100 North to return to Veterans Memorial Park and end the ride.

Miles and Directions

0.0 Start at Veterans Memorial Park, 100 North and 1st East, Monticello. Turn left onto Main Street.

0.1 Go straight at the traffic signal at Central Street.

0.2 Turn right onto 200 South.

0.5 Road bends left then right; now on Abajo Drive.

1.1 Begin steady climb.

2.5 Cattle guard.

2.6 Enter Manti-La Sal National Forest; now on North Creek Road.

4.0 Cattle guard.

4.8 Cattle guard.

5.3 Dalton Springs Campground on the left.

5.5 Restrooms on the right.

6.4 Cattle guard.

6.8 Buckboard Campground on the left.

7.3 Grade eases.

7.9 Cattle guard.

8.2 Restrooms and small lake on the right.

10.5 Begin 8 percent descent (stay on main road; now on Hart's Draw Road).

12.7 Scenic view pullout on the right; warning: sharp downhill curves ahead.

15.0 Grade eases; begin rolling hills and false flats.

16.3 Leave Manti-La Sal National Forest; cattle guard.

19.0 At the stop sign, turn right onto SR 211. Begin gradual downhill.

21.5 End downhill; begin gradual climb.

23.3 Flood crossing.

23.8 Cattle guard.

24.4 Crest of climb; begin false flats.

25.1 Cattle guard.

25.4 Cattle guard; Annie's Place is on the left.

26.2 Cattle guard.

28.4 Cattle guard.

28.7 At the stop sign, turn right onto US 191. Note Church Rock at intersection.

32.4 Begin climb.

35.4 Gradient of climb increases.

36.7 Crest of climb; begin rolling hills and false flats.

38.0 San Juan County Municipal Airport is on the right.

42.1 Enter Monticello.

43.2 End of ride; turn left onto 100 North and return to Veterans Memorial Park.

Local Information

Manti-La Sal National Forest, USDA Forest Service: www.fs.fed.us/r4/mantilasal.
City of Monticello: www.monticelloutah.org.

Restaurants

Grandma's Kitchen: 133 East Center Street (US 491), Monticello; (435) 587-3017.

Los Tachos Restaurante: 280 East Center Street (US 491), Monticello; (435) 587-3094.
MD Ranch Cookhouse: 380 South Main Street, Monticello; (435) 587-3299.

Accommodations

Best Western Wayside Inn: 197 East Center Street, Monticello; (435) 587-

2261; www.bestwesternutah.com/hotels/
best_western_wayside_motor_inn.
Monticello Days Inn: 533 North Main Street,
Monticello; (435) 587-2458.
The Monticello Inn (Triangle H Motel): 164
East Center Street; (435) 587-2274.
Mountain View RV Park: 632 North Main
Street, Monticello; (435) 587-2974.
Westerner RV-Trailer Park: 532 South Main
Street, Monticello; (435) 587-2762.
Buckboard Campground: Manti-La Sal
National Forest, Abajo Drive, 6.5 miles
west of Monticello; (435) 587-2041; www
.forestcamping.com/dow/intermtn/mantinfo
.htm#buckboard.
Dalton Springs Campground: Manti-La
Sal National Forest, Abajo Drive, 5 miles

west of Monticello; (435) 587-2041; www
.forestcamping.com/dow/intermtn/mantinfo
.htm#dalton%20springs.
Devil's Canyon Campground: Manti-La Sal
National Forest, US 191, 12 miles south of
Monticello; (435) 587-2041; www.forest
camping.com/dow/intermtn/mantinfo
.htm#devil's%20canyon.

Maps
DeLorme: Utah Atlas & Gazetteer: Page 55
B5.
Benchmark: Utah Road & Recreation Atlas:
Page 79 D6.
Southern Utah, AAA Sectional Series, American
Automobile Association.

5 Arches Cruise

The Arches Cruise is a 46.4-mile out-and-back ride over rolling hills in Arches
National Park, including a couple of out-and-back spurs. The stunning scenery—
exotic enough for an Indiana Jones film (opening sequences in *Indiana Jones and the
Last Crusade*)—makes this a must-do ride. The route opens with a dramatic climb—
and closes with a similarly dramatic descent—on switchbacks. The route is entirely
on National Park Service roads; hence, the pavement is generally smooth. The elevation ranges from 4,097 feet at the Arches National Park Visitor Center to 5,173 feet
approaching Devils Garden.

Start: Arches National Park Visitor Center.
Park here and get on your bicycle. Note that
there is a $10 entrance fee for motor vehicles.
There is a $5 entrance fee for bicycles, so an
alternative is to ride to the park from Moab,
about 5 miles to the south, along US 191.
Start from Swanny City Park (400 North 100
West).
Length: 46.4 miles (out-and-back, including
two out-and-back side roads).

Terrain: Rolling; the ride begins with a steady
climb on switchbacks, followed by a number
of shorter climbs and descents. Minimum and
maximum elevations: 4,097 to 5,173 feet.
Traffic and hazards: There were 780,000
visitors to Arches National Park in 2005. There
is no park shuttle bus, so nearly all of the visitors drive the park roads. Be cognizant of the
steady traffic volumes, especially during peak
seasons. SHARE THE ROAD signs are posted.

Auto-bicycle harmony on the road into Arches National Park.

Getting there: From Moab, drive 5 miles north on US 191 to the Arches National Park entrance, located on the right. The park is 28 miles south of I-70, on US 191.

The Ride

Arches National Park is one of two national parks in Canyonlands and one of six areas in the region administered by the National Park Service (NPS). Arches is the fourth most visited NPS land in Utah, after the canyons "trinity" of Zion, Glen, and Bryce. The layout of the park is extremely thoughtful of the tourist who wants to see the majestic scenery but who is not particularly into hiking, climbing, rappelling, or fording his or her way to a viewpoint. The roads through Arches practically provide drive-through scenery. At only a few selected spots is it necessary to get out of the car—or off the bicycle—and walk to see what's out there. In that sense, bicycling through Arches National Park is *fun.* Among the bonuses of bicycling on NPS lands are the many signs that provide information about what you are seeing. Elevations within the park range from about 4,400 to 5,200 feet.

This region of Utah gets little snow, although temperatures can drop below freezing at night during the winter. Although the park can get crowded during the summer (May through September), SHARE THE ROAD signs are posted to remind drivers of the presence of cyclists. Be particularly aware of carrying enough fluids during the summer, as well as skin protection. Vegetation in the park is scant because of the dry climate (only 10 to 11 inches of precipitation per year). Shrubs and grasslands are common, as well as cottonwood trees along washes. Piñon pines and juniper trees may be seen at higher elevations. Cryptobiotic crusts have formed on top of the soil in some places, enabling the growth of specially adapted plant communities. Wild-life—mostly nocturnal—includes antelope, ground squirrels, bobcats, collared lizards, coyotes, gray foxes, kangaroo rats, mule deer, porcupines, rattlesnakes, and ringtail cats. Sorry—no roadrunners for the coyotes to chase.

Turn right to exit the Arches National Park Visitor Center and begin a 2-mile climb, via switchbacks. At the top of the switchbacks, enjoy the panorama of the La Sal Mountains, which are to the southeast. From here, you may be challenged to keep your eyes on the road, because Arches is a smorgasbord of eye candy. Various counts estimate that there are from 1,500 to 2,000 arches within the compact 116-square-mile park. (Arches are sandstone formations that have been hollowed out through the erosive action of wind and water.) In addition to arches, there are numerous other rock formations, along with varied, tantalizing landscapes. Most of the prominent for-mations have names that incite the imagination. At mile 2.7 (from the park entrance), you enter the eerie landscape of "petrified dunes"—red-hued sandstone, buckled and shifted over an unstable bed of salt after exposure to wind, water, freezing, and thaw-ing. The road is primarily downhill here.

At mile 3.7, you are surrounded by five outstanding rock formations, including The Organ, Courthouse Towers, and, a little farther up, the Tower of Babel on the right; Three Gossips and Sheep Rock are on the left. Continue descending to the crossing of Courthouse Wash, then begin to climb. Petrified dunes are on the right; rock pinnacles and The Great Wall are on the left. Balanced Rock is on the right at mile 9.0. Turn right at mile 9.2 (from the park entrance) to head toward The Windows (there are no street signs within the park). The road continues for 2.5 miles before emptying into the parking area for The Windows. Presuming that you are not planning to dismount, continue through the parking lot, around the loop, and return to the road for the return trip. Although you may not see any "Windows," you will see Ham Rock on the right on the way in, and the Parade of Elephants on the right on the way out. The Garden of Eden and Double Arch are on the right on the way out.

At the main road, turn right and continue toward the interior of the park. You have now covered 14.3 miles. The road descends, getting steeper at mile 15.5. Turn right at mile 17.6 to head toward Delicate Arch. This is Arches' most photographed arch. If you do not dismount and walk the trail at the end of the 2.2-mile road, how-ever, you will not see the arch. On the way to the Delicate Arch parking area, you will pass by Wolfe Ranch, where the Wolfe family lived from 1888 to 1910, attending to their cattle. Just beyond the ranch, on the way to Delicate Arch, is a floodwater crossing.

Return to the main road and turn right to continue into the park. You have now covered 22.3 miles. The road climbs; the arches and rock formations disappear for a while as you pass through a desert scrub landscape. Off to the right is the Fiery Furnace, an intricate maze of deep slots and narrow canyons. Spires appear on the

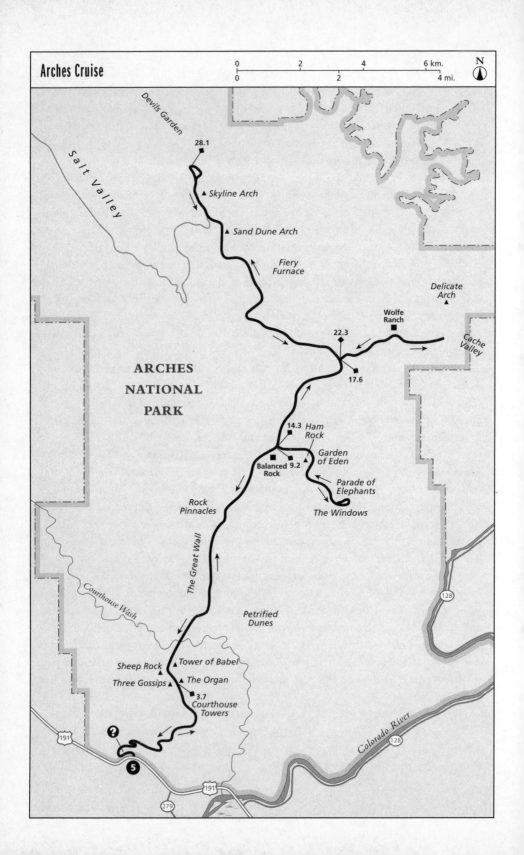

Arches Cruise

Devils Garden

Salt Valley

ARCHES
NATIONAL
PARK

28.1

▲ Skyline Arch

▲ Sand Dune Arch

Fiery
Furnace

Delicate
Arch ▲

Wolfe
Ranch ■

22.3

17.6

Cache
Valley

14.3 Ham
Rock

Garden
of Eden ▲

Balanced 9.2
Rock

Parade of
Elephants

Rock
Pinnacles

The Windows

The Great Wall

Courthouse Wash

Petrified
Dunes

128

Sheep Rock ▲ ▲ Tower of Babel

Three Gossips ▲ ▲ The Organ

3.7
Courthouse
Towers

191

❓

⑤

Colorado River

128

191

279

N

right at mile 25.0; the road crests at mile 26.3. Skyline Arch is on the right at mile 27.2. One-half mile later, you enter Devils Garden, a truly extraterrestrial landscape. If you want to see the staggering collection of arches in this area, you must get off the bicycle and hike. Otherwise, continue through the parking area, around the loop, and return to the main road.

The return trip allows a different perspective on the memorable sights seen on the outbound trip. You will not ride any of the spurs on the return. The return ride begins with a 4-mile descent, from miles 29.9 to 33.9, followed by a 1.6-mile climb. The road is level for 0.8 mile, then there is a 0.7-mile climb to Balanced Rock. From here, descend for 4.3 miles to Courthouse Wash, followed by a 2.7-mile climb to Courthouse Towers on the left, Three Gossips on the right, and the other majestic rock formations aforementioned. Viewing these magnificent structures again is a reminder that some of Arches' most breathtaking scenery is within just 3 miles of the entrance. Just beyond this area, begin to descend, on switchbacks, to the visitor center. Your inspired legs probably will not even feel as if they have just ridden 46.4 miles (especially if you remembered to bring enough fluids).

Miles and Directions

0.0 Start at the Arches National Park Visitor Center. Exit the parking area and turn right. Begin climb. (Alternatively, start at Swanny City Park at 400 North 100 West in Moab. Head west on 400 North; turn right onto 500 West. Stop at Main Street (US 191) and turn left. Head north across the Colorado River—narrow shoulders—and continue northward to Arches National Park.)

1.9 Crest of climb.

3.7 Courthouse Towers on the right. Also nearby, on the right, are The Organ and the Tower of Babel.

4.5 Cross Courthouse Wash and begin climb; note "petrified dunes" on the right.

8.8 Road levels.

9.0 Balanced Rock is on the right.

9.2 Turn right to head toward The Windows. Ham Rock is less than 1 mile in, on the right.

11.7 Enter The Windows parking area; watch for backing vehicles. Continue through the lot and around the loop. You may catch a glimpse of the Parade of Elephants on the right.

14.3 Stop at Arches main road (no street sign); turn right.

15.5 Begin steep descent; panorama of Cache Valley to the right.

17.6 Turn right to head toward Delicate Arch.

18.9 Floodwater crossing.

19.0 Begin gradual climb, followed by a descent.

19.8 Keep right; enter Delicate Arch parking area.

20.0 Exit parking lot and return to Delicate Arch road.

20.9 Floodwater crossing.

21.5 Begin climb.

22.3 Stop at Arches main road; turn right and begin climb.

26.3	Crest of climb.
27.2	Skyline Arch on the right.
27.7	Stay right; enter Devils Garden (one-lane road).
28.1	Enter Devils Garden parking lot; continue through and watch for maneuvering vehicles.
28.3	Exit parking lot.
28.5	End Devils Garden loop; now back on Arches main road for the return trip to the visitor center.
29.9	Begin descent.
33.9	Base of descent; begin climb.
35.5	Crest of climb; road levels.
36.3	Begin climb to Balanced Rock.
37.0	Crest; begin descent. Descent gets steeper after 1.2 miles.
41.3	Cross Courthouse Wash and begin climb.
44.0	Crest of climb; begin winding descent, on switchbacks.
46.4	End of ride; return to visitor center.

Local Information

Arches National Park Web site: www.nps.gov/arch/index.htm.

Restaurants

There are no food or beverage services inside the park. Water can be obtained at the visitor center. Moab restaurants are plentiful; a few follow; more are listed under the Colorado River Ramble.

Banditos Grill: 467 North Main Street, Moab; (435) 259-3894.

Buck's Grill House: 1393 North US 191, 1.5 miles north of Moab; (435) 259-5201; www.bucksgrillhouse.com.

Center Café: 60 North 100 West, Moab; (435) 259-4295; www.centercafemoab.com. Opens at 4:00 p.m.

Eddie McStiff's: 57 South Main Street, Moab; (435) 259-BEER; www.eddiemcstiffs.com.

Accommodations

Best Western Canyonlands Inn: 16 South Main Street, Moab; (435) 259-2300 or 800-649-5191; www.canyonlandsinn.com.

Big Horn Lodge: 550 South Main Street, Moab; (435) 259-6171 or (800) 325-6171; www.moabbighorn.com.

Castle Valley Inn: 424 Amber Lane, Castle Valley, Moab; (435-259-6012 or (888) 466-6012; www.castlevalleyinn.com. Bed-and-breakfast.

Dreamkeeper Inn: 191 South 200 East, Moab; (435) 259-5998 or (888) 230-3247; www.dreamkeeperinn.com. Bed-and-breakfast.

Gonzo Inn: 100 West 200 South, Moab; (435) 259-2515 or (800) 791-4044; www.gonzoinn.com.

Hotel Off Center: 96 East Center Street, Moab; (435) 259-4244.

Devils Garden Campground: There is camping in Arches National Park, at Devils Garden; (435) 435-259-2100 or (877) 444-6777; www.nps.gov/arch/planyourvisit/camping.htm. Additional listings are under the Colorado River Ramble.

Moab Valley RV and Campark: 1773 North US 191, Moab; (435) 259-4469; www.moabvalleyrv.com.

Riverside Oasis: 1861 North US 191, Moab; (435) 259-3424; www.riversideoasis.com.

Bicycle Shops

Chile Pepper: 702 South Main Street, Moab; (435) 259-4688 or (888) 677-4688; www .chilebikes.com.

Moab Cyclery: 391 South Main Street, Moab; (435) 259-7423 or (800) 559-1978; www .moabcyclery.com.

Maps

Arches, Arches National Park, Utah, National Park Service, U.S. Department of the Interior. Distributed at the park's visitor center.
Southern Utah, AAA Sectional Series, American Automobile Association. A detailed map of Arches National Park is included.
DeLorme: Utah Atlas & Gazetteer: Pages 46–47 D4 on page 46.
Benchmark: Utah Road & Recreation Atlas: Pages 70–71 F6 on page 70.

6 Colorado River Ramble

The Colorado River Ramble is a 32.6-mile out-and-back ride on flat terrain. The ride follows the Potash–Lower Colorado River Scenic Byway as it parallels the meandering river northwest of Moab. The elevation ranges from 3,953 feet at the "Potash" turnaround to 4,040 feet along SR 279, just west of US 191.

Start: Parking lot at trailhead off US 191 at mile marker 129, 0.8 mile north of Colorado River crossing.
Length: 32.6 miles (out-and-back).
Terrain: Flat, with a short climb and descent near the US 191/SR 279 junction. Minimum and maximum elevations: 3,953 to 4,040 feet.
Traffic and hazards: US 191: 6,145 vehicles per day between the Colorado River and SR 279 in 2005. SR 279: 345 vehicles per day.

Getting there: From Moab, head north on US 191 about 2 miles to the trailhead (0.8 mile north of the Colorado River crossing). If traveling by bicycle, note that the bridge over the Colorado River has a narrow shoulder.

The Ride

Although the Potash–Lower Colorado River Scenic Byway apparently pays homage to potassium chloride, the real "stars" of this route are the Colorado River and the Native American petroglyphs found on the adjacent cliffs. The Colorado River originates at La Poudre Pass Lake high in the Rocky Mountains in Colorado, near the Continental Divide. The river courses in a southwesterly direction, crossing western Colorado, Utah, Arizona, Nevada, California (along the Arizona border), and Mexico, eventually emptying—if not evaporating—into the Gulf of California. In Utah's Canyonlands region, the Colorado is joined by the Dolores and Green Rivers, two of its many tributaries. The Colorado River's width ranges from 200 to 1,200 feet through the Canyonlands, wide enough to restrict crossings to just three locations: at Hite near the eastern end of Lake Powell, at Dewey northeast of Moab, and on US 191 north of Moab. The river is a critical resource for the entire southwestern United States, providing water for all of the region's major cities, including Los Angeles, Phoenix, and Las Vegas. The river has never been used for major marine navigation, since it does not reach the ocean, but small vessels use it for recreation and other purposes.

Colorado River history reflects an ongoing struggle between preservation and the needs of humankind. The byway, for example, was built in 1962 to provide access to the Cane Creek potash processing plant. (Potash is produced from several chemical compounds involving potassium, including potassium carbonate, potassium chloride, and potassium chlorate. Potash is used to make glass, soap, and fertilizer.) Also, Atlas Corporation operated a uranium mine near the byway from 1956 until 1984. The mining accumulated some thirteen million tons of "tailings" (radioactive waste), stored in a pile about 800 feet from the Colorado River. Concerns over leakage of the waste into the river led to the authorization in 2007 of $23 million from the U.S. government to move the tailings to a more remote location.

The byway's industrial orientation has not otherwise damaged its scenic beauty, however, or the petroglyphs that line the highway. Most archaeologists agree that the petroglyphs—"Indian rock art"—were drawn by the Fremont culture between 600 and 1300 A.D., and the Utes more recently. The "older" art features animals, lines of hand-holding men, and figures with horns, spears and shields. The "newer" art features horsemen and hunting action. The petroglyphs are amazingly accessible: immediately adjacent the highway, with no barricades or hiking involved.

From the starting point at the trailhead, either ride along the bike path, toward the north, or along the shoulder of US 191. In either case, turn left onto SR 279 at mile 0.8. The route follows this highway—also known as the Potash-Lower Colorado River Scenic Byway—for the next 15.5 miles. The trailhead is situated adjacent the staging area for the Uranium Mill Tailings Remedial Action (UMTRA) Project, a $23 million radioactive waste removal effort that should alleviate the leaching of uranium tailings into the Colorado River. The project is scheduled for completion by 2017. Heading west on SR 279, the Colorado River will be on the left, and cliffs will be on your right. There are cliffs on the left, too, along the opposite shore of the river. The river follows a serpentine path along this route, traveling 15.5 miles over a straight-line distance of just 8 miles. The Jaycee Park Recreation Site is on the right at mile 4.8. A petroglyphs segment begins at mile 5.3. Slow down (or stop) to take a look at the ancient and intriguing artwork. Continue along the highway, adjacent the sheer cliffs. These are popular with rock climbers.

Once past Williams Bottom Campground, the highway and river make a sweeping, nearly 180-degree bend to the right. Corona Arch, a natural sandstone arch—similar to those in Arches National Park—can be viewed on the right around mile 10.9. The Gold Bar Recreation Site is also on the right here. The Denver & Rio Grande Railroad appears on the right at mile 11.9. From where did that come? From

Spectacular cliff faces along the Potash-Lower Colorado River Scenic Byway.

a 1.56-mile tunnel that allows the railroad to bypass the circuitous road. The railroad's primary destination is the potash plants at the end of the paved road. The highway negotiates another sweeping, 180-degree bend, this time to the left. Coming out of the turn, the Jug Handle Arch is visible on the right. You should also be able to see the monuments and towers of the rugged canyon country off to the right. Enter the potash industrial area at mile 15.4, as the canyon opens. The pavement ends at mile 16.3; turn around here, in "Potash." Off-roading enthusiasts can continue from here into the Shafer Basin and, with adequate ground clearance and traction, access Canyonlands National Park and Dead Horse Point State Park from their "back sides."

On the return route, the river will be on your right. On the right, on the opposite side of the river, is Jackson Hole (not to be confused with the more famous Jackson Hole adjacent the Grand Tetons in Wyoming). This lesser-known Jackson Hole is an abandoned meander of the Colorado River. Jackson Butte juts upward in the middle of the former river route, creating an interesting landscape. North of the Hole is Amasa Back, a large, finger-shaped mesa that is wrapped by the semicircular path of the Colorado River. Just beyond Jug Handle Arch, begin a 180-degree bend to the right (Amasa Back is prominent on the opposite side of the river). Coming out of the turn, look for the Gold Bar Recreation Site at mile 21.5. Also, note that the Denver & Rio Grande Railroad has disappeared into the cliffs, having retreated into its tunnel. As the highway comes out of the 180-degree curve to the right, sheer cliffs appear on the left. Look for rock climbers while keeping your eyes on the road. The

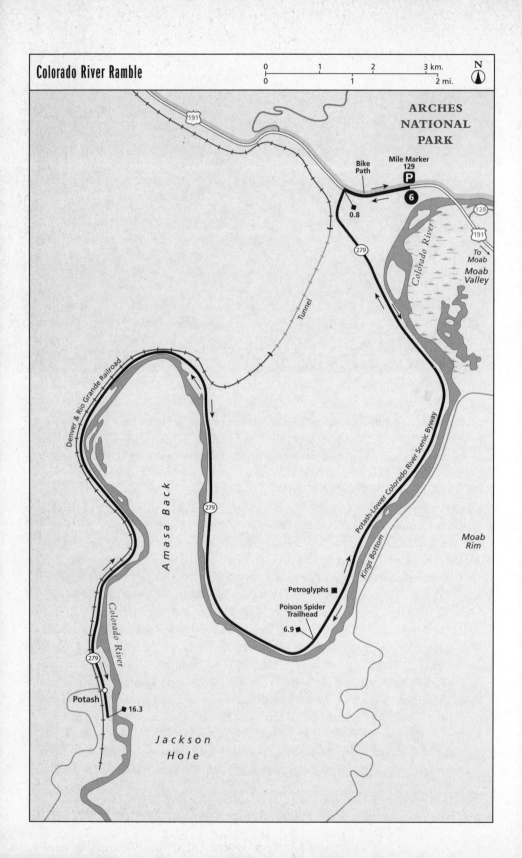

Colorado River Ramble

0   1   2   3 km.
0   1   2 mi.

N

ARCHES
NATIONAL
PARK

Bike
Path

Mile Marker
129

P

0.8

6

128

191

To
Moab

Colorado River

Moab
Valley

279

Tunnel

Denver & Rio Grande Railroad

279

Amasa Back

Potash-Lower Colorado River Scenic Byway

Kings Bottom

Moab
Rim

Petroglyphs

Poison Spider
Trailhead

6.9

Colorado River

279

Potash

16.3

Jackson
Hole

Williams Bottom Campground is on the left at mile 26.2. The petroglyphs segment begins on the left, just beyond the campground. The Jaycee Park Recreation Site, on the left at mile 27.7, marks the end of the segment. Begin a gentle upgrade at mile 30.5, as you near the terminus of SR 279. At mile 31.8, turn right onto US 191; alternatively, cross US 191 and head south on the adjacent bike path. In either case, end the ride at the parking lot adjacent the bike path at mile marker 129 on US 191. Also, in either case, be careful crossing US 191 (high-speed highway).

Miles and Directions

0.0 Start at the parking lot adjacent the trailhead at mile marker 129 along US 191, 0.8 mile north of the Colorado River crossing (about 2 miles north of Moab).

0.8 Turn left onto SR 279.

4.8 Jaycee Park Recreation Site is on the right (restrooms).

5.3 Sheer cliffs, featuring petroglyphs, begin on the right.

6.3 Williams Bottom Campground on the right.

6.9 Poison Spider trailhead (popular mountain bike route).

10.9 Gold Bar Recreation Site is on the right (restrooms).

11.9 Denver & Rio Grande Railroad track on the right.

15.4 Canyon opens; potash plant industrial area.

16.3 Pavement ends; turn around here.

20.5 Denver & Rio Grande Railroad track "disappears."

21.5 Gold Bar Recreation Site is on the left (restrooms).

24.7 Sheer cliffs begin on the left.

26.2 Williams Bottom Campground on the left.

26.8 Petroglyphs segment, on the left.

27.7 Jaycee Park Recreation Site on the left.

30.5 Begin gradual uphill.

31.8 At the stop sign, turn right onto US 191, or head straight across the highway to the adjacent bike path.

32.6 End of ride; return to parking lot adjacent trailhead.

Local Information

Potash-Lower Colorado Scenic Byway information: www.byways.org/explore/byways/2014/.
Colorado Riverway Recreation Area information, U.S. Bureau of Land Management: www.blm.gov/ut/st/en/fo/moab/recreation/recreation_areas/colorado_riverway.html.

Restaurants

Jail House Café: 101 North Main Street, Moab; (435) 259-3900. Breakfast only.
Moab Brewery: 686 South Main Street, Moab; (435) 259-6333; www.themoabbrewery.com.
Moab Diner & Ice Cream Shoppe: 189 South Main Street, Moab; (435) 259-4006; www.moabdiner.com.
Poplar Place Pub and Eatery: 11 East 100 North, Moab; (435) 259-6018.

Accommodations

Lazy Lizard Hostel: 1213 South US 191, Moab; (435) 259-6057; www.lazylizardhostel.com.

Red Rock Lodge and Suites: 51 North 100 West, Moab; (435) 259-5431 or (877) 253-5431; www.red-rocklodge.com.

Red Stone Inn: 535 South Main Street, Moab; (435) 259-3500 or (800) 772-1972; www.moabredstone.com.

Sunflower Hill Bed and Breakfast: 110 South 200 East, Moab; (435) 259-2974 or (800) MOAB-SUN; www.sunflowerhill.com.

Williams Bottom Campground: 5.5 miles west of US 191 on SR 279; (435) 259-2100; www.blm.gov/ut/st/en/fo/moab/recreation/campgrounds/hgihway_279/williams_bottom.html. *(Note that "highway" is deliberately misspelled in the Web address).*

Bicycle Shops

Poison Spider Bicycles: 497 North Main Street, Moab; (435) 259-7882 or (800) 635-1792; www.poisonspiderbicycles.com.

Slickrock Cycles: 427 North Main Street, Moab; (435) 259-1134 or (800) 825-9791.

Maps

DeLorme: Utah Atlas & Gazetteer: Page 46 D4.

Benchmark: Utah Road & Recreation Atlas: Page 70 F6.

7 Hovenweep-Navajo Classic

The Hovenweep–Navajo Classic is an 88.2-mile out-and-back route. The ride's highlights include the once-thriving, peaceful settlement of Bluff, the "loud serenity" of Navajo Nation desert wilderness, and the engineering mystique of Hovenweep. The opening and closing quarters of the route are on smooth roads, false flats, and rolling terrain; the middle half is in rugged terrain on intermittently rough roads that feature short, steep ascents and descents. The elevation ranges from 4,320 feet in Bluff to 5,220 feet at Hovenweep National Monument.

Start: Dirt lot adjacent to Cottonwood RV Park & Cabins, Main Street (US 191) and 400 West, Bluff (site of the annual Utah Navajo Fair, held each August or September).

Length: 88.2 miles (out-and-back).

Terrain: Rolling hills and false flats between Bluff and Aneth. Constant rolling hills, with a few short, steep climbs, between Aneth and Hovenweep National Monument. Minimum and maximum elevations: 4,320 to 5,220 feet.

Traffic and hazards: US 191: 1,900 vehicles per day through Bluff in 2005. SR 162: 1,750 vehicles per day between Bluff and Montezuma Creek in 2005; 2,050 vehicles per day between Montezuma Creek and Aneth in 2005.

Getting there: From Blanding, head south on US 191, 26 miles to Bluff. Enter Bluff from the east; head west to town center, then west of center to the starting point.

The Ride

At 27,000 square miles, the Navajo Nation is the largest Native American reservation in the United States. The nation straddles four states: Arizona, Colorado, New Mexico, and Utah. Within Utah, the Navajo Nation occupies the area south of the San Juan River; east of the small community of Montezuma Creek, the Nation extends north of the river, onto the McCracken Mesa, and eastward to the Hovenweep National Monument. The ancestors of the people who occupy this region migrated from Canada during the fourteenth and fifteenth centuries. They settled here; their descendants include the Navajo and the Apache. The Pueblo and the Hopi also inhabited this and nearby regions. The relatively large area of the Navajo Nation was granted by the United States, in part, to compensate for the "Long Walk." During the winter of 1863–64, U.S. Cavalry troops led by Kit Carson basically killed any Native Americans they saw, forcing a retreat into Canyon de Chelly. Once Carson's troops cornered and captured the natives, they were forced to walk 300 miles to Fort Sumner in New Mexico. Hundreds of Navajo died either along the way or at the reservation after arrival. In an amazing turnabout, Navajo natives were used during World War II in U.S. military transmissions. Their code, derived from their complex native language, could not be deciphered, helping to secure American communications during the war years. Surviving members of the Navajo Code Talkers are periodically honored at tribal functions. Today, the Navajo are the largest tribe in the United States; about half of the country's 175,000 Navajo (some sources say 250,000) live on the reservation.

The Hovenweep National Monument features ancient dwellings that actually predate the arrival of the Navajo ancestry. The Anasazi built numerous masonry structures during the early to mid-1200s, near the end of their 1,300-year stay in the region. Conjecture is that the Anasazi left during a twenty-five-year drought that began in 1274. The monument preserves six villages left behind by the Anasazi. The monument itself consists of separate units to reflect the scattered locations of the villages. Many of the ruins remain unexcavated. Preserved in the villages is a mixture of masonry towers, cliff dwellings, surface dwellings, storehouses, kivas (multiroom religious structures), and rock art. It is thought that the towers may have been used for astronomical observations.

The ride begins in Bluff, one of the oldest towns in southeastern Utah (settled in 1880). Mormon pioneers built a ranching empire that made this town one of the most affluent in the state. The town's name came from a member of the Hole-in-the-Rock Expedition, who was admiring the bluffs along the San Juan River. Although it is set in a popular location, the town has intentionally avoided commercial development. The town, not incorporated, had a population of about 320 in 2004. The town serves as a supply point for residents of the Navajo Nation, as well as an escape spot for tourists looking for a noncommercial destination. A large number of historic

The intriguing Anasazi ruins of Hovenweep await the rider.

structures date from a period of affluence that has long since passed. The town has an artisan community; employment is also provided by the town's services, as well as the area's farming, ranching, and oil exploration. Annual events include the Utah Navajo Fair, held every August or September; the Bear Dance (Ute ceremonial dances), held each Labor Day weekend; the Bluff International Balloon Festival, held each January; and the Bluff Arts Festival, held each November. Pay no mind to stories of Bluff's demise; the town is a favorite of visitors to this area, and the town's new role as an artists' haven has brought about a small rebirth.

Start from the parking lot (dirt) adjacent to the Cottonwood RV Park and Cabins. Signs posted warn against overnight parking, so be sure to complete this ride in one day if you park here. Beware that during special events held in Bluff intermittently through-out the year, parking here may be restricted. A large portion of the 88.2-mile route is in remote desert terrain with few, if any, provisions. So be sure to pack plenty of liquids and food, as well as tools, equipment, or a plan should your bicycle experience mechanical problems. Turn left to head east on US 191 (Main Street in Bluff). For an alternative, opening "promenade," turn left onto 2nd East and head toward the bluffs. Second East is the western boundary of the Bluff Historic District. Turn right onto either Black Locust Avenue or Mulberry Avenue and pedal east. Observe the pioneer houses, many of which stand in evidence of the community's wealth during the "golden" ranching era. A bro-chure titled "Historic Bluff City by Bicycle and on Foot" is available locally. In particular, look for the Bluff library, an old stone structure.

Return to US 191, making a left, then veer right onto SR 162. The route parallels the San Juan River for the next 22.4 miles and passes through a fascinating landscape of eroded sandstone bluffs on your left; the San Juan River on your right, occasionally hidden by groves of low trees; and occasional structures, including St. Christopher's Episcopal Mission about 1 mile outside of Bluff, along the San Juan River. Open areas along this part of the route feature cattle, horses, and oil-drilling derricks (the underlying ground is rich in petroleum deposits). Upon reaching Montezuma Creek, at mile 16.1, a right turn, followed closely by a left turn, keeps you on SR 162. Montezuma Creek (population 507 in 2004; unincorporated) was settled by an ex-communicated Mormon pioneer at the mouth of the same-named creek. Today, the town sits entirely within the Navajo Nation. Continue heading east, through a similar desert-scape.

At mile 23.6, just before entering the town of Aneth (population 598 in 2004; unincorporated), turn left onto CR 2414. The road sign may be hard to see; look for a small blue sign near the junction. Also, look for the HOVENWEEP NATIONAL MONUMENT sign. Get used to these signs; from this point, to the turnaround and back, all of the road signs look like these. The terrain becomes more rugged, with the road punctuated by short, steep climbs and descents. Set a steady pace here—avoid attacking the climbs, since it is likely that yet another climb lurks beyond the next (false) crest. Also, watch out for occasional rough sections along the road.

At mile 32.7, turn left onto CR 2416 (again, look for the small blue sign, as well as the HOVENWEEP sign). At mile 37.2, turn right onto CR 2422. At mile 43.2, stay right to enter Hovenweep National Monument. The visitor center is located just beyond the entrance. From here, it is a short, 1-mile loop that returns to the visitor center for the return route. But—not so fast! Why not stop briefly to experience the Hovenweep mystique? It is a short trail walk from the end of the parking lot (no cycling) to see the Square Tower ruins. These are a must-see. The Square Tower Group is the largest collection of ruins in the monument. It is thought that as many as 500 persons lived here between 1200 and 1300. A nearby spring provided water, and a dam was built to slow the runoff during storms. The architecture, ingenuity of the layout, and dramatic setting must be witnessed.

The return trip can be divided into three phases. The first phase, 19.8 miles in length, is through the rugged desert. At mile 51.0, turn left onto CR 2416. At mile 55.5, turn right onto CR 2414. The second phase begins with the right turn at mile 64.6 onto SR 162. The San Juan River is on the left, with bluffs appearing on your right. The third phase begins at mile 71.5, at the entrance to Montezuma Creek. There is a small mini-mart here, on the left. At mile 72.0, turn right, followed by an immediate left to continue heading west on SR 162. The third phase ends at mile 87.0, where the route turns left onto US 191. From here, it is a 1.2-mile ride through Bluff, from its east side to its west side, and the return to the lot adjacent to Cottonwood RV Park & Cabins.

Hovenweep-Navajo Classic

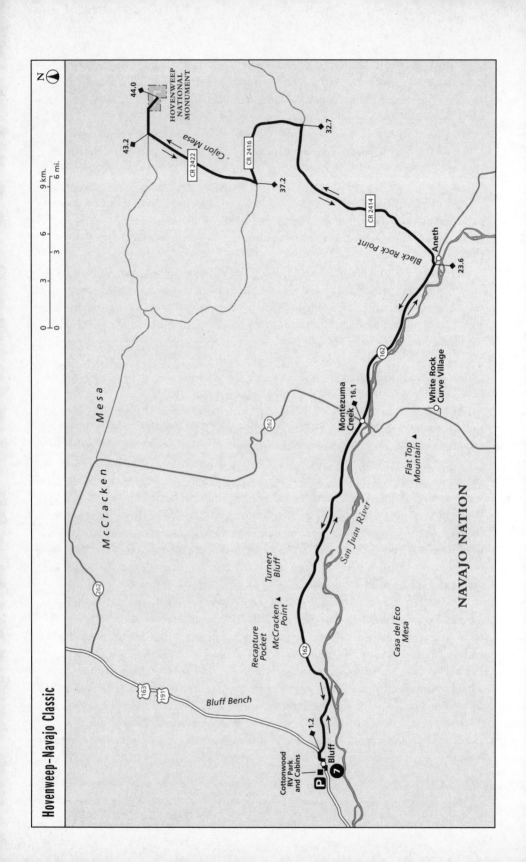

Miles and Directions

0.0 Start at the parking area adjacent Cottonwood RV Park & Cabins; turn left and head east on US 191.

1.2 Turn right onto SR 162. Leave Bluff.

4.4 Cattle guard; begin rolling terrain.

6.8 Cattle guard.

7.0 Cross wash.

9.8 Cattle guard.

11.4 Begin short, 8 percent climb.

14.0 Cattle guard.

16.1 At the stop sign, turn right to continue on SR 162.

16.2 Turn left to continue on SR 162 (eastbound); enter Montezuma Creek.

16.4 Red Mesa Express mini-mart on the right.

16.7 Leave Montezuma Creek; enter region featuring open ranges, oil-drilling derricks, and bluffs.

23.6 Turn left onto CR 2414 (posted on a small blue sign), to Hovenweep National Monument.

23.9 Cross the San Juan River; begin gradual climb.

25.3 Climb gets steeper; occasional steep climbs from here.

32.7 Turn left onto CR 2416 (toward Hovenweep National Monument).

35.1 Cattle guard; begin gradual climb.

37.1 Cattle guard; crest of climb.

37.2 Turn right onto CR 2422 (toward Hovenweep National Monument). Rolling terrain.

39.8 Cattle guard.

42.3 Cattle guard.

43.2 Stay right to enter Hovenweep National Monument.

43.4 Cattle guard; enter Hovenweep.

43.6 Visitor center (restrooms, maps, information).

44.0 Stay right; now on one-way loop that passes a campground and a trail to Holly Ruins.

44.6 Return to visitor center.

44.8 Cattle guard; exit Hovenweep.

45.0 Veer left to continue on CR 2422.

45.9 Cattle guard.

48.4 Cattle guard.

51.0 At the stop sign, turn left onto CR 2416.

51.1 Cattle guard; begin descent.

53.1 Cattle guard; end of descent.

55.5 At the stop sign, turn right onto CR 2414.

64.3 Cross the San Juan River.

64.6 At the stop sign, turn right onto SR 162.

71.5 Enter Montezuma Creek.

71.8 Red Mesa mini-mart on the left.

72.0 At the stop sign, turn right to continue on SR 162.

72.1 Turn left to continue on SR 162 (westbound).

74.2 Cattle guard.

76.8 Begin short, 8 percent descent.

79.4 Cattle guard.

81.2 Cattle guard.

81.4 Cross wash.

83.8 Cattle guard.

87.0 At the stop sign, turn left onto US 191 (Main Street in Bluff).

88.2 End of ride; turn right to reenter dirt lot adjacent Cottonwood RV Park & Cabins.

Local Information

Information on Bluff's lodgings, restaurants, attractions: www.bluffutah.com.

Information on the unincorporated town of Bluff, Utah: www.bluffutah.org.

List of historic structures in San Juan County, including Bluff: www.nationalregister ofhistoricplaces.com/UT/san+juan/state.html.

Hovenweep National Monument information: www.nps.gov/hove/index.htm.

San Juan County information and history: www.southeastutah.org.

Restaurants

Comb Ridge Coffee: 680 South US 191, Bluff; (435) 672-9931; www.combridgecoffee.com.

Cottonwood Steakhouse: US 191, west end of Bluff; (435) 672-2282; www.cottonwoodsteak house.com. Seasonal.

Cow Canyon Trading Post and Restaurant: Junction of US 191 and SR 163, Bluff; (435) 672-2208. Summer only.

Turquoise Restaurant: 3rd East US 191, Bluff; (435) 672-2433.

Twin Rocks Café & Gift Shop: 913 East Navajo Twins Drive, Bluff; (435) 672-2341 or (800) 526-3448; www.twinrockscafe.com.

Accommodations

Decker House Inn (same as Pioneer House Inn): 189 North 3rd Street, Bluff; (435) 672-2304 or (888) 637-2582; www.deckerhouse inn.com. Bed-and-breakfast.

Desert Rose Inn: 701 West Main Street, Bluff; (435) 672-2303 or (888) 475-7673; www .desertroseinn.com.

Kokopelli Inn Motel: 160 East Main Street, Bluff; (435) 672-2322; www.kokoinn.com.

Recapture Lodge, 220 East Main Street, Bluff; (435) 672-2281; www.bluffutah.org/recapture lodge/index.htm.

Cadillac Ranch RV Park: US 191, near the center of Bluff; (435) 672-2262; www.bluff utah.org/cadillacranch.

Cottonwood RV Park & Cabins: Adjacent Main Street and 400 West, Bluff; (435) 672-2287; www.cottonwoodrvpark.us. Open March 15 through November 15.

Sand Island Recreation Area: 3 miles south of Bluff; (435) 587-1504; www.blm.gov/ut/st/ en/fo/monticello/recreation/camping.html.

Maps

DeLorme: Utah Atlas & Gazetteer: Pages 62–63 C4.

Benchmark: Utah Road & Recreation Atlas: Pages 86–87 E6 on page 86.

8 Islands in the Sky Cruise

The Islands in the Sky Cruise is a 51-mile out-and-back ride over undulating terrain between and through Dead Horse Point State Park and Canyonlands National Park. The elevation ranges from 5,639 feet at Upheaval Dome, in Canyonlands National Park, to 6,184 feet on Big Flat, on SR 313 between the Canyonlands and Dead Horse Point Parks. The route is entirely on state highways and national park roads, so the pavement is generally smooth. This is one of the few rides in this book that does not begin anywhere near a city or town. That said, be prepared for this route by bringing any provisions needed—there are only limited facilities along the way. Bring cash, too, to pay park entrance fees.

Start: Dead Horse Point State Park visitor center, located 33 miles from Moab via US 191 and SR 313.
Length: 51.0 miles (out-and-back).
Terrain: Rolling hills and false flats. Minimum and maximum elevations: 5,639 to 6,184 feet.
Traffic and hazards: SR 313: 750 vehicles per day in 2005 near Dead Horse Point State Park. There are seasonal variations in the traffic volumes.

Getting there: From Moab, head north on US 191 11 miles to the junction with SR 313. Head west on SR 313 for 22 miles to the Dead Horse Point State Park visitor center.

The Ride

Canyonlands National Park is a true showcase of Utah's deep canyons, goosenecks, and buttes. The landscapes here are equally harsh, intimidating, intriguing, and alluring. There are five park districts, not all of which are accessible by paved roads. The Island in the Sky and Needles Districts are probably the most accessible to visitors. Relative to Moab, both Island in the Sky and Needles are to the southwest, although access to the former is from the northwest. The Island in the Sky District was selected for a road biking ride, in part, because it is closer to Moab than the Needles District and, in part, because Dead Horse Point State Park is adjacent. Thus, it is possible to integrate two parks into one ride. The Colorado and Green Rivers meet within Canyonlands; the two rivers' powerful actions were the main players in carving out this wonderful landscape. Surprisingly, Canyonlands is "only" Utah's fifth most visited national park. In fact, Canyonlands is not even the most popular national park in the Canyonlands region—that would be Arches. But the numbers are misleading: The scenery here is staggering, and the recreational opportunities are endless. The roads that ply the area are lightly traveled, except during peak summer months, making road biking an attractive activity. The "islands" are actually mesas, or plateaus situated at about 6,000 feet in elevation, overlooking canyons and rivers that are some 2,000 feet below. Dead Horse Point and Canyonlands' Island in the Sky District are both "islands in the sky."

Signs near the entrance to Canyonlands National Park warn that there is no water in the park. This is not entirely true—it is possible to purchase water from a vending machine at the visitor center. But there is no running water; the lavatories, for example, are modern-day outhouses.

The route involves entering and exiting a state park and a national park. Entrance fees are required for both. There is a fee for autos at Dead Horse Point State Park. Pay this, and park your car at the visitor center. Take your receipt with you on the ride as proof of payment, so that you will not have to pay again to reenter the park at the end of the ride. There is a fee for bicycles at Canyonlands National Park. Despite the fees, riding through the world's most stupendous collection of bends, buttes, canyons, cliffs, craters, mesas, and monuments is priceless.

Start at the Dead Horse Point State Park visitor center. Turn left upon exiting the parking lot, and head toward the Dead Horse Point overlook. The road undulates and winds for 1.3 miles before entering the overlook parking area. Notice the cliffs and deep canyons on either side of you. You will not be able to see the overlook unless you dismount and walk to the end of the short path, adjacent the parking area. It is worth a peek—the Colorado River winds its way through the canyon-scape some 2,000 feet below. Legend has it that cowboys used the mesa as a natural "corral" for wild mustangs. The series of flat stones along the road as you near the overlook were one of the techniques for confining the horses to a certain space. The neck here is only 90 feet wide, leaving little opportunity for any horse to escape. The good horses were chosen from the bunch, while the others were left corralled. Horses that went unselected eventually died on the point from thirst (a sad ending; no horses were known to leap into the canyon).

Return to the main park road and head toward the visitor center, taking time once again to view the remarkable cliffs and canyons. Head past the two entrance stations; now you are on SR 313. The terrain throughout the entire ride is rolling, with short climbs, short descents, and false flats. The self-explanatory "The Knoll" appears on your right as you near the junction with the main road into Canyonlands National Park (Grandview Point Road; also referred to as Island in the Sky Road). Turn left here, at mile 9.2, and begin heading south over Big Flat. Enter the park at mile 13.6. The entrance station is at mile 14.8; pay the $5 fee and proceed. The visitor center is on the right, 1.1 miles later. There are lavatories and a vending machine. Continue into the park. While you may have been unimpressed thus far with the scenery, you cross The Neck at mile 16.6, just 0.7 mile beyond the visitor center, and your perception changes.

As you cross The Neck, look left to see Shafer Canyon, which plunges deeply (and steeply) to the Colorado River below. The elevation here is 5,800 feet. Do not fail to look right, as well, for views of multiple springs and canyons. The road begins to wind and roll across the fanciful landscape. At mile 22.1, turn right to head toward Upheaval Dome. On the right is Aztec Butte, a masterpiece of slickrock. About 2

Painted sandstone bluffs captivate a cyclist in Canyonlands National Park.

miles into this road, you will be surrounded by some mighty nature: cliffs on the right, and uplifts and monuments of Holman Spring Canyon on the left. Whale Rock is on the right at mile 26.0. Enter the parking area for Upheaval Dome at mile 26.8. The Dome is directly in front of you—or, more precisely, looming above you. At this point, you can circle through the lot and return to Upheaval Dome Road. Or— better yet—dismount and hike out on Crater View Trail to at least see what's inside the dome. Geologists have surmised that Upheaval Dome is actually a crater that was formed by the impact of a meteor. The crater is 3 miles across and about 1,200 feet deep.

Return to Upheaval Dome Road for the trip back to the entrance of Canyon-lands National Park. The left turn onto Grandview Point Road comes at mile 31.7. Enjoy the winding, gentle descent near The Neck. The visitor center appears on the left at mile 37.9, and the entrance station is at mile 39.0. From here, it is 5.6 miles back to the intersection with SR 313. Turn right here and return to Dead Horse Point State Park. You will arrive at an entrance station at mile 49.0. There are two entrance stations; signs indicate where you should stop to confirm payment of entry fee. The second entrance station is at mile 51.0; turn left to enter the visitor center parking lot immediately past this point.

Miles and Directions

0.0 Start at the Dead Horse Point State Park visitor center. Turn left onto main park road, heading toward Dead Horse Point. Terrain is rolling.

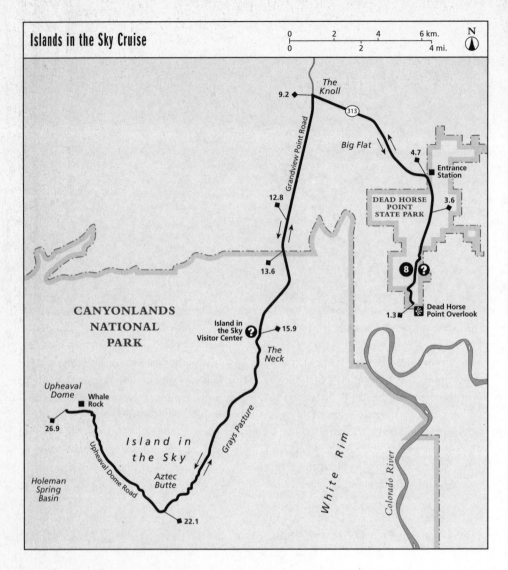

0 2 4 6 km.

0 2 4 mi.

N

The Knoll
9.2

313

Big Flat
4.7

Entrance Station

12.8

DEAD HORSE POINT STATE PARK
3.6

Grandview Point Road

13.6

8 ?

CANYONLANDS NATIONAL PARK

Island in the Sky Visitor Center ? 15.9

The Neck

Dead Horse Point Overlook
1.3

Upheaval Dome Whale Rock

26.9

Island in the Sky

Grays Pasture

White Rim

Colorado River

Holeman Spring Basin

Upheaval Dome Road

Aztec Butte

22.1

1.3 Enter loop and parking area for Dead Horse Point overlook.

1.4 . Exit loop and return to main park road.

2.7 Visitor center on the right.

2.8 Entrance station; no need to stop if the signal is green.

3.6 Enter Grand County.

4.7 Stop at entrance station; proceed (no exit fee required)—now on SR 313.

5.0 Cattle guard.

9.2 Stop at T intersection with Grandview Point Road; turn left (toward Canyonlands National Park).

12.8 Enter San Juan County.

13.6 Enter Canyonlands National Park.

14.8 Stop at entrance station; pay $5 fee (per bicycle).

15.9 Visitor center on the right (lavatories, vending machine, and information).

16.6 The Neck (elevation 5,800 feet); begin climb.

17.7 Crest of climb; begin false flats and rolling terrain.

22.1 Turn right onto Upheaval Dome Road and head toward Upheaval Dome.

22.3 Aztec Butte on the right.

26.0 Whale Rock on the right.

26.8 Stay right; enter parking area for Upheaval Dome.

27.0 Exit loop and return to Upheaval Dome Road.

30.8 Aztec Butte is now on the left.

31.7 Stop at main park road (Grandview Point Road); turn left.

37.9 Visitor center is on the left.

39.0 Stop at entrance station; proceed (no exit fee required).

41.0 Enter Grand County.

44.6 Turn right onto SR 313 (toward Dead Horse Point State Park).

48.7 Cattle guard; enter Dead Horse Point State Park.

49.0 Stop at entrance station; confirm payment of entrance fee either here or at second entrance station.

50.2 Enter San Juan County.

51.0 Stop at entrance station; confirm entry fee payment. End of ride; turn left and enter parking lot.

Local Information

Canyonlands National Park Web site: www.nps.gov/cany/index.htm.

Dead Horse Point State Park information: www.utah.com/stateparks/dead_horse.htm.

Restaurant

Bar M Chuckwagon Supper: 541 South Mulberry Lane, Moab; (435) 259-BARM or (800) 214-2085; www.barmchuckwagon.com. Cowboy supper and live western show, located 7 miles north of Moab.

Accommodations

The nearest hotels and motels are in Moab, 33 miles from Dead Horse Point State Park (see Arches Cruise and Colorado River Ramble). Camping is available in the park; (435) 259-2614; www.utah.com/stateparks/dead_horse.htm.

Maps

Canyonlands, Canyonlands National Park, Utah, National Park Service, U.S. Department of the Interior. Distributed at the park visitor centers. Southern Utah, AAA Sectional Series, American Automobile Association. A detailed map of Canyonlands National Park is included.

DeLorme: Utah Atlas & Gazetteer: Page 46 E3.

Benchmark: Utah Road & Recreation Atlas: Page 70 H5.

Castle Country

Castle Country is just east of the geographic center of Utah and includes Carbon and Emery Counties. The 2008 population of 30,059 was spread over 5,915 square miles, although settlement is limited, roughly, to the legs of a triangle bound by the Book Cliffs and US 191 on the east, I-70 on the south, and the Wasatch Plateau and SR 10 on the west. Castle Country was so named because of the numerous rock formations that the early settlers thought resembled castles. At the apex of the triangle is Price, the seat of Carbon County and the largest city in Castle Country (population 8,039 in 2008). Along the western side of the triangle are a string of communities, all in Emery County, including Huntington, Castle Dale (seat), Orangeville, Clawson, Ferron, and Emery. Other than a few additional communities near Price (Helper, Spring Glen, Carbonville, Wellington, Sunnyside), Scofield in northwestern Carbon, and Green River along I-70, Castle Country is sparsely settled. The center of the triangle is dominated by the San Rafael Swell, an anticlinal uplift of colorful layers, towers, crags, buttes, and deep canyons. The Swell, about 80 miles long and 30 miles wide, is wild and remote—barely accessible by motor vehicle and as yet undesignated by the Bureau of Land Management. At one time, the Swell served as a hideout for outlaws. All the communities in Castle Country were founded by Mormon pioneers, the first probably being Castle Dale in 1877. Many towns developed around coal mining. The discovery of coal brought the railroad into Castle Country, along with a diverse populace. Coal mining continues to be a major industry in many locations.

Mormon pioneers were not the first to settle in Castle Country, though. Nine Mile Canyon, located to the northeast of Price (and actually much longer than 9 miles), offers a stunning display of the Fremont culture's history. The Fremonts were a Native American tribe that inhabited the area (and other parts of Utah) about 900 years ago. Hundreds of petroglyphs are etched into the cliffs and boulders along the canyon. It remains a mystery as to what happened to the Fremonts after they left Utah around 1250, or why they left. Before the Fremont era—long, long before—dinosaurs occupied Castle Country. The Cleveland-Lloyd Dinosaur Quarry, located 30 miles south of Price, features an astounding display of the dinosaurs that roamed here about 147 million years ago. More than 12,000 bones from fourteen different species of dinosaur have come from the site.

Castle Country has not captured as much of the recreational market as other areas in Utah. Mountain biking has been gaining popularity, as riders have started to discover (and even create) some excellent trails. Annual mountain biking events are now held in the Book Cliffs, as well as the San Rafael Swell. A triathlon is held annually near Scofield. Other than these events, the roads in Castle Country are lightly used by cyclists, waiting to be discovered.

9 Coal Country Ramble

The Coal Country Ramble is a 19.6-mile loop with moderate elevation changes. The route makes a "skinny" loop between Price, the Carbon County seat, and Helper, *True West* magazine's top western town in 2006. The preferred direction is counterclockwise, such that all turns on and off of busy US 6/US 191 are to the right. The ride features a mixture of state highways and city streets; the road surface is generally good, although the city streets present a few rough sections. The elevation ranges from 5,500 feet on SR 10 in Price to 5,960 feet in western Helper.

Start: Carbon County Ballpark, adjacent the Carbon County Fairgrounds.
Length: 19.6 miles (loop).
Terrain: Rolling hills. Minimum and maximum elevations: 5,500 to 5,960 feet.
Traffic and hazards: SR 139: 1,600 vehicles per day in 2005. SR 157: 2,100 vehicles per day between SR 139 and SR 244. SR 244: 2,500 vehicles per day in "downtown" Helper. US 6/US 191: 11,900 vehicles per day between Helper and Price. The segment of US 6/US 191 that this route uses has a speed limit of 65 mph. There is a wide shoulder, however, and the highway has four lanes. The shoulder does not have a rumble strip and is safe for bicycling.

Getting there: Price is about 120 miles southeast of Salt Lake City via I-15 to Spanish Fork, then US 6 over Soldier Summit, through Castle Gate and into Carbon County. Once in Price, head west on 100 North. Pass under US 6/US 191 and continue westward, now on Westwood Boulevard. Turn left onto Fairgrounds Road. The road curves to the left at the crest of the climb. Carbon County Ballpark is on the right, 0.3 mile downstream of the turn.

The Ride

Price, established as a Mormon community in 1879, transformed rapidly in 1883 with the discovery of coal nearby and the completion of the railroad through town. A wave of foreign immigrants came into the area and established roots. Communities along the "coal" corridor, including Helper, Kenilworth, Spring Glen, and Carbonville, sprouted as the mining intensified. Coal mining remains the area's primary industry; uranium and natural gas are also key to the aptly named Carbon County economy. Resistance to the area's diversity came to a head in the 1920s, when a local chapter of the Ku Klux Klan was regularly burning crosses on a hillside in Spring Glen, to the north of Price. Eventually the Klan lost its fire, and today a Slovenian cemetery is on the site. The College of Eastern Utah—the only Utah higher education institution located outside of the I-15 and US 89 corridors—was established in 1937 in Price. An excellent prehistoric museum, with a superb collection of dinosaur and mammoth skeletons, is associated with the college. The legacy of Price and Carbon County's diversity is evident today; the county has more religious and political persuasions than any other in Utah.

Start at the Carbon County Ballpark, adjacent the Carbon County Fairgrounds in so-called West Price. Exit the ballpark's parking area and turn right onto Fairgrounds Road. The road descends through a residential area. At the bottom of the hill, turn left onto 1250 South. The road intersects with SR10 (Carbon Avenue) just 1 block later; turn left here and head north. After passing a mini-mart on the right and a convenience store on the left, the highway passes under US 6/US 191. Once you emerge from the underpass, welcome to Price. Price is the Carbon County seat, at an elevation of 5,566 feet, and is the largest city between the Provo–Orem area and Grand Junction, Colorado. The city was named after William Price, a Mormon bishop who explored the area during the late 1860s. As you near Price's downtown, take a look at the Price Main Post Office at 95 South Carbon Avenue, and Price Tavern-Braffet Block at 100 South. Both of these buildings/complexes are on the National Register of Historic Places (NRHP).

After slowing for traffic signals at Main Street and 100 North, continue north of downtown into another of Price's neighborhoods. Observe the Notre Dame de Lourdes Catholic Church at 200 North Carbon Avenue, as well as the Moynier House at 284 North Carbon Avenue. Both of these structures are on the NRHP. Turn left onto 400 North at the T intersection and leave Price. The road curves to the right, becoming Wood Hill Road. After 1.4 miles of rural riding, turn right onto 750 West. Head north and enter the small community of Carbonville. Although there is history galore along this course, Carbonville was settled relatively recently, and is not part of the local folklore. The route winds through Carbonville on its narrow residential streets, eventually emerging onto Mountain States Road. Follow this road to its T intersection with 1500 West. Turn left here, cross the two railroad tracks, and turn right onto Carbonville Road. About twenty trains per day cross at this location—serving the busy mining industry—so there may be a delay here.

Head north on Carbonville Road to the junction with US 6/US 191 and turn right. This is the main highway through Carbon County; ending up on this road is somewhat inevitable. Stay to the right and take the next exit, SR 139 (Spring Glen Road). Spring Glen was settled in 1880 as one of several "spoke" towns radiating from Helper, which was a center of activity at the time. Spring Glen ultimately became a community of Eastern European immigrants, including Slavs and Slovenians, who established deep roots here. The route uses Spring Glen Road, bypassing the history-laden, parallel Main Street. But you may wish to hang a right at 3550 North, followed by a quick left onto Main Street to take the parallel "history" route. Turn left at Kenilworth Road (SR 157) to return to SR 139. Beware of railroad crossings at both ends of the "detour." The detour adds no more than about 0.25 mile to the trip. Along Main Street, check out Martin Millarich Hall (also known as Slovenian National House) and the Topolovec Farmstead Building, both of which are on the

Helper's nationally registered central district is steeped in history.
ANN COTTRELL

NRHP. Whether you take the detour or not, plenty of history lies ahead, including the Clerico Commercial Building at 4985 North Spring Glen Road. At mile 9.7, the route enters the chock-full-of-history city of Helper (population 1,876 in 2008). While several of Helper's "spoke" towns have become all but ghost towns, Helper itself has remained vital. The city has been able to capitalize on its mining history and is now an emerging tourist spot, in addition to being quite scenic. Note the dramatic, mountainous backdrop of the Book Cliffs as you travel north on Main Street. The city was named for the "helper" locomotives that were used to power trains through the surrounding steep terrain. Helper was quite busy during the heydays of mining: Miners would descend from the canyons and spoke towns on the weekends to dance, swim, watch movies, drink, and carouse. The annual Helper Music and Arts Festival, held in August, has partially transformed the city into an artists' community. Some of the buildings along Main Street are empty, but artists have been discovering them, converting several into lofts.

The route enters Helper at the southern end of Main Street, on SR 244. The entire stretch of Main Street, from Locust Street on the south to Janet Street on the north, is on the NRHP. Two primary attractions worth stops are the Western Mining and Railroad Museum at 296 South Main Street and the Helper Main Post Office at 45 South Main Street. Continue along Main Street to the north end of the Helper Commercial District, where the road bends left. Cross over the Price River and then cross under US 6/US 191. A Shell station and mini-mart are on the corner, just beyond the underpass. At the stop sign, turn left onto Bryner Street. Turn left onto Canyon Street; the road bends right to become Vernal Street, then left to become Hill Street, all while passing through a Helper residential area. After another bend to the right, Hill Street descends to intersect with US 6/US 191. There is an awesome view of the Price River Valley to the left. Turn right onto US 6/US 191. The next 6.0 miles are along the (wide) shoulder of this high-speed (65 mph) highway. The wide shoulder provides a safe path for bicycles; be cognizant of traffic turning right off the highway (although there are few opportunities for right turns). Take exit 240 as you near Price. Turn right at the end of the off-ramp and head west on Westwood Boulevard. The road climbs gradually to the stop sign at Fairgrounds Road. Turn left here and climb toward the Carbon County Fairgrounds. At the crest, Fairgrounds Road bears left. Follow the bend. Carbon County Ballpark is on the right, 0.3 mile after making the turn.

Miles and Directions

0.0 Start at Carbon County Ballpark on Fairgrounds Road, adjacent Carbon County Fairgrounds (393 South Fairgrounds Road). Turn right and head southeast on Fairgrounds Road.

1.3 Turn left onto 1250 South.

1.4 At the stop sign, turn left onto SR 10 (Carbon Avenue).

1.6 Walkers' mini-mart on the right; Market Express (convenience store) on the left.

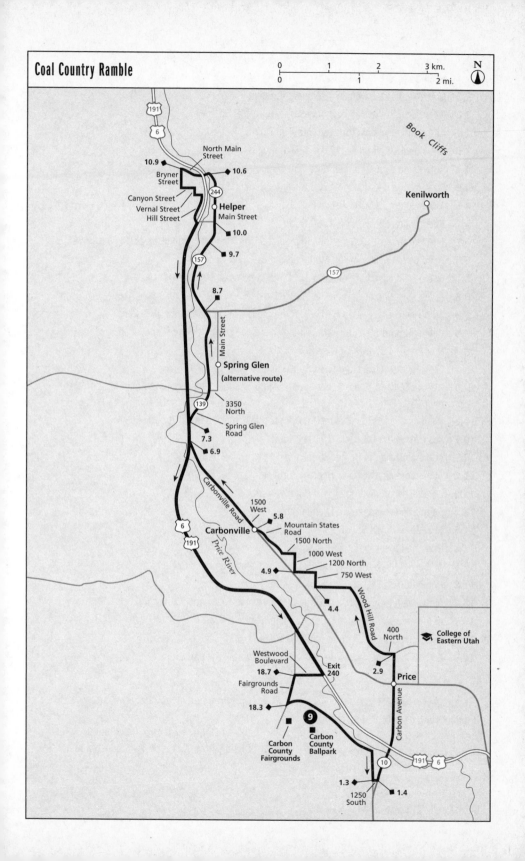

Coal Country Ramble

0   1   2   3 km.
0   1   2 mi.

N

Book Cliffs

191
6

North Main
Street

10.9

10.6

Bryner
Street

244

Canyon Street
Vernal Street
Hill Street

Kenilworth

Helper
Main Street

10.0

9.7

157

157

8.7

Main Street

Spring Glen
(alternative route)

139

3350
North

Spring Glen
Road

7.3

6.9

Carbonville Road

1500
West

5.8

Mountain States
Road

Carbonville

1500 North

6

191

Price River

1000 West

1200 North

4.9

750 West

4.4

Wood Hill Road

400
North

College of
Eastern Utah

2.9

Price

Westwood
Boulevard

18.7

Exit
240

Fairgrounds
Road

18.3

Carbon Avenue

9

Carbon
County
Ballpark

Carbon
County
Fairgrounds

10

191
6

1.3

1.4

1250
South

1.7 Go straight at the traffic signal at US 6/US 191 northbound ramps.

2.4 Railroad crossing (two tracks).

2.5 Go straight at the traffic signal at Main Street.

2.6 Go straight at the traffic signal at 100 North (SR 55).

2.9 At the T intersection, turn left onto 400 North.

3.0 Road bends right; now on Wood Hill Road.

4.4 At the stop sign, turn right onto 750 West.

4.6 Road bends left; now on 1200 North (entering Carbonville).

4.9 Turn right onto 1000 West.

5.1 Road bends left; now on 1500 North.

5.2 Turn left onto 1100 West, then immediately turn right to continue on 1500 North.

5.4 Road bends right; now on Mountain States Road.

5.7 At the yield sign, turn left onto 1500 West and cross two railroad tracks.

5.8 At the stop sign at Carbonville Road, turn right.

6.9 At the yield sign at US 6/US 191, turn right—stay in right-hand "exit" lane.

7.3 Turn right onto SR 139 North (Spring Glen Road). Enter Spring Glen.

8.7 Now on SR 157 (Spring Glen Road).

9.7 Enter Helper. Associated Food Store is on the left.

10.0 Now on SR 244 (Main Street), north of Poplar Street. Phillips 66 and mini-mart on the right.

10.6 Road curves left to cross the Price River (now on North Main Street).

10.7 Pass under the US 6/US 191 highway.

10.9 At the stop sign at Bryner Street, turn left.

11.2 At the stop sign at Canyon Street, turn left.

11.3 Go straight at the stop sign at Uintah Street.

11.4 Road bends right; now on Vernal Street.

11.5 Turn left onto Hill Street.

11.6 Road bends right; still on Hill Street.

11.8 At the yield sign at US 6/US 191, turn right—stay on the shoulder.

17.8 Exit right (exit 240: PRICE, US 6 BUSINESS LOOP).

18.3 At the traffic signal at 100 North, turn right onto Westwood Boulevard.

18.7 At the stop sign at Fairgrounds Road, turn left.

19.3 Road bends left; still on Fairgrounds Road.

19.6 End of ride; turn right to enter Carbon County Ballpark parking lot.

Local Information

Castle Country Travel Office: 81 North 200 East, Price; (435) 636-3701 or (800) 842-0789; www.castlecountry.com.

Carbon County Web site: www.carbon.utah.gov.

City of Helper Web site: www.helpercity.net.

City of Price Web site: www.priceutah.net.

Restaurants

El Salto Mexican Food: 19 South Carbon Avenue, Price; (435) 637-6545.

Farlaino's Café: 87 West Main Street, Price; (435) 637-9217.

Greek Streak: 30 West 100 North, Price; (435) 637-1930.

Groggs Pinnacle Brewing Company: 1653 North Carbonville Road, Helper; (435) 637-2924.

Accommodations

Best Western Carriage House Inn: 590 East Main Street, Price; (435) 637-5660; www .bestwesternutah.com/hotels/best-western-carriage-house-inn/index.html.

Greenwell Inn & Convention Center: 655 East Main Street, Price; (435) 637-3520 or (800) 666-3520; www.greenwellinn.com.

Holiday Inn and Suites: 838 Westwood Boulevard, Price; (435) 637-8880; www.ichotels group.com/h/d/hi/1/en/hotel/prcut.

Super 8 Motel: 180 North Hospital Drive, Price; (435) 637-8088; www .super8.com/Super8/control/Booking/ property_info?propertyId=07207.

Bicycle Shops

Bicycle Works: 710 West Price River Drive, Price; (435) 637-BIKE; www.fuzzysbicycle works.com.

Decker's Bicycle: 77 East Main Street, Price; (435) 637-0086; www.deckersbicycle.com.

Maps

Your Map to Adventure in...Utah's Castle Country, Southeastern Utah. Carbon County Travel Bureau.

DeLorme: Utah Atlas & Gazetteer: Pages 36–37 B5 on page 37.

Benchmark: Utah Road & Recreation Atlas: Pages 60–61 D7 on page 61.

10 Green River Ramble

The Green River Ramble is a 21.4-mile out-and-back ride on mostly flat terrain; there are some false flats, plus one short, steep climb and descent. The ride parallels the Green River from the namesake city to Swasey's Beach and back. The elevations range from 4,073 feet in Green River to 4,200 feet approaching the turnaround point.

Start: City Park, Solomon Street (100 East) and Main Street, Green River.

Length: 21.4 miles (out-and-back).

Terrain: Mostly flat, accented by one short, steep climb and descent. Minimum and maximum elevations: 4,073 to 4,200 feet.

Traffic and hazards: SR 19: 4,450 vehicles per day in central Green River in 2005.

Getting there: From points west and east: I-70 to Green River exit; proceed into town. From points north: US 6 south to I-70, then east to Green River exit.

The Ride

The Green River originates in the Wind River Mountains in Wyoming, where it heads south, into Colorado, then into Utah, eventually joining the Colorado River. The Green River is the Colorado's largest tributary. Through most of Utah the Green River is deep, powerful, and navigable. The river is frequented by boaters, river rafters, and anglers. A long stretch of the river passes through a region of Utah that is completely uninhabited, with no paved roads. The region was not explored or mapped until the latter half of the nineteenth century, making it one of the "last unknown" areas of the continental United States. The river remains the best means of accessing remote upstream spots, which bear names such as Desolation Canyon and Poverty Creek. "Unknown" is, of course, relative, since there is plenty of evidence that the Fremonts explored and possibly lived in the canyons of the Green River and its tributaries during the first millennium. In fact, numerous petroglyphs can be seen in the cliffs and canyons.

The town of Green River was established at a major crossing point. Early Native Americans used it, calling it Ute Crossing. The Old Spanish Trail crossed the river here. A settlement was eventually established in 1876 to serve as a ferry crossing for the U.S. Mail. In 1883 the Denver & Rio Grande Railroad bridged the river here. The railroad firmly established Green River as a town.

The boom lasted only until 1892, however, when the railroad switched most of its regional operations to Helper, about 73 miles away. During the first half of the twentieth century, uranium mining became Green River's primary economic base. During the 1960s, the U.S. Air Force established the Green River Launch Complex just outside of the city. The base was used as a testing facility for nuclear missiles headed for the White Sands Missile Range in New Mexico, until the last launch in 1973. Today, the city's primary economic asset is its location along I-70. Green River is at a crossroads for east-west traffic on the I-70 freeway, and north-south traffic on US 6/ US 191. Green River is the largest settlement within a 63-mile radius and the only city along I-70 between Utah's Sevier Valley and Fruita, Colorado. Green River is also a logical launching point for recreational activities along the real Green River.

Green River had a population of 923 in 2008. The city straddles Emery and Grand Counties, thereby straddling Utah's Castle Country and Canyonlands regions. About 90 percent of the city's population, as well as all governing offices, are in Emery County. The city has plenty of motels and eateries. Green River State Park, located on the south side of the city, is a popular portal to the Green River. The city's Melon Days come every September, with a parade, golf tournament, exhibits, and delicious, juicy melons.

Start this ride at City Park in the center of Green River. Leave the park via Main Street and head east. After crossing the Green River and entering Grand County, there is a slight upgrade to the east side of the city. Turn left onto Hastings Street (1200 East) and head north. The road surface from here is generally good, although not of the same quality as a state highway. The Green River will eventually appear on your left and will continue to provide a reference point (and some pleasant scenery) for the duration of the ride. The roadside becomes less and less developed as you travel north. The terrain dates from the Pleistocene epoch, evidenced by plenty of erosion and glacial deposits. The Book Cliffs loom in the distance, so named because the surface features resemble the pages of open books; with one open book set next to another. At mile 7.8, the road dips to traverse a flood crossing—the road could be underwater after a storm. The ride starts to become more intimate with the Green River as you enter the mouth of Lower Gray Canyon. The pavement ends, unfortunately, at Swasey's Beach—just as the ride was getting really interesting! If you want to continue heading north, then switch to an off-road bike. The beach is small and serene, and may be a nice break before making the return trip.

The Green River will be on your right during the return ride. Do not be fooled by the river's placid appearance in this area—the river rages along certain sections both upstream and downstream of Green River (city). The terrain that you see along the side of the road, similarly to many other areas in Utah, is often covered in low desert "scrub": xerographic plants, essentially weeds, which have adapted to drought-like environments. Civilization gradually begins to appear as the road nears Green River: a few houses, a few animals, and a little roadside junk. At mile 20.0, turn right onto Main Street and head west. Cross the Green River; at mile 21.4, slow down and turn right onto Solomon Street (100 East), and return to City Park. A short ride west to 134 West Third Avenue to view the Green River Presbyterian Church, which is on the National Register of Historic Places, is recommended.

Miles and Directions

0.0 Start at City Park, Solomon Street (100 East) and Main Street, Green River. Turn left onto Main Street (SR 19).

0.8 Cross the Green River.

1.2 Begin slight uphill grade.

1.4 Turn left onto Hastings Street (1200 East).

3.7 Green River is visible on the left.

4.1 Cattle guard.

5.6 Begin climb.

6.0 Crest of climb.

6.6 Cattle guard.

7.8 Begin short, steep descent.

8.0 Bottom of descent; crossing can be flooded after a storm.

9.0 Cattle guard; road surface gets rougher.

10.7 End of pavement, Lower Gray Canyon Recreation Site; turn around here.

12.4 Cattle guard.

13.4 Road dips at flood crossing; begin short, steep uphill.

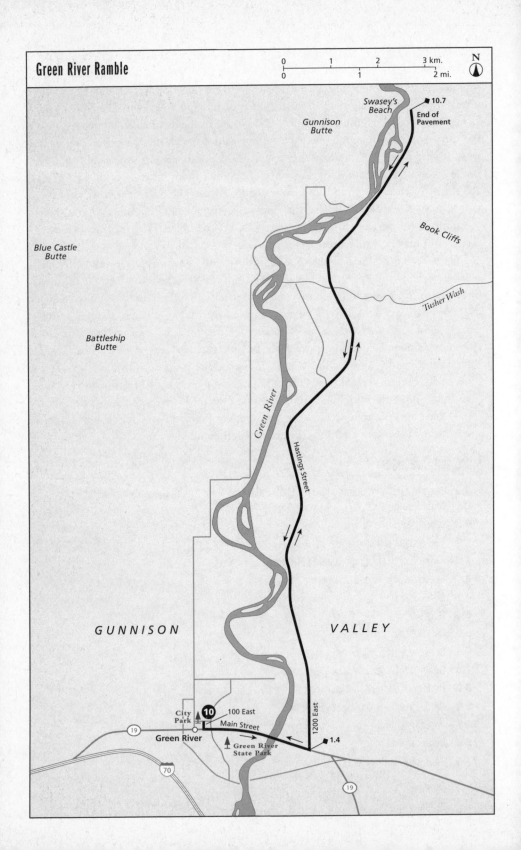

Green River Ramble

0   1   2   3 km.
0   1   2 mi.

N

Swasey's
Beach
■ 10.7
End of
Pavement

Gunnison
Butte

Book Cliffs

Blue Castle
Butte

Tusher Wash

Battleship
Butte

Green River

Hastings Street

GUNNISON   VALLEY

City
Park
10   100 East
19   Main Street
Green River

1200 East

■ 1.4

Green River
State Park

19

70

13.8 Grade eases.

14.8 Cattle guard.

15.5 Begin short downhill.

17.3 Cattle guard.

20.0 At the stop sign, turn right onto Main Street (SR 19).

20.6 Cross the Green River.

21.4 End of ride; turn right onto Solomon Street (100 East) and return to City Park.

Local Information

City of Green River Web site: www.greenriver utah.com.

"Unofficial" City of Green River Web site: www.greenriverutah.org.

Listing of historic places in Emery County, including Green River: www.nationalregisterof historicplaces.com/UT/Emery/state.html.

Restaurants

Ben's Café: 115 West Main Street, Green River; (435) 564-3352.

Ray's Tavern: 25 South Broadway, Green River; (435) 564-3511.

Tamarisk Restaurant: 870 East Main Street, Green River; (435) 564-8109.

Accommodations

Best Western River Terrace Motel: 1740 East Main Street, Green River; (435) 564-3401; www.bestwesternutah.com/hotels/best-western-river-terrace/index.html.

Book Cliff Lodge: 395 East Main Street, Green River; (435) 564-3406 or (435) 564-3447; www.bookclifflodgeut.com.

Comfort Inn: 1065 East Main Street, Green River; (435) 564-3300; www.comfortinn.com/hotel-green_river-utah-UT424.

Green River State Park: 450 South Green River Boulevard, Green River; (435) 564-3633; www.utah.com/stateparks/green_river.htm.

KOA Campground: 550 South Green River Boulevard, Green River; (435) 564-8195 or (800) 562-5734; www.koa.com/where/UT/44154/.

Shady Acres RV Park: 350 East Main Street, Green River; (435) 564-8290 or (800) 537-8674; www.shadyacresrv.com.

United Campground: 910 East Main Street, Green River; (435) 564-8195.

Maps

DeLorme: Utah Atlas & Gazetteer: Page 46 A1.

Benchmark: Utah Road & Recreation Atlas: Page 70 B1.

Color Country

C olor Country occupies the southwestern corner of Utah. Five counties are included in this, Utah's largest region: Beaver, Garfield, Iron, Kane, and Washington. The population in 2008 was 199,526, spread over 17,370 square miles. About 75 percent of the population is concentrated in the cities of Cedar City, Enoch, Hurricane, Ivins, La Verkin, St. George, Santa Clara, and Washington. Where is the color? Everywhere! Starting from the southwestern tip of Utah and heading in a northeasterly direction, the colors become more startling and vivid as the terrain generally becomes increasingly rugged. While the westernmost areas of Color Country—including the western halves of Beaver, Iron, and Washington Counties—feature deserts, forests, and a few mountains, the eastern areas feature plateaus, cliffs, canyons, folds, mesas, more mountains, and more forests. "Kaleidoscope Country" may be a more descriptive moniker, as the colors of the landscape include a mesmerizing blend of red, orange, yellow, cream, pink, green, black, brown, and even blue. Garfield and Kane Counties—the least populated of the five-county region—are especially blessed, touting such features as Bryce Canyon National Park, Grand Staircase-Escalante National Monument, Glen Canyon National Recreation Area, Coral Pink Sand Dunes State Park, Kodachrome Basin State Park, Escalante Petrified Forest State Park, Box-Death Hollow Wilderness, a portion of Capitol Reef National Park, and other areas. Although Beaver, Iron, and Washington Counties are more heavily populated, they claim their own outstanding natural features, including Cedar Breaks National Monument, Zion National Park, Snow Canyon State Park, Dixie National Forest, the Parowan Gap petroglyphs (surprisingly not a state park), and other areas. It is not possible to incorporate all of the remarkable scenery into a small set of bike rides; this chapter emphasizes the highlights.

Color Country features the widest range of elevations of any Utah region. The city of St. George—the population center of this region—sits at an elevation of 2,840 feet, while the Tushar Mountains east of Beaver reach to a breathtaking height of 12,319 feet. One of St. George's attractions is its elevation: The ambient temperature is consistently higher than in any other area in Utah, and the city rarely gets clobbered with snow during the winter. Hence, the city makes a great year-round base for traveling in the region. Bicycling in Color Country can be an extremely pleasant experience. Even the tensest cyclist will find himself or herself becoming immersed in the surroundings. Forget about excessive motor vehicle traffic, noise, air pollution, and road rage (except in the heart of St. George)—this is cycling nirvana. That said, cyclists should always be aware of the presence of motor vehicles, even on quiet back roads. Nature can also be unfriendly: Temperatures at the lower elevations in Color Country can easily exceed 100 degrees F during the summer, so be sure to bring plenty of fluids. Rainstorms in January 2005 softened snowpacks in the mountains, eventually leading to flooding in the St. George area. The Virgin River got so high that an important bridge on the Virgin River Trail (a bike path) was washed out (and had yet to be replaced as of the writing of this book). Along a few corridors that are heavily traveled during the summer—such as Red Canyon near Bryce Canyon, and Zion Canyon—there are alternative, parallel bike paths. Riders should use these paths rather than the highways. Know about road conditions and the weather forecast before venturing into the mountains during all but the summer months. Some highways are closed during the winter—know which ones these are, to avoid having to retrace your route.

11 Beaver Dam Mountains Classic

The Beaver Dam Mountains Classic is a 66.9-mile out-and-back ride through mountain and desert terrain. The ride starts in Santa Clara, ascends the Beaver Dam Mountains in extreme southwestern Utah, and then descends through an increasingly barren landscape, crossing into Arizona before entering the settlement of Beaver Dam. The return route reverses the outbound route. The elevation ranges from 1,880 feet in Beaver Dam, Arizona, to 4,721 feet at the crest of "Utah Hill," in the Beaver Dam Mountains. The elevation in Beaver Dam, Arizona, is lower than Utah's lowest elevation and is the lowest altitude reached by any course in *Road Biking Utah*. The region is typically dry, hot, and windy, especially during the summer months, so be sure to bring plenty of fluids. Water can be replenished at the Dam Store or Dam Deli at the turnaround; otherwise, be self-sufficient.

Start: Santa Clara City Park (also referred to as Canyon View Park), 1400 Canyon View Drive, Santa Clara (adjacent the Spencer Gunn Memorial Fields).
Length: 66.9 miles (out-and-back).
Terrain: Mountainous, with one long climb and descent outbound, followed by the same

inbound. Minimum and maximum elevations: 1,880 to 4,721 feet.
Traffic and hazards: Old Highway 91: 10,560 vehicles per day in central Santa Clara in 2005; 5,275 vehicles per day in Ivins; 1,160 vehicles per day between Ivins and Shivwits.

Getting there: From I-15, head west on St. George Boulevard to Bluff Street. Turn right onto Bluff Street, then left onto Sunset Boulevard. Head west on Sunset Boulevard to Canyon View Drive. Turn right onto Canyon View Drive; look for the City Park on the right, just beyond the high school signs.

The Ride

The Beaver Dam Mountains are located in the extreme southwest corner of Utah, straddling the border between Utah and Arizona. The mountains are a collection of contrasts, at times jagged and at other times gently sloping; at times populated with trees and scrub and at other times barren. Also, despite the peak elevation of 7,680 feet (West Mountain), the region immediately adjacent the mountains includes Utah's lowest elevation land. Regarding the trees, a large sector of the mountains is designated as the Joshua Tree Wilderness. The Joshua Tree is of the yucca genus, and is found almost exclusively in the Mojave Desert. The name was concocted by Mormons who crossed the Mojave during the nineteenth century; the unusual shape of the tree reminded them of a biblical story in which Joshua reaches his hands up to the sun. The tree is known for its heavy branches, slow growth, and longevity. Animals indigenous to the Beaver Dam Mountains area include bighorn sheep, desert tortoise, raptors, and lizards.

The northeastern side of the mountains, along with a portion of the adjacent Santa Clara River valley, is dedicated to the Shivwits Reservation, home to a band of the southern Paiute people. The southern Paiutes are a peaceful tribe that was subjected to the "slave raids" of the Navajo tribes that dated from the pre-nineteenth century. The practice was abruptly ended with the "Long Walk" (see Hovenweep-Navajo Classic), as well as the influences of Mormon settlers. The southern Paiutes and Mormons, in fact, shared water sources for a time during the late nineteenth century. The Mormon missionary Jacob Hamblin was partially responsible for the diplomacy. The so-called Pah Ute wars—a series of raids and ambushes by the Paiutes in 1860—disrupted the establishment of a Pony Express route. Some theories have circulated that Paiute chiefs participated in the Mountain Meadows Massacre (see the Escalante Valley Ramble). Other theories even claim that the Paiutes were entirely responsible for the executions. It is likely, however, that the Mormon militiamen were looking for a group on which to place blame and that the Paiutes actually had little to do with the massacre. The violence of the era finally ended in 1865, when the Paiutes and the federal government agreed to a peace treaty, although the treaty was never ratified by the U.S. Senate. The Shivwits Reservation was established in 1891, and a Paiute agency under the Bureau of Indian Affairs was set up in 1927 in Cedar City.

The passage through the Beaver Dam Mountains is along Old Highway 91, a north-south route that formerly stretched from California to Canada. Although portions of the highway currently exist—designated as US 91—most of the older segments have been replaced by I-15. The route through the mountains also follows the Old Spanish Trail, used in the early nineteenth century to connect Santa Fe, New Mexico (which was then part of Mexico), with Los Angeles, California. The route avoided the extremes of the Mojave Desert and established a trade route between the United States and Mexico.

The ride explores a remote corner of Utah and ventures into northwestern Arizona. This part of Arizona is effectively cut off from the rest of Arizona; passage to other parts of Arizona (on paved roads) from here requires travel through either Utah or Nevada. The ride starts at Santa Clara City Park—also referred to as Canyon View Park—in the city of Santa Clara. Santa Clara, a suburb of St. George, had a population of 6,866 in 2008. The city is named after the river that flows through the city on its course from the Pine Valley Mountains to the Virgin River. The name also refers to the region's good weather. Head south on Canyon View Drive to Santa Clara Drive. Turn right at the traffic signal. Enter the Santa Clara Historic District at mile 0.8. There are a number of historic buildings along Santa Clara Drive, including the George and Bertha Graff House at 2865 Santa Clara Drive, the Frederick and Anna Maria Reber House at 2988–2990 Santa Clara Drive, the Hans George Hafen House at 3003 Santa Clara Drive, the Santa Clara Relief Society House at 3036 Santa Clara Drive, the Santa Clara Tithing Company at 3105 Santa Clara Drive, and the Frederick and Mary F. Reber House at 3334 Santa Clara Drive. Also, the Jacob Hamblin House (the Mormon missionary) is just off Santa Clara Drive, near the western end of the district.

The road curves right at mile 1.8, leaving the historic district. Begin climbing at mile 2.0. The gradient eases at mile 2.8, although the road continues uphill. Note the reddish color of the ground in this area. The imposing mountains on the right are named the Red Mountains. The highway traverses the western edge of Ivins starting around mile 3.9. There is a short descent at mile 4.8, followed by rollers. Enter the Shivwits Paiute Reservation at mile 6.4. The highway crests at mile 7.5, followed by a descent to a crossing of the Santa Clara River. Beyond the crossing, the highway starts to wind and climb. Stay left at the junction at mile 9.3, toward Old Highway 91. You are now following the Old Spanish Trail. Note the red rocks on the surrounding hillsides ("red rocks" is a theme heard and seen repeatedly throughout Utah). The highway continues to roll upward through this landscape; there are several false crests, and the roadway width varies between two and three lanes to accommodate climbing segments. Enter the Beaver Dam Mountains at mile 13.2—from here, the hillsides "close in" on the highway as it winds toward the summit. During my field visit in July 2008, most of the surrounding trees were blackened, as evidence of a recent wildfire. Exit the Shivwits Paiute Reservation at mile 15.2. The trees and desert scrub become denser around mile 16.4, an indicator of the higher elevation. The highway crests at mile 16.9; a long descent begins here.

The landscape becomes increasingly barren around mile 19.3. The vista is wide and encompassing. The mountains in the far distance include Bunkerville Ridge and the Black Rock and Virgin ranges. The floor of the Virgin Valley can be seen clearly below; the highway eventually takes you there. Enter the Joshua Tree Wilderness around mile 20.7. These protected yucca trees have an unusual shape—nearly all branches, with very little trunk. The trees can survive the harsh desert environment, provided that there is some rainfall and at least one winter freeze. The trees are pollinated entirely by the yucca moth. Enter Arizona at mile 26.2; you are now in Mohave County, on CR 91. The downhill gradient eases at mile 28.4. After a long, straight segment, the highway finally bends right at mile 31.6. Enter the Beaver Dam settlement at mile 32.2. The I-15 freeway is less than 2 miles from here. Beaver Dam, and the immediately adjacent Littlefield settlement, are located about 10 miles from the booming border town of Mesquite, Nevada. Turn around at Old Pioneer Road, just past the bridge over Beaver Dam Wash, adjacent the Dam Store. Note that the Dam Deli and Dam Bar are next door, making this a dam good place to turn around. This would also be a good place to restock on fluids.

Climbing begins almost immediately after crossing the Beaver Dam Wash, heading back. A steep climb leads away from the settlement and back into the desert. The land slopes upward toward the Beaver Dam Mountains in the distance. Joshua trees begin to appear, initially on the left and then on the right (particularly beyond mile 38.5). The highway also gets noticeably steeper here. Cross under an easement (overhead power lines) at mile 39.9 and enter Utah at mile 40.6. Unlike the outbound route, there is no sign here welcoming you to Utah. The climb gets steeper at mile 44.0; enter the Beaver Dam Mountains at mile 45.2. From here, the highway winds to negotiate the generally barren slopes of the mountains. Blackened trees begin to appear at mile 48.2. The highway crests at mile 50.0. Notice that, at the upper elevations, the trees—mostly pinyon pines and junipers—are fairly dense. The highway descends from here. The gradient varies; watch your speed on the steeper segments. Enter the Shivwits Paiute Reservation at mile 51.7. The vistas of the red cliffs in the distance are frequently awesome. After crossing the Santa Clara River at mile 58.8, the Shivwits settlement appears on the left at mile 59.3. The long descent ends here; rolling terrain begins at mile 60.8, as you enter Ivins. Ivins had a population of 7,870 in 2008 and was growing rapidly. Ivins is known for the Kayenta development (luxury homes that accentuate the surrounding red cliffs), the Tuacahn outdoor amphitheater, and Snow Canyon State Park (see the Dixie Legacy Classic). Enter Santa Clara at mile 64.1. The road curves left, widening to accommodate a bike lane and entering the Santa Clara Historic District. The tree-lined street is a welcome contrast to the harsh desert and mountains. After leaving the historic district, turn left onto Canyon View Drive (mile 66.4). After a short climb, the ride ends at Crestview Drive, adjacent Canyon View Park (Santa Clara City Park; mile 66.9).

Miles and Directions

0.0 Start at Santa Clara City Park (Canyon View Park) at Canyon View Drive and Crestline Drive. Head south on Canyon View Drive.

0.1 Begin downhill.

0.4 At the traffic signal at Santa Clara Drive, turn right.

0.8 Enter historic district.

1.8 Road curves right; exit historic district.

2.0 Begin climb; road surface condition changes to "fair."

4.8 Grade eases; begin descent.

5.4 Begin rolling hills, with net elevation gain.

6.4 Enter Shivwits Paiute Reservation.

7.5 Crest of climb; begin descent.

8.0 Cross Santa Clara River; begin winding climb.

9.3 Stay left at junction (i.e., follow Old Highway 91).

13.2 Enter Beaver Dam Mountains; highway varies from two to three lanes, depending on steepness.

15.2 Leave Shivwits Paiute Reservation.

16.9 Crest of climb; begin descent.

20.7 Enter Joshua Tree Wilderness.

24.3 Woodbury Desert Study Area on the left.

26.2 Enter Arizona; now on Mohave County Route 91.

28.4 Downhill grade eases; now on false flat.

31.6 Highway bends right.

32.2 Enter Beaver Dam community.

33.2 Cross Beaver Dam Wash.

33.4 Turn around adjacent Dam Store and Old Pioneer Road.

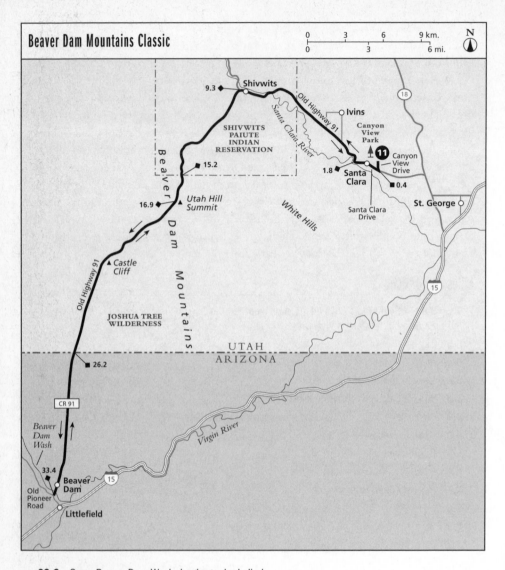

Beaver Dam Mountains Classic

33.6 Cross Beaver Dam Wash; begin gradual climb.

34.0 Climb gets steeper.

34.7 Gradient eases; continue gradual uphill.

35.1 Highway bends left.

38.6 Gradient increases; Joshua trees on left and right.

39.9 Cross under easement (overhead power lines).

40.6 Enter Utah (no sign).

42.5 Woodbury Desert Study Area on the right.

44.0 Climb gets steeper.

45.2 Enter Beaver Dam Mountains; begin curves. Highway width varies from two to three lanes.

50.0 Crest of climb; begin winding descent.

51.7 Enter Shivwits Paiute Reservation.

58.8 Cross Santa Clara River.

59.1 End descent; begin slight uphill.

59.3 Shivwits settlement on the left.

60.5 Begin descent.

60.8 Enter Ivins; begin series of "rollers."

64.1 Enter Santa Clara.

64.9 Road curves left; begin bike lane (enter historic district).

66.1 Leave tree-lined historic district.

66.4 Traffic signal at Canyon View Drive; turn left.

66.5 Begin short climb.

66.9 End ride at Crestview Drive; Canyon View Park is on the right.

Local Information

City of Ivins Web site: www.ivins.com.

City of Santa Clara Web site: www.santa claracityutah.com.

Beaver Dam Mountains Wilderness information (Bureau of Land Management): www.wilderness.net/index.cfm?fuse=NWPS&sec=wildView&WID=33.

Restaurants

Burger Bar: 1025 North Lava Flow Drive, Santa Clara; (435) 652-4141.

J.J. Hunan Chinese Restaurant: 1973 West Sunset Boulevard, St. George; (435) 628-7219.

Scaldoni's Restaurant & Bar: 929 West Sunset Boulevard, St. George; (435) 674-1300; www.scaldonis.com. Opens at 4:00 p.m.

Accommodations

Best Western Abbey Inn: 1129 South Bluff Street, St. George; (435) 652-1234; www .bestwesternutah.com/hotels/best-western-abbey-inn/.

Best Western Coral Hills: 125 East St. George Boulevard, St. George; (435) 673-4884 or (800) 542-7733; www.coralhills.com.

Green Gate Village Historic Bed & Breakfast Inn: 76 West Tabernacle, St. George; (435) 628-6999 or (800) 350-6999; www.green gatevillage.com.

Seven Wives Inn Bed & Breakfast: 217 North 100 West, St. George; (435) 628-6737 or (800) 600-3737; www.sevenwivesinn.com.

McArthur's Temple View RV Resort: 975 South Main Street, St. George; (435) 673-6400 or (800) 776-4410; www.templeviewrv .com.

St. George Campground: 2100 East Middleton Drive, St George; (435) 673-2970.

Snow Canyon State Park (located in Ivins): (435) 628-2255; http://stateparks.utah.gov/ parks/snow-canyon.

Maps

Street Map of St. George and Cedar City (including Santa Clara). North Star Mapping, 2001.

DeLorme: Utah Atlas & Gazetteer: Page 56 D4.

Benchmark: Utah Road & Recreation Atlas: Page 80 F5.

12 Dixie Legacy Classic

The Dixie Legacy Classic is an 80.7-mile out-and-back ride featuring long, steady climbs and descents and some rolling hills. The route starts and finishes in St. George and visits the Legacy Loop Highway, Dixie National Forest, and Snow Canyon State Park. The cyclist should be prepared for high desert temperatures during the summer months, although the middle part of the route is at higher elevations, where temperatures are cooler. The elevation ranges from 2,560 feet at the start in St. George to 6,576 feet at the turnaround in Pine Valley. The route incorporates city streets, state highways, paved bike trails, a state park road, and county highways that were all in good condition as of this writing.

Start: Tonaquint Park at 1851 South Dixie Drive, just north of 600 West, in St. George.
Length: 81 miles (out-and-back, with a detour through Snow Canyon State Park on the return).
Terrain: Long, steady climbs and descents, with some rolling terrain. Minimum and maximum elevations: 2,560 to 6,576 feet.
Traffic and hazards: SR 18: 14,705 vehicles per day north of Snow Canyon Parkway in St. George in 2006; 10,630 vehicles per day at the St. George northern limits; 3,715 vehicles per day at Snow Canyon Drive; 2,630 vehicles per day through Veyo; 1,660 vehicles per day at Pine Valley Highway. Dixie Drive: 10,615 vehicles per day in 2005. Snow Canyon Drive: 1,745 vehicles per day in 2005.

Getting there: From I-15, take exit 6 (Bluff Street); head north on Bluff Street, then turn left onto Hilton Drive. The road curves to the right, becoming Dixie Drive after crossing Tonaquint Drive. Look for Tonaquint Park on the right, just north of 600 West.

The Ride

The city of St. George is located about 300 miles south of Salt Lake City and 120 miles northeast of Las Vegas, Nevada. All three cities are connected by the I-15 freeway. The city is also at the approximate halfway point between Los Angeles and Salt Lake City. St. George was founded during the 1850s under the direction of Mormon church leader Brigham Young. The city was probably named in honor of one of the church's apostles, George A. Smith. St. George was the eighth most populous city in Utah as of year 2008 (72,718). As of 2005, the St. George metropolitan area had the second-fastest growth rate in the country, and was growing slightly faster than the Las Vegas area. Growth is evident in St. George, as the city has sprawled in all directions except directly to the north and to the southeast. It is a challenge for development to blend in with the stunning landscape, while accommodating the needs of the population and avoiding extremely rugged spots.

Traffic volumes can be heavy on the city's major roads and at major intersections. Cyclists in St. George can avoid a lot of the street traffic by using the city's "trail" system, which is actually a network of paved bike paths. Since paths are not built to the same standards as roads, they are susceptible to damage; for example, flooding along the Virgin River in 2005 washed out an important bridge on the Virgin River Trail. St. George is a haven for retirees and recreationalists, the latter of whom are drawn by the area's year-round temperate climate. The flooding was an anomaly; most of the time the climate is relatively dry, and the Virgin River is merely a trickle. St. George is considered to be a gateway to Color Country; its proximity to Zion National Park verifies its choice location.

The climate is a critical factor: Annual snowfall averages 3.2 inches, with no recorded accumulation. One promo is that St. George "is where Utah's summer sun spends the winter." Why is the region referred to as Utah's "Dixie"? Early settlers attempted to grow cotton in the area during the Civil War, when productivity was low. Yields were low, so Utah's cotton "era" was short-lived, but the moniker has endured. Plus, this is "southern" Utah, hence the forbearance of Dixie. Some of St. George's attractions include the St. George Temple (dedicated in 1877), the Brigham Young Winter Home, the Daughters of Utah Pioneers Museum, the University of Utah's Dixie Campus (formerly Dixie State College), the Rosenbruch Wildlife Museum, the Johnson Farm Dinosaur Tracks (dilophosaurus and ceolophysis), the St. George Marathon (held every October), and the Huntsman World Senior Games (an Olympic-style competition open to athletes age fifty and over). Cyclists are hoping that the former "Tour of St. George," a stage race, will return someday. The Southwestern Utah Bicycle Touring Association (SWUBTA) is a very active club that has weekly ride events year-round. One of their major events is the Cactus Hugger Century, held every April. Other cycling events include the Red Rock 200, Tour of Southern Utah, and the Hoodoo 500—the 200 and 500 are *long* races that take in portions of some of *Road Biking Utah*'s Color Country courses.

Start the ride at Tonaquint Park, located at 1851 South Dixie Drive in St. George. Exit the park and turn right onto Dixie Drive. The shoulder width varies along this stretch of road, as does the number of lanes. The St. George Municipal Airport sits atop the mesa to your right, some 200 feet above the city. It is an interesting, out-of-the-way place to locate an airport. Turn right onto 540 North at mile 3.2 and then immediately bear left to enter the trailhead to the Halfway Wash Bike Trail. This is a paved bike path that allows you to avoid busy crossings at Sunset Boulevard and Snow Canyon Parkway. The trail crosses under Snow Canyon Parkway at mile 5.2. Just beyond the underpass, turn right onto the connector path and then turn left onto the path that parallels Snow Canyon Parkway. The path is little more than a striped sidewalk along this stretch. Follow the path as it turns left at the intersection with SR 18. The path parallels SR 18 for the next 7.5 miles. Although the path is an alternative to SR 18, which gets less busy as you travel farther north, the path is actually more physically demanding than the highway. While the highway negotiates gentle grades and false flats, the path undulates over steep climbs and descents. Take your pick. There are a few crossings along the path that will require you to watch for cross-traffic. The path ends at Snow Canyon Drive at mile 13.2, adjacent the entrance to Snow Canyon State Park. Turn right here to return to SR 18. Turn left onto SR 18 and continue heading north.

The highway begins to climb north of Snow Canyon Drive as you head into the aptly named Red Mountains. The climb finally crests at mile 17.0. Once you are beyond the confines of the mountain range, the Bull Valley Mountains in the distance come into view. The Pine Valley Mountains are to the east. Enter the Dammeron Valley area at mile 19.0. Dammeron Valley is a planned community, nestled against the Cedar Bench, established around 1976.

A 7 percent descent takes you out of the Dammeron Valley and toward the wash of the Santa Clara River, at mile 21.9. Veyo Volcano is the prominent peak on the left. Although the volcano has not erupted anytime since at least 1,000 years ago, it represents one of the youngest eruption centers in the St. George region. The volcanism in the region has suggested the presence of geothermal energy resources. Enter the community of Veyo shortly after crossing the wash. There are a couple of mini-marts along the highway. Veyo was settled in 1911 as Glen Cove but was later renamed by Mormon "Beehive" girls (twelve- to thirteen-year-old participants in a young women's organization of the Mormon church). The young girls created "Veyo" as an acronym of virtue, enterprise, youth, and order. Very clever! The highway climbs out of Veyo, roughly following the reverse course of the Santa Clara River. From Veyo north to Central, the course traces a portion of the route of the Red Rock 200 bike race. The climb crests at mile 23.6; begin false flats, followed by rolling terrain, and then a descent at mile 26.0. The downhill gets steeper at mile 27.5. At mile 29.1, turn right onto Pine Valley Highway, in the community of Central (population 415). Central is the starting point for the St. George Marathon, held each October.

Enter the Dixie National Forest at mile 30.7 and begin a steady climb. The Pine Valley Mountains, shooting up to 10,365 feet (Signal Peak), are on the horizon. The gradient eases at mile 35.5, from which the terrain rolls and then descends. The highway bends right at mile 36.7, becoming Grass Valley Road. As the gradient eases, the road enters the community of Pine Valley.

The descent into Pine Valley seems to be from a storybook. The legend is that the valley was "discovered" by Isaac Riddle, an early Mormon settler, who wandered "up into the hills" to find a stray cow. Pine Valley was settled in the mid-1850s and was so named for the abundance of ponderosa pines, along with conifers, in the area. Lumbering was the community's first industry, but today the town attracts recreationalists and seasonal "getaway" homeowners. Turn left onto Main Street at mile 37.4. The Pine Valley Chapel and Tithing Office are on the corner. The chapel is the oldest functioning Mormon chapel in Utah and is on the National Register of Historic Places. The building was designed by Ebenezer Bryce, the namesake of Bryce Canyon. Bryce, a former shipbuilder from Australia, applied his seafaring knowledge by designing the church to resemble the hull of an upside-down ship.

Head east up Main Street, toward the mountains. The peacefulness may, unfortunately, be broken by the proliferation of ATVs (all-terrain vehicles). The road enters

Cyclists enjoying the stupendous beauty of Snow Canyon's eroded sandstone.

the Pine Valley Recreation Area after 1 mile; this is the turnaround point. On the way up Main, you may have noticed the Pine Valley Lodge (and cafe) and Brandin' Iron Steakhouse. Any of these may be worth a visit (rest stop) before embarking on the return trip.

Now on the return trip, Main Street descends to the intersection with Grass Valley Road, at mile 40.4. Turn right here to leave the Pine Valley community. As the road curves left to become Pine Valley Highway and you begin to climb (mile 40.9), feel free to take a look back at the lovely valley setting. After a segment of rolling terrain, the highway starts to descend at mile 42.3. The highway starts to wind around mile 46.1—watch your speed in the curves. Leave the Dixie National Forest at mile 47.5 and return to the community of Central. Red Butte (elevation 5,810 feet) is in the foreground, with the Bull Valley Mountains serving as a backdrop. Turn left onto SR 18 at mile 49.0 and head south. Begin to descend at mile 51.0. SR 18 forms one segment of the Legacy Loop Highway through southwestern Utah. The highway follows portions of the Old Spanish Trail, the main route through this area long before the construction of I-15. The highway's other legacy is its proximity to Mountain Meadows, which is described under the Escalante Valley Ramble.

Enter Veyo at mile 55.1; there are mini-marts on both sides of the highway starting at mile 55.7. Runners in the St. George Marathon appreciate the awe-inspiring sight of Veyo Volcano to the right, but they do not appreciate the climb that starts at mile 56.3. The climb continues, with an interim respite, through Dammeron Valley, eventually cresting at mile 60.2. After a few miles of rolling terrain, begin a 6 percent descent at mile 63.6. Turn right onto Snow Canyon Drive at mile 65.0.

Enter Snow Canyon State Park at mile 65.1. There are stations at either end of the park, and one or both of them may be manned. In any case, be prepared to pay the $5 entrance fee either via self-service or a park ranger. Begin the descent into the park. The desert scrub and forestation of the first three-fourths of the ride gives way to the barren but extremely colorful sandstone of Snow Canyon. Upon entering the park, your first thought might be "this could be a national park." The park is part of the much larger Red Cliffs Desert Preserve, a federally designated area designed to protect the habitats of the desert tortoise. Wildlife also includes coyotes, kit foxes, canyon tree frogs, leopard lizards, roadrunners, quail, and gopher snakes, along with the protected peregrine falcons and Gila monsters. Plant life includes creosote bush, blackbrush, desert willow, sand sage, and narrow-leaf yucca, along with scrub oak. The canyon descent can be completed fairly rapidly, but take time to absorb some of the desert life. Exit the park and enter Ivins at mile 71.0. An access road to the Tuacahn Amphitheater is on the right, just ahead. The outdoor theater features live productions and concerts from March until December. Performers in 2008 included the Beach Boys, Colbie Caillat, and Kenny Loggins.

The town of Ivins is blessed with a spectacular red-cliff backdrop that changes shades with different positions of the sun, and in creeping and receding shadows. The setting seems natural but was a challenge because of the lack of water. A couple of ingenious civil engineers, Leo A. Snow and Clarence S. Jarvis, conceived of constructing an 8-mile canal to the Santa Clara River, and then storing the water in a new reservoir. Despite their contribution, the town is named for Anthony W. Ivins, a Mormon apostle. Turn left onto Snow Canyon Parkway at mile 72.5. Leave Ivins and enter St. George. The parkway passes through some of the newer residential areas of St. George. The parkway widens from two to four lanes as it sweeps toward the southeast, then east. Turn right onto 1300 West at mile 76.1, just as the road begins to climb. Turn right again at the next street, 1390 North, to access the Halfway Wash Bike Trail. Bear left onto the trail and begin the gradual 2-mile descent past more St. George neighborhoods. The trail's speed limit is 20 mph, which is certainly an upper limit given the sharp curves. The trail ends abruptly at the intersection of 540 North and Dixie Drive, at mile 77.4. Cross Dixie Drive, turn left, and head south. The road crosses the ever-present Santa Clara River at mile 78.2. There is a mini-mart on the left at mile 78.8. Continue heading south; the stately West Black Ridge is to the left. The ride ends at the entrance to Tonaquint Park, which is on the left at mile 80.7, just north of 600 West. The park is a pleasant place to cool down, with a water conservation garden, nature center, restrooms, and drinking water.

Miles and Directions

0.0 Exit Tonaquint Park and turn right onto Dixie Drive.

1.9 Sinclair mini-mart on the right.

2.5 Cross the Santa Clara River.

3.2 Turn right onto 540 North, then immediately turn left onto the Halfway Wash Bike Trail.

5.2 Snow Canyon Parkway underpass. After 0.05 mile, turn right onto bike path connector.

5.3 Bear left to continue on bike path paralleling Snow Canyon Parkway.

5.4 Go straight at the stop sign at Sonoran Drive.

5.7 Path bends left at SR 18; now riding parallel to SR 18.

8.0 Short steep climb, followed by undulations.

9.6 Cross 4200 North.

9.8 Cross 4400 North.

10.5 Cross Ledges Parkway (under construction as of this writing).

12.3 Cross maintenance access road.

13.2 End of bike path at Snow Canyon Drive; turn right, cross SR 18 (watch for traffic), and turn left.

13.5 Begin climb.

17.0 Crest of climb; begin false flats.

19.0 Enter Dammeron Valley area.

20.8 Begin 7 percent descent.

21.9 Cross Santa Clara River (may be dry); begin climb.

22.2 Enter community of Veyo; mini-marts are adjacent.

23.6 Crest of climb; begin false flats.

25.0 Begin rolling terrain.

26.0 Begin gradual downhill.

27.5 Downhill gets steeper.

29.1 Turn right onto Pine Valley Highway; watch for potholes in turn. Enter Central.

30.6 Cattle guard.

30.7 Enter Dixie National Forest; begin steady climb.

33.4 Cattle guard; gradient eases.

34.2 Resume climbing.

35.5 Crest of climb; begin rolling terrain.

35.9 Cattle guard.

36.7 Begin descent; highway bends right—now on Grass Valley Road.

37.0 Gradient eases; enter Pine Valley.

37.4 At the stop sign at Main Street, turn left.

38.4 Lodge and cafe on the right, steakhouse on the left.

38.9 Cattle guard; entrance to Pine Valley Recreation Area—turn around here.

40.4 Turn right onto Grass Valley Road.

40.8 Road bends left; now on Pine Valley Highway.

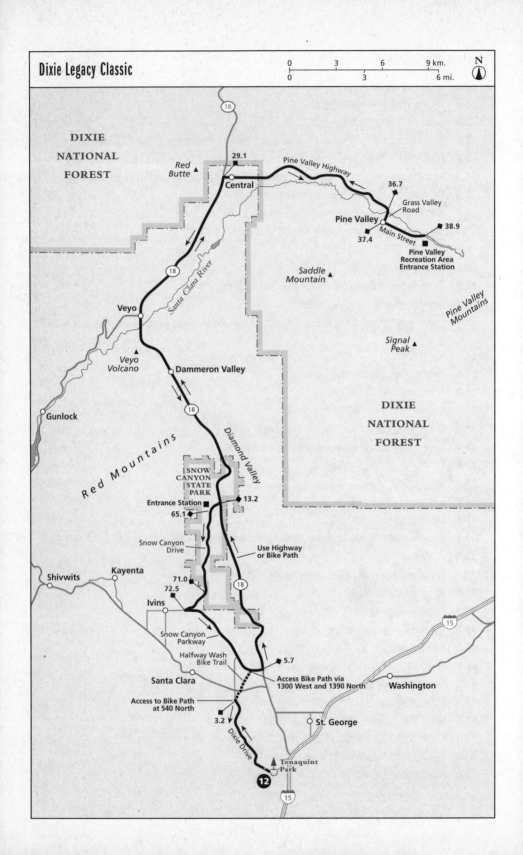

Dixie Legacy Classic

0 3 6 9 km.
0 3 6 mi.

N

DIXIE
NATIONAL
FOREST

Red Butte ▲

29.1

Central

Pine Valley Highway

36.7

Grass Valley
Road

Pine Valley

38.9

Main Street

37.4

Pine Valley
Recreation Area
Entrance Station

*Saddle
Mountain* ▲

Santa Clara River

18

Veyo

*Veyo
Volcano* ▲

Dammeron Valley

18

*Pine Valley
Mountains*

*Signal
Peak* ▲

DIXIE
NATIONAL
FOREST

Gunlock

Diamond Valley

Red Mountains

SNOW
CANYON
STATE
PARK

Entrance Station

13.2

65.1

Snow Canyon
Drive

Use Highway
or Bike Path

Shivwits

Kayenta

71.0

72.5

Ivins

18

Snow Canyon
Parkway

Halfway Wash
Bike Trail

5.7

Access Bike Path via
1300 West and 1390 North

Santa Clara

Washington

15

Access to Bike Path
at 540 North

3.2

St. George

Dixie Drive

✠ *Tonaquint
Park* ▲

12

15

40.9 Cattle guard; begin climb.

41.3 Crest of climb; begin rolling terrain.

41.9 Cattle guard.

42.3 Begin descent.

44.8 Cattle guard.

46.1 Winding descent; watch speed in curves.

47.5 Leave Dixie National Forest.

47.6 Cattle guard; gradient eases. Enter Central.

49.0 At the stop sign at SR 18, turn left.

51.0 Begin gradual downhill.

55.1 Enter Veyo.

55.7 Mini-marts on the left and right.

56.2 Cross Santa Clara River.

56.3 Begin climb.

57.5 Crest of climb; begin rolling terrain.

58.3 Begin ascent; enter Dammeron Valley area.

60.2 Crest of climb; begin rolling terrain.

63.6 Begin 6 percent descent.

65.0 Turn right onto Snow Canyon Drive.

65.1 Enter Snow Canyon State Park; begin descent. Pay $5 entrance fee here or at exit station.

71.0 Exit Snow Canyon State Park; pay $5 fee here if not paid at entrance. Enter Ivins; gradient eases.

72.5 At the stop sign at Center Street and Snow Canyon Parkway; turn left onto Snow Canyon Parkway. Bike path parallels Snow Canyon Parkway, on left side of road.

73.2 Traffic circle; stay on Snow Canyon Parkway.

73.4 Enter St. George.

76.1 Turn right onto 1300 West.

76.2 Turn right onto bike path at 1390 North "Units 4-6" (as signed).

76.3 Bear left onto Halfway Wash Bike Trail.

77.4 The bike path ends at the stop sign at 540 North and Dixie Drive. Cross Dixie Drive and head south (left).

78.2 Cross Santa Clara River.

78.8 Mini-mart on the left.

80.7 End of ride; turn left to enter Tonaquint Park, just north of 600 West.

Local Information

Interagency Information Center: U.S. Bureau of Land Management, 345 East Riverside Drive, St. George. Located in lobby of Bureau of Land Management Office; (435) 688-3246; www.blm.gov/ut/st/en/fo/st_george.

html. Guidebooks and maps on southwestern Utah, national parks, state parks, and national monuments.

Utah State Parks' Snow Canyon State Park Web site: http://stateparks.utah.gov/parks/snow-canyon.

City of Ivins official Web site: www.ivins.com.
Town of Pine Valley Web site: http://pinevalley
utah.org
City of St. George official Web site: www
.sgcity.org.

Restaurants

Bear Paw Coffee Company & Café: 75 North
Main Street, St. George; (435) 634-0126;
www.bearpawcafe.com.
Painted Pony Restaurant: 2 West St. George
Boulevard #22, St. George; (435) 634-1700;
www.painted-pony.com.
**Pancho & Lefty's Mexican Restaurant &
Cantina:** 1050 South Bluff Street, St. George;
(435) 628-4772.
The Pasta Factory: Ancestor Square, 2 West
St. George Boulevard (435) 634-3753; www
.ancestorsquare.com/business/pasta.php.
Paula's Cazuela: 745 West Ridge View Drive,
St. George; (435) 673-6568.
Sullivan's Rococo Steakhouse & Inn: 511
South Airport Road, St. George; (435) 628-
3671; www.rococo.net/steakhouse.html.

Accommodations

Best Western Abbey Inn: 1129 South Bluff
Street, St. George; (435) 652-1234; www
.bestwesternutah.com/hotels/best-western-
abbey-inn/.
Best Western Coral Hills: 125 East St. George
Boulevard, St. George; (435) 673-4884 or
(800) 542-7733; www.coralhills.com.
**Green Gate Village Historic Bed & Breakfast
Inn:** 76 West Tabernacle, St. George; (435)
628-6999 or (800) 350-6999; www.green
gatevillage.com.

Seven Wives Inn Bed & Breakfast: 217 North
100 West, St. George; (435) 628-6737 or
(800) 600-3737; www.sevenwivesinn.com.
McArthur's Temple View RV Resort: 975
South Main Street, St. George; (435) 673-
6400 or (800) 776-4410; www.templeviewrv
.com.
St. George Campground: 2100 East Middleton
Drive, St George; (435) 673-2970.
Snow Canyon State Park (located in Ivins):
(435) 628-2255; http://stateparks.utah.gov/
parks/snow-canyon.

Bicycle Shops

Bicycles Unlimited: 90 South 100 East, St.
George; (435) 673-4492 or (888) 673-4492;
www.bicyclesunlimited.com. Rentals available.
Desert Cyclery: 1091 North Bluff Street
#1530, St. George; (435) 674-2929;.
Moke Sport Outdoors: 25 North Main Street,
St. George; (435) 652-4499. Rentals available.
Red Rock Bicycle Company: 446 West 100
South, St. George; (435) 674-3185; www
.redrockbicycle.com. Rentals available.
Sunset Cycles: 140 North 400 West, St.
George; (435) 215-4251; www.sunset-cycles
.com.

Maps

City of St. George Parks, Trails and Facilities,
City of St. George, Utah, 2005.
Street Map of St. George and Cedar City, North
Star Mapping, 2001.
DeLorme: Utah Atlas & Gazetteer: Page 56
D4.
Benchmark: Utah Road & Recreation Atlas:
Page 80 G5.

13 Escalante Desert Ramble

The Escalante Desert Ramble is a 30-mile loop on mostly flat terrain. Elevations range from 4,968 feet in Milford to 5,280 feet in Minersville. The change in elevation is almost imperceptible along this ride. The ride covers the Milford Flat subregion of the Escalante Desert; conditions are typically dry, so be sure to stock up on fluids. The first half of the ride is on a state highway (SR 21), and the second half is on city streets and secondary roads. The pavement is generally smooth on the state highway, but there may be some rough segments on the secondary roads (Highway 129 was under construction during my field visit in July 2008, repairing damage caused by the Milford Flat fire).

Start: Milford Veterans Park at 600 South and Main Street, Milford.

Length: 30.0 miles (loop, with a short out-and-back segment at the start and finish).

Terrain: False flats, with one railroad overpass.

Minimum and maximum elevations: 4,968 to 5,280 feet.

Traffic and hazards: SR 21: 1,655 vehicles per day between Milford and Minersville in 2005. SR 130: 1,090 vehicles per day in Minersville.

Getting there: From I-15, take exit 112 at Beaver and head west on SR 21. The distance is 17 miles (west) to Minersville, followed by 13 miles (north) to Milford.

The Ride

Franciscans Atanasio Dominguez and Silvestre Velez de Escalante intended to travel from Santa Fe, New Mexico, to Monterey, California, in 1776. The Dominguez-Escalante expedition failed to reach California and ultimately traced a large circle through New Mexico, Arizona, Utah, and Colorado. Although the trip failed, the party was the first group of "white men" to explore this region. Their route passed along the eastern edge of present-day Escalante Desert, a high desert region (minimum elevation of over 5,000 feet) covering about 3,000 square miles in southwestern Utah (mostly in Iron County). The desert receives only about 8 inches of rainfall per year. The desert is part of the much larger Great Basin Desert, which stretches from western Utah, across Nevada, and into eastern California and southeastern Oregon.

A subregion of the Escalante Desert is Milford Flat, a flat, agricultural plain located immediately to the south of the town of Milford, in the northeastern corner of the desert. In July 2007, Milford Flat was the scene of the largest wildfire in Utah history. The fire was started by lightning and eventually burned a 567-square-mile area. The fire was 100 percent contained after an eight-day battle involving up to 400 firefighters. The blaze moved toward the east and northeast, ultimately requiring the closure of long stretches of the I-15 freeway. Two highway fatalities, a five-car pileup, and the abandonment of several cargo loads were all attributed to the fire.

Perhaps the bike rack is not needed—parking at the community pool in Minersville.

Milford, located in Beaver County, had a population of 1,399 in 2008. The city was originally established as a community for miners who worked in the nearby hills and mountains. Cattle-raising became an important activity later. The introduction of the Southern Utah Line in the 1880s made the city an important division terminal. The Union Pacific Railroad continues to operate through the area. Mining activities eventually slowed down, but the construction of a huge geothermal power plant 13 miles northeast of town—serving Utah Power and Light—sustained the city. The city remains relatively quiet, with few tourist amenities, but it has been recognized as a "thorough representative of all aspects of frontier life." Nearby recreational opportunities include Minersville Reservoir, located about 20 miles to the southeast, a few ghost towns, and old mines awaiting (safe) exploration.

The ride begins at the southern end of Milford, at the city's Veterans Park. Turn right onto Main Street (SR 21) and negotiate the railroad overpass. The highway quickly leaves the city environs, entering the Milford Flat area. The Mineral Mountains parallel the highway on the left. Despite the name (prompted, perhaps, by wishful thinking), few minerals have been found in these mountains. After a very gradual but steady upgrade beginning at mile 5.5, the highway crests at mile 11.9; from here, the town of Minersville can be seen in the distance. Turn right onto SR 130 after a short, gradual descent to mile 13.4. Cross the Beaver River and enter Minersville at mile 13.6. Minersville had a population of 817 in 2008. This small town was named in honor of the miners who worked the area. Today, with little mining activity in the region, the name is somewhat misleading. The town is the hub of the Great Utah Bicycle Festival, held in September and featuring road and mountain bike races and rides. After crossing the river, turn right onto Main Street and head west, through town. Minersville City Hall, at 60 West Main Street, is on the National Register of Historic Places (NRHP). A little farther down the road, at 113 West Main Street, is the Rollins-Eyre House. The building dates from the late nineteenth century and is also on the NRHP.

Turn right at 400 West and head north. Turn left onto Thermo Road at mile 14.5 and head west. Next, turn right onto Highway 129 at mile 16.2. This is a former state highway that heads northward through the heart of Milford Flat, past grazing areas, open space, and a few residences. Although the road appears to be pancake flat, the traverse is actually a net descent. The Star Range is off to the left, the scene of mining activity in bygone days. The intriguingly named "Mollies Nipple" is one of the higher peaks in the range, located toward the northeast (of the range). Pray for a tailwind as you negotiate the 13 miles along Highway 129. Turn left at mile 29.3 onto SR 21. The highway curves left, then to the right over the railroad overpass that signals the entrance into Milford. Once in town, turn left almost immediately onto 600 South to return to Veterans Memorial Park and conclude the ride.

Miles and Directions

0.0 Exit the small parking area adjacent Milford Veterans Park in Milford. Turn left onto 600 South, then right onto Main Street (SR 21).

0.2 Begin railroad overpass.

2.3 Highway speed limit increases to 65 mph.

5.5 Begin gradual upgrade.

11.9 Crest of upgrade; begin gradual descent.

13.4 Turn right onto SR 130.

13.6 Cross the Beaver River and enter Minersville. Now on Center Street.

13.7 Turn right onto Main Street.

14.1 At the stop sign at 400 West, turn right.

14.5 At the stop sign at Thermo Road, turn left.

15.6 Cattle guard.

16.2 Turn right onto Highway 129.

29.3 At the stop sign at SR 21, turn left.

30.0 End of ride; turn left onto 600 South and return to Veterans Memorial Park.

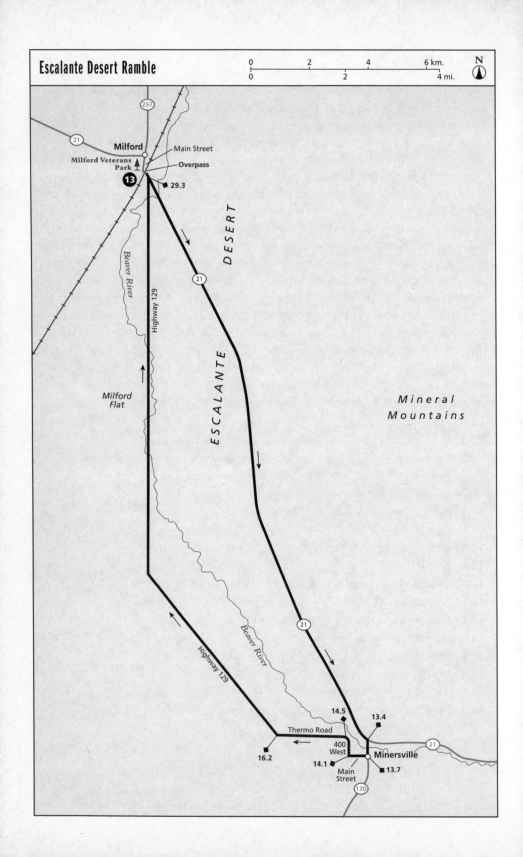

Escalante Desert Ramble

0   2   4   6 km.
0   2   4 mi.

N

257

21

Milford — Main Street

Milford Veterans Park — Overpass

13

■ 29.3

Beaver River

Highway 129

DESERT

21

Milford Flat

ESCALANTE

Mineral Mountains

21

Highway 129

Beaver River

14.5 ■

■ 13.4

Thermo Road

400 West

■ 16.2

14.1 ■

Main Street

Minersville

■ 13.7

21

130

Local Information

City of Milford official Web site: www.milford ut.com.

Restaurants

Hong Kong Café: 433 South Main Street, Milford; (435) 387-2251. Oldest restaurant in southern Utah.

Joe Yee's Station Restaurant: 425 South 100 West, Milford; (435) 387-2804.

Penny's Diner: 777 West Highway 21, Milford; (435) 387-5266.

Accommodations

Affordable Motel (also referred to as Milford Station Motel): 485 South 100 West, Milford; (435) 387-2482.

Oak Tree Inn: 777 West Highway 21, Milford; (435) 387-5266.

Maps

DeLorme: Utah Atlas & Gazetteer: Pages 41, 49 E8 on page 41.

Benchmark: Utah Road & Recreation Atlas: Page 73 A10.

14 Escalante Valley Ramble

The Escalante Valley Ramble is a 23.7-mile out-and-back ride on false flats and gentle rollers, with a few short climbs and descents. The route travels from Enterprise, past Hebron (ghost town), and into the Dixie National Forest where the two Enterprise reservoirs and the intriguing Honeycomb Rocks can be viewed. The elevation ranges from 5,310 feet in Enterprise to 5,715 feet at the Upper Enterprise Reservoir.

Start: Daughters of Utah Pioneers Park, Main and Center Streets, Enterprise.
Length: 23.7 miles (out-and-back).
Terrain: False flats and gently rolling, with a

few short climbs and descents. Minimum and maximum elevations: 5,310 to 5,715 feet.
Traffic and hazards: SR 219 (Main Street): 2,855 vehicles per day in Enterprise in 2005.

Getting there: From St. George, head north on SR 18 to the SR 219 junction; turn left here to get to Enterprise. From Cedar City, head west on SR 56 to Beryl Junction. Turn left onto SR 18 and head south. Continue straight at the SR 18/SR 219 junction, thereby accessing SR 219. Keep straight into Enterprise.

The Ride

The Escalante Valley forms the transitional zone between the Escalante Desert to the north and the Markagunt Plateau and Bull Valley Mountains to the east and south, respectively. The Dominguez–Escalante expedition skirted the edge of the valley during their 1776 trek. Elevations in the valley range from about 5,000 feet on the fringes of the desert to 11,000 feet in the mountains. Proximity to the mountains enables the capture of runoff for the irrigation of crops and for stocking water supplies. Portions of the Escalante Valley were at one time described as being in the Escalante Desert. The discovery of aquifers (pools of water underground) and the introduction of irrigation, however, transformed some of the desert lands into valley areas. There is some concern over ongoing reductions in groundwater levels in the valley, though. Several new fissures (deep cracks in the ground formed by the subsidence of groundwater levels) have been observed in the valley.

Settlement of the Escalante Valley began in the mid-1860s in a community named Hebron, located at the junction of the forks of Shoal Creek, at the foot of the Bull Valley Mountains. The community was named after the more famous ancient city in Palestine. A 1902 earthquake with magnitude 6.0 caused extensive damage in Hebron. Further damage was caused by the 1906 San Francisco earthquake, despite the epicenter being over 500 miles away. The two events, among other issues, were enough to convince the Hebron residents to pack their bags and move 10 miles east to the community of Enterprise. The new residents boosted the population of Enterprise, leading to its incorporation as a city.

A honeycomb rocks formation is dwarfed by the Bull Valley Mountains in Utah's "Dixie."

Enterprise was initially settled by Mormons who worked on a dam project on nearby Shoal Creek. The dam created Enterprise Reservoir, southwest of the city. Enterprise is the nearest city to the Mountain Meadows Massacre site, the scene of an infamous incident in 1857. In this, a local Mormon militia slaughtered the Fancher-Baker party, which had emigrated from Arkansas, heading for California. About 120 men, women, and children were executed. The slaughter was thought to be a form of retaliation against previous acts of maliciousness toward the Mormons, having only recently escaped persecution in Illinois. Nine indictments were eventually issued to members of the militia. Justice was only partially served, however, when just one person was convicted and, eventually, executed. The settlement of Enterprise some forty years later represented a new beginning, being entirely unrelated to the massacre.

Start at the Daughters of Utah Pioneers Park at the corner of Main and Center Streets, in central Enterprise. Turn left onto Main Street and head west. Main Street is SR 219 to the edge of town. Leave Enterprise at mile 0.8 and enter a rural environment of country residences, agriculture, horses, cattle, and false flats. The road surface condition ranges from fair to good. There is a short hill at mile 4.1. Cross Shoal Creek at mile 6.2. Just before the bridge, signs pointing toward the ghost town of Hebron are posted. Turn left immediately after the bridge crossing, following the sign toward Honeycomb Rocks Campground. The road makes a very gradual climb to the Enterprise reservoirs, approximately 300 feet above the elevation of the city. The road negotiates several cattle guards as it winds into the Bull Valley Mountain foothills. Enter Dixie National Forest at mile 8.5. Do not expect to see dense forestation, though; the trees are generally small conifers, including pinyon pines and junipers. Cross Little Pine Creek at mile 10.0. Begin a short climb at mile 10.2. Lower Enterprise Reservoir appears on the right. The road crests at mile 10.7; begin a short, steep descent. The road bends right at 11.2—watch for a poor road surface in the turn. Begin another short climb at mile 11.6. Enter the Honeycomb Rocks Campground area at mile 11.9; Upper Enterprise Reservoir is on the right. Turn around here, adjacent the campground entrance and outhouse. After turning, note the rock formations ahead and to the right. It is quite evident how the site was named! The honeycombs are common in sandstone, which are subject to the formation of tiny cavities (tafoni) in the presence of water. Wind and erosion gradually enlarge the cavities, leading to the creation of some surreal formations.

Head back down the hill adjacent the campground area; turn left at mile 12.5 to return to the main road. Begin a long roller, with a short, steep descent followed by a short, steep ascent. Lower Enterprise Reservoir is on the left. Cross Lone Pine Creek at mile 13.7. Note the creek flowing on the right side of the road. Leave Dixie National Forest at mile 15.2. After negotiating a few cattle guards, turn right at mile 17.4. Cross Shoal Creek immediately after the turn. The road rolls gently through the Shoal Creek valley, adjacent nestled farming and grazing lands. The mountains in the far distance are the Pine Valley range to the right, and the Harmony and Iron ranges toward the center and the left. Enter Enterprise at mile 23.0. The road surface

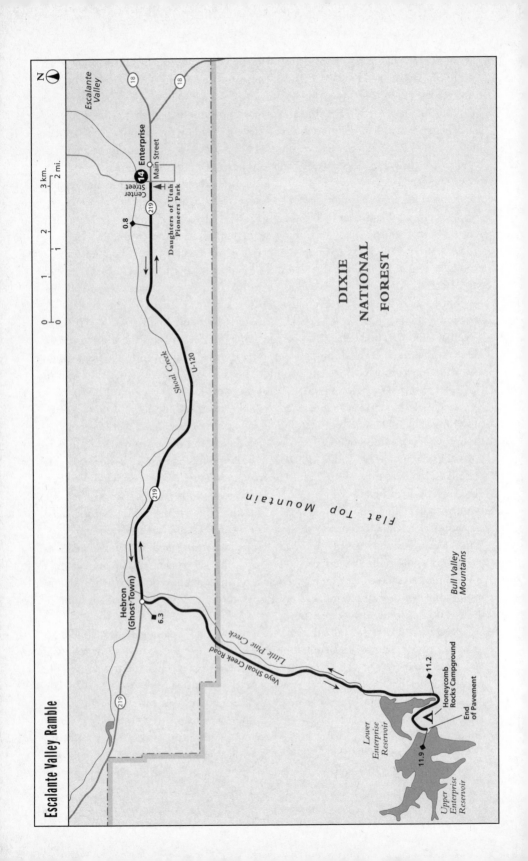

Escalante Valley Ramble

DIXIE NATIONAL FOREST

Flat Top Mountain

Bull Valley Mountains

Escalante Valley

Enterprise

14

Main Street

Center Street

Daughters of Utah Pioneers Park

Shoal Creek

U-120

Hebron (Ghost Town)

Veyo Shoal Creek Road

Little Pine Creek

Honeycomb Rocks Campground

End of Pavement

Lower Enterprise Reservoir

Upper Enterprise Reservoir

0.8

6.3

11.2

11.9

N

3 km.
2 mi.

improves; you are now on Main Street (SR 219). After a short jaunt past some of Enterprise's cozy homes, turn right onto Center Street (mile 23.7). Return to Daughters of Utah Pioneers (DUP) Park. There is a small museum in the park; a much larger memorial museum is located in Salt Lake City, at the DUP headquarters.

Miles and Directions

0.0 Start at Daughters of Utah Pioneers Park, Main and Center Streets, Enterprise. Turn left and head west on Main Street (SR 219).

0.8 End of SR 219 and Main Street; the road continues westward as U-120.

4.1 Short climb.

6.2 Bridge across Shoal Creek.

6.3 Turn left toward Honeycomb Rocks Campground (no other street sign). Cattle guard after turn.

7.4 Cattle guard.

8.0 Cattle guard.

8.5 Enter Dixie National Forest.

10.0 Bridge across Little Pine Creek.

10.2 Short hill; Lower Enterprise Reservoir on the right.

10.4 Restrooms on the right.

10.7 Crest of climb; begin short, steep descent.

11.2 Road bends right (poor road surface in turn).

11.6 Begin short climb. Restrooms on the left.

11.9 Enter Honeycomb Rocks Campground area; Upper Enterprise Reservoir on the right. Turn around here; outhouse adjacent.

12.3 Restrooms on the right.

12.5 Curve left (poor road surface in turn).

12.7 Begin long roller, including a short, steep descent and ascent.

13.1 Lower Enterprise Reservoir on the left.

13.7 Bridge across Little Pine Creek.

15.2 Leave Dixie National Forest.

15.7 Cattle guard.

16.3 Cattle guard.

17.4 Cattle guard, followed by stop sign; turn right to continue.

17.5 Bridge across Shoal Creek.

23.0 Enter Enterprise; now on Main Street (SR 219).

23.7 End of ride; turn right on Center Street and return to Daughters of Utah Pioneers Park.

Local Information

City of Enterprise official Web site: www .enterpriseutah.org.

Dixie National Forest, USDA Forest Service: www.fs.fed.us/r4/dixie.

Restaurants

Carter's Market: 167 East Main Street, Enterprise; (435) 878-2239. Grocery store.

Tropical Sno Stand: Main and Center Streets (mobile); Enterprise; (435) 878-2554.

Tuck's American Favorites: 590 East Main Street, Enterprise; (435) 878-8825.

Accommodations

Jinglebob Inn: 341 South 475 East, Enterprise; (435) 231-0052. Bed-and-breakfast.

Sleep E Motel: SR 18 and SR 219 (855 East Main Street), Enterprise; (435) 878-8802.

Honeycomb Rocks Campground: Dixie National Forest (adjacent Upper Enterprise Reservoir); (435) 688-3246 or (877) 444-6777; www.fs.fed.us/r4/dixie/recreation/campgrounds/honeycombrocks.html.

Bicycle Shops

Enterprise Bicycles: 270 East 400 South, Enterprise; (435) 878-2657.

Maps

DeLorme: Utah Atlas & Gazetteer: Page 56 A3.

Benchmark: Utah Road & Recreation Atlas: Page 80 B4.

15 Iron Mountains Challenge

This is a 62.4-mile out-and-back ride along flat and hilly terrain. The ride starts and finishes in Cedar City, venturing into the Iron Mountains to the west, along the Legacy Loop Highway. The route is flat for the opening 7 miles, climbs for 13 miles, and then descends for 11 miles before retracing the profile in the reverse direction. The route ascends and descends the Iron Mountains in both directions. The elevations range from 5,450 feet on SR 56 just east of the Iron Mountains to 6,560 feet at the Iron Mountains summit. Most of the course is on SR 56, so the pavement is generally smooth. The highway actually passes between several mountain ranges: The Swett Hills are on the right upon leaving the city; the Iron Mountains are immediately to the west. The Harmony Mountains are to the left (i.e., on the south side of SR 56). You probably will not notice the difference when you are riding, though—they will all be mountains.

Start: Bicentennial Park at 1045 North and North Cedar Boulevard, Cedar City.
Length: 62.4 miles (out-and-back).
Terrain: 25 percent flat; 75 percent climbing and descending. Minimum and maximum elevations: 5,450 to 6,560 feet.

Traffic and hazards: SR 56: 5,475 vehicles per day west of I-15 in Cedar City in 2005; 1,860 vehicles per day through the Iron Mountains. Airport Road: 3,920 vehicles per day between SR 56 and Kitty Hawk Drive.

Getting there: Cedar City is 250 miles south of Salt Lake City, 50 miles north of St. George, and 180 miles north of Las Vegas, all along I-15. To get to Bicentennial Park, head east on 200 North to 400 West. Turn left here and head north. At the end of 400 West, turn left onto Coal Creek Road. Turn right onto 1045 North; Bicentennial Park is on the right.

Soloing away from the chase pack and the Iron Mountains, near Cedar City.

The Ride

Iron ore was discovered in the mountains west of Cedar City in 1850. Iron was being produced in small quantities until 1858, when cheaper iron was brought in from the East. Production resumed in the 1920s following discoveries of large quantities of iron ore. Iron production peaked during the 1960s but continues to this day. Utah remains the fourth-largest iron producer in the United States. The mountains contain several iron mines, as well as a few abandoned ones, and a ghost town (Irontown). Cedar City is located 15 to 20 miles east of the mountains. The local economy has not depended on mining for some time, having expanded into cultural (Utah Shakespearean Festival), educational (Southern Utah University), sporting (Utah Summer Games), and other arenas. The city had a population of 28,667 in 2008, making it the second-largest city in southern Utah after St. George. Despite being only 50 miles apart, the two cities do not share the same climate. While St. George sits at an elevation of 2,700 feet, Cedar City is at a gasping 5,840 feet. Cedar City is served by I-15 as well as by commercial flights at the local airport. Its accessibility has made the city an alternative base for exploring southern Utah; Cedar City, in fact, is closer to Bryce Canyon National Park and Cedar Breaks National Monument than St. George.

The summer months are busy in Cedar City, with the Utah Summer Games in June and the Utah Shakespearean Festival running from June until August, with a second season in the fall. Although lodging facilities are plentiful, occupancy can approach 100 percent during this period.

Mormon settlers arrived in present-day Iron County from Salt Lake City in 1850. The first band was preceded by the 1776 Dominguez-Escalante expedition and the 1826 Jedediah Smith trek. All of these parties were predated, however, by the Fremont and Anasazi cultures and, later, the southern Paiutes. An iron empire was envisioned by the Mormon pioneers. The going was tough initially, as there were crop failures, floods, harsh winters, and shortages of skilled workers. About three-quarters of a century of hard work finally led to successful mining and agricultural activities. Today, tourism is a major aspect of the economy. In recent years, a number of high-tech companies have established headquarters in Cedar City, possibly attracted to the growth, strong economic climate, and availability of workers. Unlike many Utah cities and towns that have stabilized, and possibly still living in the past, Cedar City's history is still being written.

Cycling has a "presence" in Cedar City. The Utah Summer Games' cycling competitions are held on the roads near Cedar City, including a criterium, hillclimb, road race (using most of the Iron Mountains Challenge course), and time trial. The Color Country Cycling Club has regular rides.

Begin the ride at Bicentennial Park on the north side of Cedar City, at 1045 North and North Cedar Boulevard. Turn left onto 1045 North; at the stop sign, turn right onto Coal Creek Road. The road flies over I-15 and then bends to the right, becoming Bulldog Road (in reference to a local high school mascot). Turn left onto Kitty Hawk Drive. As suggested, you are near the Cedar City Regional Airport. Turn left onto Airport Road at mile 0.9 and head south. At the traffic signal, turn right onto 200 North (SR 56). You are now on the western edge of the city, heading away from town and toward the distant mountains. The highway gradually narrows to two lanes, and the speed limit gradually increases to 65 mph. The road bends to the left at mile 6.2—stay on the main highway. At mile 6.6, you will notice that the pedaling starts to become labored as the highway starts to climb. The climbing begins in earnest at mile 9.5—the mountains are ahead.

Enter a forested area at mile 13.2; the highway brushes by Dixie National Forest, which is to the south. The climb is steady along this section, although the gradient varies. Underneath the trees, underground, are the veins of ore that keep mining active in the Cedar City area. The veins are the result of reactions between Paleozoic and Mesozoic limestone and volcanic magma. Iron, copper, silver, and gold can be found; history recorded that the industrious Brigham Young did not care much for gold and silver, however. The climb reaches a "preliminary" crest at mile 18.0. The landscape is picturesque, with rolling hills dotted with low trees (pinyon pine and juniper). After a short descent, the climbing continues to mile 18.6, after which the highway begins to roll. This is the crest through the Iron Mountains; the descent down the west side of the mountains begins at mile 20.0. An expansive vista opens up at mile 21.7. Silver Peak (elevation 7,273 feet), which appears somewhat hostile, is off to the right. The highway continues to descend toward Escalante Valley, then levels at mile 30.5; enter Newcastle at mile 30.9. Newcastle is a small farming community (population unknown) that is home to some excellent geothermal resources. The possibility of producing electricity here was being considered. Turn around at Main Street (mile 31.2; convenience mart on the corner) to begin the return trip. You are now heading east on SR 56.

Begin climbing at mile 32.0. The grade eases, briefly, at mile 32.8 and then increases at mile 33.2. Silver Peak is now on the left; notice its bald top. The landscape is desert scrub interspersed with low trees—a frequent scene in Utah. The grade eases at mile 36.4 then increases again at mile 37.6. Notice the scarring on the adjacent mountainsides, the result of mining activities. A false crest comes at mile 42.2; after a short false flat, the real summit is crossed at mile 43.1. After a 1-mile descent, one final, short climb awaits. Restart the descent at mile 44.5. The mountains in the far distance are the Hurricane Cliffs. Cedar Valley is spread out before you as you descend. The highway is essentially flat by mile 52.8. The road bends right at mile 56.1. Move toward the center lane around mile 60.0 to prepare for a left turn onto Airport Road (signalized intersection). Be patient and cautious when making the turn. Head north on Airport Road to Kitty Hawk Road (mile 61.4) and turn right. The airport is to the left. Turn right onto Bulldog Road and cross over I-15. The road bends left, becoming Coal Creek Road. Turn left onto 1045 North and look for Bicentennial Park on the right (mile 62.4).

Miles and Directions

0.0 Start at Bicentennial Park, 1045 North and North Cedar Boulevard in Cedar City. Exit the park and turn left onto 1045 North.

0.15 At the stop sign at Coal Creek Road, turn left.

0.2 I-15 overpass.

0.4 Road bends right; now on Bulldog Road.

0.45 Turn left onto Kitty Hawk Drive.

0.9 At the stop sign at Airport Road, turn left.

1.6 Railroad crossing (single track).

2.0 At the traffic signal at 200 North (SR 56), turn right.

2.6 Railroad crossing (skewed single track—be careful).

6.2 Highway bends left.

6.6 Begin gradual climb.

9.5 Grade increases (eases and increases intermittently for the next several miles).

13.2 Enter forested area (near Dixie National Forest).

18.0 Crest of climb; begin short descent.

18.4 Foot of descent; begin short climb.

18.6 Crest of climb; now on false flats.

20.0 Begin descent.

Iron Mountains Challenge

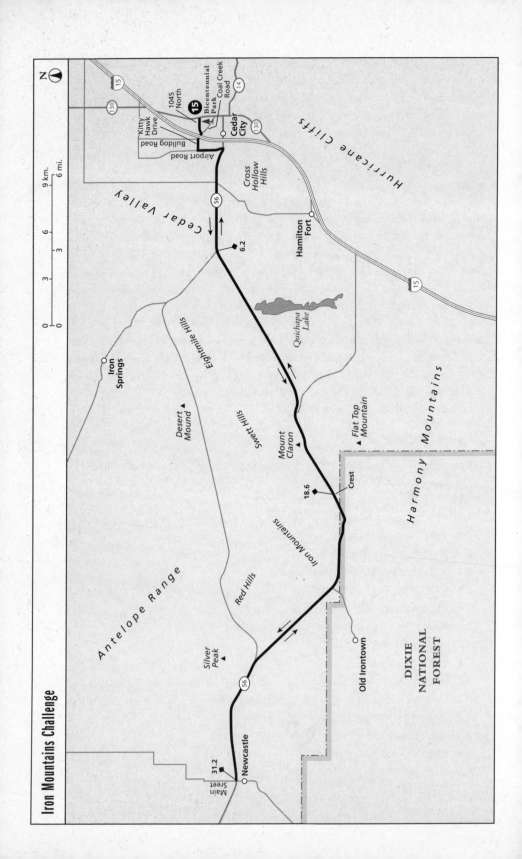

24.8 Grade eases; now on false flat.

27.4 Descent resumes.

30.5 Base of descent; highway is now level.

30.9 Enter Newcastle.

31.2 Turn around at Main Street; mini-mart on the right.

32.0 Begin climb (now heading east on SR 56).

33.2 Grade increases.

36.4 Grade eases; now on false flat.

37.6 Climbing resumes.

42.2 Crest of climb; now on false flats.

43.1 Summit (6,560 feet); begin short descent.

44.1 Begin short climb.

44.5 Crest of climb; begin descent.

52.8 Grade eases; highway is now on flat section.

56.1 Highway bends to the right.

59.7 Railroad crossing (skewed single track—be careful).

60.4 At the traffic signal at Airport Road, move into left turn lane (highway has 5 lanes) and turn left.

60.8 Railroad crossing (single track).

61.4 Turn right onto Kitty Hawk Drive.

61.9 At the stop sign at Bulldog Road, turn right—road bends left at I-15 overpass to become Coal Creek Road.

62.2 Turn left onto 1045 North.

62.4 End of ride; return to Bicentennial Park, on the right.

Local Information

City of Cedar City official Web site: www .cedarcity.org.

Color Country Cycling Club, based in Cedar City: www.colorcountrycycling.org.

Restaurants

Market Grill: 2290 West 400 North, Cedar City; (435) 586-9325; http://marketgrill.net.

The Pastry Pub: 86 West Center Street, Cedar City; (435) 867-1400; www.cedarcitypastry pub.com.

Pizza Factory & Pasta: 131 South Main Street, Cedar City; (435) 586-3900.

Sullivan's Café & Sulli's Steak House: 301 South Main Street, Cedar City; (435) 586-6761; www.sullivanscafe.com.

Accommodations

One hundred percent occupancy is reached at times during the summer (reservations recommended).

Abbey Inn: 940 West 200 North, Cedar City; (435) 586-9966 or (800) 325-5411; www .abbeyinncedar.com.

Baker House Bed & Breakfast: 1800 Royal Hunte Drive, Cedar City; (435) 867-5695 or (888) 611-8181; www.bbhost.com/ bakerhouse/.

Bard's Inn Bed & Breakfast: 150 South 100 West, Cedar City; (435) 586-6612; http:// bards.qwestoffice.net.

Best Western El Rey Inn & Suites: 80 South Main Street, Cedar City; (435) 586-6518; www.bestwesternutah.com/hotels/best- western-el-rey-inn-and-suites/.

Best Western Town & Country Inn: 189 North Main Street, Cedar City; (435) 586-9900; www.bestwesternutah.com/hotels/best-western-town-and-country-inn/.
Cedar City KOA: 1121 North Main Street, Cedar City; (435) 586-9872 or (800) 562-9873; www.koa.com/where/ut/44125/.
Country Aire RV Park: 1700 North Main Street, Cedar City; (435) 586-2550.

Bicycle Shops
Bike Route: 70 West Center Street (University Avenue), Cedar City; (435) 586-4242.
Cedar Cycle: 38 East 200 South, Cedar City; (435) 586-5210; www.cedarcycle.com.

Maps
Street Map of St. George and Cedar City, North Star Mapping, 2001.
DeLorme: Utah Atlas & Gazetteer: Pages 48, 49 E7 on page 49.
Benchmark: Utah Road & Recreation Atlas: Pages 73, 80, 81 H10 on page 73.

16 Johnson Canyon Cruise

The Johnson Canyon Cruise is a 50.8-mile out-and-back course. The elevations range from 4,985 feet in Kanab to 5,950 feet at the turnaround. The ride begins at the Grand Staircase- Escalante National Monument (GSENM) Visitor Center on the eastern edge of Kanab. The route spends very little time in Kanab, immediately heading toward the expansive sagebrush flats east of town and the wonderful landscape of the GSENM.

Start: Grand Staircase-Escalante National Monument Visitor Center, 745 East Highway 89, Kanab (hours: 8:00 a.m. to 5:00 p.m. seven days a week, mid-March through mid-November; 8:00 a.m. to 4:30 p.m. mid-November through mid-March).
Length: 50.8 miles (out-and-back).

Terrain: Rolling hills and false flats. Minimum and maximum elevations: 4,985 to 5,950 feet.
Traffic and hazards: US 89: 2,450 vehicles per day east of Kanab in 2005; 2,120 vehicles per day at Big Water; 3,190 vehicles per day at the Arizona state line.

Getting there: From I-15 in the St. George area, exit to SR 9 and head east to Hurricane. In Hurricane, get onto SR 59. This highway proceeds through Hilldale and enters Arizona at Colorado City, before terminating at US 89A in Fredonia. Turn left and head north on US 89A to Kanab. Once in Kanab, turn right and head east on US 89. The GSENM Visitor Center is at the eastern edge of Kanab.

The Ride

Kanab (population 3,782 in 2008) is the seat of Kane County, located in a rugged region of southern Utah. Kanab is bordered by the Vermilion Cliffs on the north, the Kaibab Plateau and Shinarump Cliffs on the south, the Moquith Mountains and several canyons on the west, and, prior to the damming that formed Lake Powell, the Colorado River on the east. The region is so rugged that, in fact, it was one of the last areas of the continental United States to be mapped. Kanab, at an elevation of 4,925 feet, was once considered to be one of the most isolated towns in the United States; before the introduction of highways into the area, access was a challenge. The Anasazi, Desert, and Southern Paiute cultures all inhabited the valleys and canyons surrounding Kanab during different eras, before "white men" established a settlement. The name "Kanab" is, in fact, a derivative of a Southern Paiute word meaning "willow basket," which was used to carry a baby on a mother's back. Early white settlers abandoned Kanab initially when they experienced hostilities from the Native American tribes. Just a few years later, however, around 1870, Mormon pioneers returned to Kanab and established a peaceful community.

During the twentieth century, Kanab established itself as "Little Hollywood," serving as the scene for over 150 "western"-themed films and television shows. Frontier Movie Town in Kanab is a permanent movie-set replica. A number of actual movie sets exist in the undeveloped areas around town, but they are generally on private lands. If you have seen any of the movies shot in and around Kanab—*The Outlaw Josey Wales, Rin Tin Tin, The Greatest Story Ever Told, The Lone Ranger, My Friend Flicka, Planet of the Apes*, and others—then you will sense an eerie familiarity with the area.

More recently, Kanab has become one of the gateways to the Grand Staircase-Escalante National Monument (GSENM). In 1996 flags in Kanab flew at half-mast when the 1.7-million-acre GSENM was officially designated by President Bill Clinton. Why? Because the GSENM is rich in coal and petroleum, and it was a fleeting hope for locals that the region would generate potentially high-paying jobs and extensive industrial development. The GSENM is managed by the Bureau of Land Management (BLM) rather than the National Parks Service. The Johnson Canyon Cruise explores a small sector of the GSENM.

Exit the visitor center onto Fairway Drive, turning left to cross US 89. Once across US 89, turn left onto Chinle Drive—watch for gravel in the turn. This 5.0-mile stretch of road is Old Highway 89, and it serves as a practically car-free alternative to the main highway. Old Highway 89 is used for the bike portion of the annual Kanab Triathlon. Turn left onto 8-Mile Gap Road (4400 East) at mile 5.1. At mile 5.2, turn right to continue eastward on US 89. (I observed that new residential construction in July 2008 was extending Chinle Drive farther eastward). Although the speed limit on US 89 is 65 mph, there is a shoulder, and the traffic volume was fewer than 2,500 vehicles per day in 2005. Turn left onto Johnson Canyon Road at mile 8.9 and begin the northbound trek into Johnson Canyon, amidst the Vermilion Cliffs, with the White Cliffs in the distance adding to the cornucopia of colors. The road is gradually uphill, although you may not notice as you gaze at the mixture of red, cream, and pink cliffs.

About 6 miles up the canyon, take note of the structures on the right. The some-what familiar-looking buildings were featured regularly in the television series *Gunsmoke*. The buildings were also used occasionally in *Have Gun Will Travel*, *Death Valley Days*, and *Wagon Train*. While observing the cliffs and the "historical" buildings, also be sure to notice the periodic "sinks" that appear on the right. The soft layers of Chinle shale have eroded to form these sinks; the surrounding cliffs, however, are composed of hard layers of Navajo sandstone. Enter the GSENM at mile 20.6. The gradient increases beyond this point as you snake between the walls of Wygaret Terrace. The walls recede at mile 24.5, and the vista now includes the Pink Cliffs and Skutumpah Terrace. You never actually get there, though, as the pavement ends at mile 25.4. The now dirt road splits—to the left as Johnson Canyon Road (also known as Alton Amphitheater Scenic Backway), and to the right as Skutumpah Road—but pay these no mind, as it is time to turn around.

The return trip begins with a descent through the narrow canyon that you just climbed. On the way back, you may want to pay attention to the plant and bird life along the route. Larks, sparrows, vultures, swallows, thrashers, wrens, eagles, hawks, and falcons are common sightings. A trained eye may be needed to see some of the less

The White Cliffs of Johnson Canyon beckon a riderless bike.

common birds that have been sighted in the GSENM, including grebes, loons, herons, pelicans, doves, and roadrunners. Box elder, cottonwood, juniper, and pinyon pines are abundant in the canyon. As you near US 89, the panorama includes the Shinarump Cliffs; farther in the distance are the mountains and trees of the Kaibab National Forest. Still farther is the Grand Canyon, directly south of Johnson Canyon and Kanab, although you cannot actually see the canyon from here. Turn right onto US 89 at mile 41.9. Look for the left turn onto 8-Mile Gap Road (4400 East) at mile 45.6. Watch for vehicular traffic when making the turn. At the stop sign, turn right onto Chinle Drive. Enjoy the view of the colorfully eroded cliffs on the right, as well as the city of Kanab, as you head westward. At mile 50.7, at the stop sign, turn right onto 700 East. After a stop at US 89, continue across, where the road becomes Fairway Drive. The GSENM Visitor Center is on the right. For your convenience and refreshment, a Walker's mini-mart and Wendy's are on the left, across the street from the visitor center.

Miles and Directions

0.0 Exit Grand Staircase-Escalante National Monument (GSENM) Visitor Center parking lot (east side); turn left onto Fairway Drive, then left again to continue on Fairway Drive. Walker's mini-mart and Wendy's are adjacent.

0.05 Stop at US 89; proceed across—now on 700 East.

0.1 At the stop sign, turn left onto Chinle Drive.

0.9 Begin climb.

1.7 Crest of climb; begin rolling terrain.

5.1 Turn left onto 8-Mile Gap Road (4400 East).

5.2 At the stop sign at US 89, turn right.

8.9 Turn left onto Johnson Canyon Road.

19.6 Cattle guard.

20.6 Enter GSENM.

24.5 Cattle guard.

25.4 End of pavement at Y intersection with Skutumpah Road; turn around here and begin return trip.

26.3 Cattle guard.

30.2 Leave GSENM.

31.2 Cattle guard.

41.9 At the stop sign at US 89, turn right.

45.6 Turn left onto 8-Mile Gap Road (4400 East).

45.7 At the stop sign at Chinle Drive, turn right (no street sign).

49.1 Begin descent.

49.9 Base of descent.

50.7 Turn right onto 700 East. After 0.05 mile, go straight at the stop sign at US 89; now on Fairway Drive.

50.8 End of ride; turn right and enter the GSENM Visitor Center parking lot.

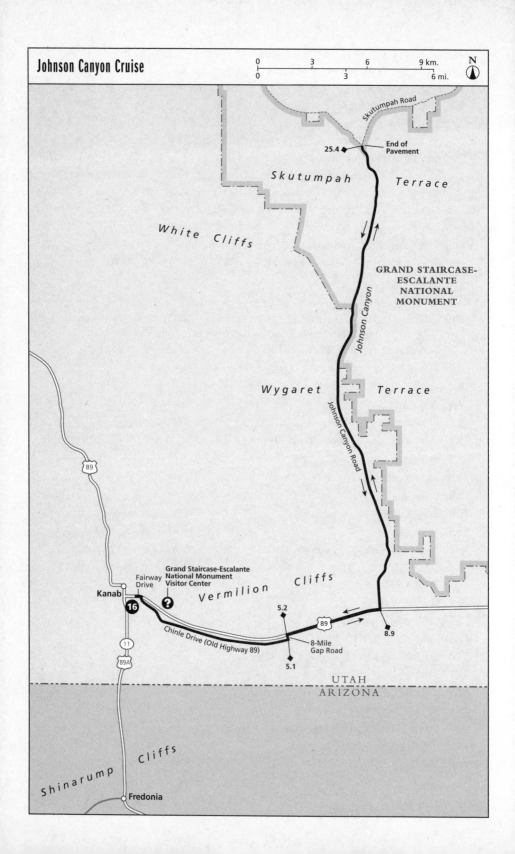

Johnson Canyon Cruise

Local Information

City of Kanab official Web site: http://kanab
.utah.gov.
Grand Staircase Escalante National Monument information: www.blm.gov/ut/st/en/fo/
grand_staircase-escalante.html.

Restaurants

Escobar's Mexican Restaurant: 373 East 300
South, Kanab; (435) 644-3739.
Houston's Trail's End Restaurant: 32 East
Center Street, Kanab; (435) 644-2488; www
.houstons.net. Open April through October.
Nedra's, Too: 310 South 100 East, Kanab;
(435) 644-2030; www.nedrascafe.com.
Rocking V Café: 97 West Center Street, Kanab;
(435) 644-8001; www.rockingvcafe.com. Open
March through November.
Vermillion Espresso Bar and Café: 4 East
Center Street, Kanab; (435) 644-3886. Open
November through February.
Wok Inn: 86 South 200 West, Kanab; (435)
644-5400. Open March through October.

Accommodations

Best Western Red Hills: 125 West Center
Street, Kanab; (435) 644-2675 or (800) 830-
2675; www.bestwesternredhills.com.

Holiday Inn Express: 815 East US 89, Kanab;
(435) 644-3100 or (888) HOLIDAY; www
.ichotelsgroup.com/h/d/ex/1/en/hotel/knbut.
Located directly across from the GSENM Visitor
Center.
Parry Lodge: 89 East Center Street, Kanab;
(435) 644-2601 or (888) 289-1722; www
.parrylodge.com.
Rodeway Inn: 70 South 200 West, Kanab;
(435) 644-5500; www.rodewayinn.com/hotel-
kanab-utah-UT144?promo=gglocal.
Crazy Horse Campark: 625 East 300 South,
Kanab; (435) 644-2782. Open mid-April
through late October.
Hitch'n Post RV Park: 196 East 300 South,
Kanab; (435) 644-2142 or (800) 458-3516;
www.hitchnpostrvpark.com.
Kanab RV Corral: 483 South 100 East, Kanab;
(435) 644-5330; www.kanabrvcorral.com.

Maps

DeLorme: Utah Atlas & Gazetteer: Page 58
D2.
Benchmark: Utah Road & Recreation Atlas:
Pages 75, 76 G11 on page 75.

17 Journey Through Time Challenge

The Journey Through Time Challenge is a 58.1-mile out-and-back ride over rolling terrain with several steep climbs and descents. The ride travels SR 12, an All-American Highway (i.e., *very* scenic) between Escalante and Boulder in the Grand Staircase-Escalante National Monument. Bike handling skills are a must in negotiating the winding descents, and stamina is needed to surmount the climbs. The elevation ranges from 5,820 feet in Escalante, to 5,204 feet at the Escalante River crossing, to 6,775 feet to the southwest of Boulder. The route is entirely on SR 12, except for a turnaround loop along city of Boulder streets.

Start: Escalante Ranger District, Glen Canyon National Recreation Area and Grand Staircase-Escalante National Monument (long name), 755 West Main Street (SR 12), Escalante.
Length: 58.1 miles (out-and-back).

Terrain: Almost constantly rolling, with several steep climbs and descents. Minimum and maximum elevations: 5,204 to 6,775 feet.
Traffic and hazards: SR 12: 1,375 vehicles per day in Escalante in 2005; 740 vehicles per day between Escalante and Boulder.

Getting there: From I-15, take exit 95 and head east on SR 20. Turn right onto US 89 at the junction and head south. Once past Panguitch, staying on US 89, turn left onto SR 12, toward Bryce Canyon National Park. Continue on SR 12 beyond the park, passing through the communities of Tropic, Cannonville, and Henrieville. The next community is Escalante, where the ride starts. The ranger station is at the entrance to town, on SR 12.

The Ride

Grand Staircase-Escalante National Monument (GSENM) was designated in 1996 after a controversial decision-making period and debate, the latter of which had lasted for decades. The federal government acted, in part, amidst fears that mining operations would destroy the landscape and the area's archaeological ruins. Local communities were not pleased with the federal intervention, as they had looked forward to further agricultural and economic development in some of these areas. Making the dedication at the Grand Canyon—in Arizona, not Utah—further damaged the locals' trust in "them Easterners" handling of Utah's lands. One decade later, the controversy still simmers, but the communities have been gradually adapting to the new ecotourism. It is hard to argue against the need for preservation of these lands after a visit and after learning about the geological and human history that is so rich here: A vast inland sea once covered this area, dinosaurs once walked here, the Anasazi tribe once settled here, leaving behind some archaeological treasures, and Spanish and American explorers mapped and established communities here.

The GSENM covers a vast 1.9 million acres and includes three distinct districts: Escalante River canyons and wilderness in the east, Kaiparowits Plateau in the center, and the Grey, White, and Pink Cliffs of the Grand Staircase in the west. The GSENM is the largest parkland in the southwestern United States. The Grand Staircase is a series of small plateaus that descend, in giant steps, from Bryce Canyon in the north to Grand Canyon in the south. The Staircase is part of the much larger Colorado Plateau, which covers all of Utah east of the Wasatch Plateau. The Journey Through Time is the official name of SR 12, a 124-mile U.S. scenic byway and "All-American Road." The "journey" retraces some 300 million years of evolution and change that can be visualized along and off the highway. The Bureau of Land Management (BLM) has divided the GSENM into four zones; the Monument Front (near SR 12, other paved roads, and settlements) is the most accessible and frequented. Settlements are found on the northern and southern fringes of the monument. The largest is Escalante (population 763 in 2008). The city has been transformed by the establishment of the GSENM: What was formerly a blip along the highway, famous for potato farming, is becoming an important base for monument visitors. Escalante is named in honor of the Spanish explorer who ventured through this area in 1776 but actually passed nowhere near the current site of the town. The town was originally named "Potato"; potatoes still grow wildly in the area. Although the Anasazi occupied these environs during the early centuries of the first millennium, white men did not "discover" the Escalante area until the mid-nineteenth century. Even then, the discovery was merely a circumstance of the Black Hawk War, during which a group of Mormon cavalry came upon the Escalante area while pursuing Native Americans.

State Highway 12 (SR 12) was completed in 1935 under President Franklin D. Roosevelt's Civilian Conservation Corps. The highway cost $1 million to construct, making it one of the most expensive roads of the time. Before the road, the only access to the Escalante-Boulder area was by horse or pack mule. The 15-mile segment from the Calf Creek Recreation Area to Boulder, which is part of the Journey Through Time Challenge, is extraordinary, not to mention exhausting, with its steep climbs and descents.

Start the ride at the Escalante Ranger District office located on SR 12 on the western edge of Escalante. The office was established in 2003 and represents several agencies (BLM, USDA Forest Service, National Parks Service). Walk your bicycle to the highway (unpaved parking lot) and begin the ride. Head east on SR 12, passing through Escalante. This would be a good time to pick up provisions. Leave Escalante at mile 2.0, on a slight uphill. False flats and rolling terrain begin shortly thereafter. The scenery for the next 4 miles is relatively ordinary: desert scrub, low trees, and a few sinks. Enter the GSENM at mile 5.8 and start heading across Big Flat. The first truly steep part of the route begins at mile 10.4: an 8 percent downgrade. You are now at the Head of Rocks, overlooking Escalante Canyon from various vantage points; the view is occasionally obscured because of the numerous curves. A short climb begins at mile 12.7; the route rolls for 1 mile after cresting at mile 13.1. Another 8 percent downgrade follows, passing through a spectacular cut that demonstrates the challenges of penetrating this rugged region. The Kiva Koffeehouse, seemingly in the

Riders cruise through Escalante after a "journey through time."

middle of nowhere, appears on the left at mile 14.9. If you are in need of a caffeine boost, then this would be the place to get it. The cliffs are spectacular here. Cross the Escalante River at mile 15.5. The Calf Creek Recreation Area is on the left at mile 16.1. This is a great place for a picnic or hike, particularly to see Lower Calf Creek Falls plunging 126 feet from the rock walls into a pool surrounded by shade trees. The hike is 5.5 miles, however, which may sap some of the energy needed to complete this ride. Back to the road, begin to climb beyond here.

The climbing continues for the next few miles, getting quite steep at mile 18.9. The reward is at the crest, at mile 19.1; you are now entering "The Hogsback"—also referred to as New Home Bench—in which the highway travels along a narrow ridge, with steep drop-offs on both sides. To your left is the Phipps–Death Hollow Outstanding Natural Area (part of the GSENM); on your right is Boulder Creek Canyon. The highway winds along the ridge to mile 21.3, where the highway straightens. Boulder Mountain is in the far distance. Begin a steep (8 percent) downhill at mile 25.1. The highway begins to level at mile 27.3 on the outskirts of Boulder (population 186 in 2008). The Boulder Creek valley is quite scenic. Begin a gradual climb into town at mile 27.8. At mile 28.2, SR 12 makes a hard bend to the left; bear right at this point onto Boulder-Bullfrog Scenic Road. The Boulder Mesa Restaurant is on the left. Turn left at mile 28.6 onto Lower Boulder Road (no street sign). The road winds through a quiet residential area before returning to SR 12. Turn left onto SR 12 at mile 29.3 to begin the return trip. Note that this turn is somewhat west of the center of Boulder. If you have need for provisions, you may go off-course and head east on SR 12, into town to obtain food and beverage. Alternatively, there is a mini-mart at mile 30.7, just outside of town on the return trip.

The return ride features a net elevation loss of about 900 feet, including a net 1,500-foot drop to the Escalante River. From the river, however, there is a net elevation gain of 620 feet. The highway descends out of Boulder, making a sharp bend to the right as you exit town. The mini-mart mentioned above is on the right at mile 30.7. Begin an 8 percent climb at mile 31.3. Beyond the crest, at mile 36.7, is The Hogsback. You are now getting a different perspective on this ridge and the deep canyons on the left and right. The highway continues to roll and wind through the intriguing landscape. The highway descends quite steeply (14 percent) at mile 38.8; rolling terrain, generally downhill, follows. Calf Creek Recreation Area is on the right at mile 42.0. The steep cliffs of the Haymaker (on the left) and Bowington (on the right) Benches are just as engaging now as they were on the outbound trip. Cross the Escalante River at mile 42.6 and begin to climb. The road crests and straightens at mile 43.9; there is a short downhill at mile 45.1, followed by a climb at mile 45.5. This is the last strenuous climb of the route, taking you to the top of Big Flat. Enter Escalante at mile 56.7; the road through town is gradually uphill. The Escalante Ranger District office is on the left at mile 58.1. Turn left and enter the parking area to end the ride.

Miles and Directions

0.0 Start at Escalante Ranger District office at 755 West Main Street (SR 12), Escalante. Walk bicycle to highway, turn right, and head east.

1.2 Slight uphill.

1.8 Mini-mart on the right (and other marts and eateries).

2.0 Leave Escalante. Begin false flats and rolling terrain.

5.8 Enter Grand Staircase-Escalante National Monument (no entrance fee).

10.4 Begin 8 percent downgrade.

11.6 Cattle guard; continue winding descent.

12.7 Begin short climb.

13.1 Crest of climb; begin rolling terrain.

14.1 Begin 8 percent downgrade.

14.9 Kiva Koffeehouse on the left.

15.5 Cross Escalante River.

16.1 Calf Creek Recreation Area on the left; begin climb.

16.7 Cattle guard; climb becomes steeper.

18.2 Crest of climb; begin rolling terrain.

18.9 Begin steep climb.

19.1 False crest; continue rolling terrain.

20.5 Begin The Hogsback.

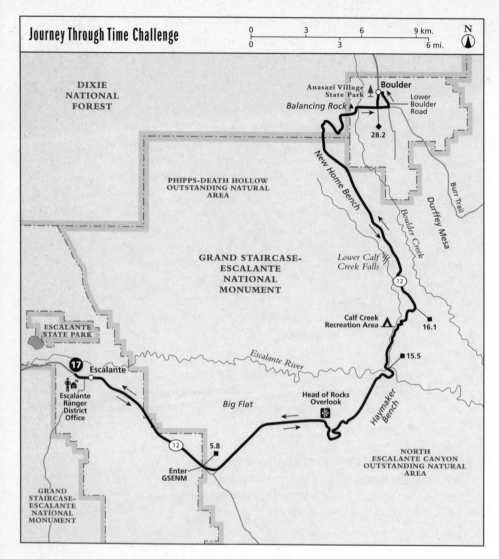

Journey Through Time Challenge

0   3   6   9 km.
0   3   6 mi.

N

DIXIE
NATIONAL
FOREST

Anasazi Village
State Park

Boulder

Balancing Rock

Lower
Boulder
Road

28.2

New Home Bench

Boulder Creek

Durffey Mesa

Burr Trail

PHIPPS-DEATH HOLLOW
OUTSTANDING NATURAL
AREA

GRAND STAIRCASE-
ESCALANTE
NATIONAL
MONUMENT

*Lower Calf
Creek Falls*

12

ESCALANTE
STATE PARK

Calf Creek
Recreation Area

16.1

Escalante River

15.5

17 Escalante

Escalante
Ranger
District
Office

Big Flat

Head of Rocks
Overlook

Haymaker Bench

12   5.8

Enter
GSENM

NORTH
ESCALANTE CANYON
OUTSTANDING NATURAL
AREA

GRAND
STAIRCASE-
ESCALANTE
NATIONAL
MONUMENT

21.3   Leave The Hogsback; highway straightens—begin false flats.

25.1   Begin 8 percent downgrade.

26.3   Enter Boulder.

27.3   Road levels. Hills of Hollows Mini-mart on the left.

27.8   Begin climb into town.

28.2   Bear right onto Boulder-Bullfrog Scenic Road.

28.6   Turn left onto Lower Boulder Road (no street sign).

29.2   Road bends left.

29.3   At the stop sign at SR 12, turn left to begin return trip.

29.8   Highway curves to the right; continue descending.

31.0	Cross Boulder Creek; short climb, then rolling terrain.
31.7	Begin series of false crests, false flats, and rolling sections.
36.7	Enter The Hogsback.
38.8	Begin 14 percent downgrade, interspersed with rollers.
42.0	Calf Creek Recreation Area on the right.
42.6	Cross Escalante River; begin climb.
43.2	Kivea Koffeehouse on the right.
43.9	Crest of climb; begin rollers on straightened highway.
45.1	Begin short downhill.
45.5	Begin climb.
46.5	Cattle guard.
56.7	Enter Escalante; mini-mart on the right.
57.3	Begin gradual upgrade through town.
58.1	End of ride; turn left to enter Escalante Ranger District office parking area.

Local Information

Official Escalante Chamber of Commerce Web site: www.escalante-cc.com.
Grand Staircase-Escalante National Monument Web site (Bureau of Land Management): www.ut.blm.gov/monument.

Restaurants

Boulder Mesa Restaurant: 155 East Burr Trail Road, Boulder; (435) 335-7447; www.bouldermesa.com.
Esca-Latté Espresso and Pizza Café: 310 West Main Street, Escalante; (435) 826-4266 or (866) 455-0041; www.escalanteoutfitters.com.
Hell's Backbone Grill: 20 North Highway 12, Boulder; (435) 335-7464; www.hellsbackbonegrill.com. Open mid-March through Thanksgiving.
Kiva Koffeehouse: On SR 12 overlooking the Escalante River Canyon, at mile marker 73.86; (435) 826-4550; www.kivakoffeehouse.com. Open April through October.
Trailhead Café & Grill: 125 East Main Street, Escalante; (800) U-EXPLORE *(Note that this phone number, provided on the café's website, seems to have too many digits);* http://excursionsofescalante.com/html/trailhead_cafe.html.

Accommodations

Boulder Mountain Lodge: 20 North Highway 12, Boulder; (435) 335-7460; www.boulderutah.com.
Circle D Motel: 475 West Main Street, Escalante; (435) 826-4297;www.escalantecircledmotel.com.
Escalante Outfitters: 310 West Main Street, Escalante; (435) 826-4266 or (866) 455-0041; www.escalanteoutfitters.com. Single-room cabins and on-site camping.
Escalante's Grand Staircase B&B/Inn: 280 West Main Street, Escalante; (435) 826-4890; www.escalantebnb.com.
Prospector Inn: 380 West Main Street, Escalante; (435) 826-GOLD; www.prospectorinn.com.

Maps

DeLorme: Utah Atlas & Gazetteer: Pages 51, 52 D8 on page 51.
Benchmark: Utah Road & Recreation Atlas: Page 82 G3.

Dinosaurland

D inosaurland occupies three counties in eastern Utah: Daggett, Duchesne, and Uintah. The population of the region was 47,684 in 2008, spread over an area of 8,424 square miles. The region is dominated by the Uintah Basin, an expansive plateau bound by the Uinta Mountains on the north, the Wasatch Mountains on the west, Colorado on the east, and plateaus and cliffs on the south. In the early 1900s, a rich treasure trove of dinosaur fossils was discovered near the Utah–Colorado border. Dinosaur National Monument, located east of Vernal (see Dinosaur Country Cruise), was created to preserve and showcase one of the richest deposits. The paleontologist who discovered the dinosaur bones, Earl Douglass, was actually looking for mammal fossils. Despite his famed finding, he continued to search for mammal bones. Dinosaurs occupied Utah from the Triassic (245 million years ago) to the end of the Cretaceous period (65 million years ago), when a giant asteroid collided with the earth, splitting continents and forever changing the climate. Among the fossils found in Dinosaurland are those of the allosaurus, apatosaurus, barosaurus, brontosaurus, camarasaurus, camptosaurus, ceratosaurus, diplodocus, dryosaurus, stegosaurus, and torvosaurus—an impressive quarry. Despite the plethora of dinosaur museums and replicas in Dinosaurland, and elsewhere in Utah, there is no "Jurassic Park" here. But imaginations can run wild, envisioning an era when dinosaurs roamed these lands.

A more current Dinosaurland history is that of the Native Americans, who have occupied the region for the last 1,800 years. The Fremont peoples lived here from about 200 to 1300 A.D., leaving extensive rock art. The Utes (from which Utah gets its name) arrived after the Fremonts and were still living in the Basin when the first European Americans arrived in 1776. To protect the Utes from intervention by trappers, traders, and Mormon settlers, President Abraham Lincoln established the two-million-acre Uintah Indian Reservation in 1861, incorporating most of the Uintah Basin. Later, another two-million-acre reservation for the Ouray peoples was established immediately to the south. The two reservations merged in 1886. Since then, chunks of land have been withdrawn from the reservation by the federal government for various reasons. For example, in 1888, 7,004 acres containing valuable Gilson deposits were withdrawn from the eastern end of the reservation. In 1905, 1,100,000 acres were withdrawn to be incorporated into the Uinta National Forest; in 1909 another 56,000 acres were withdrawn for the Strawberry Valley Reclamation Project. By then, the reservation consisted of 250,000 acres of grazing reserve, plus 103,265 acres of individual allotments. A 1934 federal act eventually returned 726,000 acres to the reservation, and in 1986 the Northern Ute tribe was granted legal jurisdiction over three million acres.

White settlement brought a trail of outlaws to the Uintah Basin during the 1880s and 1890s. Vernal (see the Dinosaur Country Cruise) was along the path between places of refuge to the north and south that were heavily used by outlaws on the run. Agriculture and mining were developed in the early twentieth century, and oil was discovered in 1948. A huge oil field exists in the southeastern quadrant of the Basin, although the deposits have not yet been fully exploited. One of the region's primary economic mainstays is the Central Utah Project, a massive water reclamation effort that draws from the Colorado River and other sources to provide irrigation water throughout central and eastern Utah. Although the project was started in 1959, various components of it are still being developed.

The geography of Dinosaurland is distinguished by the Uinta Mountains to the north, which include Kings Peak, the tallest mountain in Utah at 13,528 feet. Most of the basin sits at an elevation of about 1 mile, keeping temperatures relatively mild in the summer and chilly in the winter. The region is known for its Outlaw Trail and Northern Ute Pow-Wow Festivals, rodeos, fishing, history, the Ouray National Wildlife Refuge (more than 200 species of migratory birds), scenic drives, and dinosaur fossils. Winter sports and hunting are popular, as well. Dinosaurland is not a "hotbed" of cycling activity, but there is some excellent riding here on low-volume roads through some eye-popping scenery.

18 Dinosaur Country Cruise

The Dinosaur Country Cruise is a 48.1-mile out-and-back ride over gently rolling hills and false flats. The ride journeys from Vernal, into the Dinosaur National Monument as far as the pavement stretches, and returns. The pavement surface is good along the outer ends of the route (i.e., in Vernal and approaching and in Dinosaur National Monument) but is fair to rough along Brush Creek Road, in the middle section of the course. There are ten cattle guard crossings. The elevation ranges from 5,359 feet in Vernal to 4,757 feet along SR 149 near Dinosaur National Monument.

Start: Vernal City Park on 900 West south of 500 North.
Length: 48.1 miles (out-and-back).
Terrain: Gently rolling hills. Minimum and maxi-
mum elevations: 4,757 to 5,359 feet.
Traffic and hazards: SR 149: 680 vehicles per day approaching Dinosaur National Monument in 2005.

Getting there: From Salt Lake City, take I-80 east to the US 40 exit (Silver Creek Junction). Head south then east on US 40 to Vernal (140 miles from the junction).

The Ride

Dinosaur National Monument was the site, in 1909, of the discovery of a rich cache of dinosaur fossils. The discovery forever changed Utah's role in paleontological history. The discovery led to the creation of the Dinosaur National Monument, along with other dinosaur-related attractions in Utah (such as the Dinosaur Diamond Prehistoric Byway). Dinosaur National Monument straddles Utah and Colorado, extending from northeastern Uintah County into northwestern Moffat County. The monument began as a quarry; today, a visitor center allows the general public to view the ongoing process of fossil evaluation, as well as an authentic dig. Later, the site was expanded to include opportunities for river rafting, hiking, scenic drives, and geological exploration in the Yampa and Green River Canyons. Although the monument headquarters is located in Dinosaur, Colorado, the Utah side features the visitor center and the Green River. (The visitor center was closed to the general public because of some structural issues, as of this writing.)

The ride begins in Vernal, Dinosaurland's largest city and center of commercial activity (population 8,696 in 2008). Several facts distinguish Vernal: One of the few Utah towns founded by non-Mormons, and the largest city in the United States with no railroad are two of the city's claims to fame. Monuments to Tyrannosaurus rex and a creature that resembles Barney stand at two of the city's gateways. The city has a hard, rural, industrial feel, perhaps because of its outlaw past and the work involved in water reclamation and oil-extraction projects. But the city has a "soft" side, with plenty of outfitters providing for the region's recreational opportunities, museums, and a few outstanding examples of architecture.

Biking the dinosaur; cuestas and tilted rocks in Dinosaur National Monument.
ANN COTTRELL

Start the ride at Vernal City Park; head east on 500 North from 900 West. Where 500 North curves to the right to become 500 West, turn left to continue on 500 North (mile 0.3). Cross Vernal Avenue and continue heading east. The roadsides become increasingly rural through here: open space, pasture, and fewer houses. At the fork in the road (mile 3.9), veer right onto Brush Creek Road. The pavement surface gets rough here; watch out for potholes. The vista is of a desolate, dry landscape. The road turns downhill at mile 7.3; stay right at the Y intersection at mile 7.8. Climb out of this "saddle" to mile 8.5 and then begin another steep downhill. Reach the foot of the descent at mile 9.0; enter Brush Creek Valley. There are a few houses through here and a prominent bluff on your left. The pavement surface improves at mile 9.7, except for a rough, narrow bridge at mile 11.9. Turn left at mile 12.5 onto 9600 East (SR 149) and head north. This lightly used state highway (680 vehicles per day in 2005) provides direct access to Dinosaur National Monument. After passing some lovely meadows, with bluffs on your left and the Green River on your right, enter the monument at mile 14.3.

The monument's entrance station is at mile 16.0; you may be required to pay a fee here, although the station was unmanned when I visited in early September 2007. The visitor center (not the quarry, which is up the adjacent hill) is on the left; stop here for restrooms, refreshments, and information. The mountains in the foreground appear to "bubble" over the landscape; the tall peak in the background is Split Moun-

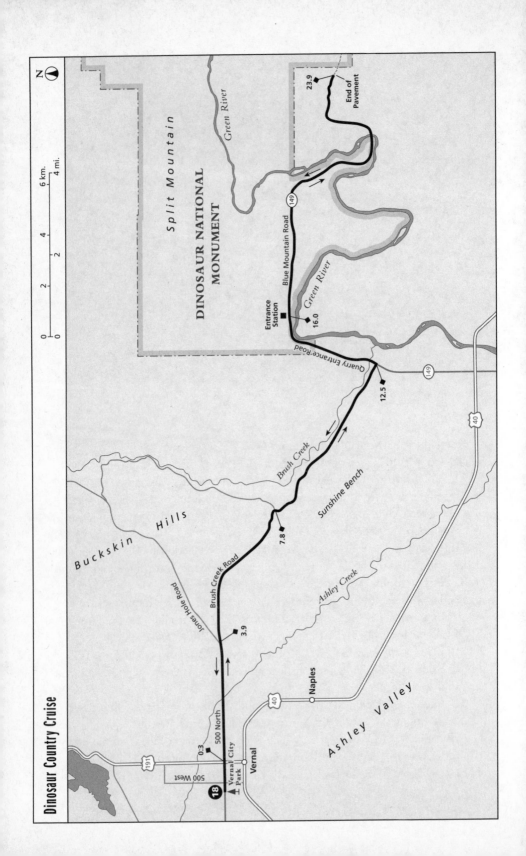

Dinosaur Country Cruise

tain (elevation 7,609 feet). The road through the monument reveals a mixture of tilted sedimentary rocks, hogbacks (steep ridges that are narrow at the top and broad at the bottom), flatirons (successions of hogbacks), and cuestas (asymmetrical ridges). There are also sections of desert scrub, along with panoramas of the Green River and nearby Yampa Plateau. Cross the Green River at mile 21.5 and begin a gradual climb. The rocky ridges have a very bright sand color that accentuates their ruggedness. The grade eases at mile 23.2, and the road narrows at mile 23.9. Turn around here; beyond this point, the road continues to narrow, becoming unpaved. On the return ride, cross the Green River at mile 26.1 and begin to climb. The road crests at mile 27.8; check out the expansive vista at mile 29.2. You are looking at the broad draw of the Green River. The famous Dominguez-Escalante expedition passed through this area in 1776. The visitor center appears on the right at 31.7; exit the monument at mile 33.8. After crossing Brush Creek, turn right onto 3500 South (Brush Creek Road; mile 35.5) and start the westerly journey back toward Vernal.

Cross the rough, narrow bridge at mile 36.1; the pavement surface becomes consistently rough at mile 38.4. The road climbs at mile 39.1. After cresting at mile 40.0, the road makes a sharp descent; stay left at the Y intersection and watch for gravel in the turn. The road makes a short, steep climb before entering rolling terrain. This area, through which you passed earlier, is particularly desolate, with only patchy scrub. The high mountains in the far distance are the Uintas, Utah's tallest range. The pavement surface improves at mile 42.4. Vernal can be seen in the distance at the crest in the road at mile 43.4. Turn left onto 500 North (no street sign) at mile 44.2. Development slowly returns after you cross Ashley Creek at mile 45.5. Cross Vernal Avenue at mile 47.2. At mile 47.7, turn right at 500 West to continue on 500 North. The ride ends at 900 West (mile 48.1); turn left here to return to Vernal City Park, which is on your right after making the turn.

Miles and Directions

0.0 Start at Vernal City Park on 900 West south of 500 North; turn right onto 500 North and head east.

0.3 Turn left at 500 West, where 500 North bends right (to stay on 500 North).

0.9 Go straight at the stop sign at Vernal Avenue.

2.5 Cross Ashley Creek.

3.6 Begin upgrade; road gets bumpy.

3.9 False crest; cattle guard—veer right at fork in road onto Brush Creek Road (no street sign).

4.7 Crest of hill; begin downgrade and rolling terrain.

7.3 Steep downhill.

7.8 Stay right at fork in road; begin climb after junction.

8.5 Crest of hill; begin steep downhill (watch for potholes).

9.0 Foot of descent; now in Brush Creek Valley.

9.7 Pavement surface improves.

11.7   Cattle guard.

11.9   Narrow bridge over Brush Creek; rough surface.

12.5   At the stop sign, turn left onto 9600 East (SR 149).

12.7   Cross Brush Creek; begin false flats.

14.3   Cattle guard; enter Dinosaur National Monument.

16.0   Dinosaur National Monument entrance station; visitor center on the left.

20.0   Begin downhill.

21.4   Cattle guard.

21.5   Cross Green River; begin upgrade.

22.8   Cattle guard.

23.2   Gradient eases.

23.9   Road narrows; turn around here.

25.0   Cattle guard.

26.1   Cross Green River; begin upgrade.

26.3   Cattle guard.

27.8   Crest of hill.

28.8   Begin downhill.

31.7   Visitor center on the right.

32.0   Entrance station to Dinosaur National Monument.

33.8   Cattle guard; leave Dinosaur National Monument.

35.3   Cross Brush Creek.

35.5   Turn right onto 3500 South (Brush Creek Road).

36.1   Narrow bridge across Brush Creek (rough surface).

36.4   Cattle guard; begin rolling terrain.

38.4   Rough pavement surface.

39.1   Begin climb.

40.0   Crest of climb; begin descent.

40.2   Stay left at fork in road; gravel in turn—end of descent.

40.3   Begin climb.

40.6   Pavement surface improves; intermittent rough spots.

41.1   Begin rolling terrain.

42.4   Pavement surface improves.

43.4   Crest of climb; begin slight downhill.

44.2   At the stop sign, turn left onto 500 North.

45.5   Cross Ashley Creek.

47.2   Go straight at the stop sign at Vernal Avenue.

47.7   At the stop sign at 500 West, turn right to continue on 500 North.

48.1   End of ride; turn left on 900 West to return to Vernal City Park (on the right).

Local Information

Northeastern Utah's Dinosaurland Travel Guide: Dinosaurland Travel Board, Vernal (published annually).
Uintah County official Web site: www.co.uintah.ut.us.
Dinosaur National Monument, National Park Service Web site: www.nps.gov/dino.
City of Vernal official Web site: www.vernalcity.org.

Restaurants

Betty's Café: 416 West Main Street, Vernal; (435) 781-2728.
Casa Rios Restaurant: 2750 West Highway 40, Vernal; (435) 789-0103.
Curry Manor: 189 South Vernal Avenue, Vernal; (435) 789-0789 or (435) 789-2289.
La Cabaña Restaurant: 56 West Main Street, Vernal; (435) 789-9055.
7-11 Ranch Café: 77 East Main Street, Vernal; (435) 789-1170; www.711ranchrestaurant.com.

Accommodations

Best Western Antlers: 423 West Main Street, Vernal; (435) 789-1202; www.bestwesternutah.com/hotels/best-western-antlers/.
Best Western Dinosaur Inn: 251 East Main Street, Vernal; (435) 789-2260; www.bestwestern.com/dinosaurinn.

Landmark Inn & Suites: 301 East 100 South, Vernal; (435) 781-1800 or (888) 738-1800; www.landmark-inn.com. Bed-and-breakfast.
Split Mountain Motel: 1015 East Highway 40, Vernal; (435) 789-9020.
Weston Lamplighter: 120 East Main Street, Vernal; (435) 789-0312.
Weston Plaza Hotel: 1684 West Highway 40, Vernal; (435) 789-9550; www.westonplazavernal.com.

Bicycle Shops

Altitude Cycle: 580 East Main Street, Vernal; (435) 781-2595 or (877) 781-2460; www.altitudecycle.com.
Basin Saw & Cycle: 460 West Main Street, Vernal; (435) 781-1226.
Red Rock Cycle: 1147 West Highway 40, Vernal; (435) 789-2695.

Maps

City Street Map: Park City, Heber City, Price, Vernal. GM Johnson City Map Series.
DeLorme: Utah Atlas & Gazetteer: Pages 28–29 A4 on page 28.
Benchmark: Utah Road & Recreation Atlas: Pages 54–55 B6 on page 54.

19 Flaming Gorge Classic

The Flaming Gorge Classic is a 75.0-mile out-and-back ride over mountainous terrain at high altitude (exceeding 6,000 feet). The route traces an approximate semicircle around the southern perimeter of Flaming Gorge Reservoir, along the Drive Through the Ages Scenic Byway, from Manila to Dutch John and back. Elevations range from 6,006 feet at the Flaming Gorge Dam to 8,060 feet near Leona Spring in the Flaming Gorge National Recreation Area. Chilly temperatures limit the optimal period for completing this ride to late spring, summer, and early fall. Although the ride is long, the breath-boosting scenery, which is constantly changing, increases the adrenaline needed to sustain your energy.

Start: Daggett County Centennial Park, 2nd West, north of SR 43, Manila.
Length: 75.0 miles (out-and-back).
Terrain: Mountainous, with several lengthy climbs and descents. Minimum and maximum elevations: 6,006 to 8,060 feet.
Traffic and hazards: SR 43: 2,460 vehicles per day in Manila in 2005. SR 44: 1,525 vehicles per day between Greendale Junction (US 191) and Sheep Creek Geological Area; 830 vehicles per day between Manila and Sheep Creek Geological Area. US 191: 1,305 vehicles per day between Greendale Junction (SR 44) and Flaming Gorge Reservoir; 940 vehicles per day at Dutch John.

Getting there: From Vernal, head north on US 191 to Greendale Junction; turn left onto SR 44 and head north to Manila. Turn left at SR 43, then right onto 2nd West to access Daggett County Centennial Park. From I-80, take exit 34 (in Wyoming) to Business Route 80. At the Urie junction, turn right onto SR 414. Head southeast through Mountain View, Lonetree, Burntfork, and McKinnion, all in Wyoming, before entering Utah (SR 414 becomes SR 43). Enter Manila; turn left onto 2nd West to access Centennial Park.

The Ride

Where is Utah's most breathtaking scenery? Color Country? Canyonlands? How about the northeastern corner of the state, near the Flaming Gorge Reservoir? The Flaming Gorge National Recreation Area (NRA) straddles Utah and Wyoming. The main attraction is Flaming Gorge Reservoir, a sprawling lake that spans 91 miles north–south and covers over 40,000 acres when full. The reservoir is at an elevation of 6,045 feet. It was formed by the Flaming Gorge Dam, which towers 502 feet above the bedrock. The dam corrals waters from the Green River; the river continues south of the reservoir to eventually merge with the Colorado River in Utah's Canyonlands. The land surrounding the reservoir is within the Ashley National Forest. State Highway 44, along with US 191, make a rough trace of the southern perimeter of the Flaming Gorge NRA; the highways both form the Flaming Gorge-Uintas Scenic Byway. The scenic route also goes by the moniker "Drive Through the Ages" or "Wildlife Through the Ages." Similarly to Highway 12 in southern Utah (see the

Journey Through Time Challenge), the scenic byway literally passes through the geologies of several ancient eras. Some twenty interpretive signs along the highway inform the traveler of the era to which the adjacent landscape pertains. With some background information to supplement that on the signs, the route is akin to traveling in a time machine. Nature trails are abundant along the byway, offering numerous opportunities for off-road exploration. There is plenty to see from the road as well. There is so much to see, in fact, that one could probably ride this route every day for a year and still not fully absorb the array of colors, various plants and animals, different vistas, human and natural histories, geological characteristics, and changing seasons, all while getting in a strenuous cycling workout at high altitude.

Although most of Flaming Gorge Reservoir is in Wyoming, Utah is where the Green River cuts into the Uinta Mountains. The clash of these two giants of nature creates imposing, 1,500-foot-high cliffs, twisted rock formations, and stupendous, fiery colors. Under the proper lighting, the waters of the reservoir are a clear, sparkling blue, creating a fabulous contrast to the reds and greens of the surrounding landscape. Given that the entire area sits at an elevation of at least 6,000 feet, white (from snow) becomes the dominant color in the winter. Wildlife in the NRA and adjacent national forest is abundant and includes bighorn sheep, black bears, bobcats, eagles, foxes, minks, and pronghorn antelope. Birds are staggeringly abundant as well, with bluebirds, chickadees, cormorants, cranes, creepers, crows, doves, ducks, egrets, falcons, geese, grebes, grosbeaks, grouse, gulls, hawks, herons, hummingbirds, ibises, jays, larks, loons, mockingbirds, nighthawks, owls, pelicans, pheasants, pigeons, rails, shrikes, sparrows, starlings, swallows, swans, swifts, tanagers, terns, vultures, warblers, woodpeckers, and wrens (and others!) all seen in the region.

Flaming Gorge Dam was completed in 1964. The Flaming Gorge Classic crosses the dam near the turnaround point in the community of Dutch John. Dutch John was established in 1957 by the U.S. Bureau of Reclamation to house dam workers. At its peak, the town was the largest in Daggett County, home to about 3,500 persons. Today, Dutch John's population is about 150, primarily dam maintenance and operations personnel, USDA Forest Service workers, and their families. The community's name paid tribute to "Dutch" John Hanselena, an early 1860s horse trader and miner from Prussia. John had a strong accent, but it was probably not Dutch, given that Prussia covered present-day northern Germany. The Flaming Gorge Classic starts in Manila, the Daggett County seat. Manila had a population of 324 in 2008 and is the largest settlement in Utah's least-populated county. The town was named to commemorate the United States' capture of Manila, Philippines, in 1898. The capture coincided with the subdivision of the town site. Today, Manila is home to the Flaming Gorge NRA Headquarters, county government activities, and community events, and serves as a takeoff point for recreational tourism.

The ride starts in Manila at Daggett County Centennial Park. The park is located on 2nd West, just north of SR 43. The annual Cow Country Rodeo is held here each July. Head south on 2nd West (short dirt road) and turn left onto SR 43. Turn right

Cycling through the ages in Flaming Gorge, on the descent to Sheep Creek.
ANN COTTRELL

onto SR 44 at the junction in the center of town. A convenience mart and small grocery store are adjacent. Stock up on provisions here, as there are few services along the route. Start the ride with a short descent at mile 0.6. The first of about twenty interpretive signs appears at mile 1.0. The signs describe the period and formation to which the adjacent geology is attributed. At mile 1.0, the Mancos (shale) Formation dates from the Cretaceous period (146 to 65 million years ago). Begin rolling terrain at mile 1.6. At mile 2.4, the Frontier (sandstone) Formation also dates from the Cretaceous period. At mile 3.1, the Curtis Formation dates from the Jurassic period (208 to 246 million years ago). Begin an 8 percent descent at mile 4.2. Enter the Flaming Gorge NRA at mile 4.7. At mile 4.8, the adjacent Entrada (sandstone) Formation is from the Jurassic period. The evolution is fast, as the Carmel Formation (Jurassic) comes into view; at mile 5.9, the Navajo (sandstone) Formation (Jurassic) is prominent. The entrance to the Sheep Creek Geological Loop is on the right at mile 6.0. The loop is a highly recommended diversion, but the pothole-strewn road (unpaved in some places) is not recommended for road bikes. Begin to climb at mile 7.4. Sheep Creek Bay can be seen on the left at mile 8.1. At mile 8.6, the Park City Formation from the Permian period (286 to 245 million years ago) is adjacent. The highway enters a winding segment with sharp curves here. At mile 10.1, look right to see deep into the "flaming" gorge (but keep your eyes on the road). The 4-mile climb crests at mile 11.7. A 0.8-mile descent then a 0.7-mile climb follows.

Cross Sheep Creek at mile 13.4. Enter deep forestation at mile 14.6. Ponderosa pines typically abound around 8,000 feet in elevation, as well as Douglas firs. Begin to climb at mile 14.9, with the gorge on the left. The adjacent geological formation is from the Uinta Mountain Group of the Pre-Cambrian Time (4.5 billion to 500 million years ago). It is estimated that this group was deposited about one billion years ago, representing one of the oldest formations in the region. Descend starting at mile 17.6; cross Burnt Creek at mile 17.9. Take note again of the mixture of trees. In addition to pines and firs, aspens and blue spruce can also be seen. The descent gets steeper at mile 18.7, finally leveling at mile 20.7. An access road to Red Canyon is on the left at mile 24.6. Although the scenery along the highway is sufficiently spectacular, the view at Red Canyon is of 1,360-foot sheer cliffs descending to the reservoir below. The terrain rolls through this area. The highway reaches Greendale Junction at mile 28.0. Bear left here to head north on US 191.

The sights and attractions along this stretch of highway are frequent and of historical interest. An access road leading to Swett Ranch National Historic Site is on the left at mile 28.5. The ranch is an exhibit of early twentieth-century homesteading, with a historic house, cabins, blacksmith shop, horse barn, cow shed, and other outbuildings. The access road is 1.3 miles long and gravel, so a side trip on a road bike is not recommended. The Flaming Gorge Resort is on the left at mile 30.1. There are a restaurant and store here, along with raft rentals and guided fishing trips (and restrooms). The Firefighters Memorial is on the right at mile 30.6. The marker memorializes three firefighters who lost their lives battling a blaze that was ignited by lightning in July 1977 in Ashley National Forest. Begin to descend at mile 31.0, with sharp curves starting at mile 31.8. Note that, at these lower elevations, pinyon pine and juniper are the dominant tree types. Rabbit brush (yellow flowers bloom in September) can also be seen—and smelled: The plant is known for its strange odor. Cross Francis Creek at mile 33.3. An interpretive sign at mile 33.7 indicates that the adjacent geology is from the Browns Park Formation of the Pre-Cambrian Time. A short descent at mile 33.8 leads to Flaming Gorge Dam, at mile 34.1. A visitor center is on the left. Beyond here, the highway edges along the cliffs, with the dam plummeting downward some 500 feet to the right. The highway climbs away from this precarious segment at mile 34.6, cresting at mile 35.7. The cuts and layers in the adjacent cliffs are extraordinary. After a descent, enter the Dutch John environs at mile 36.6. Turn right onto South Boulevard at mile 36.8 to enter Dutch John. There is a mini-mart at the Conoco on the corner. Make a short loop through town by turning left onto Fifth Avenue, left onto South Center Street, and left onto Sixth Avenue. Turn right onto South Boulevard to exit Dutch John. Turn left at mile 38.1 to return to US 191 southbound.

The return ride reverses the outbound route. Climb away from the Dutch John area, cresting at mile 39.0. Descend from here to Flaming Gorge Dam, which starts at mile 40.4. The visitor center is on the right at mile 40.8. Cross Francis Creek at 41.4 on the Cart Creek Bridge; begin to climb on the opposite end. The climb continues to the Firefighters Memorial at mile 44.2. The gradient eases here. The Flaming Gorge Resort is on the right at mile 44.7. If you were planning to complete the ride over a two-day period—or if you are uncertain about making it back to Manila—then this may be a good place to spend the night. Enter the Greendale community at mile 45.0, where the ascent continues. The forestation is dense through this portion of the Ashley National Forest. Turn right onto SR 44 at mile 46.9 to begin a long stretch of false flats and rolling hills through the forest. Access to Red Canyon is on the right at mile 50.3. You may be able to catch a glimpse of the steep cliffs that plummet into the "fire" of Flaming Gorge as you ride past. The high point of the course (8,060 feet) is reached within the next few miles. The highway begins to descend at mile 56.2.

Cross Burnt Creek at mile 57.1, followed by Deep Creek at mile 58.3. The gorge comes into view on the right at mile 59.3. The strata in the adjacent rock, right along the roadside, are magnificent. Cross Carter Creek at mile 59.9 and enter the formation of the Uinta Mountain Group at mile 60.1. Start another climb. Spirit Lake Lodge is on the left at mile 61.5. Reach the crest of the climb at mile 61.7 and start a short descent. The gorge is on the right. Another climb begins at mile 62.4, cresting at mile 63.3. An 8 percent descent follows; watch your speed and handling on the sharp curves. Flaming Gorge Reservoir appears on the right then on the left as the highway negotiates the twisting downhill. Access to the Sheep Creek Geological Loop is at mile 66.6. The base of the descent is at mile 67.7; observe the craggy peaks of this supernatural area, to your right and just ahead. The northern end of the Sheep Creek loop is at mile 68.8; begin to climb from here. The climb and ensuing descent accelerates the time machine, taking you through successive geological formations representing different eras. The climb crests at mile 70.7, followed by a sharp, 8 percent descent. The roller coaster continues; reach the base of the descent at mile 71.8 and then start another climb! After another crest, descent, climb, and descent, the highway finally levels at mile 74.6, at the entrance to Manila. Turn left onto SR 43 at mile 74.7 and head west. The journey concludes at mile 75.0, at 2nd West. Turn right here, dismounting (dirt road), and return to Daggett County Centennial Park.

Miles and Directions

0.0 Start at Daggett County Centennial Park, 2nd West, north of SR 43, Manila. Head south on 2nd West (dirt road) and turn left onto SR 43.

0.2 Turn right onto SR 44.

0.6 Begin descent.

1.0 End of descent; begin flat segment.

1.6 Begin rolling terrain.

4.2 Begin 8 percent descent.

4.7 Enter Flaming Gorge National Recreation Area.

6.0 Entrance to Sheep Creek Geological Area on the right.

6.4 Willows Campground on the left.

6.9 Mann's Campground on the left.

7.4 Begin climb.

8.1 Sheep Creek Bay visible on the left.

8.6 Begin winding highway.

10.1 Gorge visible on the right.

11.7 Crest of climb; begin 8 percent descent.

12.5 End of descent; begin climb.

13.2 Crest of climb; begin descent.

13.4 Cross Sheep Creek.

14.3 Dowd Mountain Campground on the left.

14.9 View of gorge on the left; begin climb.

15.1 Cross Carter Creek.

16.2 Gradient of climb eases.

16.6 Deep Creek Campground (access) on the right.

17.6 Begin descent.

17.9 Cross Burnt Creek.

20.7 Gradient of descent decreases; now on false flats.

24.4 Cattle guard.

24.6 Access road to Red Canyon on the left.

25.4 Skull Creek Campground on the left.

28.0 Bear left onto US 191 northbound (Greendale Junction).

28.5 Access to Swett Ranch National Historic Site on the left; begin descent.

29.8 Cattle guard.

29.9 Greendale Campground on the left.

30.1 Flaming Gorge Resort on the left (mini-mart).

30.6 Firefighters Memorial (and campground) on the right.

31.0 View of reservoir on the left; gradient of descent increases.

31.8 Begin sharp curves.

32.5 Cedar Springs Campground on the left.

33.3 Bridge over Francis Creek.

33.8 Begin descent.

34.1 Flaming Gorge Dam crossing; visitor center on the left (restrooms).

34.2 Begin cliff-side segment and gradual climb; deep gorge on the right.

35.0 Arch Dam Campground on the right.

35.7 Crest of climb; begin descent.

36.6 Dutch John Campground on the left.

36.8 Turn right onto South Boulevard; enter Dutch John community.

37.2 Begin gradual climb and counterclockwise loop through town.

Flaming Gorge Classic

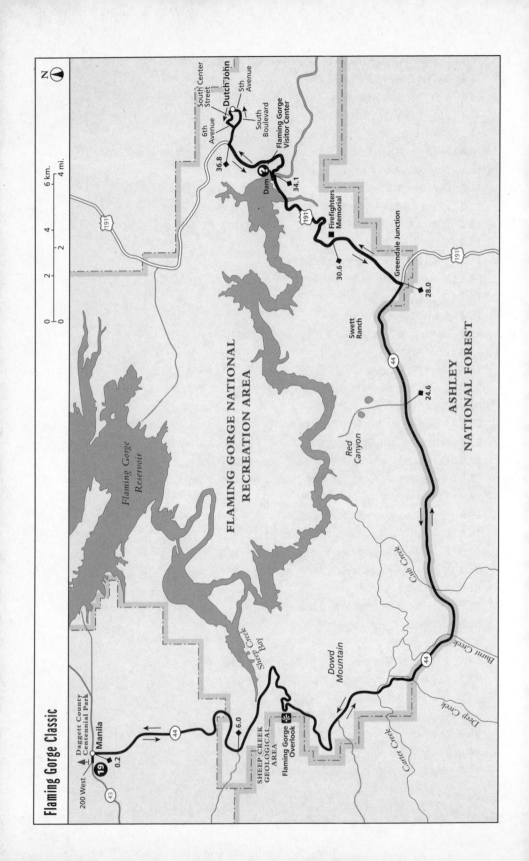

37.4   Turn left onto Fifth Avenue.

37.5   Turn left onto South Center Street.

37.6   Turn left onto Sixth Avenue.

37.7   At the stop sign, turn right onto South Boulevard.

38.1   At the stop sign, turn left onto US 191 southbound.

38.4   Begin climb.

39.0   Crest of climb; begin descent. Flaming Gorge Reservoir on the right.

39.9   Arch Dam Campground on the left.

40.8   Visitor center on the right.

41.4   Bridge across Francis Creek.

41.6   Begin climb.

42.3   Cedar Spring Campground on the right.

44.2   Firefighters Memorial on the left; gradient of climb decreases.

44.7   Flaming Gorge Resort on the right.

45.0   Greendale Campground on the right; cattle guard.

46.3   Swett Ranch National Historic Site access on the right.

46.9   At the stop sign, turn right onto SR 44 (Greendale Junction).

47.0   Begin false flats and rolling terrain.

49.6   Skull Creek Campground on the right.

50.3   Access road to Red Canyon on the right.

50.5   Cattle guard.

56.2   Begin descent.

57.1   Cross Burnt Creek.

58.3   Cross Deep Creek.

59.9   Cross Carter Creek.

60.1   Begin climb at Uinta Mountain Group.

60.7   Dowd Mountain Campground on the right.

61.5   Spirit Lake Lodge on the left.

61.7   Crest of climb; begin descent—deep gorge on the right.

62.4   Sharp curve to the right; begin climb.

63.3   Crest of climb; begin descent—reservoir on the right.

63.5   Begin winding segment; careful—sharp curves.

67.7   End descent.

68.0   Mann's Campground on the right.

68.5   Willows Campground on the right.

68.8   Sheep Creek Geological Area; entrance on the left—begin climb.

70.2   Leave Flaming Gorge National Recreation Area.

70.7   Crest of climb; begin 8 percent descent.

71.8   End descent; begin climb.

72.4   Crest of climb; begin descent.

73.0 End descent; begin short climb, followed by descent.

74.4 Highway levels.

74.6 Enter Manila.

74.7 At the stop sign, turn left onto SR 43.

75.0 End of ride at 2nd West (dirt road); turn right to access Centennial Park.

Local Information

Flaming Gorge-Uintas Scenic Byway information: www.byways.org/explore/byways/2008.
Daggett County official Web site: www.daggettcounty.org.
Flaming Gorge National Recreation Area, Ashley National Forest Web site: www.fs.fed.us/r4/ashley/recreation/flaming_gorge/index.shtml.
City of Manila official Web site: www.manilautah.us.
Flaming Gorge National Recreation Area information: www.utah.com/nationalsites/flaming_gorge.htm.

Restaurants

Flaming Gorge Recreation Services: 1050 South Boulevard, Dutch John; (435) 885-FISH or (435) 885-3342. Grill.
Flaming Gorge Resort: 1100 East Flaming Gorge Lodge, Dutch John; (435) 889-3773 or (877) FG-TROUT; www.flaminggorgeresort.com. Restaurant and convenience store.
Red Canyon Lodge: 790 Red Canyon (or 2450 West Red Canyon), Dutch John; (435) 889-3759. www.redcanyonlodge.com/dining.html. Restaurant open every day during the summer and on weekends October through May. Also a convenience store.
Slaugh's Chevron: Highway 43 and Main Street (Highway 44), Manila; (435) 784-3363. Grill and mini-mart.
Trout Creek Flies, Inc.: Highway 191 and Little Hole Road, Dutch John; (435) 885-3338 or (435) 885-3355; www.fishgreenriver.com. Grill.

The Villa: Highway 43, one-quarter mile east of Highway 44, Manila; (435) 784-3015; www.endweb.net/villa/index.html.

Accommodations

Flaming Gorge Motel & Café: Highway 43 and Highway 44, Manila; (888) 4FG-MOTL; www.fgmotel.com.
Flaming Gorge KOA (camping): Highway 43 and 3rd West, Manila; (435) 784-3184 or (800) 562-3254; www.koa.com/where/ut/44114/. Open April 15 through November 1.
Flaming Gorge Resort: 1100 East Flaming Gorge Lodge, Dutch John; (435) 889-3773 or (877) FG-TROUT; www.flaminggorgeresort.com.
Red Canyon Lodge: 790 Red Canyon (also listed as 2450 West Red Canyon), Dutch John; (435) 889-3759; www.redcanyonlodge.com.
Vacation Inn: 250 West Highway 43, Manila; (435) 784-3259.
Note: There are numerous campgrounds along the route in the Flaming Gorge National Recreation Area; (877) 444-6777; www.fs.fed.us/r4/ashley/recreation/flaming_gorge/index.shtml.

Maps

DeLorme: Utah Atlas & Gazetteer: Page 13 B5.
Benchmark: Utah Road & Recreation Atlas: Page 38 B2.

Golden Spike Empire

The Golden Spike Empire occupies the extreme northwestern corner of Utah. Box Elder, Davis, Morgan, and Weber Counties comprise the 6,526-square-mile region (population 580,503 in 2008). Davis and Weber Counties are heavily urbanized. Box Elder County (named for the box elder tree, a type of maple) is urbanized along the I-15 corridor, but the western part of the county is sparse and remote. Morgan County, despite being immediately to the east of Davis County and close enough to Salt Lake City to be part of that city's metropolitan area, is predominantly rural; it does not border the Great Salt Lake. The Golden Spike (replaced by an iron one almost immediately) was driven to connect the Central Pacific and Union Pacific Railroads on May 10, 1869. The historic event occurred at Promontory Point, in Box Elder County, immediately to the north of the Great Salt Lake. The event changed the western United States forever, chopping the transcontinental travel time from an epic six months to a reasonable six days. Progress in railroad engineering and alignment led to the construction of the Lucin Cutoff in 1904, a causeway across the northern reaches of the Great Salt Lake, somewhat south of the Golden Spike alignment. The cutoff diverted the railroad to the south, leaving Promontory Point as an inactive, but significant historical site. The old railroad tracks have since been removed. In 1942 a ceremony was held to "remove" the Golden Spike—but the name lives on.

Geologically, the Golden Spike Empire is characterized by two main features: the Great Salt Lake, about half of which is in the Empire, and the Great Salt Lake Desert. The latter is located west of the Great Salt Lake, in Box Elder County, and is unpopulated. The very extreme northwestern corner of Box Elder County, and of Utah, has a few mountains and forested lands—there are few towns in this area. The eastern edge of the Empire abuts the Wasatch Front; hence, the interior areas of all four Empire counties are mountainous. A lesser-known geological feature of the Empire is the Bear River. The river empties into the Great Salt Lake after snaking some 500 miles; the final miles of its long course are in Box Elder County. Prehistoric Lake Bonneville, which at one time occupied almost 25 percent of Utah's area, once covered all but the extreme northwestern corner of the Golden Spike Empire. Hence, the land is etched with the geographical memory of the onetime larger lake, as well as by earth

131

movement along the Wasatch Fault. Many of the Empire's features, such as the Blue Spring Hills, Antelope Island, an alluvial plain in east-central Box Elder County, and the Wellsville Mountains, resulted from either faulting or lake deposits. West of the Wasatch Front, the Golden Spike Empire is extremely flat, except for the scattered narrow ranges and tilted fault blocks. All of the population centers "hug" the mountains, however, so cycling in the Empire invariably involves some climbing. About 21 percent of Utah's population lives in the Golden Spike Empire. The four Golden Spike Empire routes thereby serve a large clientele.

20 Antelope Island Cruise

The 46.8-mile Antelope Island Cruise includes a short ride from Syracuse to the Antelope Island Causeway, on Lake Bonneville deposits, a flat causeway trip across the Great Salt Lake, and an out-and-back ride on picturesque Antelope Island. Elevations range from 4,200 feet on the Antelope Island Causeway (just above lake level) to 4,440 feet on Antelope Island. Be sure to bring enough cash for the $3 Antelope Island Causeway toll, plus a little extra for the vending machines that you will find on the island.

Start: Joseph Holbrook Centennial Park, 1800 South 2000 West, Syracuse.
Length: 46.8 miles (out-and-back).
Terrain: Mostly flat between Syracuse and the island; rolling hills on the island. Minimum and maximum elevations: 4,200 to 4,440 feet.
Traffic and hazards: SR 127: 2,220 vehicles per day at the SR 110 junction in Syracuse in 2005. Antelope Island Causeway: 525 vehicles per day.

Getting there: From I-15, take exit 335 (Layton); turn left and head west on Antelope Drive (SR 108). Continue westward into Syracuse. Turn left onto 2000 West; the park is on the left.

The Ride

Antelope Island is located in the Great Salt Lake, 7 miles west of the mainland. The island is a mountain ridge, with lake-filled grabens (valleys formed by parallel, down-thrusting faults) on either side. Rocks on Antelope Island, especially those toward its southern end, are some of the oldest in Utah, having been around since prehistoric Lake Bonneville days. The island is a state park; a 7-mile toll causeway connects the island with the city of Syracuse. Use of the island has transformed over the years. Early trapper Osborne Russell spotted antelope and buffalo on the island in 1841. Once fresh water was found to be flowing on the island, Mormon pioneers, including Brigham Young, established sheep and horse ranches. In the 1860s the island was used as a prison; there was never any fencing or barbed wire, however. Prison use was discontinued when it was observed that a prisoner could easily escape by walking across the surrounding sandbars when lake levels were low. In 1923 the silent film *The Covered Wagon* was shot on the island, with scenes featuring some of the 350-strong bison herd. There are about 600 bison on the island now. The state assumed ownership of the island in the 1960s, taking over all ranches as well as wildlife management. The causeway was submerged for ten years starting in 1982 after record rainfalls raised lake levels. It was reopened in 1992—lake levels have not approached those record heights since. As long as Mother Nature stays within normal hydrological patterns, the island should remain accessible to a large urban audience. A ride to the island and back is part of the annual Cycle Salt Lake Century, held each May. There is also a "moonlight" bike ride, generally held each July, in which cyclists ride 22 miles at night on the island.

The Antelope Island Cruise starts at Joseph Holbrook Centennial Park in Syracuse. There were several Josephs in the Holbrook lineage, ultimately purchasing a farm in Syracuse where several generations of Holbrooks had worked. Exit the park and turn left onto 2000 West. Bear right at the traffic circle at mile 0.8; look for the second "exit" onto 2700 South westbound. Although this area is rapidly developing, as of the time of this writing, there were few residences out here. The area is mostly open space, with some agricultural development. Although you are heading toward the Great Salt Lake, it is difficult to see (unless you are very tall) because of the flatness of the land. The road bends right at mile 2.9, becoming 4000 West. Turn left at 1700 South (SR 127) and head west, toward the Great Salt Lake. This is a high-speed road (55 mph, decreasing to 45 mph), with narrow shoulders, so be particularly cautious. Enter Antelope Island State Park at mile 4.7.

Pull up to the Antelope Island Causeway booth at mile 4.8 and pay the $3 toll. The ride along the causeway is pancake flat, frequently windy, and a little smelly (the odor is probably from decaying brine shrimp). The Great Salt Lake is on either side of the 7-mile causeway; if it is not windy, then the waters are peaceful and calm. Insects occasionally congregate along here; the best defense is to keep moving. Although the ride can be monotonous, the island looms in the distance, constantly reminding you of your destination. The shoulders on the causeway are wide. Once on the island, at mile 11.8, bear left at the Y intersection. A small marina is on the right; there are lavatories and vending machines here. Make the short climb onto "Ladyfinger," an elevated ridge that juts in the direction of the causeway. Buffalo Bay is on the left. The road parallels the coastline adjacent the bay, then turns inland. Turn left at mile 12.5, toward "The Ranch," to start the long trek along Antelope Island's east side. Farmington Bay is to the left. The most arduous climb on the route starts at mile 12.9. The road crests at mile 14.0, then, after a false flat, descends for about 1 mile. The road levels at mile 15.5, beginning a series of false flats and short climbs and descents. The road winds through desert grassland, with relatively barren slopes on your right. Out here, you may get to see some of the island's wildlife, including bison, bobcats, coyotes, elk, and bighorn sheep. Bison, in fact, are known to cross the road to access grazing areas. Be sure to give them plenty of space; these critters are more punchy than playful. Although the cities of Davis County can be seen across the bay on the left, the peaceful island environment is in stark contrast. The road ends at mile 23.3, entering the parking area for the Fielding Garr Ranch.

The Fielding Garr Ranch was started in 1848 by Fielding Garr as a small log cabin. The ranch eventually grew, under the direction and operation of the Mormon church, as a place to manage tithing herds of cattle. Fielding elected to develop the ranch at Garr Springs, one of forty springs on the island. The ranch changed ownership over the years. One of the more legendary owners was John Dooly Jr., who introduced one dozen bison to the island in 1893 in an effort to preserve the species. Sheep ranching was established for a while but was deemed unprofitable by the 1950s. Cattle ranching again became the dominant enterprise on the island. Ranching activities continued until 1981, when the island was converted into a state park. Archaeological digs on the island have estimated

A cycling critical mass on the Antelope Island Causeway.

that occupancy predated Fielding Garr by over 900 years. Antelope were reintroduced to the island in 1993 after an extensive absence. Feel free to take a break and spend some time exploring the ranch, which is on the National Register of Historic Places.

Exit the ranch by looping the parking lot perimeter. Return to the main road and turn right. After a short climb, the road descends and then enters a series of false flats. Farmington Bay is on the right. The slopes to the left are underlain with Precambrian rocks—gneiss and schist—estimated to be 2.6 billion years old. Begin to climb at mile 31.3, with the grade getting steeper at mile 31.6. The climb crests at mile 32.6. The reward is a commanding view of Buffalo Bay ahead and to the right, and the curvilinear path of the Antelope Island shoreline. After a fast descent and short uphill, turn right at the T intersection toward MARINA-EXIT. After a nifty 0.6-mile descent, the road bears right adjacent the marina, at mile 34.9. Vending machines and restrooms are on the left. You are now entering the Antelope Island Causeway, hopefully leaving with no souvenirs from the island's voracious mosquitoes.

On the horizon during the return ride on the 7-mile causeway are the Wasatch Mountains and the urbanization of Davis County. Once past the tollbooth (mile 42.0), continue on SR 127 to 4000 West. Turn right here (mile 42.8); the road bends left at mile 43.9 and becomes 2700 South. At the somewhat confusing traffic circle at mile 45.9, circulate and take the fourth exit, onto 2000 West northbound. The ride ends at mile 46.8, at Centennial Park. For post-ride refreshments, there is a retail center directly opposite the signalized intersection located just north of the park.

Miles and Directions

0.0 From Joseph Holbrook Centennial Park at 1800 South 2000 West in Syracuse, turn left and head south on 2000 West.

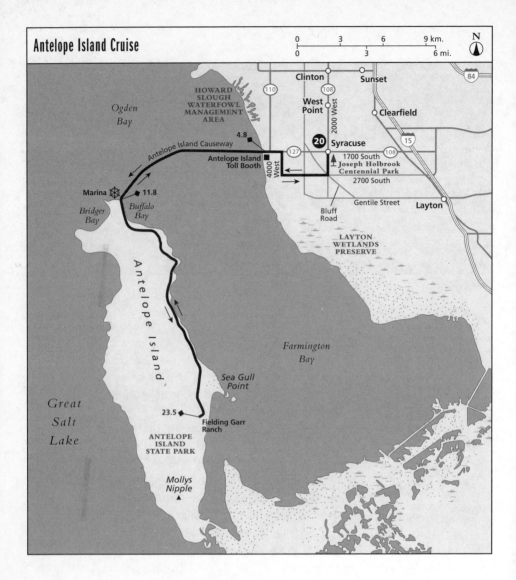

Antelope Island Cruise

0.8 Bear right at traffic circle, onto 2700 South.

2.9 Road bends right; now on 4000 West.

3.9 At the stop sign at 1700 South (SR 127), turn left.

4.4 End SR 127—continue onto Antelope Island Parkway.

4.7 Enter Antelope Island State Park; restrooms on the left.

4.8 Stop at toll booth and pay fee ($3 per bicycle).

11.8 End of causeway; vending machines and restrooms on the right. After 0.05 mile, bear left at Y intersection (no street signs); begin climb.

12.5 Turn left toward RANCH (no street sign).

12.9 Begin climb.

13.2 Gate (closed at dusk).

14.0 Crest of climb; begin false flat.

14.4 Begin downhill.

15.5 Gradient eases; now on false flats.

20.5 Begin climb.

20.7 Enter Fielding Garr Ranch area.

21.2 Crest of climb; begin false flats.

22.3 Begin climb.

23.0 Crest of climb; begin descent.

23.3 Enter Fielding Garr Ranch parking area; make a counterclockwise circle around lot.

23.5 At the stop sign at the main road, turn right—begin short climb.

23.8 Crest of climb; begin downhill, followed by false flats.

31.3 Begin climb; steeper at mile 31.6.

32.2 Gradient of climb eases.

32.6 Crest of climb; begin false flat.

33.6 Begin downhill.

34.3 At the stop sign at the crest of a short hill, turn right toward Marina—Exit (no street sign)—begin downhill.

34.9 Bear right onto Antelope Island Causeway; now leaving island. Restrooms and vending on the left.

42.0 Stop at Antelope Island toll booth; proceed (no fee).

42.1 Restrooms on the right. Now on SR 127 (1700 South).

42.8 Turn right onto 4000 West.

43.9 Road bends left; now on 2700 South.

45.9 Yield at traffic circle; take fourth "exit" onto 2000 West northbound.

46.8 End of ride; turn right to enter Centennial Park.

Local Information

City of Syracuse official Web site: www
.syracuseut.com.
Antelope Island State Park information: www
.utah.com/stateparks/antelope_island.htm.
Fielding Garr Ranch information: www.utah
outdooractivities.com/fieldingranch.html.

Restaurants

Syracuse Town Center, located adjacent the
intersection of Antelope Drive (1700 South)
and 2000 West (diagonally opposite Centennial Park), was under development as of this
writing. Several fast food eating establishments
were planned.

Accommodations

I am not aware of any lodging facilities in
Syracuse. There is camping on Antelope Island,
near the northwest beach. Please see the East
Layton Cruise for accommodations nearby in
Layton.

Bicycle Shops

Bingham Cyclery: 2317 North Main Street,
Sunset; (801) 825-8632; www.bingham
cyclery.com.

Map

Benchmark: Utah Road & Recreation Atlas:
Pages 42–43 C7 on page 43.

21 Bear River Valley Ramble

The Bear River Valley Ramble is a 17.2-mile clockwise loop on flat and gently rolling terrain. The route is through the Bear River Valley, a spacious, agricultural valley situated between the Blue Spring Hills on the west, and the Wellsville Mountains on the east. The ride starts and ends in Garland and visits Collinston, Deweyville, and Tremonton. The valley offers numerous, lightly traveled roads that are ideal for cycling. The Bear River Valley Ramble incorporates only a selection of these roads.

Start: Garland City Park, 100 North and 600 East, Garland.
Length: 17.2 miles (clockwise loop).
Terrain: Flat and some gently rolling hills. Minimum and maximum elevations: 4,216 to 4,303 feet.
Traffic and hazards: Garland Road (4400 West): 790 vehicles per day northeast of Garland in 2005. SR 30: 5,590 vehicles per day between SR 30 and SR 38. SR 38: 2,015 vehicles per day through Collinston and Deweyville. SR 82: 2,265 vehicles per day near SR 13 in Garland; 6,890 vehicles per day north of SR 102 in Tremonton; 5,240 vehicles per day in "central" Garland. SR 102: 2,140 vehicles per day across the Bear River in Deweyville. 7,695 vehicles per day between SR 13 and SR 82 in Tremonton.

Getting there: Take I-15 to exit 381; turn right and head east on 12000 North into Garland. Turn left onto Main Street (SR 82) and go north. Turn right onto Factory Street (also SR 82) and head east. Turn left onto 500 East and then right onto 100 North to enter Garland City Park.

The Ride

The Bear River follows an incredibly long course—500 miles—in snaking its way from northeastern Utah, through southwestern Wyoming, into southeastern Idaho, into and out of Bear Lake, and back into northern Utah, before emptying into the Great Salt Lake. The river originates high in the Uinta Mountains. By the time the Bear River reaches Box Elder County, it is in its last phase, having merged with the Malad River flowing out of southern Idaho. The river meanders through a picturesque, predominantly agricultural region in Box Elder before flowing into a muddy delta at the northeastern corner of the Great Salt Lake. The delta is protected as the Bear River Migratory Bird Refuge, located directly west of Brigham City (Box Elder County's largest city). About sixty species of birds nest in the refuge, and a total of 200 species pass through, including ducks, geese, pelicans, swans, and shorebirds.

The route passes through several cities and towns on a pleasant tour of the scenic Bear River Valley. Water is always nearby, in the form of irrigation facilities, ponds, and, of course, the Bear River. The Wellsville Mountains provide a stately backdrop on the east side of the valley. The ride begins in Garland, a city with a population of 2,059 in 2008. Garland is located just to the northeast of the junction between the I-15 and I-84 freeways in Tremonton. The city was settled in 1890 and was named for William Garland, known for leading the construction of the Bothwell Canal (diverts

With a Wellsville Mountains backdrop, a cyclist crosses the Bear River.

water from the Bear River to an area west of Tremonton). Garland also helped to develop the sugar beet industry in the area. After leaving Garland, the route passes through Collinston, named for Collin Fulmer, a conductor on the Utah Northern Railroad. Collinston is unincorporated and is the likely location at which John C. Frémont crossed the Bear River in 1843. The community was settled around 1867. Frémont's expedition led to the laying of the Oregon Trail, and to setting off a wave of emigration to the western United States. Just south of Collinston is Deweyville, a town with a population of 334 in 2008. Deweyville was settled in 1864, eventually being named for John C. Dewey, a Mormon immigrant from England. The town was a railroad stop on the Utah Northern, a defunct line that operated during the 1870s and 1880s (and was later absorbed by the Union Pacific Railroad). Before returning to Garland, the route enters Tremonton (see the Golden Spike Challenge).

Start at Garland City Park. The parking area is gravel. To exit the park, head west on 100 North, then south on 500 East. Turn left onto Factory Street (SR 82) and head east. The road dips steeply to negotiate an underpass of SR 13; the descent is followed by a short, steep climb. Underneath all of the concrete and asphalt is the Malad River, making its run toward the Great Salt Lake. The road curves left at mile 1.0, becoming Garland Road (4400 West). The Corinne Canal appears on the right; the road crosses the canal at mile 2.1. The mountains in the far distance are the

Clarkstons, which extend northward into Idaho. Turn right onto SR 30 at mile 4.2 and head east. The highway dips at mile 4.6 to cross the Bear River, probably near the John C. Frémont crossing. The highway climbs steeply then gradually beyond the Bear River. Turn right onto SR 38 at mile 6.1 and begin a gradual descent into Collinston. A pleasant view of Bear River Valley is on the right as you negotiate the rollers along SR 38. Enter the northern reaches of Deweyville at mile 9.2. The imposing Wellsville Mountains are to the immediate left.

Turn right onto SR 102 and head west. Notice the building at 3274 West; this private residence was formerly the Fryer Hotel. The building is on the National Register of Historic Places (NRHP). A short descent to a crossing of the Bear River comes at mile 11.9. The crossing is followed by a short ascent. Enter Tremonton at mile 13.2. The "crossroads" (junction of SR 13 and SR 102) is at mile 13.7. Keep straight here; there are a couple of eating establishments on the corner. You are now on Main Street in Tremonton. Turn right at the traffic signal, onto 300 East (SR 82). The road passes through a pleasant residential area. The Holmgren Farmstead Building at 460 North 300 East is on the NRHP. Enter Garland at mile 15.6. You are now on Main Street in Garland. The Bear River High School Science Building at 1450 South Main Street is on the NRHP. Turn right onto Factory Street at mile 16.8. You are still on SR 82. Turn left onto 500 East at mile 17.1. The ride ends at 100 North, at mile 17.2. Turn right here to return to Garland City Park.

Miles and Directions

0.0 Start at Garland City Park, 100 North and 600 East, Garland. Head west on 100 North to 500 East. Turn left onto 500 East and head south.

0.1 At the stop sign at Factory Street, turn left.

0.5 SR 13 underpass; steep descent, followed by steep ascent.

1.0 Road curves left; now on Garland Road (4400 West).

2.1 Cross Corinne Canal.

4.2 At the stop sign at SR 30 (15200 North), turn right.

4.6 Begin 6 percent descent.

4.9 Cross Bear River.

5.1 Begin climb.

6.1 Turn right onto SR 38; begin gradual descent.

6.6 Enter Collinston.

7.0 Begin false flats and rolling terrain.

9.2 Enter the north end of Deweyville.

11.1 Turn right onto SR 102 (watch for gravel in turn).

11.3 Railroad crossing (two tracks).

11.9 Begin short descent.

12.4 Cross Bear River.

12.5 Begin short climb.

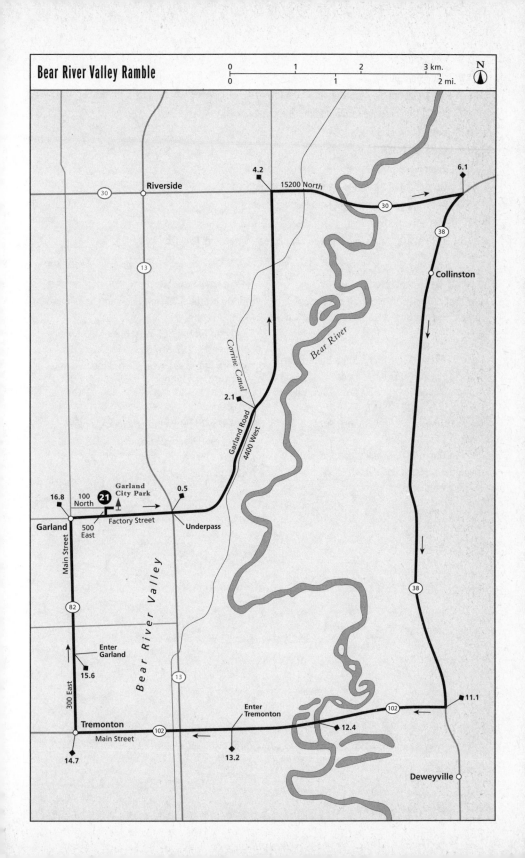

Bear River Valley Ramble

0   1   2   3 km.

0   1   2 mi.

N

Riverside

15200 North

4.2

6.1

30

30

38

13

Collinston

Corrine Canal

Bear River

2.1

Garland Road

4400 West

Garland
City Park

0.5

16.8

100
North

21

Underpass

Garland

500
East

Factory Street

Main Street

82

Bear River Valley

Enter
Garland

15.6

300 East

13

38

102

Enter
Tremonton

11.1

12.4

Tremonton

102

Main Street

13.2

14.7

Deweyville

12.9 Crest of climb.

13.2 Enter Tremonton.

13.7 Go straight at the stop sign at SR 13 (1550 East).

14.7 At the traffic signal, turn right onto 300 East (SR 82).

14.9 Begin short climb.

15.2 Crest of climb.

15.6 Enter Garland.

15.7 Go straight at the traffic signal at 1400 South.

16.8 At the stop sign, turn right onto Factory Street.

17.1 Turn left onto 500 East.

17.2 Yield at 100 North; turn right—end of ride at entrance to Garland City Park.

Local Information

Box Elder County official Web site: www
.boxeldercounty.org.

Restaurants

Figaro's Pizza: 1387 South Main Street, Garland; (435) 257-9988.

Munn's Sweet Shoppe: 20 West 1400 South, Garland; (435) 257-3947.

Outpost Tavern: 91 East Factory Street, Garland; (435) 257-0880.

The Pie Dump & TL Steakhouse: 20 West 1400 South, Suite B, Garland; (435) 257-3947; www.thepiedump.com.

Accommodations

Marble Motel: 116 North Tremont, Tremonton; (435) 257-3524.

Sandman Motel: 585 West Main Street, Tremonton; (435) 257-5675.

Western Inn: 2301 West Main Street, Tremonton; (435) 257-3399.

Map

Salt Lake City & Vicinity Including Logan, Ogden, and Provo, 5th edition, 2003. Rand McNally, Chicago, IL. Pages 27–29, 35–36 AH19 on page 28.

22 East Layton Cruise

The East Layton Cruise is a 37.2-mile out-and-back route with loops on both ends. The ride starts and finishes in Kaysville and visits Farmington, Fruit Heights, Layton, South Weber, and Uintah in Davis and Weber Counties. There are two long climbs (and two descents) along the course, with ample flat and false flat "recovery" segments in between. The ride elevation ranges from 4,349 feet in Kaysville to 4,800 feet along US 89.

Start: Utah Transit Authority or Utah Department of Transportation Park-and-Ride Lot at 200 North and 600 West, Kaysville. (As of this writing, a temporary lot at 381 North 400 West, Kaysville, was being used.)
Length: 37.2 miles (out-and-back, with loops on both ends).
Terrain: Flat and false flats; two long climbs and two long descents. Minimum and maximum elevations: 4,349 to 4,800 feet.

Traffic and hazards: SR 273: 14,300 vehicles per day between I-15 and Main Street in 2005; 19,650 vehicles per day between 200 North and 50 West. US 89: 30,500 vehicles per day in Kaysville and Layton; 42,800 vehicles per day between SR 193 and SR 60 in Layton and South Weber. SR 60: 3,200 vehicles per day in South Weber. Sunset Drive: 7,500 vehicles per day in Kaysville.

Getting there: From I-15, take exit 328 (200 North, Kaysville). Head west on 200 North; after passing under the freeway, turn left on 600 West. The park-and-ride lot is on the left. Alternatively, to get to the temporary park-and-ride lot, head east on 200 North at the freeway exit; turn left on 400 West. The lot is on the left at 381 North. Utah Transit Authority route 472 serves the park-and-ride lot on its express run between downtown Ogden and downtown Salt Lake City. Route 470 also runs between Ogden and Salt Lake City but serves Main Street, a few blocks east of the park-and-ride lots.

The Ride

Layton is the largest city in Davis County (population 65,514 in 2008). It is the only city in the county that stretches from the "flatlands" in the west to the Wasatch Mountains "bench" in the east. The centerpiece of the East Layton Cruise is US 89, which runs north–south along the bench. Despite its high motor vehicle traffic volumes, US 89 is heavily used by cyclists, as it is the most convenient way to get from points south to points north. The highway has four lanes and wide shoulders on both sides, but the cyclist must be alert and cautious when using the road. Hill Air Force Base is to the west and south of the northernmost roads of the route. Hill is a large, active military base with about 20,000 workers. You may observe Air Force fighter jets on training exercises during your ride.

Start at the Utah Transit Authority/Utah Department of Transportation (UTA/UDOT) park-and-ride lot at 200 North and 600 West in Kaysville, just west of the I-15 freeway. (As of this writing, a temporary lot at 381 North 400 West in Kaysville was being used during commuter railroad–related construction at 200 North, just west of the freeway.)

Kaysville (population 25,820 in 2008) is Layton's sister city, although the two entities have not always been friendly. The two cities grew simultaneously after the first settlers arrived in 1849. Kaysville was named for William Kay, the first Mormon bishop of the new settlement, while Layton was named for Christopher Layton, another Mormon bishop. Although the two settlements were distinct, Kaysville officials claimed Layton as part of their territory and began to tax the residents. A lawsuit filed by a Layton citizen eventually trekked all the way to the U.S. Supreme Court. A task force of Mormon apostles was formed to settle the differences, although they decided to keep church and state separate. Matters were finally settled when Layton declared independence, becoming an incorporated city, in 1902. Can't we all just get along?

Exit the lot; turn right onto 600 West, then right onto 200 North. Pass under I-15 and continue on 200 North, past a strip of commercial and retail development. (From the temporary lot, head south on 400 West and turn left onto 200 North—watch for traffic.) There are a couple of mini-marts along this stretch, so this may be a good place to stock up on fluids before embarking on the journey. Turn right onto Main Street at the signal. Then, where Main Street curves to the left, bear right onto 50 West. This road passes by the Utah Botanical Gardens (on the left) at mile 1.9, and Ponds Park (on the right) at mile 2.3. The road becomes East Frontage Road at mile 3.4, as it borders a residential area. Continue to the end of the road, turn left at Shepard Lane (1225 North), and enter Farmington (population 17,217). Farmington is the seat of Davis County. Although the city is only the eighth largest in the county, it is geographically central. The city is also the crossroads to all of Davis County's main highways: I-15, US 89, and the Legacy Parkway. Turn left onto Shepard Parkway (1075 West) and head north. Heritage Park is on the left at mile 4.8. At the end of the short climb north of the park, turn right onto Main Street. Cross over US 89 and turn left onto Mountain Road. The road curves back toward US 89, then again to head north, roughly paralleling the highway. This is the start of a 3.6-mile climb, but there is a restful downhill segment at the midpoint.

Once on Mountain Road, parallel to US 89, the route enters Fruit Heights (population 5,312). Although the city has attracted a substantial number of new subdivisions in recent years, there are still a few fruit orchards, from which the city gets its name. Take note of the Grandison Raymond House at 88 South Mountain Road—it is on the National Register of Historic Places (NRHP). Fruit Heights is a "bench" community, nestled against the dramatic peaks of the Wasatch Front. The high point, to your right, is Francis Peak, topping out at 9,547 feet. The white structure at the summit is a radar station. Turn left at the stop sign at 400 North, then make an immediate right at the traffic signal onto US 89. Climbing resumes here. You will return to Kaysville for a short stretch before entering Layton. There are a few small subdivisions to your right as you travel along busy US 89, but most of the city is sprawling to your left. There are mini-marts at the intersection with Cherry Lane, at mile 10.8. A 0.7-mile climb is next, followed by a rapid descent toward the Weber River valley. Just after the descent begins, it is advisable to take exit 404, for Clearfield Hill Air Force Base, and then immediately reenter US 89. This strategy avoids the discomforting situation of having motor vehicles merging onto the highway from your right. Continue the steep descent toward the valley; take exit 405 for South Weber Drive. Turn left at the stop sign, onto South Weber Drive. The opening up of the valley before your eyes as you descend is a special experience.

South Weber Drive is a low-volume road that is the city of South Weber's main thoroughfare. The road gradually gets narrower as you traverse the city. South Weber is a growing (population 6,167) suburb bordering the north rim of Hill Air Force Base. Strong winds whipping through the Weber River canyon to and from the east are quite common in South Weber. Turn right at 475 East at mile 17.9. Cross I-84 and turn right onto Cottonwood Drive. The road becomes 6600 South upon entering the town of Uintah (population 1,258). Uintah, formerly called Easton, at one time had a population of 5,000. The town's main attraction was a Union Pacific Railroad station, logistically situated at the mouth of Weber Canyon. The station was eventually relocated to Ogden, to the north, and the town's population waned. Trains continue to pass through Uintah, however; although there is no stop here, railroad tracks define the fabric of the community. You will ride parallel to the tracks, along 6600 South, as you pass through the town.

At the end of 6600 South, you come to the hairiest part of the course: the return to US 89. Turn right and begin to merge left, watching for motor vehicles exiting US 89 to access I-84 westbound. Once clear of this juncture, watch for motor vehicles entering US 89 from the I-84 loop ramp on your right. If that is not enough, also watch for motor vehicles exiting US 89 to access I-84 eastbound. Use hand signals, make eye contact, and watch the road—all at the same time—and you will be fine. Seriously, the interchange should probably be avoided during the morning and evening rush hours. During the other hours of the day, and on the weekends, there should be plenty of "gaps" in the traffic stream.

Once past the I-84 interchange, prepare to exit US 89 to South Weber Drive. Continue straight across this road and reenter US 89. Begin the 1.5-mile climb to Layton. Near the crest of the climb, do not take exit 404—stay on the highway. You will have to move left to avoid the off-ramp; so, again, watch for exiting motor vehicles and use hand signals. Once past the crest, watch for traffic entering US 89 from the right, although my experience is that this ramp is not heavily used. Once in Layton, US 89 rolls for a few miles before descending toward Fruit Heights. Turn left at the signal at 400 North; prepare for the turn by moving left, into the center lane, in advance of the intersection. The turn comes at mile 28.8. Turn right onto Mountain Road immediately after making the left turn and enter Fruit Heights. Mountain Road climbs to mile 29.5 before making a rapid descent toward Farmington. Turn right at Main Street, cross US 89, and then turn left onto Shepard Parkway (1075

West). After a short descent, Heritage Park will be on your right. Turn right onto Shepard Lane (1225 North). There are outdoor vending machines on the left, at the golf course, at mile 33.0. Continue onto the I-15 overpass, entering Kaysville on the other side. The road is rough in places, curving to the right and left before making a hard right at mile 34.5 to become Sunset Drive. Follow this street past some of Kaysville's newest residences. Sunset Drive is along the route of the annual Cycle Salt Lake Century (each May). At mile 36.3, the road bends right to become Old Mill Lane. The road bends left at mile 37.0 to become 600 West. Head north for 0.2 mile to the UTA/UDOT park-and-ride lot to end the ride.

Miles and Directions

0.0 Exit UTA/UDOT park-and-ride lot at 200 North and 600 West; turn right onto 600 West—at the stop sign at 200 North, turn right. (From temporary park-and-ride lot at 381 North 400 West, exit lot and turn right onto 400 West—at the stop sign at 200 North, turn left).

0.1 Go straight at the traffic signal at I-15 southbound ramps.

0.2 Go straight at the traffic signal at I-15 northbound ramps; now on SR 273.

0.7 At the traffic signal at Main Street, turn right. Still on SR 273.

1.0 Turn right onto 50 West (Frontage Road).

1.9 Utah Botanical Center on the left (lavatories, water).

2.3 Ponds Park on the right (lavatories, water).

3.4 Now on East Frontage Road (1400 North).

3.8 At the stop sign at Shepard Lane (1225 North), turn left.

4.3 At the stop sign at Shepard Parkway (1075 West), turn left.

4.8 Heritage Park on the left (lavatories, water).

5.3 At the stop sign at Main Street (SR 273), turn right. After 0.05 mile, go straight at the traffic signal at US 89 southbound ramps.

5.4 Go straight at the traffic signal at US 89 northbound ramps.

5.5 Turn left onto Mountain Road (1800 North); begin climbing.

5.6 Go straight at the stop sign at Northridge Road.

6.4 Fruit Heights city offices and park on the left (lavatories, water).

7.3 Crest of climb; begin gradual descent.

8.0 At the stop sign at 400 North; turn left.

8.1 At the traffic signal at US 89, turn right, begin climbing.

9.1 Crest of climb.

10.8 Go straight at the traffic signal at Cherry Lane. Mini-marts on the corner. Begin climb.

11.5 Crest of climb.

12.4 Take exit 404, CLEARFIELD, HILL AIR FORCE BASE.

12.7 Go straight at the traffic signal at SR 193; begin downhill.

13.0 Reenter US 89 from on-ramp.

13.9 Take exit 405 for South Weber Drive.

14.2 At the stop sign at South Weber Drive (SR 60), turn left.

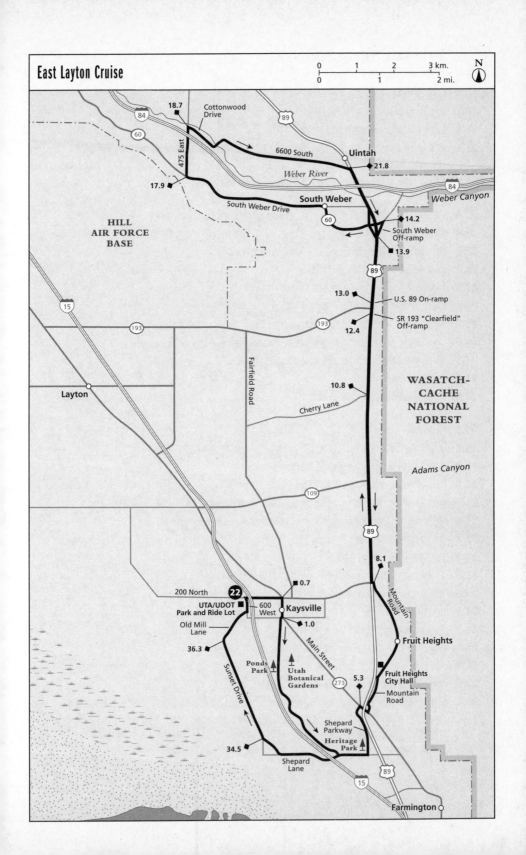

East Layton Cruise

0 1 2 3 km.
0   1   2 mi.

N

18.7 Cottonwood Drive
84
89
60
475 East
6600 South
Uintah
21.8
Weber River
17.9
South Weber Drive
South Weber
84
Weber Canyon
60
14.2
South Weber Off-ramp
13.9
89
13.0 U.S. 89 On-ramp
15
193
193
12.4 SR 193 "Clearfield" Off-ramp
Fairfield Road
Layton
10.8
Cherry Lane
WASATCH-CACHE NATIONAL FOREST
HILL AIR FORCE BASE
Adams Canyon
109
89
8.1
Mountain Road
0.7
200 North
22
UTA/UDOT Park and Ride Lot
600 West
Kaysville
1.0
Old Mill Lane
36.3
Fruit Heights
Main Street
Ponds Park
Utah Botanical Gardens
273
5.3
Fruit Heights City Hall
Mountain Road
Sunset Drive
34.5
Shepard Parkway
Heritage Park
Shepard Lane
89
15
Farmington

16.2 Road narrows; shoulder surface is poor.

17.9 Turn right onto 475 East.

18.6 I-84 overpass.

18.7 Turn right onto Cottonwood Drive.

19.4 Enter Uintah; now on 6600 South.

21.8 At the stop sign at US 89, turn right. Move left. Watch traffic from behind exiting US 89 and entering I-84.

21.9 Go straight at the traffic signal at I-84 northbound on-ramp—a turn would put the rider on the freeway.

22.1 Go straight at the traffic signal at I-84 southbound off-ramp.

22.4 Move right to exit US 89 at exit 405.

22.7 Go straight at the stop sign at South Weber Drive.

23.0 Reenter US 89; continue climbing.

23.9 Move left—do *not* take exit 404.

24.2 Crest of climb; watch for vehicles entering US 89 from the right.

25.0 Go straight at the traffic signal at Sunset Drive.

26.0 Go straight at the traffic signal at Cherry Lane—mini-marts on the corner.

27.1 Go straight at the traffic signal at Oak Hills Drive.

28.1 Begin descent.

28.8 At the traffic signal at 400 North, turn left, and then turn right onto Mountain Road—begin climb.

29.5 Crest of climb.

29.8 Begin descent.

31.2 Go straight at the stop sign at Northridge Road.

31.3 At the stop sign at Main Street, turn right.

31.4 Go straight at the traffic signal at US 89 northbound ramps.

31.5 Go straight at the traffic signal at US 89 southbound ramps; move left.

31.6 Turn left onto Shepard Parkway (1075 West).

32.1 Heritage Park on the right.

32.5 At the stop sign at Shepard Lane (1225 North), turn right.

33.0 Vending machines on the left (at Oakridge Country Club).

33.5 Enter Kaysville.

34.5 Bear right onto Sunset Drive.

36.3 Road bends right; now on Old Mill Lane.

36.9 Railroad crossing (four tracks).

37.0 Road bends left; now on 600 West.

37.2 End of ride, just south of 200 North; turn right and enter UTA/UDOT park-and-ride lot. To return to temporary lot, turn right onto 200 North; proceed under I-15 (traffic signals at ramps on either side). Turn left onto 400 West and head north—the lot is on the left.

Local Information

City of Farmington official Web site: www
.farmington.utah.gov.
City of Fruit Heights official Web site: www
.fruitheightscity.com.
City of Kaysville official Web site: www
.kaysvillecity.com.
City of Layton official Web site: www.layton
city.org.
City of South Weber official Web site: www
.southwebercity.com.

Restaurants

Dylan's Drive-Inn Restaurant: 185 North Main
Street, Kaysville; (801) 498-7777; http://
dylans-warrens.com.
Granny Annie's Family Restaurant: 286 North
400 West, Kaysville; (801) 544-8817.
Jake's Over the Top: 315 North Main Street,
Kaysville; (801) 444-3230.
Pepperbellys: 141 North Main Street,
Kaysville; (801) 444-3132; www.pepperbellys
.net.

Accommodations

Courtyard by Marriott: 1803 North Woodland
Park Drive, Layton; (801) 217-2300; www
.marriott.com/hotels/travel/slccl-courtyard-
salt-lake-city-layton/.
Hilton Garden Inn: 762 West Heritage Park
Boulevard, Layton; (801) 416-8899; http://
hiltongardeninn.hilton.com/en/gi/hotels/
index.jhtml;sessionid=ERMJNE3CSINXICSGBJC
4D4Q?ctyhocn=SLCLAGI.
Towneplace Suites by Marriott: 1743 Woodland Park Drive, Layton; (801) 779-2422; www
.marriott.com/hotels/travel/slctl-towneplace-
suites-salt-lake-city-layton/.
Cherry Hill Recreation Park: 1325 South
Main Street, Kaysville; (801) 451-5379 or
(800) 4GO-CAMP; www.cherry-hill.com. Camping and amusement park.

Bicycle Shop

The Biker's Edge: 232 North Main Street,
Kaysville; (801) 544-5300; www.bebikes.com.

Map

*Rand McNally: Salt Lake City Street Guide:
including Logan, Ogden, and Provo, 6th edition.* Pages 1173, 1229, 1230, 1282–1284,
1345 and 1346; starting grid: E5 on page
1282.

23 Golden Spike Challenge

The Golden Spike Challenge is a 57.7-mile ride combining a 42-mile loop with a 16-mile out-and-back segment. The origin and destination are the city of Tremonton and the Golden Spike National Historic Site, respectively. In between, the route skirts the perimeter of the ATK Thiokol facility and attacks the Blue Spring Hills. Significant climbs are featured in the latter, and on the road to Golden Spike. The elevation ranges from 4,291 feet just west of Tremonton to 5,420 feet at the crest of the Blue Spring Hills.

Start: Tremonton City Meadow Park, 600 West between 720 South and 800 South in Tremonton.

Length: 57.7 miles (loop, with 16-mile out-and-back segment).

Terrain: Long false flats, plus two significant climbs and descents. Minimum and maximum elevations: 4,291 to 5,420 feet.

Traffic and hazards: SR 83: 2,650 vehicles per day between SR 102 and Lampo Junction (road to Golden Spike) in 2005; 2,050 vehicles per day west and north of Lampo Junction. SR 102: 2,075 vehicles per day between SR 83 and Thatcher.

Getting there: I-15 north to I-84 north; take exit 41 (Tremonton) and turn right onto 11200 North. The road becomes Main Street upon entering Tremonton. Turn right onto 1000 West (Iowa String Road) and head south. Turn left onto 600 South, then turn right onto 634 West. The road curves left, becoming 720 South. Meadow Park is adjacent, on the right. Park on the opposite side of the park, near 800 South and 660 West.

The Ride

On May 10, 1869, a golden spike was driven between the final two eastbound and westbound rails of the transcontinental railroad, linking the western and eastern United States for the first time in history. The golden spike was driven at Promontory Point, immediately north of the Great Salt Lake in what is now Box Elder County. The historic event was preceded by the furious pace-setting of Central Pacific and Union Pacific railroad workers. The Central Pacific line came from the west, while the Union Pacific line came from the east. The Central Pacific used Chinese laborers who would sleep on the ground, next to the tracks, before resuming their daily duties. The Union Pacific used Irish and German immigrants who had more comfortable accommodations. The federal government was offering land grants and subsidies for each mile of track laid. The summit meeting involved not one spike, but two gold, one silver, and one composite spike. Service continued along the Promontory Point segment until 1904, when the Lucin Cutoff was constructed across the northern part of the Great Salt Lake. The bypass reduced traffic along the Promontory Point route drastically. By 1942, the railroad tracks on this route, having been all but abandoned, were ripped up and sold for scrap (the materials were sorely needed during World

War II). The significance of the site was not lost; some have argued that this was the most important American event of the nineteenth century. The Golden Spike National Historic Site (NHS) was authorized by Congress in 1965. An annual Last Spike Ceremony reenacts the events of May 10, 1869.

Tremonton is the closest city to the Golden Spike NHS. The city of Tremonton (population 6,789 in 2008) was founded in 1888, although it had been settled earlier by French-Canadian trappers. The city was originally named Tremont, but the name was changed to Tremonton in the early 1900s to avoid confusion with the city of Fremont. It is located at the junction of the I-15 and I-84 freeways and is an important crossroads. The city is home to La-Z-Boy and Malt-o-Meal, both familiar brand names. Tremonton is also the closest city to one of ATK Thiokol's plants, a rocket and missile propulsion development company. Thiokol has produced the Pershing, Minuteman, Trident I and II, and other missiles, as well as rocket motors, low-earth orbiting vehicles, ski lifts, and other innovative technologies. The Golden Spike Challenge passes by the ATK Thiokol facilities, giving the cyclist a chance to see some of their products on display.

Start by heading south from Tremonton City Meadow Park on 660 West. Turn right onto 1200 South (Rocket Road) at mile 0.3 and head west. Turn left onto Iowa String Road (1000 West) and head south, passing under I-84. Turn right onto 10400 North at mile 0.9 (also called Rocket Road) and head west. The road passes through some of the agricultural areas of the fertile Bear River Valley, with the Blue Spring Hills looming in the distance. Continue straight at mile 6.0 onto SR 102, the main road through this area. The road negotiates a series of left- and right-hand bends over the next 10 miles. The highway passes through a series of unincorporated communities along this stretch, including Bothwell, Thatcher, and Penrose. Bothwell was named in honor of John R. Bothwell, the principal in charge of the construction of the Bothwell Canal (see the Bear River Valley Ramble). Thatcher was named for Moses Thatcher, a Mormon apostle. Penrose was named for Charles W. Penrose, a Mormon church official, editor (*Deseret News* newspaper), poet, and composer (lyrics for several Mormon hymns). Highway 102 ends at mile 15.7; leave this interesting area by turning right onto SR 83 and heading west.

SR 83 is a barn-burner of a highway: relatively straight, flat, and very fast. The highway provides a convenient connection between I-15 and ATK Thiokol, which this ride visits. There are wide shoulders, though, so the highway is suitable for cycling. The Great Salt Lake is across the spacious mud flats on the left. Turn left at Lampo Junction (mile 19.2), toward Golden Spike NHS. The visitor center is open from 9:00 a.m. to 5:00 p.m. The road climbs into the Promontory Mountains at mile 21.5. The hillsides are laced with rocks that date from the Cretaceous period. The climb crests at mile 23.4; here, you are surrounded by desert scrub, possibly wondering if you took the wrong road. The road bends left at mile 25.9 and...behold! Enter the Golden Spike NHS at mile 26.7. The railroad crossing at mile 26.9 confirms that this

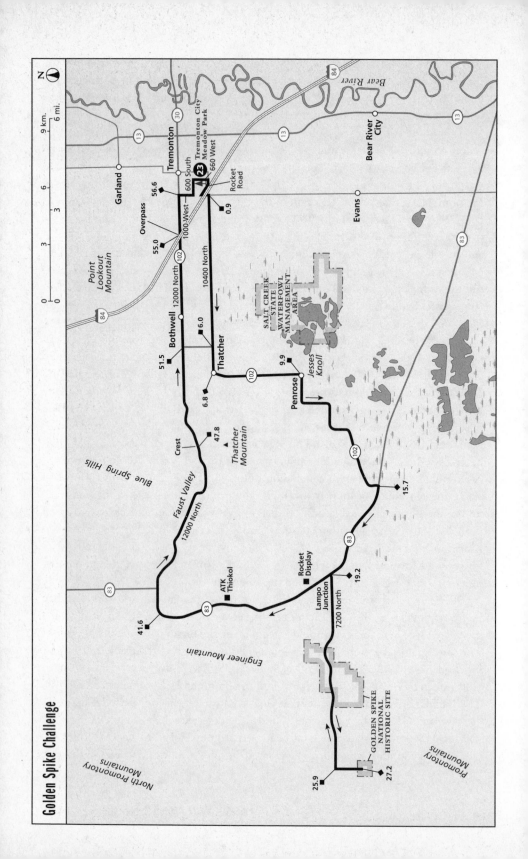

Golden Spike Challenge

is indeed where the eastern and western United States "joined hands." Turn right to enter the visitor center parking lot at mile 27.0. Take time to refresh and to learn about the transcontinental railroad. Complete the lot loop and return to the main road. Head out, turning right at mile 28.5 to continue on the main park road. The road turns downhill at mile 30.9 (watch your speed) and levels at mile 33.1. End the out-and-back segment at mile 35.2 by turning left to head northwest on SR 83.

The ATK Thiokol rocket display appears on the right at mile 37.0. One of the items on display is a space shuttle reusable solid rocket motor. Continue on SR 83, passing Engineer Mountain on the left. The highway makes a large horseshoe around the perimeter of the ATK Thiokol plant, eventually turning eastward at mile 41.6. The road becomes 12000 North at mile 42.6 (keep straight at the T intersection) and begins to climb into the Blue Spring Hills. There are five cattle guards over the next 5.6 miles. The road gets steeper in stair-steps, finally cresting at mile 47.8. From the top, the view of the Bear River Valley floor is commanding. Begin a fast descent here—watch your speed in the curves. The highway starts to level at mile 51.0 as you return to some outlying residences. A couple of the residences have some intriguing outdoor displays. At mile 51.5 you are once again on SR 102. The I-84 overpass at mile 55.0 announces the entry into town. There are several convenience marts and eateries along this stretch. Enter Tremonton at mile 55.4 and cross under I-15 at mile 56.0 (now on Main Street). Turn right onto 1000 West at mile 56.6 and head south. Turn left onto 600 South at mile 57.1 and enter a Tremonton residential area. Turn right onto 634 West; the road bends left, becoming 700 South. Meadow Park is on your right. To return to the start, continue along the border of the park. The ride ends at 800 South and 660 West, at mile 57.7.

Miles and Directions

0.0 Start at Tremonton City Meadow Park, 600 West between 720 South and 800 South. Begin by heading south on 660 West from 800 South.

0.3 At the stop sign, turn right onto 1200 South (Rocket Road).

0.6 At the stop sign, turn left onto 1000 West (Iowa String Road). After 0.05 mile, you come to the I-84 underpass.

0.9 Turn right onto 10400 North (Rocket Road).

3.2 Road dips to cross Salt Creek.

6.0 Yield at the sign at SR 102; now on SR 102.

6.8 Road bends left (still on SR 102); enter Thatcher.

9.9 Road bends right; enter Penrose.

10.9 Road bends left; still on SR 102.

11.3 Begin series of left-hand and right-hand bends.

15.7 Yield at the sign at SR 83; turn right.

19.2 Turn left onto 7200 North (Lampo Junction; to Golden Spike NHS).

21.5 Begin climb.

21.7 Enter Golden Spike National Historic Site.

23.4 Crest of climb; begin false flats.

25.9 Road bends left.

26.7 Pass Golden Spike National Historic Site sign.

26.9 Railroad crossing (two tracks).

27.0 Turn right into visitor center (restrooms); loop parking lot.

27.2 At the stop sign at the parking lot exit, turn left to return to main road.

27.5 Railroad crossing (two tracks).

28.5 Turn right to continue on main park road (no street sign); begin false flats.

30.9 Begin downhill.

33.1 End downhill.

35.2 At the stop sign at SR 83, turn left and head west.

37.0 ATK Thiokol rocket display on the right.

41.6 Highway bends right.

42.6 Begin uphill and curves; now on 12000 North.

43.2 Climb gets steeper; begin stair-steps—steep climbs interspersed with false crests.

43.9 Cattle guard.

45.1 Cattle guard.

46.8 Cattle guard; climb gets steeper.

47.5 Cattle guard; climb gets even steeper.

47.8 Crest of climb; begin fast descent.

48.2 Cattle guard, followed by curves (watch speed).

51.0 Gradient eases.

51.5 Now on SR 102 eastbound.

54.1 Cross Salt Creek.

55.0 I-84 overpass.

55.4 Enter Tremonton; convenience stores and fast food on left and right.

56.0 I-15 underpass.

56.6 Turn right onto 1000 West.

57.1 Turn left onto 600 South.

57.4 Turn right onto 634 West.

57.5 Road bends left; now on 700 South. After 0.05 mile, turn right onto 660 South.

57.6 At the stop sign at 800 South, turn right.

57.7 End of ride at 660 West; turn right to enter Meadow Park parking area.

Local Information

Box Elder County official Web site: www
.boxeldercounty.org.
**Golden Spike National Historic Site, National
Park Service Web site:** www.nps.gov/gosp.
City of Tremonton official Web site: www
.tremontoncity.com.

Restaurants

Bear River Bowl (Connie's Corner): 1410
West Main Street, Tremonton; (435) 257-1997.
JC's Country Diner: 10260 North State Road
13 (5200 West), Elwood; (435) 257-1867.
Mack's Family Drive-In: 80 East Main Street,
Tremonton; (435) 257-3712.
Saigon Towers: 26 South Tremont, Tremonton;
(435) 257-0443.

Accommodations

Marble Motel: 116 North Tremont, Tremonton;
(435) 257-3524.
Sandman Motel: 585 West Main Street, Tremonton; (435) 257-5675.
Western Inn: 2301 West Main Street, Tremonton; (435) 257-3399.

Maps

DeLorme: Utah Atlas & Gazetteer: Pages
11–12 C1 on page 12.
*Rand McNally: Salt Lake City Street Guide:
including Logan, Ogden, and Provo:* Map of
Tremonton on pages 520, 521, 584; starting
grid: D7 on page 520.
Benchmark: Utah Road & Recreation Atlas:
Page 48 G2.

A rider enters the site of arguably the most significant U.S. event of the nineteenth century.

Great Salt Lake Country

Great Salt Lake Country encompasses two counties in Utah: Salt Lake and Tooele. The region had a population of 1,079,592 in 2008, spread over an area of 7,687 square miles, making it Utah's most populous (and most densely populated) region. About 40 percent of the state's population lives in Great Salt Lake Country, making this region the center of the heavily urbanized Wasatch Front. Salt Lake City is, in fact, the largest city within a 330-mile radius that reaches beyond Utah and into neighboring states. If the *Road Biking Utah* ride selection procedure were based on population only, then 40 percent of the rides would be in Great Salt Lake Country. As such, only seven courses are in this region— to leave room for complete coverage of the state.

The region's name pertains to the Great Salt Lake, arguably Utah's most prominent and well-known feature. The Great Salt Lake is the largest salt lake in the Western Hemisphere (the Caspian Sea is the largest in the world), the fourth-largest terminal lake in the world (i.e., the lake has no outlet), and the thirty-third-largest lake in the world. The lake's size fluctuates quite a bit, ranging from an all-time low of just 950 square miles in 1963 to a high of 3,300 square miles in 1987. The latter size was associated with some flooding. The lake is a "watered-down" version of ancient Lake Bonneville, which once blanketed most of western and northern Utah. As of the writing of this book, lake levels were lower than average. The lake serves as a habitat for a large number of waterfowl, brine shrimp, and shore birds. Solar evaporation ponds on the edges of the lake collect the lake's abundant salt, after which it is transformed into table salt, potash, ice-melt, and other useful chemicals. Brine shrimp are also harvested. There is limited lake-oriented recreation, mainly because of the unpredictable lake levels, as well as the putrefying odor of decaying insects, brine shrimp, and other wildlife. But a few facilities take advantage of the lake's recreation potential, including the Great Salt Lake State Park Marina, Willard Bay State Park, Bear River Migratory Bird Refuge, and Antelope Island State Park (see the Antelope Island Cruise under Golden Spike Empire).

Salt Lake County contains four of Utah's five largest cities. The largest, Salt Lake City (population 181,698 in 2008), is the state capital, the Salt Lake County seat, the headquarters of the Utah Department of Transportation, home to the University of Utah, and the worldwide headquarters of the Mormon Church. Utah's present-day settlement patterns effectively fanned out from Salt Lake City, starting in 1847. Today, Salt Lake Valley development continues to push toward physical boundaries: the Great Salt Lake in the northwest, the Oquirrh Mountains in the west, and the Wasatch Mountains in the east. If the world did not "recognize" Salt Lake City as much more than the center of the Mormon Church prior to 2002, then the staging of the 2002 Winter Olympic Games perhaps changed that perception. Since the Games, the number of visitors to the area has increased, and the city has attracted major conferences and sporting events.

The city is laid out in a grid pattern that is duplicated by nearly every town in Utah. Nearly all cities, for example, have a north–south Main Street and/or State Street, and an east–west Center Street. The intersection between these streets is usually treated as the center of town. Temple Square is Salt Lake City's origin. Wide streets—wide enough to "turn a wagon team around without resorting to profanity" (Brigham Young)—are also characteristic of Salt Lake City and other Utah cities and towns. In general, streets ending in "North" or "South" run east–west, and streets ending in "East" or "West" run north–south.

Cycling is a popular activity in Great Salt Lake Country. Traffic volumes are high in the thick of urbanization, so the best cycling is on the perimeter of the cities and in the canyons leading up into the mountains. Salt Lake City, somewhat surprisingly, does not have a well-developed bike path network. One path, however, the Jordan River Parkway, is worth checking out (see the Jordan River Ramble). Numerous cycling clubs are based in Great Salt Lake Country; some emphasize recreational riding, while others focus on competitive racing. The Cycle Salt Lake Century, starting from the Utah State Fairgrounds in Salt Lake City, is held every May, and the Salt Lake City Marathon Bicycle Tour, on the Salt Lake Marathon course, is held every April. The Bonneville Bicycle Touring Club hosts several centuries and rides of other distances in Great Salt Lake Country and neighboring regions. Race events can change from year to year, but as of the writing of this book, there were two weekly criteriums in West Valley City, a biweekly time trial in Saltair, annual criteriums in Salt Lake City and Draper, an annual circuit race in Salt Lake City, an annual time trial in Tooele County's Skull Valley, and hillclimbs up five of the Wasatch Mountain canyons. A very active racer, in fact, might find up to five events per week during the peak spring-summer racing season. The Tour of Utah, a multiday stage race attracting top U.S. professionals, featured a couple of routes in Great Salt Lake Country in 2006. The event was cancelled in 2007 and returned in 2008; all or part of the 2009 route's six stages were held in the region.

It can be argued that Utah's most important bicycling-related advisories, policies, and regulations are generated in Great Salt Lake Country. The Salt Lake County Bicycle Advisory Committee (SLCBAC), the Utah Bicycle Coalition (based in Salt Lake City), Safe-Route Connection, Inc., and the Salt Lake Bicycle Collective all serve the cycling community by developing maps, staging special events, posting bicycle-related laws, lobbying for bicycling improvements, and functioning as information clearinghouses. The efforts of these groups have had an impact on cycling in the entire state.

24 Big Cottonwood Canyon Challenge

The Big Cottonwood Canyon Challenge is a 37.2-mile mountain climb and descent, starting in Mount Olympus with 4 miles of rolling hills, followed by a 14-mile climb up the canyon to Brighton, a 14-mile descent, and 4 miles of rolling hills to return to the starting point. The elevations range from 4,840 feet at the start at Olympus Hills Park to 8,730 feet at the turnaround. The course is on well-maintained county roads and state highways, so the pavement is generally smooth. The highway through Big Cottonwood Canyon is subject to closure during inclement weather, although the road is plowed during the winter to enable access to the Solitude and Brighton ski resorts.

Start: Olympus Hills Park, 3131 East 4500 South, Mount Olympus (unincorporated community).
Length: 37.2 miles (out-and-back).
Terrain: Rolling hills followed by a 14-mile climb to Brighton, then a 14-mile descent and rolling hills to return to the start. Minimum and maximum elevations: 4,840 to 8,730 feet.
Traffic and hazards: SR 266: 14,395 vehicles per day on I-215 in 2005. SR 190: 4,145 vehicles per day east of SR 210, entering Big Cottonwood Canyon; 830 vehicles per day at Brighton (subject to seasonal variations).

Getting there: From central Salt Lake City, head south on I-15 to I-80 east to I-215 south. Exit at 4500 South and turn right. Olympus Hills Park is adjacent the freeway. Or take Utah Transit Authority (UTA) route 45 from the 4500 South TRAX (light rail) station to Olympus Hills Park. Bus service every fifteen minutes.

The Ride

The Wasatch Mountains that form the Salt Lake Valley's impressive backdrop are drained through several canyons. The paved ones include City Creek, Emigration, Parleys, Big Cottonwood, and Little Cottonwood. Big Cottonwood is home to two ski resorts—Brighton and Solitude—as well as plentiful camping, climbing, cycling, fishing, hiking, and picnicking. Observers of wildflowers appreciate the diverse array of plants in the canyon, including the Wasatch shooting star, which is known to grow only in Big Cottonwood. Despite the popularity of Brighton and Solitude among skiers and snowboarders, and the proximity of the canyon to Salt Lake City (25 miles from downtown), none of the 2002 Winter Olympic Games events were held here. Utah is home to several Cottonwood Canyons, all of which refer to the cottonwood tree that is common here. The tree has shiny (green), triangular leaves that tend to "shine" and shake in the wind. Female trees produce fluffy white seeds that resemble cotton (the trees do not produce cotton). Big Cottonwood Creek occasionally flows with force, providing power and water (the canyon is a watershed) to Salt Lake Valley residents. The moniker Big Cottonwood implies that there is a Little Cottonwood;

Along the bench adjacent Mount Olympus, on Wasatch Boulevard.

indeed, there is—it is the next most southerly canyon in the Wasatch. It is not readily clear why one canyon is "Big" and the other is "Little," although the "Big" canyon is a couple of miles longer than the "Little" one.

Big Cottonwood Canyon has been designated as a scenic byway by the Utah Department of Transportation. Big Cottonwood Canyon is also a popular route for cyclists. The annual Big Cottonwood Canyon Hillclimb is held during the summer. The canyon was the scene of an unfortunate fatality in September 2004, however, when a young University of Utah student was hit by a sport-utility vehicle while ascending the canyon. The event raised the awareness of the cycling community to a greater extent than other bike-car collisions. An annual memorial ride that has attracted over 1,000 participants has been held since the incident. The incident also spurred the legislation of a "3-feet rule" in Utah, which effectively requires drivers to give cyclists a 3-foot gap when passing (similar laws exist in other states). The canyon continues to be a popular cycling route.

The ride begins at Olympus Hills Park, in the shadow of Mount Olympus, in Mount Olympus (a census-designated place that is part of Millcreek Township). Millcreek Township was established in 2002. Although it is an unincorporated community, the township had a population of 69,293 in 2004, making it the seventh-largest urban conglomeration in Utah. Turn left upon exiting the park and begin the short, steep climb to Wasatch Boulevard via 4430 South (SR 266). At the top of the climb, after crossing over the I-215 freeway, turn right onto Wasatch Boulevard. The road descends along "the bench," with an outstanding view of the Salt Lake Valley. To your left is Mount Olympus, which reaches up to 9,026 feet above sea level. Wasatch Boulevard curves to the left, and then to the right around mile 3.1. Start moving left here, in preparation for the left turn at the upcoming T intersection and traffic signal. The left turn actually keeps you on Wasatch Boulevard. Swing wide, onto the shoulder, after making the turn and begin the gentle climb to the mouth of Big Cottonwood Canyon. You are now in Cottonwood Heights (population 35,418 in 2008), Salt Lake County's newest city, incorporated in 2005. The city is home to Overstock.com and JetBlue Airways. You continue to have an outstanding view of the valley on your right.

Turn left at the traffic signal, toward Big Cottonwood Canyon (SR 190), and begin the climb. From this point, the fastest hillclimb to Brighton, the turnaround point, appears to be one hour and twenty-two seconds, set by professional cyclist Jeff Louder in 2007. The climb begins gradually; enter the Wasatch-Cache National Forest at mile 4.8. From mile 5.9 and beyond, notice the spectacular cuts made in excavations for the highway. The Stars Station water treatment plant then at mile 6.2. Water flowing down the canyon is processed here and then consumed by Salt Lake Valley residents. Pretreated water is kept clean by prohibiting pets and other animals from entering the canyon. The climb gets noticeably steeper at mile 6.4. The Storm Mountain Picnic Area is at mile 7.0; Storm Mountain towers to the right, peaking at 9,524 feet. The grade eases while passing the picnic area, but the steep climb resumes just beyond here. A pair of hairpin curves follows at mile 8.4. The gradient eases at mile 9.3; the highway climbs gradually for the next 5 miles.

The steep climb resumes at mile 14.2, at Spruces' Campground, remaining steep all the way to Brighton. The Silver Fork Lodge is on the right at mile 15.3. Silver Fork is actually a small, canyon community with a few seasonal residents. The Solitude ski area is on the right at mile 16.3. The accompanying Solitude Mountain Resort is on the right at mile 16.7. This pre- and après-ski spot has eateries, as well as restrooms. The gradient finally eases at mile 18.1, just before entering Brighton. Bear right at the Y intersection and begin a counterclockwise, one-way loop. The Solitude Nordic Center (cross-country skiing and snowshoeing) is on the right at mile 18.3 (restrooms). The Brighton ski area is on the right at mile 18.5. All along the loop, watch for entering and exiting motor vehicles. The highway crests at mile 18.6, and the loop ends at mile 18.9.

The highway starts to descend steeply at mile 19.1. You may generate quite a bit of speed here, zipping past the Solitude Mountain Resort (mile 20.5) and Solitude ski area (mile 20.8). Silver Fork is at mile 21.8. While descending, you may notice gates spaced intermittently along the road. The gates are part of the canyon's snow avalanche control system; when the avalanche risk is high, the at-risk segment of the highway is closed until the risk is reduced. The grade eases at mile 23.4; the descent continues, but pedaling may be needed to maintain a high speed. Steep descending resumes at mile 26.7. Enter a series of hairpin turns at mile 28.6—watch your speed here, and avoid crossing the centerline. Leave the Wasatch-Cache National Forest at mile 32.3 and enter Cottonwood Heights. Hit the brakes in preparation for the right turn onto Wasatch Boulevard at mile 32.9. Turn right again at mile 33.8 to remain on Wasatch Boulevard. The road climbs for about 0.7 mile before leveling off along "the bench." Enjoy the valley view on the left. Enter Millcreek Township at mile 35.4. After a gradual climb, turn left at the traffic signal onto 4500 South (SR 266). The road descends sharply, crossing over I-215. Just beyond the overpass, turn right, into Olympus Hills Park, to conclude the ride.

Miles and Directions

0.0 Start at Olympus Hills Park at 3131 East 4500 South (actually 4430 South; SR 266) in Mount Olympus; turn left onto 4430 East and head east, climbing toward "the bench."

0.1 I-215 overpass; continue steep climb.

0.2 At the traffic signal at Wasatch Boulevard, turn right—begin downhill.

3.1 Move left to prepare for left turn.

3.3 At the traffic signal at Wasatch Boulevard, turn left to continue on Wasatch Boulevard. Now on SR 190; enter Cottonwood Heights.

4.3 At the traffic signal at SR 190, turn left to enter Big Cottonwood Canyon and continue on SR 190—begin climb.

4.8 Gate (closed during inclement weather); enter Wasatch-Cache National Forest.

6.2 Stars Station on the right.

6.4 Climb gets steeper.

7.0 Picnic area; gradient eases.

7.5 Steep grade resumes.

8.4 Hairpin curve to the left, followed by hairpin curve to the right.

9.3 Gradient eases; gradual climb for the next 5 miles.

14.2 Steep climb resumes.

15.3 Silver Fork Lodge on the right.

16.3 Solitude ski area on the right.

16.7 Solitude Mountain Resort on the right (eateries, restrooms).

18.1 Gradient eases.

18.2 Bear right; enter Brighton—begin counterclockwise, one-way loop.

18.3 Solitude Nordic Center on the right (restrooms, information).

18.5 Brighton ski area on the right—watch for entering and exiting vehicles.

18.6 Crest of climb.

18.9 End of one-way loop.

19.1 Begin steep descent.

20.5 Solitude Mountain Resort on the left.

20.8 Solitude ski area on the left.

21.8 Silver Fork Lodge on the left.

23.4 Gradient eases; still descending.

26.7 Gradient increases (descent gets steeper).

28.6 Hairpin curve to the left, followed by hairpin curve to the right.

29.3 Gradient eases.

30.0 Sharp bends—descent gets steeper; highway winds.

30.8 Gradient eases.

32.3 Leave Wasatch-Cache National Forest; enter Cottonwood Heights.

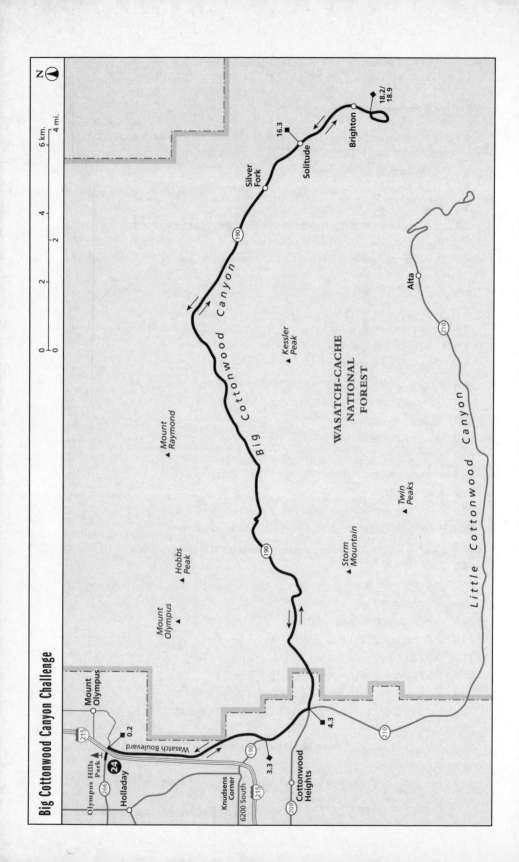

Big Cottonwood Canyon Challenge

N

6 km.
4 mi.

Olympus Hills Park
24
266
Holladay
Mount Olympus
Mount Olympus
215
0.2
Wasatch Boulevard
190
3.3
Knudsens Corner
6200 South
215
4.3
Cottonwood Heights
209
210

Mount Olympus
Mount Raymond
Hobbs Peak

190

Big Cottonwood Canyon

Kessler Peak

Storm Mountain

Twin Peaks

WASATCH-CACHE NATIONAL FOREST

190

Silver Fork

16.3
Solitude

Brighton
18.2/ 18.9

Alta
210

Little Cottonwood Canyon

32.9 At the traffic signal at Wasatch Boulevard, turn right.

33.8 At the traffic signal at Wasatch Boulevard, turn right to continue on Wasatch Boulevard—begin climb.

34.5 Gradient eases; now on false flat.

35.4 Enter Millcreek Township.

36.2 Begin gradual climb.

37.0 At the traffic signal at 4500 South (SR 266), turn left—begin descent.

37.1 I-215 freeway overpass.

37.2 End of ride; turn right to enter Olympus Hills Park.

Local Information

City of Cottonwood Heights official Web site: www.cottonwoodheights.utah.gov.
Millcreek Township official Web site: www.millcreektownship.org.
Big Cottonwood Canyon Scenic Byway information: www.utah.com/byways/big_cottonwood.htm.

Restaurants

Café Madrid: 2080 East 3900 South, Millcreek Township; (801) 273-0837; www.cafemadrid.net. Dinner only.
Log Haven: 6451 East Millcreek Canyon Road, Mount Olympus; (801) 272-8255; www.loghaven.com. Dinner only.
Market Street Grill & Oyster Bar—Cottonwood: 2985 East 6580 South (Cottonwood Parkway), Cottonwood Heights. Grill: (801) 942-8860; www.ginc.com/cottmsg/index.html. Oyster Bar: (801) 942-8870; www.ginc.com/cottoyst/index.html.
Mikado Cottonwood—Japanese Fusion Cuisine and Sushi Bar: 6572 South Big Cottonwood Canyon Road, Cottonwood Heights; (801) 947-9800.
Porcupine Pub and Grille "at the Mouth": 3698 East Fort Union Boulevard, Cottonwood Heights; (801) 942-5555; www.porcupinepub.com.
Tuscany/Club Tuscany: 2832 East 6200 South, Cottonwood Heights; (801) 277-9919; www.tuscanyslc.com. Weekdays: lunch and dinner; weekends: dinner.

Accommodations

Candlewood Suites: 6990 South Park Centre Drive, Cottonwood Heights; (801) 567-0111 or (877) 226-3539; www.ichotelsgroup.com/h/d/cw/1/en/hotel/slcfu.
Millcreek Inn: 5803 East Millcreek Canyon Road, Mount Olympus; (801) 278-7927; www.millcreekinn.com.
Residence Inn Salt Lake Cottonwood: 6425 South 3000 East, Cottonwood Heights; (801) 453-0430; www.marriott.com/hotels/travel/slctt-residence-inn-salt-lake-city-cottonwood.

Bicycle Shops

Hyland Cyclery: 3040 South Highland Drive, Salt Lake City; (801) 467-0914; www.hylandcyclery.com.
Millcreek Bicycles: 3969 Wasatch Boulevard (Olympus Hills Mall), Holladay; (801) 278-1500; www.canyonbicycles.com.
REI (Recreational Equipment Inc.): 3285 East 3300 South, East Millcreek; (801) 486-2100; http://rei.com/stores/19.
Spin Cycle: 4233 South Highland Drive, Holladay; (801) 277-2626 or (888) 277-SPIN; www.spincycleut.com.

Map

Rand McNally: Salt Lake City Street Guide: including Logan, Ogden, and Provo: Pages 2072, 2178, 2182, 2183 B2 on page 2072.

25 Bingham Canyon Cruise

The Bingham Canyon Cruise is a 14.8-mile out-and-back ride that starts in a pleasant West Jordan neighborhood, ascends Bingham Canyon to the Kennecott Copper Mine gate, then turns around for the descent and return to the start. The return route makes a short detour through the township of Copperton. The elevation ranges from 4,790 feet at the start to 5,520 feet just outside of Copperton.

Start: Teton Estates Park, Targhee Drive and Laurel Ridge Drive, West Jordan.
Length: 14.8 miles (out-and-back).
Terrain: Steady but not steep ascent to the turnaround, followed by a descent to the finish.

Minimum and maximum elevations: 4,790 to 5,520 feet.
Traffic and hazards: SR 48: 1,590 vehicles per day through Copperton in 2005.

Getting there: From I-15, take exit 295 and head west on 9000 South (into West Jordan). Turn left onto 4000 West and head south. Turn right onto Laurel Ridge Drive. Teton Estates Park is located adjacent the 90-degree right-hand bend in the road, at Targhee Drive. Utah Transit Authority route 90 runs east-west along 9000 South between the Sandy TRAX (light rail) station and West Jordan every thirty minutes on weekdays. Route 348 runs between downtown Salt Lake City to West Jordan during commute periods only. Both buses stop at 4000 West and 9000 South. In both cases, head south on 4000 West and then right onto Laurel Ridge Drive to Teton Estates Park.

The Ride

Bingham Canyon, in the southwest corner of the Salt Lake Valley, is home to the largest open copper mining pit in the world. The pit can be seen from outer space. Mining began in Bingham Canyon in 1863. Gold, silver, and lead were extracted initially, but the attention turned to copper in 1906. The mine has since yielded a total of twelve million tons of copper. To access the mineral, deeper and deeper cuts have created a pit that was 2.5 miles in diameter and 0.5 mile deep as of this writing. The pit is the world's largest excavation and is a National Historic Landmark. The town of Bingham, adjacent the mine, once was home to 15,000 persons, including miners and their families. The town was disincorporated in 1971 after it had been nearly overrun by pit expansion. The town had also been subjected to fires, floods, and avalanches during its history. The town of Copperton, located about 1 mile east of the fringes of the mine, continues to exist. Copperton was built in 1926 by the Utah Copper Company when Bingham became overcrowded. The community is home to about 800 residents, about 50 percent of whom work at the mine. Although the Bingham Canyon Cruise does not venture into the pit, the mine has a visitor center.

Bingham Canyon is located in the Oquirrh Mountains, which form the western boundary of the Salt Lake Valley. The Salt Lake Valley is actually bound on three sides,

Ascending Bingham Canyon, near the township limits of Copperton.

with the north–south Oquirrh range continuing into the east–west Traverse Mountains, which connect to the north–south Wasatch Mountains. Unlike the Wasatch,
there are no ski resorts in the Oquirrhs. This is partially because of their ruggedness.
Paleozoic limestone in the Oquirrhs, however, is rich in the minerals that have been
extracted for nearly one-and-one-half centuries in Bingham Canyon. The Bingham
Canyon Cruise rides up the canyon to the copper pit gate and then turns around.

The ride starts in West Jordan, one of Salt Lake City's rapidly growing suburbs.
West Jordan (named as such for being "west" of the Jordan River) was settled in 1848,
just one year after Mormon pioneers first set foot in the Salt Lake Valley. West Jordan
had a population of 104,447 in 2008, making it the fourth-largest city in Utah, and
the fourth to crack the 100,000 barrier. The route also traces the northern boundary
of the city of South Jordan. South Jordan had a population of 51,131 in 2008. The
western half of South Jordan, leading up to the flanks of Bingham Canyon and the
Oquirrh foothills, was undeveloped as of this writing. The so-called Daybreak Community was being planned for this region, however, with the potential for doubling
South Jordan's population. Currently, cyclists can enjoy the relative tranquility of this
part of the Salt Lake Valley. The tranquility may not last, unfortunately.

Start at Teton Estates Park, at Targhee Drive and Laurel Ridge Drive, in West
Jordan. Head north on Targhee Drive through a West Jordan neighborhood. Turn

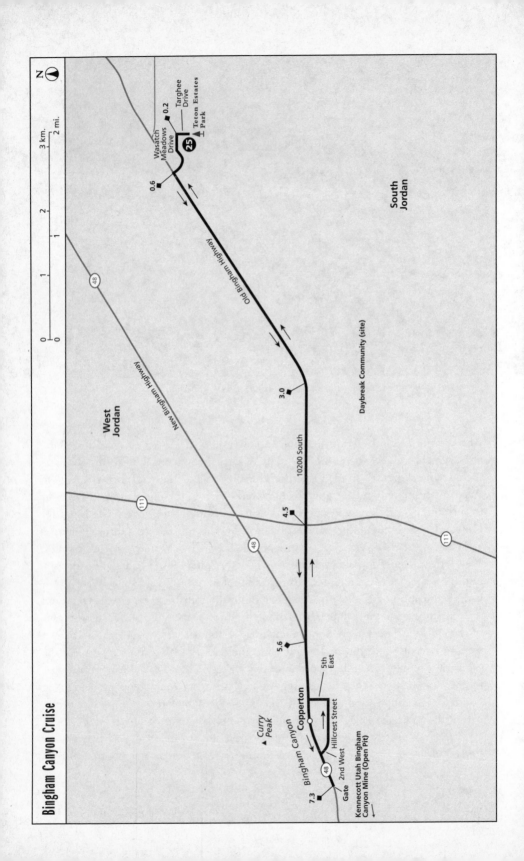

Bingham Canyon Cruise

N

3 km.
2 mi.

Wasatch Meadows Drive

0.2
Targhee Drive
Teton Estates Park

25

0.6

Old Bingham Highway

South Jordan

West Jordan

New Bingham Highway

48

Daybreak Community (site)

3.0

10200 South

111

4.5

48

111

5.6

Curry Peak

Bingham Canyon
Copperton

Hillcrest Street

5th East

2nd West

48

Gate

7.3

Kennecott Utah Bingham Canyon Mine (Open Pit)

left onto Wasatch Meadows Drive. The road bends right and "Ts" into Old Bingham Highway at mile 0.65. Turn left here to begin the ascent toward Bingham Canyon. Just FYI, there is a "New" Bingham Highway, paralleling the old one about 0.5 mile to the north. The new highway is a faster and more direct east–west route than the old highway, enabling the latter to have comparatively light traffic volumes. The Oquirrh Mountains serve as the backdrop during the ascent. Exercise caution at the skewed railroad track crossing at mile 2.1. Cross SR 111 at mile 4.5; turn left onto SR 48 at mile 5.6. You have now merged with the "New" Bingham Highway and are in the canyon's alignment. Enter Copperton after passing under a railroad structure. Notice the cozy dwellings on the left; the entire Copperton township is a National Historic District. The highway continues to climb, finally cresting at mile 6.7. After passing underneath a conveyor structure, the highway descends toward the mine. The overhead conveyor is 5 miles long, ending at the Copperton concentrator located some distance off to your right. Some of the terraces of the mining operation, unseen during the climb, are now in plain view. The famous pit cannot be seen from here, and is actually to the southwest. The height and depth of these terraces, though, give some indication of the size of the mining operation. The highway makes a short descent to a locked gate (this is not the main public entrance to the mine). The One Horse Saloon is on the right. Turn around here.

The "descent" of Bingham Canyon actually begins with a short climb. Once past the conveyor structure, at mile 7.7, the highway enters Copperton. Bear right onto West Park Street, then right again—immediately—onto 2nd West. You are now on one of Copperton's residential streets. The road curves left, becoming Hillcrest Street. Notice the steep drop-off to the right. The town was built on Rattlesnake Flat, in an area that was suitable for development. A single architectural firm designed all of the houses. The houses, in fact, have similar floor plans, but the exterior treatments differ. A few community facilities, including Copperton Park, are located along Hillcrest Street. The road curves left again, becoming 5th East. Turn right at SR 48 (the sign reads STATE HIGHWAY) at mile 8.7, to continue the return trip. After leaving town, bear right at the WEST JORDAN sign, onto Old Bingham Highway, at mile 9.3. The Wasatch Mountains are in the far distance. Enjoy the view of the Salt Lake Valley floor. Cross SR 111 at mile 10.4 and continue the descent. Carefully cross the skewed railroad track at mile 12.8. At mile 13.3, notice the sign for RAD CANYON BMX. A sanctioned BMX track is located about 0.5 mile to the south, at 9800 South 5200 West (in South Jordan). If you are doing the Bingham Canyon Cruise on a BMX bicycle, a detour to the track may be tempting. Turn right onto Wasatch Meadows Drive (4400 West) at mile 14.2 and reenter the Teton Estates neighborhood of West Jordan. The road curves left; turn right onto Targhee Drive at mile 14.6. The ride ends at Teton Estates Park, which is on the left adjacent the corner of Targhee Drive and Laurel Ridge Drive.

Miles and Directions

0.0 Start at Teton Estates Park, Targhee Drive and Laurel Ridge Drive in West Jordan. Head north on Targhee Drive.

0.2 Turn left onto Wasatch Meadows Drive (9230 South).

0.3 Go straight at the stop sign at Teton Estates Drive (4250 West).

0.5 Road curves right; now on 4570 West (still on Wasatch Meadows Drive).

0.6 Railroad crossing (one track). After 0.05 mile, at the stop sign at Old Bingham Highway (9180 South), turn left (begin steady climb).

1.0 Go straight at the traffic signal at 4800 West.

2.1 Railroad crossing (one track; skewed—caution).

3.0 Road curves right.

4.5 Go straight at the stop sign at SR 111 (7230 West).

5.6 At the stop sign, turn left onto SR 48.

5.9 Railroad underpass.

6.0 Enter Copperton.

6.7 Crest of climb.

6.8 Pass under overhead conveyor structure.

7.0 Begin descent; view of mining pit terraces ahead.

7.3 One Horse Saloon on the right—gate ahead; turn around here.

7.5 Begin short climb.

7.7 Crest of climb.

7.9 Bear right onto West Park Street, then immediately right again onto 2nd West.

8.0 Road curves left; now on Hillcrest Street.

8.3 Copperton Park on the left.

8.5 Road curves left; now on 5th East.

8.7 At the stop sign, turn right onto SR 48 (STATE HIGHWAY).

9.0 Railroad underpass.

9.3 Bear right at WEST JORDAN sign, onto Old Bingham Highway.

10.4 Go straight at the stop sign at SR 111.

11.8 Road curves left.

12.8 Railroad crossing (one track; skewed—caution).

13.8 Go straight at the traffic signal at 4800 West.

14.2 Turn right onto Wasatch Meadows Drive (4400 West). After 0.05 mile, come to a railroad crossing (one track).

14.3 Road curves left; now on 9260 South (still on Wasatch Meadows Drive).

14.5 Go straight at the stop sign at Teton Estates Drive.

14.7 At the stop sign at Targhee Drive (4170 West), turn right.

14.8 End of ride at Teton Estates Park, on left (at Laurel Ridge Drive).

Local Information

Township of Copperton official Web site: www.copperton.org.
Kennecott Utah Copper, information on Bingham Canyon mine: www.kennecott.com.
City of South Jordan official Web site: www.southjordancity.org.
City of West Jordan official Web site: www.wjordan.com.

Restaurants

Several familiar chain outlets are in West Jordan, including Arby's (two locations), IHOP, and McDonald's (three locations).

Accommodations

Country Inn & Suites by Carlson-Salt Lake City-South Towne: 10499 South Jordan Gateway, South Jordan; (801) 553-1151 or (800) 456-4000; www.countryinns.com/saltlakecityut_south.

River Oaks Apartments & Suites: 9051 South 1075 West, West Jordan; (801) 545-5600. Extended stay only (30-night minimum).
Camping at the RAD Canyon BMX facility: 9800 South 5200 West, South Jordan; (801) 699-9575; www.radcanyonbmx.com.

Bicycle Shops

Golsan Cycles: 10445 South Redwood Road, South Jordan; (801) 446-8183; www.golsancycles.com.

Maps

H.M. Gousha Co., Salt Lake City (city map). Rand McNally, Sandy/Orem/Provo, Utah (street map).

26 Bonneville Salt Flats Ramble

The Bonneville Salt Flats Ramble is a 19.5-mile out-and-back ride on level roads on the western edge of the Great Salt Lake Desert. The ride starts and ends in Wendover, on the Utah–Nevada border. The desert is arid and dry (and *hot* during the summer), so be sure to properly hydrated and to bring plenty of fluids on the ride. There is a mini-mart at the 4.6-mile and 14.8-mile marks of the course (same mart), perhaps perfectly located for a refreshment stop.

Start: Ball fields, Uinta Avenue (200 South) at 200 East, Wendover.
Length: 19.5 miles (out-and-back).
Terrain: Flat, except for a freeway overpass. Minimum and maximum elevations: 4,214 to 4,252 feet.
Traffic and hazards: SR 58 (Wendover Boulevard): 10,350 vehicles per day near the Nevada border in 2005; 5,850 vehicles per day at the eastern limits of Wendover.

Getting there: Take I-80 west from Salt Lake City to exit 1 (Wendover; Aria Boulevard). Turn left at the end of the ramp, onto Aria Boulevard, and head south. Cross Wendover Boulevard (SR 58); you are now on 1st Street (100 East). Turn left onto Uinta Avenue (200 South) and head east to 200 East, adjacent the ball fields.

The author contemplates his failed attempt at a speed record at the Bonneville Salt Flats.
ANN COTTRELL

The Ride

The Great Salt Lake Desert occupies about 4,000 square miles west of the Great Salt Lake, in Tooele and Box Elder Counties. The desert is actually larger than its namesake Great Salt Lake. Part of the much larger Great Basin Desert, it is arid and barren, practically devoid of vegetation. The curvature of the earth can be viewed across the horizon of the desert's vast, flat expanses. The desert was once the lakebed of Lake Bonneville, the giant ancestor of the Great Salt Lake, before the former broke through the Sawtooth Mountains in Idaho and receded. A large portion of the Great Salt Lake Desert is used for military testing and is not accessible to the public. The area north of the I-80 freeway, however, has historically been used for racing. This corner of the desert is referred to as the Bonneville Salt Flats, occupying some 159 square miles. Although the flats are not pure salt, there is a high concentration of salt in the soil. A speedway—seasonal, since the desert is subject to inundation during periods of rain—is "built" by the Bureau of Land Management each year. The speedway is 10 miles long and 80 feet wide. Racing on the speedway is generally against the clock, with the primary objective being to set land speed records.

The legacy of the speedway is actually in bicycling, as it was W. D. Rishel who discovered the potential of the flats when scouting a location for bike racing in the mid-1890s. After the discovery, the flats saw the land speed record increase from just over 100 mph to over 600 mph. Although the Bonneville Speedway can no longer claim the automobile speed record (the Black Rock Desert in Nevada now owns that title), the bicycle speed record (152.2 mph!) was set at Bonneville. Olympic cyclist John Howard rode a specially constructed bicycle, drafting behind the large tail fairing of a streamlined motor vehicle, in 1985 to set the record. The dangers of setting such a record were apparent when John Howard described how he "scraped a pedal" during a practice run, and the pedal "disintegrated"!

The harshness of the Great Salt Lake Desert leaves it virtually uninhabited. At the far western edge of the desert is the city of Wendover, at the Nevada border. Wendover had a population of 1,632 in 2008. Although the city seems separated from the rest of Utah by the vast expanses of the desert, the city is adjacent the I-80 freeway, making it remarkably accessible. Wendover's "sister" city, West Wendover, is located just across the border in Nevada. West Wendover thrives on a gaming economy, with five casino resorts as of this writing. Wendover suffers in lacking this economic stimulus; the city's residents, in fact, voted in favor of annexation by West Wendover (thus becoming part of Nevada). The annexation would require congressional approval, however. The Wendover Airfield, located on the south side of the city, was very busy during World War II. The city was home to about 20,000 residents during this period, and the base was the training ground for the Enola Gay crew (the plane that dropped the atomic bomb on Hiroshima). The airfield was deactivated in the 1960s but is currently used for private and charter flights. Renewed investment in Wendover's schools, lodging facilities, and airport was stimulating the economy on the "Utah side" of the border as of this writing. Perhaps this ride can add to the stimulus.

Start adjacent the ball fields in Wendover, at the intersection of Uinta Avenue (200 South) and 200 East. Head west on Uinta—the pavement surface was poor during my July 2008 field visit. Turn right on 1st Street and head north, then turn right onto Wendover Boulevard (SR 58). To the left of this intersection is the Utah–Nevada border—little more than a white line painted across the road. Two large resort casinos abut the border, announcing the entry into Nevada's gaming environment. Despite the temptation, turn right here and head east. The road quickly leaves Wendover, passing the rocky flanks of Wendover Peak. Turn right onto Frontage Road at mile 1.3. The road parallels I-80 (on the left) and the Union Pacific railroad (on the right). There is some industry out here: Sand across the road and some rough patches are indicators of heavy truck activity. Cross a skewed railroad spur at mile 3.2—exercise caution here. Turn left at the I-80 sign at mile 4.0 and head north. The road crosses over I-80 and then passes a mini-mart. The Silver Island Mountains are in the distance (when viewed from a much greater distance, the mountains appear to be an island floating in a sea…of salt). Enter the Bonneville Salt Flats Recreation Area at mile 5.2. The road curves right at mile 5.7 to head east toward the vast expanses of the parched

Bonneville Salt Flats Ramble

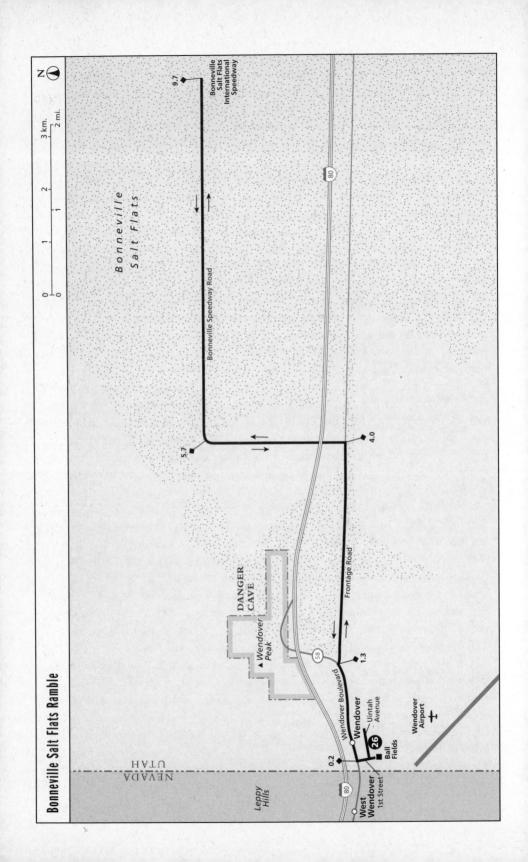

desert. It is easy to underestimate distances in this environment, but the end of the road, where you may see some activity, is 4 miles away. The road ends in a cul-de-sac at mile 9.7. A descriptive sign marks this spot as the Bonneville Salt Flats International Speedway. It is possible to drive (or ride) across the flats during the dry season, but this route prefers to stay on pavement.

After gazing across the desert, and possibly talking with a speedster, turn around for the return trip to Wendover. The road curves left at mile 13.6. Leave the Salt Flats Recreation Area at mile 14.2. The mini-mart is on the left at mile 14.8. After crossing over I-80, turn right onto Frontage Road (TO WENDOVER). Be cautious at the railroad crossing at mile 16.2. Turn left onto Wendover Boulevard (SR 58) at mile 18.0. A healthy rock outcrop on the flanks of Wendover Peak serves as a gateway to the city. After passing several motels and services, turn left onto 1st Street. Turn left onto Uinta Avenue (poor pavement) and head east to 200 East to conclude the ride.

Miles and Directions

0.0 Start at the ball fields, Uinta Avenue (200 South) at 200 East, Wendover. Head west on Uinta Avenue.

0.1 At the stop sign at 1st Street (100 East), turn right.

0.2 At the stop sign at Wendover Boulevard (SR 58), turn right.

0.8 Leave Wendover.

1.3 Turn right onto Frontage Road.

3.2 Railroad crossing (one track, skewed—exercise caution).

4.0 Turn left onto unnamed road (TO I-80).

4.2 I-80 overpass.

4.6 Sinclair (mini-mart) on the right.

5.2 Enter Bonneville Salt Flats Recreation Area.

5.7 Road curves right; now heading east.

9.7 End of pavement at Bonneville Salt Flats International Speedway; turn around here.

13.6 Road curves left; now heading south.

14.2 Leave Bonneville Salt Flats Recreation Area.

14.8 Sinclair (mini-mart) on the left.

15.2 I-80 overpass.

15.4 At the stop sign at Frontage Road (TO WENDOVER), turn right.

16.2 Railroad crossing (one track, skewed—exercise caution).

18.0 At the stop sign at Wendover Boulevard (SR 58), turn left.

18.6 Enter Wendover.

19.3 Turn left onto 1st Street.

19.4 Turn left onto Uinta Avenue (200 South).

19.5 End of ride at 200 East, adjacent the ball fields.

Local Information

Bonneville Salt Flats Recreation Area, Bureau of Land Management: www.blm.gov/ut/st/en/fo/salt_lake/recreation/bonneville_salt_flats.html.

Utah Salt Flats Racing Association Web site: www.saltflats.com.

Bonneville Salt Flats information: www.utah.com/playgrounds/bonneville_salt.htm.

Restaurants

There are additional places in West Wendover.

Subway: 42 East Wendover Boulevard, Wendover; (435) 665-2310.

Taco Poblano: 600 East Wendover Boulevard, Wendover; (435) 665-0458.

Accommodations

Best Western Salt Flat Inn: 895 East Wendover Boulevard, Wendover; (435) 665-7811; www.bestwesternutah.com/hotels/best-western-salt-flat-inn/.

Bonneville Inn: 375 East Wendover Boulevard, Wendover; (435) 665-2540; http://bonnevilleinn.us.

Knights Inn (formerly Heritage Motel): 505 East Wendover Boulevard, Wendover; (435) 665-7744 or (800) 457-5927.

Western Motel: 645 East Wendover Boulevard, Wendover; (435) 665-2230 or (800) 566-2215.

Camping (primitive) is allowed in the Bonneville Salt Flats Recreation Area: (801) 539-4001; www.blm.gov/ut/st/en/fo/salt_lake/recreation/bonneville_salt_flats.html. Camping is prohibited on the salt flats.

Map

Nevada Street and Road Map with Recreation Guide. Includes a street map of West Wendover (and Wendover). Compass Maps, Inc., Modesto, CA, 1993.

27 City Creek Canyon Ramble

The City Creek Canyon Ramble is a 13.6-mile out-and-back ascent and descent of City Creek Canyon in Salt Lake City, starting and finishing at the state capitol. Although the elevation difference between the start–finish and the turnaround point is over 1,500 feet (4,500 to 6,084 feet), the route is not as challenging as the other canyon ascents in the Salt Lake City area. There are some steep pitches along the climb—the average gradient exceeds 9 percent over the upper half of the route—but it is classified as a ramble because the distance is short, the speed is controlled (15 mph limit), the narrow, car-free road is typically shared with runners, walkers, and other cyclists, and the pavement surface on the upper part of the route is of a poor quality (further limiting the pace).

Start: East Capitol Street and 300 North adjacent Utah State Capitol, Salt Lake City.

Length: 13.6 miles (out-and-back).

Terrain: Steady ascent to the turnaround point, followed by a descent. Minimum and maximum elevations: 4,500 to 6,084 feet.

Traffic and hazards: Bonneville Boulevard: 525 vehicles per day in 2006; most of the ride is on roads that are closed to motor vehicles.

Getting there: Head north on State Street from downtown Salt Lake City, to the Utah State Capitol. Turn right onto 300 North; the road bends left, becoming East Capitol Street. Park on the canyon side of the street. By bicycle, head north on Main Street to 200 North; turn right onto 200 North. After crossing State Street, the road bends left, becoming East Capitol Street. Start the ride at 300 North after tackling the climb from 200 North (on a rough road). Utah Transit Authority route 500 travels between downtown Salt Lake City and the Utah State Capitol every fifteen minutes, from 5:30 a.m. until 6:30 p.m., on weekdays (only).

The Ride

City Creek originates in the mountains northeast of downtown Salt Lake City. The waters flow down a ravine popularly known as City Creek Canyon. After exiting the canyon, the creek travels in an underground conduit to the Jordan River, on the west side of Salt Lake City. City Creek, just 14.5 miles long, was Salt Lake City's chief water supply until 1882. Today, the creek continues to provide drinking water to the Avenues district northeast of the downtown and some other northern parts of the city. The creek flows year-round, fed by snowmelt from the mountains and by natural springs. The creek really flowed in 1983, when heavy precipitation led to flooding. A single, gated road snakes up City Creek Canyon. The gate controls access to the road, such that no motor vehicles are allowed up during the "off-season" (October 1 until Memorial Day). During the "season" (Memorial Day through September 30), bicycles are allowed up only on odd-numbered days, and motor vehicles are allowed on the even days. The prospect of a road with no cars makes the canyon very popular with recreationalists. The narrow road is shared by cyclists, runners, and walkers, so the speed is restricted to 15 mph. Picnicking spots (and restrooms) are at frequent intervals along the road, so there are numerous opportunities for rest stops.

City Creek Canyon is easily accessible by bicycle, and somewhat less so by motor vehicle. The canyon has two "mouths." The upper mouth is located at a hairpin turn in Bonneville Boulevard, a one-way road (for motor vehicles) that travels east to west along an upper bench of the Avenues district. One lane of Bonneville Boulevard is set aside for cyclists and pedestrians for travel in *both* directions, making the upper mouth accessible from either the east (Avenues district) or the west (state capitol area). The lower mouth of the canyon is accessed through Memory Grove, a park dedicated to Utah veterans. A road (no motor vehicles) paralleling City Creek heads up the lower canyon for about 1 mile, to intersect with Bonneville Boulevard's hairpin turn.

The City Creek Canyon Ramble starts adjacent the Utah State Capitol, accessing the canyon from Bonneville Boulevard. There is plenty of on-street parking on the east side of the Capitol—on East Capitol Street, north of 300 North. This is the staging area for the ride. The Utah State Capitol, on the National Register of Historic Places (NRHP), was completed in 1916. The Capitol building is the centerpiece of a complex of structures and monuments that sprawl over forty acres. East Capitol Street was part of the course used in Stage 5 of the 2006 Tour of Utah. The Tour returned to the Capitol in 2009 for the opening time trial; East Capitol Street and Bonneville Boulevard were on the course.

To the southeast of City Creek Canyon is the Avenues district, an eclectic Salt Lake City neighborhood. The entire district, stretching from State Street in the west to Virginia Street in the east, and from First Avenue on the south to Ninth Avenue to the north, is a National Historic District. Most of the Victorian-era homes were built between 1880 and 1920. The Avenues' grid system violates the standard ten-acre block grid pattern of the rest of Salt Lake City. As such, the Avenues' streets are narrower, and the blocks are smaller than elsewhere in the city. The deviance is somewhat emblematic of the traditionally diverse population of the district.

Start the ride adjacent the Utah State Capitol, at East Capitol Street and 300 North in Salt Lake City. To the right is the deep cut of lower City Creek Canyon; Memory Grove is below. A 1996 tornado (extremely rare in Utah) traveled through downtown Salt Lake City, over Capitol Hill, across Memory Grove, and across the northwest corner of the Avenues, knocking down trees and destroying power lines. The grounds of the State Capitol were heavily wooded before the tornado struck. Trees in Memory Grove were also uprooted. Head north on East Capitol Street, immediately starting to climb. Just as you start to feel the burn, turn right onto Bonneville Boulevard. A DO NOT ENTER sign applies to motor vehicles only. The right lane of this road is for the exclusive use of bicycles and pedestrians. Bonneville Boulevard winds along a canyon terrace. This segment of the route is commonly referred to as "Gravity Hill," since it has the illusion of being flat or even downhill, when it actually is a climb. At the 180-degree bend in Bonneville Boulevard (mile 1.2), turn left onto City Creek Canyon Road. After a short segment, there is a gate (no fee). As explained earlier, the canyon is accessible to bicycles year-round, except between Memorial Day and September 30, when it is open to bicycles on odd-numbered days only. Presumably, you have chosen the correct day for this ride!

Once inside the gate, the narrow, meandering road starts a gradual climb. Although there are a few open sections, most of the route passes through a dense canopy of trees. Numerous bird species have been spotted fluttering around these trees, including bunting, chickadee, crow, gnatcatcher, grosbeak, hummingbird, robin, sparrow, and swallow. A variety of four-legged animals have been observed in the canyon as well, including badgers, cougars, deer, elk, and moose. There are numerous designated picnicking spots along the creek side of the road, many of which also have lavatories. A water treatment plant is on the right at mile 4.5. From here, the road narrows and gets steeper and rougher. One of the steeper segments comes just before the entrance to Rotary Park, at mile 6.0. This park was established in 1921 through support from the local Rotary Club. Overuse of the canyon, resulting in the pollution of City Creek, led to its closure in 1952. Following the construction of the water treatment plant, and a "cleansing" period, the canyon was reopened in 1967. The Rotary Club renewed its support of Rotary Park in 1991. The road climbs through the park, sometimes steeply, crossing Rotary Bridge at mile 6.7. After another steep segment, the

Enjoying a car-free road in the dense vegetation of City Creek Canyon.
ANN COTTRELL

road comes to an end (mile 6.8). There are lavatories and picnicking facilities here, including a covered area. Turn around here to begin the descent.

The descent of City Creek Canyon begins steeply. Watch your speed here. Not only is the speed limit 15 mph, but also the road is poor, making it worthwhile to slow down enough to react to potholes and rocks. Exit Rotary Park at mile 7.6. The narrow road continues to wind and descend to mile 9.1; here, the road widens and becomes smoother as you pass the water treatment facility. Continue to check your speed. A maintenance worker in a pickup truck once yelled at me for descending too rapidly through here. It is not possible to see the Salt Lake Valley on the descent, but there are some nice views of the canyon ahead. Signs warn of the entrance gate as you get closer to the mouth of the canyon. Slow down here and move left, to exit via the side gate. It may be necessary to walk through. Continue along the short segment to Bonneville Boulevard at mile 12.4. Turn right here. You have the option of riding on the left or the right. The right lane is shared with motor vehicles, while the left lane is for bicycles and pedestrians. I felt most comfortable in the right lane, because of the downhill speed. Turn left onto East Capitol Street at mile 13.3. The State Capitol is on the right. The ride ends at 300 North, on the south side of the Capitol. While watching for approaching motor vehicles, turn left (or hang a U-turn) to return to the parking area on the opposite side of the street.

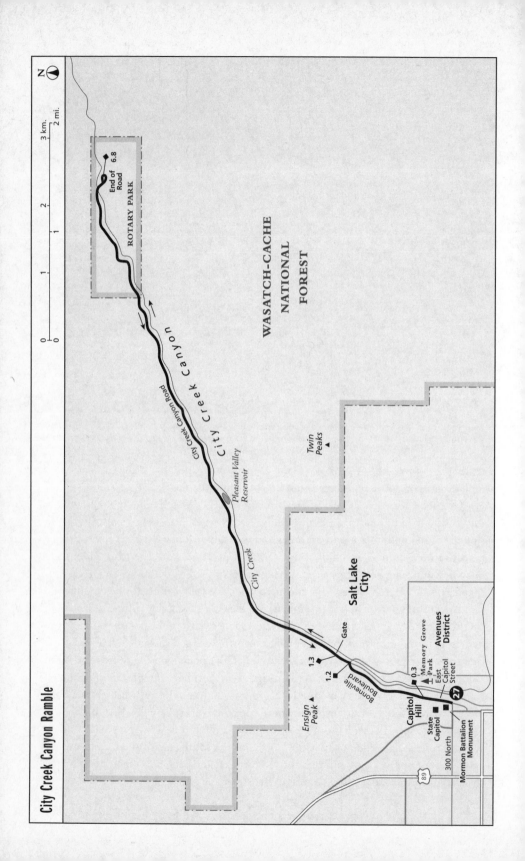

City Creek Canyon Ramble

Miles and Directions

0.0 Start adjacent the Utah State Capitol, at East Capitol Street and 300 North in Salt Lake City. Head north (uphill) on East Capitol Street.

0.3 Turn right onto Bonneville Boulevard—use right lane (bicycles and pedestrians only).

1.2 Turn left onto City Creek Canyon Road (at 180-degree bend in Bonneville Boulevard).

1.3 Gate: open to cyclists daily October 1 through Memorial Day; open to cyclists on odd-numbered days only Memorial Day through September 30. No fee. Begin City Creek Canyon climb.

4.5 Water treatment facility on the right; road narrows and steepens. Watch for potholes.

6.0 Enter Rotary Park.

6.7 Cross Rotary Bridge (over City Creek).

6.8 End of pavement at upper end of Rotary Park; turn around here (begin descent).

6.9 Cross Rotary Bridge.

7.6 Leave Rotary Park; watch for steep sections, potholes, and blind corners. Speed limit: 15 mph.

9.1 Water treatment facility on the left.

12.3 Gate; slow down and move left to pass through narrow side gate.

12.4 At the stop sign at Bonneville Boulevard, turn right. Ride in right or left lane.

13.3 At the stop sign at East Capitol Street, turn left.

13.6 End of ride at 300 North; carefully bear left and return to on-street parking area.

Local Information

City of Salt Lake City official Web site: www.ci.slc.ut.us.

Maps and description of City Creek Canyon: www.saltlakecycling.com.

State of Utah, Utah State Capitol information: www.utahstatecapitol.utah.gov.

Restaurants

Café Trang—Downtown: 307 West 200 South, Salt Lake City; (801) 539-1638; www.cafetrangrestaurant.com.

Lamb's Grill Café: 169 South Main Street, Salt Lake City; (801) 364-7166; http://lambsgrill.com.

Market Street Grill—Downtown: 48 West Market Street, Salt Lake City; (801) 322-4668; www.ginc.com/msg/index.html.

Market Street Oyster Bar—Downtown: 54 West Market Street, Salt Lake City; (801) 531-6044; www.ginc.com/oyster/index.html.

Metropolitan: 173 West Broadway (300 South), Salt Lake City; (801) 364-3472; www.themetropolitan.com.

New Yorker: 60 West Market Street (340 South), Salt Lake City; (801) 363-0166; www.gastronomyinc.com/ny/index.html.

Red Rock Brewing Company L.C.: 254 South 200 West, Salt Lake City; (801) 521-7446; www.redrockbrewing.com.

Accommodations

The Grand America Hotel: 555 South Main Street, Salt Lake City; (800) 621-4505; www.grandamerica.com.

Hilton Salt Lake City Center: 255 South West Temple, Salt Lake City; (801) 328-2000; www1.hilton.com/en_US/hi/hotel/SLCCCHH-Hilton-Salt-Lake-City-Center-Utah/index.do.

Hotel Monaco: 15 West 200 South, Salt Lake City; (801) 595-0000 or (800) 805-1801; www.monaco-saltlakecity.com.

Little America Hotel: 500 South Main Street, Salt Lake City; (801) 596-5700 or (800) 281-7899; www.littleamerica.com/slc.

Marriott Salt Lake City Downtown: 75 South West Temple, Salt Lake City; (801) 531-0800; www.marriott.com/SLCUT.

Peery Hotel: 110 West Broadway, Salt Lake City; (801) 521-4300 or (800) 331-0073; www.peeryhotel.com.

Bicycle Shops

Salt Lake City Bicycle Company: 177 East 200 South, Salt Lake City; (801) 746-8366; www.slcbike.com.

Wasatch Touring: 702 East 100 South, Salt Lake City; (801) 359-9361; www.wasatch touring.com.

Wild Rose Mountain Sport: 702 Third Avenue, Salt Lake City; (801) 533-8671; www.wild rosesports.com.

Maps

Salt Lake City Green Bikeways Map, Salt Lake City Department of Transportation, 2006.

Rand McNally: Salt Lake City Street Guide: including Logan, Ogden, and Provo: Pages 1754, 1755, 1858 D2 on page 1858. Annotated map of City Creek Canyon: www.bikely.com/maps/bike-path/City-Creek-Canyon.

28 Emigration Trail Classic

The Emigration Trail Classic is a history-laden, 80.6-mile out-and-back route, including a 12-mile loop at the turnaround end. The ride starts in eastern Salt Lake City and incorporates all or a portion of Emigration Canyon, East Canyon, Main Canyon, the Emigration (Mormon Pioneer Memorial) Trail, the California Trail, and the Pony Express Trail. The ride visits three counties: Salt Lake, Summit, and Morgan. There are three summits: Little Mountain, Big Mountain, and Hogback. Three canyons, three trails, three counties, three summits. The elevation ranges from 4,920 feet at This Is the Place State Park to 7,420 feet at Big Mountain (Salt Lake–Morgan County line).

Start: This Is the Place State Park, 2601 East Sunnyside Avenue, Salt Lake City.
Length: 80.6 miles (out-and-back, including a 12-mile loop at the turnaround).
Terrain: Three long climbs and descents outbound, followed by three long climbs and descents inbound. Minimum and maximum

elevations: 4,920 to 7,420 feet.
Traffic and hazards: SR 65: 890 vehicles per day between Emigration Canyon Road and the Salt Lake–Morgan County line in 2005; 1,105 vehicles per day in Henefer at the I-84 interchange.

Getting there: From Salt Lake City, head east on 800 South, which becomes Sunnyside Avenue east of 1300 East. Continue past Foothill Boulevard to This Is the Place State Park (across the street from Hogle Zoo). Utah Transit Authority (UTA) route 228 makes trips to Hogle Zoo during summer months. UTA routes 21, 313, 354, and 810 all stop near the intersection of Sunnyside Avenue and Foothill Boulevard, which is about 0.7 mile from This Is the Place State Park.

The Ride

Emigration Canyon is legendary in the annals of Utah history; it was through this canyon that the Mormon pioneers first caught sight of the Salt Lake Valley in 1847, declaring in unison "This is the place!" after their long journey from Nauvoo, Illinois. Actually, Brigham Young, the leader of the caravan, made the declaration, stating, "This is the right place. Drive on." Also, the caravan could see the Salt Lake Valley from Big Mountain, about 15 miles northeast of the mouth of Emigration Canyon. This Is the Place State Park was dedicated on July 24, 1947, one hundred years after the pioneers first caught sight of the Salt Lake Valley. The park is located just west of the mouth of Emigration Canyon. July 24, Pioneer Day, is a state holiday in Utah. The park also pays homage to other explorers who journeyed down the same canyon before and after the Mormons' historic trek, including Catholic missionaries from Spain, fur traders and trappers, and California-bound immigrants.

Emigration Canyon is shared by the Mormon Pioneer, California, and Pony Express National Historic Trails. Geologically, the canyon is one of several that drain the Wasatch Mountains into the delta of the former, massive Lake Bonneville. Jurassic Nugget sandstone, colored pink and tan, is quite common in the canyon. The sandstone has been harvested as an attractive and sturdy material for buildings in the Salt Lake City area. Jurassic limestone, used in the manufacture of cement, is found farther up the canyon (particularly in the Henefer area, near the turnaround point for the Emigration Trail Classic).

The California National Historic Trail extends from Missouri to California. Some 250,000 persons traveled along this trail during the 1840s and 1850s, mostly forty-niners (gold seekers) and farmers in search of rich lands. It was the greatest mass migration in U.S. history. The trail passed through Emigration Canyon on its way west. The Pony Express also barreled down this canyon during its short life from 1860 to 1861. Stations were spaced at 10-mile intervals. A rider would change to a fresh horse at each station; the intervals were chosen to allow the horses to travel at full gallop before fatiguing. Operations ceased just two days after the Transcontinental Telegraph reached Salt Lake City, thereby supplanting the need to deliver hand-held messages. The route was also used by the Donner-Reed Party, which preceded the Mormon Pioneer trek by about one year, in 1846. The Donner-Reed group was headed for California from Missouri, only to become snowbound in the Sierra Nevada during the 1846–47 winter. Their ill-fated trek, along with the treks of other California-bound groups, is memorialized in the California National Historic Trail.

Start at This Is the Place State Park, located at 2601 East Sunnyside Avenue in Salt Lake City. The park extends along Sunnyside Avenue for some distance; exit the park at the far eastern end. Turn left onto Sunnyside Avenue, being ever watchful of motor vehicles, and head east. Enter Emigration Canyon at mile 0.1. The shoulder was narrow (and under construction) as of this writing. The road was being widened to include bike lanes for several miles up the canyon. The Emigration Canyon climb is gradual, unlike the climbs of the other Wasatch Mountain canyons. Partly for this reason, the canyon is a popular route for local cyclists. Ruth's Diner is on the right just 2 miles up the canyon. Watch for motor vehicles turning in and out of the parking lot. The restaurant may make a pleasant stop at the end of the ride. Continue climbing as the shoulder narrows at mile 3.7. The Sun and Moon Café is on the left at mile 5.2. At mile 6.1, the road makes a 180-degree bend to the right. Beyond this point, the climb gets noticeably steeper. After the bend, you are traveling in a southerly direction, enabling a wonderful view of the canyon and the Salt Lake Valley. The road bends 180 degrees to the left at mile 7.3. The crest of the climb (Little Mountain) comes at mile 7.9. The elevation is 6,227 feet here; there is a Mormon pioneer monument at the summit.

Begin the descent to Little Dell Reservoir. The descent is not steep, but there is a series of sharp curves starting at mile 8.5. Stop and turn left onto SR 65 at mile 9.4. Little Dell Reservoir is on the right; restrooms are available at mile 9.9. There is a gate at mile 10.1—SR 65 is closed during the winter (November through March). Begin to climb gradually at mile 10.7. There is a trailhead, with restrooms, on the right at mile 11.6. The climb gets steeper here. Affleck Park is on the left at mile 12.3. The climbing gets "serious" at mile 13.3, as the highway enters a series of switchbacks. The forestation is also notable, as the highway ascends into an alpine environment. The highway crests at mile 15.5; enter Morgan County here. The elevation is 7,420 feet. There are a trailhead and restrooms on the right. Begin the descent toward East Canyon.

The descent features a couple of sharp left-hand curves—be particularly cautious on the second one, as your speed will probably be high here. East Canyon Resort appears on the left at mile 21.8. This is an off-the-beaten-path facility located adjacent East Canyon Reservoir. There are a store and restrooms, as well as a restaurant. The highway continues lakeside from here, although the reservoir level was well below the road at the time of my field research. The lakeside elevation is 5,760 feet. East Canyon State Park, located on the opposite side of the reservoir from SR 65, provides boating access. The Big Rock Campground is on the left (restrooms) at mile 22.6. After a pleasant, winding stretch, SR 65 junctions with SR 66 at the north end of the reservoir. Stay to the right to remain on SR 65. The highway begins to climb from here toward Hogback Summit. The climb gets noticeably steeper just before the summit, which comes at mile 28.9 (elevation 6,240 feet). The highway enters Summit County. From here, the highway descends through Main Canyon, through some lovely pastoral settings. The town of Henefer lies just beyond the mouth of the canyon.

Pass Henefer Road on the left at mile 34.0. This is the beginning of a counterclockwise loop; you will return to this point after covering 11.8 miles. Enter Henefer (elevation 5,333 feet) at mile 34.1. Henefer, first settled in 1859, had a population of 680 in 2008. The town is set in the picturesque and cozy Henefer Valley. The I-84 freeway runs just to the east, giving the town easy access to the more heavily urbanized areas to the west. Turn right onto Henefer's Main Street at mile 34.6 and head southeast. The road curves left at mile 35.1, then crosses over the Weber River and I-84. Turn left onto East Henefer Road at mile 35.6. This narrow road curls its way toward Lost Creek Canyon, climbing and descending before cresting at mile 39.3. The road enters Morgan County here, while starting a swift downhill. The road curves sharply to the right at mile 39.7—watch your speed here. At mile 40.0, prepare to yield and turn left onto 1900 North (no street sign). You are now in the unincorporated community of Croydon. The community was settled in 1862 as Lost Creek. The name was eventually changed to Croydon because most of the settlers were from Croydon, England (a borough of London). The road bends left at mile 40.7. There is some pavement surface damage around mile 41.5, adjacent the large cement plant. The road curves sharply to the left at mile 41.8, just beyond a Weber River crossing.

Things get busy here—there is a railroad underpass at mile 41.9, followed by an I-84 underpass at mile 42.0. Amidst all of the commotion, remember to look right (and up) to catch a glimpse of Devil's Slide, an interesting geological formation. The slide is actually two parallel Jurassic limestone reefs set 20 feet apart. The reefs protrude up to 40 feet above the slopes of the cliff, thereby resembling a chute. The road curves left here; stay right to prepare for I-84 freeway entry. Stay to the right of the shoulder to avoid the rumble strip. Take the very next exit (Henefer); turn right onto Henefer Road at the end of the ramp. This road curves around the west side of Henefer Valley, along a pleasant, undulating, and quiet route. Turn right onto SR 65 at mile 45.8 to begin the return route.

Now that you are heading back toward the Salt Lake Valley, you are retracing history along the same route used by Mormon pioneers, California-bound travelers, and the Pony Express. You may wish to envision yourself as a member of one of these groups (perhaps a Pony Express rider, charging through the canyons at full gallop?). The highway begins to climb gradually toward Hogback Summit; the gradient increases at mile 48.6. Reach Hogback Summit at mile 50.9 and begin a sharp descent toward East Canyon Reservoir. The Dixie Hollow Pony Express Station was located along this descent; you may be able to catch the marker along the road. Bear left at the junction at mile 53.3; that is, head toward the "left" side of the reservoir. East Canyon Reservoir will be on your right. The highway winds lakeside for several miles. Taylor Hollow Use Area is on the right at mile 56.2 (restrooms); Big Rock Campground is on the right at mile 57.6 (restrooms). East Canyon Resort is on the right at mile 58.0. The highway begins to climb at mile 59.2; the Bauchmanns Pony Express Station was located near here (look for a marker). There is a gate (closed in winter) at mile 59.6. The highway ascends Big Mountain. During the second stage of the 2008 Tour of Utah, Blake Caldwell from the United States and Daniel Lill from South Africa attacked the leading group on the Big Mountain climb, riding away to the stage victory—and overall race lead—for Caldwell. The summit comes at mile 64.8 (7,420 feet). The descent features a series of switchbacks through steep terrain, so exercise caution when heading down. Affleck Park is on the right at mile 68.3; restrooms are on the left at mile 69.0. The Ephraim Hanks Pony Express Station is nearby; look for a marker. Little Dell Reservoir is on the left at mile 70.5 (restrooms); the highway begins to climb gradually here. Turn right at mile 71.2 (Emigration Canyon Road) and continue the climb.

The final phase of the ride consists of a short climb to Little Mountain summit (mile 72.7), followed by the descent of Emigration Canyon. There are sharp, 180-degree turns at miles 73.3 and 74.5. Exercise caution through these turns. It is a gradual, fun descent through Emigration Canyon. Ruth's Diner is on the left at mile 78.6. Continue the descent, exiting the canyon at mile 80.5. An entrance to This Is the Place State Park is on the right at mile 80.6. Turn right here to end the ride. Be sure to spend some time checking out the artifacts and history at the park. Hogle Zoo is directly across the street.

Miles and Directions

0.0 Start at This is the Place State Park at 2601 East Sunnyside Avenue; exit the park at the east end of the park; turn left and head east on Sunnyside Avenue (watch for traffic).

0.1 Enter Emigration Canyon and begin climbing.

0.6 Begin bike lane (the first 0.5 mile was under construction as of this writing).

2.0 Ruth's Diner on the right.

3.7 Road shoulder narrows.

5.2 Sun and Moon Café on the left.

6.1 180-degree curve to the right; climb gets steeper.

7.3 Road curves to the left 180 degrees.

7.9 Crest of climb (Little Mountain summit); monument on the right—begin descent.

8.5 Sharp curve to the right.

8.8 Sharp curve to the left.

9.2 Sharp curve to the right.

9.4 At the stop sign, turn left onto SR 65 north.

9.9 Little Dell Reservoir on the right (restrooms).

10.1 Gate (closed in the winter).

10.7 Begin gradual climb.

11.6 Trailhead and restrooms on the right; climb gets steeper.

12.3 Affleck Park on the left.

13.3 Begin series of switchbacks (uphill).

15.5 Big Mountain summit: enter Morgan County—trailhead and restrooms on the right; begin descent.

15.8 180-degree curve to the left.

17.7 180-degree curve to the left.

20.9 Road levels.

21.8 East Canyon Resort, restaurant, store, and restrooms on the left.

22.6 Big Rock Campground (restrooms) and East Canyon Reservoir on the left.

26.5 SR 66 junction; stay right to remain on SR 65—begin climb.

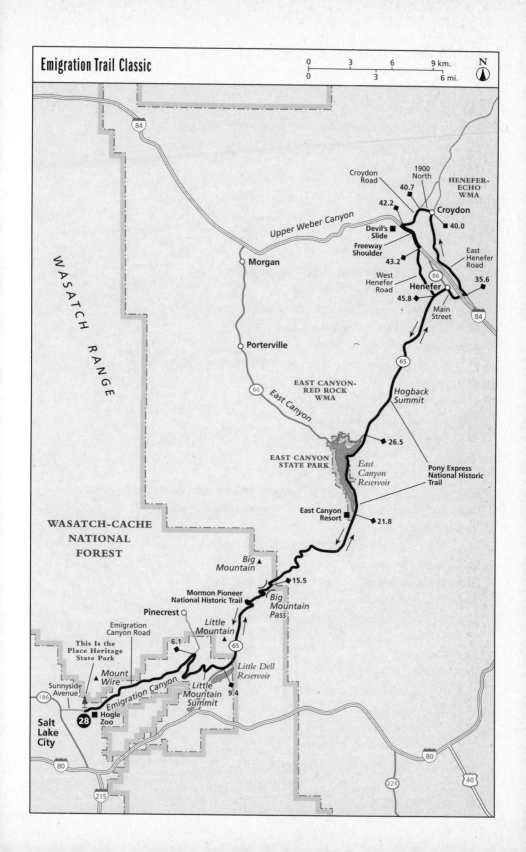

Emigration Trail Classic

0 3 6 9 km.
0   3   6 mi.

N

WASATCH RANGE

WASATCH-CACHE
NATIONAL
FOREST

84

Upper Weber Canyon

Croydon
Road

1900
North

40.7

42.2

Croydon

40.0

HENEFER-
ECHO
WMA

Devil's
Slide

Morgan

Freeway
Shoulder

43.2

West
Henefer
Road

86

East
Henefer
Road

35.6

Henefer

45.8

Main
Street

84

Porterville

66

East Canyon

EAST CANYON-
RED ROCK
WMA

65

Hogback
Summit

26.5

EAST CANYON
STATE PARK

East
Canyon
Reservoir

Pony Express
National Historic
Trail

East Canyon
Resort

21.8

Big
Mountain

15.5

Mormon Pioneer
National Historic Trail

Big
Mountain
Pass

Pinecrest

Little
Mountain

65

Emigration
Canyon Road

6.1

Little Dell
Reservoir

This Is the
Place Heritage
State Park

Mount
Wire

Little
Mountain
Summit

9.4

Sunnyside
Avenue

186

Emigration Canyon

Salt
Lake
City

28

Hogle
Zoo

80

80

224

40

215

28.9 Hogback Summit; enter Summit County and begin descent.

31.2 Grade eases; still traveling downhill.

34.0 Highway levels.

34.1 Enter Henefer.

34.6 At the stop sign, turn right onto Main Street (still on SR 65).

35.1 Road curves left.

35.3 I-84 overpass.

35.6 Turn left onto East Henefer Road.

36.8 Begin gradual climb.

37.3 Begin descent.

37.7 Road levels.

38.2 Begin gradual climb.

39.3 Crest of climb; enter Morgan County—begin downhill.

39.7 Road curves right—watch your speed.

40.0 At the yield sign, turn left onto 1900 North (no street sign).

40.7 Road curves left; now on Croydon Road.

41.5 Some road damage.

41.8 Road curves left sharply, just after Weber River crossing.

41.9 Railroad underpass.

42.0 I-84 underpass; road curves left.

42.1 Cattle guard; stay right.

42.2 Enter I-84 freeway—stay on shoulder (move right to avoid rumble strips).

43.0 Enter Summit County.

43.2 Exit I-84 freeway (Henefer exit, SR 86 East).

43.5 Cattle guard. At the stop sign 0.05 mile farther at Henefer Road, turn right.

45.8 At the stop sign at SR 65, turn right and begin gradual upgrade.

48.6 Gradient increases.

50.9 Hogback Summit; enter Morgan County—begin descent.

51.4 Descent gets steeper.

53.3 Junction with SR 66; bear left to stay on SR 65.

56.2 Taylor Hollow Use Area on the right (restrooms).

57.6 Big Rock Campground on the right (restrooms).

58.0 East Canyon Resort on the right.

59.2 Begin climb.

59.6 Gate (closed in winter).

64.8 Big Mountain summit; enter Salt Lake County (restrooms on left)—begin descent.

65.1 Begin series of switchbacks—watch speed.

68.3 Affleck Park on the right.

69.0 Restrooms on the left.

70.5 Foot of climb (adjacent Little Dell Reservoir—restrooms).

71.2   Turn right onto Emigration Canyon Road—continue climb.

72.7   Little Mountain summit; begin descent.

73.3   180-degree curve to the right—watch speed.

74.5   180-degree curve to the left—exercise caution.

75.4   Sun and Moon Café on the right.

78.6   Ruth's Diner on the left.

80.5   Exit Emigration Canyon.

80.6   End of ride; turn right, enter This Is the Place State Park.

Local Information

Salt Lake City official Web site: www.ci.slc .ut.us.

Information on Emigration Canyon, including planning, history, and other links: www .emigrationcanyon.org.

California National Historic Trail, National Park Service: www.nps.gov/cali.

Mormon Pioneer Historic Trail, National Park Service: www.nps.gov/mopi.

Pony Express National Historic Trail, National Park Service: www.nps.gov/poex.

This Is the Place Heritage Park Web site: www.thisistheplace.org.

Bicycling along the Emigration Canyon Trail: www.utah.com/bike/trails/emigration.htm.

Restaurants

Cedars of Lebanon: 152 East 200 South, Salt Lake City; (801) 364-4096; www.cedarsof lebanonrestaurant.com. Dinner only.

Desert Edge Brewery at the Pub: 273 Trolley Square (602 South 500 East), Salt Lake City; (801) 521-8917.

Fresco Italian Café: 1513 South 1500 East Salt Lake City; (801) 486-1300; www.fresco italiancafe.com. Dinner only.

Ichiban Sushi and Japanese Cuisine: 336 South 400 East, Salt Lake City; (801) 532-7522. Set in a former Lutheran church.

The Lion House Pantry Restaurant: 63 East South Temple, Salt Lake City; (801) 539-3257; www.diningattemplesquare.com/pantry.html.

Market Street Broiler—University: 260 South 1300 East, Salt Lake City; (801) 583-8808; www.ginc.com/broiler/index.html.

Oasis Café: 151 South 500 East, Salt Lake City; (801) 322-0404; www.oasiscafeslc.com.

Ruth's Diner: 2100 Emigration Canyon, Salt Lake City; (801) 582-5807; www.ruthsdiner.com.

The Sun and Moon Café: 5195 Emigration Canyon, Salt Lake City; (801) 583-8331; www. thesunandmooncafe.com.

Accommodations

Anton Boxrud Bed and Breakfast: 57 South 600 East, Salt Lake City; (800) 524-5511; www.antonboxrud.com/location.html.

The Armstrong Mansion Historic Bed and Breakfast: 667 East 100 South, Salt Lake City; (801) 531-1333 or (800) 708-1333; www.armstrongmansion.com.

The Avenues Hostel: 107 F Street (North Temple at 500 East), Salt Lake City; (801) 539-8888 or (801) 359-3855; www.saltlake hostel.com.

Inn on the Hill (Inn on Capitol Hill): 225 North State Street, Salt Lake City; (801) 328-1466; www.inn-on-the-hill.com.

International Ute Hostel: 21 East Kelsey Avenue (1160 South), Salt Lake City; (801) 595-1645; www.internationalutehostel.com.

Marriott Salt Lake City Center: 220 South State Street, Salt Lake City; (801) 967-8700 or (866) 967-8700; www.marriott.com/SLCCC.

Marriott University Park: 480 Wakara Way, Salt Lake City; (801) 581-1000; www.marriott .com/SLCUP.

Bicycle Shops

Bicycle Center: 2200 South 700 East, Salt Lake City; (801) 484-5275; www.bicyclecenter.com.

The Bike Guy: 1555 South 900 East, Salt Lake City; (801) 860-1528; www.thebikeguyslc.com.

Bingham Cyclery: 336 West Broadway (300 South), Salt Lake City; (801) 583-1940; www.binghamcyclery.com.

Contender Bicycles: 875 East 900 South, Salt Lake City; (801) 364-0344; www.contenderbicycles.com.

Cyclesmith: 250 South 1300 East, Salt Lake City; (801) 582-9870; www.cyclesmithslc.com.

Fishers Cyclery: 2175 South 900 East, Salt Lake City; (801) 466-3971; www.fisherscyclery.com.

Guthrie Bicycle: 803 East 2100 South, Salt Lake City; (801) 484-0404; www.guthriebike.com.

Maps

DeLorme: Utah Atlas & Gazetteer: Pages 17–18 D7 on page 17.

Salt Lake City Green Bikeways Map, Salt Lake City Department of Transportation, 2006.

Rand McNally: Salt Lake City Street Guide: including Logan, Ogden, and Provo: Pages 120, 121, 131, 132, 141–143, and 153; FG60 on page 153.

Benchmark: Utah Road & Recreation Atlas: Page 43 G9.

29 Ibapah Valley Ramble

The Ibapah Valley Ramble is a 24.2-mile out-and-back ride on Ibapah Road in extreme southwestern Tooele County. The route is from Ibapah, at the Deep Creek Pony Express Station, to Goshute (main community on the Goshute reservation) and back. The lightly traveled road climbs gradually from Ibapah to Goshute.

Start: Deep Creek Pony Express Station, Ibapah (on Ibapah Road).
Length: 24.2 miles (out-and-back).
Terrain: Gradual ascent, with a few rollers, to the turnaround point, followed by a descent.

Minimum and maximum elevations: 5,288 to 6,160 feet.
Traffic and hazards: Very low volumes on Ibapah Road.

Getting there: From West Wendover, Nevada, head south on US 93A. Turn left at Ibapah Road and continue heading south to the Ibapah Valley (return to Utah from Nevada). The Deep Creek Pony Express Station is 1.5 miles south of the Ibapah Trading Post. Ibapah is 59 miles south of Wendover and West Wendover.

The Ride

The Goshute tribe, once 20,000 strong, occupied a chunk of the Great Basin Desert extending from the Great Salt Lake in Utah to the Steptoe Range in Nevada. It is likely that the Shoshoneans, the ancestors of the Goshutes, entered the Great Basin from Death Valley in California about 1,000 years ago. The tribe managed to

Combined Pony Express, Lincoln Highway, Goshute, and pioneer settlers marker in Ibapah.
ANN COTTRELL

thrive in the harsh, arid Great Basin. Without any formal agricultural techniques, the Goshutes survived by eating wild seeds and roots, insects, reptiles, birds, rodents, and larger game. With the arrival of Mormon missionaries in 1859, the Goshutes learned farming methods. The Goshute population has dwindled over the years; their current estimated population is only 500. The Goshutes occupy several small reservations in Utah and Nevada, including areas in Ibapah Valley and Skull Valley. To boost their economic prospects, the Goshutes agreed to store 40,000 metric tons of spent nuclear fuel on their property in Skull Valley. The Nuclear Regulatory Commission had approved the Goshute application, but political leaders in Utah—as well as some Goshutes—were fighting the facility's placement. Despite the outrage, the Skull Valley reservation is near a nerve gas storage facility, as well as a magnesium plant having some severe environmental issues.

Ibapah Valley (also referred to as Deep Creek Valley) is located in the extreme southwestern corner of Tooele County. The valley is located just east of the Nevada border. It is, fortunately, cut off from Skull Valley's environmental concerns by the tall Deep Creek Mountains (the elevation of Ibapah Peak is 12,087 feet). The mountains leave the valley fairly isolated. In fact, the valley can be accessed by paved roads only from Nevada. The Dugway Proving Grounds, located east of the Deep Creek Range, consume a large area of the Great Salt Lake Desert through which there is no public access. To get to Ibapah Valley from Utah, therefore, the traveler is limited to unpaved roads out of Juab County, to the southeast. The valley's isolation makes it one of the most remote (if not *the* most) in Utah. Ibapah and Goshute are the primary settlements, the latter of which is the central community on the Goshute reservation.

Despite Ibapah's remoteness, it was once a key stop along several historic routes. For example, Ibapah was established as the Deep Creek Pony Express station in conjunction with the arrival of Mormon missionaries in 1859. Although the Pony Express was discontinued in 1861, Ibapah remained. Later, Ibapah was along the Overland Stage route and, still later, the Lincoln Highway (the United States' first cross-country highway). The Ibapah Valley Ramble captures some of the transportation and Native American history of this region, in traveling from Ibapah to Goshute and back.

Start at the Deep Creek Pony Express Station marker located adjacent Ibapah Road. A smaller marker on the opposite side of the road signifies the passing of the Lincoln Highway through this area. Turn right and head south on Ibapah Road. The mighty Deep Creek Range is on the left, and the wide-open expanses of Ibapah Valley, and then Nevada, are on the right. The Pony Express, Lincoln Highway, and Overland Stage routes passed around the tip of the Deep Creek Range to the north of here. To the south, the Deep Creeks gradually get higher, reaching from 7,708 feet just north of Ibapah to 12,087 feet just south of Goshute. Ibapah Road curves left at mile 0.1. The historical routes all turned right here and headed west into Nevada. Continue heading south. The undulating road climbs gradually from Ibapah (5,288 feet) to Goshute (6,160 feet). The land surrounding the road seems desolate to the untrained eye, with little more than dense, low desert scrub. An airstrip is on the right at mile 3.0. A short climb and a cattle guard at mile 11.6 announce the entry into Goshute, a small community on the Goshute reservation. A few houses and buildings line the road. Turn around at the intersection with Tempi Poi Lane (on the right) and Poho Poi Lane (on the left), adjacent a small, federally funded housing complex and school.

The downward slope of the valley is evident as you look ahead to the north. Exit Goshute at mile 12.6 (cattle guard). The gradual descent is frequently interrupted by mini-rollers (short climbs). The Deep Creek Range is to the right. The airstrip, along with a few buildings, are on the left at mile 20.7. The road curves right at mile 24.0 as you rejoin the Pony Express, Overland Stage, and Lincoln Highway routes. The ride concludes at the Deep Creek Pony Express Station marker. The station was actually located about 1 mile west of the marker. The Overland Stage continued to operate until the transcontinental railroad was completed in 1869. After a period of hibernation, transcontinental travel returned to Ibapah with the completion of the Lincoln Highway in 1912. The highway was eventually supplanted by preferred alignments, such as Route 66, and, later, the Interstate System.

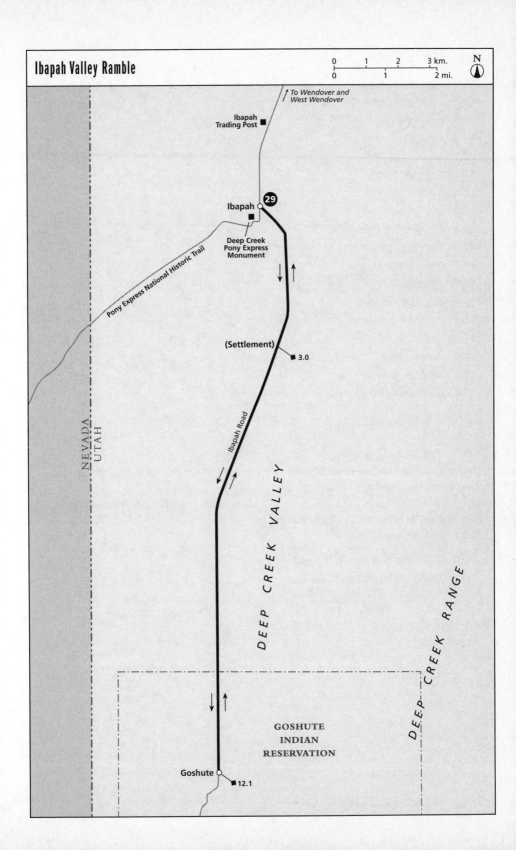

Ibapah Valley Ramble

0   1   2   3 km.
0   1   2 mi.

N

To Wendover and
West Wendover

Ibapah
Trading Post ■

Ibapah ■ ⓐ29

Deep Creek
Pony Express
Monument

Pony Express National Historic Trail

(Settlement) ■ 3.0

Ibapah Road

NEVADA
UTAH

DEEP CREEK VALLEY

DEEP CREEK RANGE

GOSHUTE
INDIAN
RESERVATION

Goshute ○ ■ 12.1

Miles and Directions

0.0 Start at the Deep Creek Pony Express Station marker on Ibapah Road in Ibapah.

0.1 Road bends left; begin false flats and "mini-rollers."

3.0 Settlement.

7.6 Cattle guard.

9.7 Cattle guard.

11.3 Begin short climb.

11.6 Cattle guard; enter Goshute settlement.

12.1 Intersection of Tempi Poi Lane and Poho Poi Lane; turn around here.

12.2 Begin gradual downgrade.

12.6 Cattle guard; leave Goshute settlement.

14.5 Cattle guard.

16.5 Cattle guard.

18.1 Begin short climb.

18.9 End of climb; resume gradual descent.

21.2 Settlement.

23.3 Road curves left

24.0 Road curves right.

24.2 End of ride at Pony Express Station marker, on the left.

Local Information

Confederated Tribes of the Goshute Indian Reservation (headquarters at Ibapah): www.goshutetribe.com.

Pony Express National Historic Trail, National Park Service: www.nps.gov/poex.

Food and Accommodations

Ibapah Trading Post (groceries): 101 Trading Post Lane, Ibapah (1.5 miles north of Deep Creek Pony Express Station marker); (435) 234-1166. There are two small motel-apartment rooms.

Maps

DeLorme: Utah Atlas & Gazetteer: Page 22 D2.

Benchmark: Utah Road & Recreation Atlas: Page 36 E6.

30 Jordan River Ramble

The Jordan Park Ramble is a 27.1-mile out-and-back ride that uses the Jordan River Parkway and connecting paths over 80 percent of the length. A 10-mile loop that, in part, uses city streets serves as the turnaround. The ride starts and finishes in the Glendale neighborhood of Salt Lake City, at Jordan Park adjacent the International Peace Gardens. The route is mostly flat, except for a few overpasses and underpasses, and some minor undulations on city streets. The elevation varies from 4,225 feet along the Jordan River in Salt Lake City to 4,365 feet on 1300 West in Taylorsville.

Start: Jordan Park, 1060 South 900 West, Salt Lake City.
Length: 27.1 miles (out-and-back, including a 10-mile loop that serves as the turnaround).
Terrain: Mostly flat, with a few mild climbs and descents. Minimum and maximum elevations: 4,225 to 4,365 feet.

Traffic and hazards: Most of the ride is on a bicycle path (no autos). A portion of the return route is on city streets. 7800 South (SR 48): 29,095 vehicles per day between the Jordan River Parkway and 1300 West in West Jordan in 2005. 1300 West: 11,165 vehicles per day between 7200 South and Winchester Street in West Jordan.

Getting there: Head west in Salt Lake City on 800 South or 900 South to 900 West. Turn left and head south to Montague Street; turn right and park. Enter the bike path at the end of the street. Utah Transit Authority routes 227, 232, and 516 all serve the neighborhood near Jordan Park. All buses emanate from downtown Salt Lake City.

The Ride

The Jordan River—not to be confused with its biblical counterpart—bisects the Salt Lake Valley via a south-to-north flow from Utah Lake to the Great Salt Lake. The river's course is about 40 miles. Jedediah Smith, a fur trader and trapper whose travels preceded the Mormon emigration, recorded that he was "very much strangled" in attempting to cross the Jordan. The river has always been slow-moving, so he was probably referring to a crossing attempt at flood stage. The river was renamed from "Utah River" in tribute to the Holy Land waterway (which, in a striking similarity, also empties into a salty body of water—the Dead Sea—which has no outlet). The Jordan River (Utah version) is not navigable and has been subjected to heavy pollution from adjacent industries in the past. Despite the "dirty water," nonindigenous species, including piranha, have turned up in the river.

Plenty of birds appear and nest along the river, including blackbirds, bluebirds, chickadees, cormorants, crows, doves, ducks, eagles, egrets, finches, flycatchers, gnatcatchers, geese, grebes, gulls, hawks, herons, hummingbirds, ibises, mallards, meadowlarks, orioles, osprey (rare), owls, pelicans, pheasants, quail, ravens, snipes, sparrows, swallows, teals, terns, thrushes, vultures, warblers, wrens, and (deep breath) others. The river has been in the process of being cleaned up with money from the Superfund. There are numerous roadway crossings of the river, with no more than about 2.5 miles between bridges.

As part of the clean-up process, segments along the river were converted into a recreational use trail. As of this writing, the trail was discontinuous, but the vision is for a path extending from the Jordan River's Utah Lake origin to a point near the Great Salt Lake outlet, at the Salt Lake-Davis County line, nearly as long as the river's 40 miles. Enough of the path was completed through the most heavily populated areas of the Salt Lake Valley, however, for inclusion as the Jordan River Ramble.

The Jordan River Ramble penetrates the heavily populated areas of Salt Lake Valley, slicing through the cities of Salt Lake City, Murray, and West Jordan, and along the borders of West Valley City, South Salt Lake, Millcreek, Taylorsville, and Midvale. The population of these cities totaled 634,314 in 2008, representing just under one-fourth of Utah's population. Logic would dictate that the Jordan River Parkway must be a crowded bike path! In general, it is not, although the path is shared with walkers, runners, children on bicycles, and others. There are plenty of long, peaceful stretches, however, that (almost) make you forget about being in the middle of an urban environment.

The ride starts and finishes in Salt Lake City, which, as Utah's largest city, offers numerous superlatives. Salt Lake City's most famous natives include Rocky Anderson (former mayor and outspoken liberal), Roseanne Barr (comedienne and actress), Jon Huntsman Sr. (billionaire), Jon Huntsman Jr. (former Utah governor and U.S. ambassador to China as of this writing), Karl Rove (political strategist), and Ryne Sanborn (actor and the so-called child-of-light of the 2002 Winter Olympics). As Salt Lake City was settled in 1847, communities immediately to the west and south were settled shortly thereafter, most as early as 1848.

Heading south through and beyond some west Salt Lake City neighborhoods, the Parkway straddles the border between West Valley City and South Salt Lake. West Valley City, with a population of 123,447, is Utah's second-largest city. The city was incorporated in 1980, consolidating several communities. West Valley City hosted men's and women's ice hockey during the 2002 Winter Olympic Games. Heading southward, the Parkway straddles the Taylorsville and Murray city borders. Taylorsville, named in honor of John Taylor, a former president of the Mormon Church, was incorporated in 1996. With a population of 58,785, Taylorsville is Utah's tenth-largest city. Murray (population 46,201) was renamed from South Cottonwood to honor Eli Murray, Utah's twelfth territorial governor. Notably, Murray was incorporated in 1903 following reaction to a fire and riot started by local smelter workers; their act generated the interest in a new city. Heading southward, the Parkway straddles the West Jordan and Midvale (population 28,129) city borders. The route leaves the Parkway at 7800 South, entering West Jordan. Although the Parkway continues for about 1 mile south of 7800 South, the path subsequently empties onto city streets as of this writing. This and other gaps in the path were to be closed subject to the availability of funding.

The ride starts at Jordan Park, located on 900 West in western Salt Lake City. Access the Jordan River Parkway from Montague Street, a cul-de-sac that juts west of 900 West on the northern boundary of the park. Bear left to head south on the Parkway. Immediately to your left will be the International Peace Gardens, which were conceived in 1939 and dedicated in 1952. The gardens are under the direction of the Salt Lake Council of Women. Twenty-six nations participated in the project, each with its own representative plot—the Holland entry, for example, features Dutch windmills, while the Japanese plot features a pagoda. The Parkway quickly bypasses the gardens as it winds its way southward through west Salt Lake neighborhoods. There is an at-grade crossing (no control) at Fremont Avenue at mile 0.3, followed by another at California Avenue at mile 0.9. Another at-grade crossing is at 1700 South (signal-controlled) at mile 1.5; south of here, there is only one more at-grade crossing; the others are grade-separated. Raging Waters (waterslide madness) is on the right, just after the 1700 South crossing.

The path generally hugs the Jordan River shoreline, except in a few places. At mile 1.95, bear right to head north along the Surplus Canal and temporarily move away from the Jordan River. This canal was constructed in 1885 for Jordan River flood control. Soon after the right turn, bear left to cross the canal; at the end of the bridge, turn left and head south. The canal is now on the left. After passing the weir (water flow control), you will be next to the Jordan River. The path passes underneath 2100 South at mile 2.25, followed by an underpass of SR 201. The Redwood Nature Area is adjacent the path south of 2100 South. The Redwood Trailhead Park is also adjacent (tables, restrooms). The path veers away from the river at mile 3.2. Turn left at mile 3.3 to continue southward on the path (continuing straight enters a West Valley City neighborhood). The path enters an undeveloped expanse that is unusually "wild" for an urban area. The path returns to the riverside, then crosses the river at mile 3.7. With the river on the right, the path continues southward, crossing under 3300 South (mile 4.3) and then over the Meadowbrook Expressway (mile 5.5). The path crosses the river just beyond the overpass and continues southward, with the river on the left. Pass underneath 4500 South at mile 7.2. Notice the Freedom Shrine Wall on the right, just beyond the underpass. The path crosses the river just upstream of the 4800 South underpass at mile 8.5. The river is now on the right. The path crosses Little Cottonwood Creek, which drains from the Wasatch Mountains into the Jordan River, at mile 8.6. The path then enters the Kennecott Nature Center of Murray, along a boardwalk. The boardwalk takes you through a lush wetlands area. (By now, you will have noticed that the Jordan River Parkway was not "built for speed." Slow down here, as well as across the narrow bridges and underpasses, while enjoying the experience.)

Exit the nature center at mile 8.8, as the path traces the edge of a Murray neighborhood. Enter Germania Park at 9.1. Bear left to enter the parking lot. Parking lot? Yes—the path resumes on the opposite side of the lot. Return to the path here; stay to the right just downstream where the path appears to split. Cross under 5400 South at mile 9.5 and continue heading south. The only at-grade crossing in this area comes at mile 10.2, at Bullion Street. Stop—look both ways!—and cross. The path splits just south of the crossing. Which way? Either one is fine—the paths converge downstream, just north of the I-215 underpass. The path crosses the river at mile 10.9; turn left after crossing and head south. The river is now on the left. The path splits again at a parking lot; stay left here and head for the Winchester Street underpass (mile 11.5). The path continues southward, past some minimally developed park-lands, passing under a railroad structure at mile 12.5. The path splits just beyond the underpass—take either route, since they converge downstream. Beyond here, the path is sandwiched between the railroad on the right and some dense vegetation on the left; the river is on the other side of the vegetation. Stay to the right as the path curves to parallel 7800 South in West Jordan. The path passes underneath a railroad structure, then empties into Gardner Village.

Gardner Village, named for Archibald Gardner, a Scottish immigrant and polyga-mist (eleven wives!), was established in 1853 as a flour mill. The site changed own-ership numerous times over the years. Nancy Long bought and restored the mill in 1980, then opened a furniture and gifts shop. A restaurant was added in 1990, followed by the addition and conversion of historic homes into retail specialty and theme shops. Feel free to linger for a few moments before exiting the historic vil-lage. Please be aware that the entry–exit road is shared with autos. Turn right onto 7800 South and head west. The next 5.2 miles of the Jordan River Ramble are on city streets. Turn right at 1300 West and head north. The street, also known as Temple Drive, travels past some West Jordan houses, entering Taylorsville at mile 14.6. After crossing Bennion Boulevard, the road becomes Canal Street and travels along the border between Taylorsville and Murray. After passing under the I-215 freeway, the North Jordan Canal appears on the right. The canal was completed in 1882 to divert water from the Jordan River for Salt Lake Valley farmers and residents. The canal is an American Water Works Association National Landmark. Continue northward to the T intersection with 4800 South (Murray–Taylorsville Road); turn right here. The road heads eastward through a Taylorsville residential community. The Wasatch Mountains loom in the distance. Turn right at the 4800 South trailhead at mile 18.0 and head south, toward the Jordan River Parkway. The "trailhead" is actually a cul-de-sac that terminates in a parking lot. Continue through the lot and onto the path. This is not the main path, but is a connector. Stay on the connector across the Jordan River. Keep straight to the next path and turn left. You are now on the Jordan River Parkway path, traveling north rather than south.

Enter the Kennecott Nature Center at mile 18.35 (boardwalk). The paved path continues beyond the boardwalk, crossing Little Cottonwood Creek (mile 18.55), passing under 4800 South (mile 18.6), and crossing the Jordan River (18.7). The path bends to the right after the crossing and continues northward. The path may be bumpy along this stretch. Pass under 4500 South at mile 19.9. Curve right to cross the Jordan River at mile 21.5; curve left on the other side and climb the Meadowbrook Expressway overpass. Continue heading north, passing under 3300 South at mile 22.8. Cross the Jordan River at mile 23.6 and curve left. The river is on the left. Note that you were traveling in the opposite direction on the opposite side of the river earlier, when heading south. After a stretch next to a series of industrial buildings, turn left to cross the river (mile 24.4). Do not miss this crossing, since the path you are on empties into the parking area for Paul Workman Park, to the north of here. The river is wide here, so this is probably one of the longest crossings. Turn right to continue heading north. Cross under SR 201 at mile 24.75, followed by 2100 South at mile 24.85. Just past the weir (which separates the Jordan River from the Surplus Canal), turn right to cross over. Turn right at the end of the crossing, then curve left to continue on the path. The river is on the right. A series of at-grade crossings welcomes your return to Salt Lake City neighborhoods, including ones at 1700 South (mile 25.6), California Avenue (mile 26.2), and Fremont Avenue (mile 26.8). The only signalized crossing is at 1700 South. Once past these crossings, and several more river crossings, the greenery of Jordan Park and the International Peace Gardens appears on the right. Follow the path as it curves to the right and empties into Montague Street, to end the ride. Although it is not advertised as a premier attraction, a visit to the International Peace Gardens is a *must*.

Miles and Directions

0.0 Start at Jordan Park, on Montague Street just west of 900 West in Salt Lake City. Head west to the end of Montague Street and enter the Jordan River Parkway path. Bear left and head south. At 0.15 mile you will see the International Peace Gardens on the left.

0.3 Go straight after stopping at Fremont Avenue.

0.5 Cross the Jordan River; keep straight after crossing.

0.9 Go straight after stopping at California Avenue. After 0.05 mile cross the Jordan River; river now on the right.

1.5 Path empties onto sidewalk. Go straight at the traffic signal (pedestrian-controlled) at 1700 South.

1.7 Railroad crossing (one track).

2.0 Cross the Jordan River; river now on the left. After 0.05 mile the path bends to the right; Surplus Canal on the left.

2.1 Curve left to cross canal. After 0.05 mile turn left at end of bridge; canal on the left.

2.3 2100 South underpass; now adjacent Jordan River, on the left.

2.4 SR 201 underpass.

3.2 Path curves right, away from river.

3.3 Turn left and keep straight to continue on path; enter undeveloped area.

3.6 Return to riverside; river on the left.

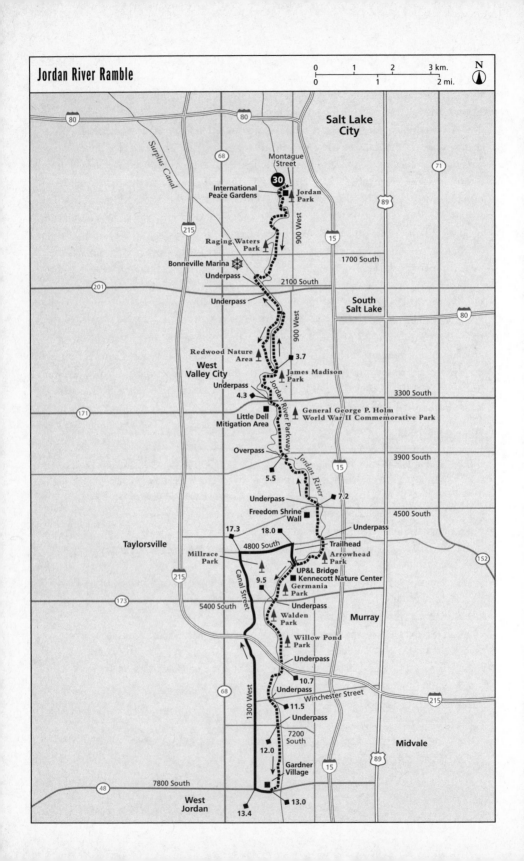

Jordan River Ramble

0   1   2   3 km.

0   1   2 mi.

N

Salt Lake City

80

80

68

Surplus Canal

Montague Street

30

International Peace Gardens

Jordan Park

900 West

215

71

89

15

1700 South

Raging Waters Park

Bonneville Marina

Underpass

2100 South

South Salt Lake

201

Underpass

900 West

80

Redwood Nature Area

James Madison Park

3.7

West Valley City

Underpass

4.3

Jordan River Parkway

3300 South

General George P. Holm World War II Commemorative Park

171

Little Dell Mitigation Area

Overpass

Jordan River

3900 South

5.5

15

Underpass

7.2

Freedom Shrine Wall

4500 South

Underpass

Taylorsville

17.3

18.0

Trailhead

152

4800 South

Arrowhead Park

Millrace Park

Canal Street

UP&L Bridge

Kennecott Nature Center

Germania Park

9.5

215

173

5400 South

Underpass

Walden Park

Murray

Willow Pond Park

Underpass

1300 West

10.7

68

Underpass

Winchester Street

215

11.5

Underpass

7200 South

Midvale

12.0

Gardner Village

15

89

48

7800 South

13.0

West Jordan

13.4

3.7 Cross the Jordan River and turn right to continue on path; river on the right.

4.3 3300 South underpass.

5.5 Meadowbrook Expressway overpass.

5.6 Cross the Jordan River and turn left to continue on path; river on the left.

7.2 4500 South underpass.

8.4 Cross the Jordan River; river on the right.

8.5 4800 South (Murray-Taylorsville Road) underpass.

8.6 Cross Little Cottonwood Creek.

8.7 Continue southward on path via boardwalk.

8.8 End boardwalk; return to pavement.

9.1 Turn left to enter Germania Park parking lot.

9.2 Exit parking lot at opposite end by turning right onto path; resume Parkway path.

9.4 Veer right to stay on path.

9.5 5400 South underpass.

10.2 Go straight after stopping at Bullion Street.

10.3 Path splits; take either path (they converge at I-215 underpass).

10.7 I-215 underpass.

10.9 Cross the Jordan River and turn left; river now on the left.

11.5 Stay left (on path) at parking lot.

11.5 Winchester Street underpass.

12.0 7200 South underpass.

12.5 Pass underneath railroad structure.

12.6 Path splits; take either direction (they converge downstream).

12.9 Path curves right to parallel 7800 South. After another 0.05 mile you pass underneath railroad structure.

13.0 End of path at Gardner Village parking area; turn left. After 0.05 mile exit parking lot; turn right onto 7800 South.

13.4 At the traffic signal at 1300 West, turn right.

14.4 Go straight at the traffic signal at 7000 South.

14.6 Enter Taylorsville.

14.8 Go straight at the traffic signal at Winchester Street.

15.4 Go straight at the traffic signal at Bennion Boulevard.

15.5 1300 West becomes Canal Street.

15.9 I-215 underpass.

16.5 Go straight at the traffic signal at 5400 South.

17.3 At the traffic signal at 4800 South (Murray-Taylorsville Road), turn right.

18.0 Turn right to enter 4800 South trailhead (to Jordan River Parkway).

18.1 Exit trailhead parking area and head south on path.

18.2 Cross Jordan River and keep straight.

18.3 Turn left onto Jordan River Parkway path; river on the left.

18.4 Begin boardwalk.

18.5 End boardwalk; return to pavement. After 0.05 mile cross Little Cottonwood Creek.

18.6 4800 South (Murray-Taylorsville Road) underpass.

18.7 Cross the Jordan River and curve right; river on the right.

19.9 4500 South underpass.

21.5 Cross the Jordan River and turn left to continue on path; river on the left.

21.6 Meadowbrook Expressway overpass.

22.8 3300 South underpass.

23.6 Cross the Jordan River and turn left to continue on path; river on the left.

24.4 Cross the Jordan River and turn right to continue on path; river on the right.

24.8 SR 201 underpass.

24.9 2100 South underpass. After 0.05 mile turn right to cross canal.

25.0 Turn right at end of bridge to continue on path; canal on the right.

25.1 Curve left to continue on path; river on the right.

25.2 Cross the Jordan River; river now on the left.

25.4 Railroad crossing (one track).

25.6 Go straight at the traffic signal (pedestrian-controlled) at 1700 South.

25.7 Continue northward on sidewalk, then veer left onto path.

26.2 Cross the Jordan River; river now on the right. Then go straight after stopping at California Avenue.

26.6 Continue on path across bridge.

26.8 Go straight after stopping at Fremont Avenue.

27.0 International Peace Gardens on the right.

27.1 End of ride at Montague Street trailhead; exit path and return to street.

Local Information

City of Salt Lake City official Web site: www.ci.slc.ut.us.

International Peace Gardens Web site: www.internationalpeacegardens.org.

City of Midvale official Web site: www.midvalecity.org.

City of Murray official Web site: www.murray.utah.gov.

City of South Salt Lake official Web site: www.ssl.state.ut.us.

City of Taylorsville official Web site: www.taylorsvilleut.gov.

City of West Jordan official Web site: www.wjordan.com.

City of West Valley City official Web site: www.wvc-ut.gov.

Restaurants

Club Room: 2177 West North Temple (at the Radisson Hotel-Airport), Salt Lake City; (801) 364-5800; www.radisson.com/hotels/SALTAIR/dinings.

Festa Tavola (at the Holiday Inn Hotel & Suites): 5001 West Wiley Post Way, Salt Lake City; (801) 741-1800; www.ichotelsgroup.com/h/d/hi/1/en/hotel/SLCFF/dining?start=1.

Grill 114 (at the Airport Hilton): 5151 Wiley Post Way, Salt Lake City; (801) 539-1515; www1.hilton.com/en_US/hi/hotel/SLCAHHF-Hilton-Salt-Lake-City-Airport-Utah/dining.do#1.

La Frontera Café: 1236 West 400 South, Salt Lake City; (801) 967-9905.

Red Iguana: 736 West North Temple, Salt Lake City; (801) 322-1489; www.rediguana.com.

Totem's Private Club & Steakhouse/Totem's Café: 538 South Redwood Road, Salt Lake City; (801) 975-0401.

Accommodations

Gateway Inn: 819 West North Temple, Salt Lake City; (801) 364-7549.
Overniter Motor Inn: 1500 West North Temple, Salt Lake City; (801) 533-8300.
Salt City Inn: 1025 North 900 West, Salt Lake City; (801) 328-8520; www.saltcityinn.com.

Bicycle Shop

SLC Bicycle Collective: 2312 South West Temple, Salt Lake City; (801) FAT-BIKE; www. slcbikecollective.org.

Maps

Salt Lake City Green Bikeways Map, Salt Lake City Department. of Transportation, 2006.
Rand McNally: Salt Lake City Street Guide: including Logan, Ogden, and Provo: Pages 1857, 1963, 2069, 2070, and 2175 E6 on page 1857.
Jordan River Trail Completion Project: www .recreation.slco.org/parks/pdf/JordanRiver Map.pdf.

The Jordan River Parkway passes through a Salt Lake City neighborhood.

Mountainland

The Mountainland region includes Summit, Utah, and Wasatch Counties in north-central Utah. The region cuts an undulating, diagonal swath across the Wasatch Front. Mountainland is not entirely mountainous—the profile trace, from west to east, starts with the comparatively low areas of Utah Lake and Utah Valley, leaps upward to Mount Timpanogos (11,750 feet) in the Wasatch Front, drops down into Parleys Park, Heber Valley, and Kamas Valley, then heads upward again into the Uinta Mountains. The Uinta Mountains are the only east-west range in the continental United States. The range contains Utah's highest peaks (Kings Peak, at 13,528 feet, although this mountain is actually in Dinosaurland). Mountainland could arguably be named "Waterworld," given the abundance of liquid. Utah Lake, Utah's largest freshwater lake (area: 151 square miles), is near the western boundary of the region. Other lakes and reservoirs, including Deer Creek, Echo, Jordanelle, and Rockport, are in the region. In addition, the Uinta Mountains are home to numerous high-altitude lakes. The Bear, Green, Provo, and Weber Rivers all originate in the Uinta Mountains, and many of the canyons in the region feature creeks and springs.

Mountainland's valleys are populated, while the mountains are unpopulated national forest lands and wilderness areas. Mountainland covers 5,050 square miles and had a population of 588,003 in 2008. The greatest concentration of settlement is Utah Valley, sandwiched between Utah Lake to the west and the steep and powerful Wasatch Mountains to the east. The cities of Provo, Orem, American Fork, Lehi, and others are found here, along with Brigham Young University, Utah Valley University, and many other institutions and places of interest. The cities of Utah Valley were originally developed as part of the "Mormon corridor" extending southward from Salt Lake City along present-day US 89. Brigham Young's vision was for settlements to be spaced about one mile apart along a north–south spine spanning the length of Utah Territory. The spaces between the towns in Utah Valley filled in long ago as the area urbanized. Utah Valley has a rich cultural heritage that continues to be dominated by the Mormon religion, although the Winter Olympic Games in 2002 (Provo hosted some of the ice hockey matches) introduced a diverse audience to the region (and vice versa).

To the northwest of Utah Valley is Parleys Park, one of several high-altitude basins situated between the Wasatch Front in the west and the Uinta Mountains in the east. Park City, nestled against the "back side" of the Wasatch Front (i.e., the "Wasatch Back"), is located here. Park City's easy access to the slopes makes the nearby mountains, along with the city's historic Main Street, ideal for winter sports and resorts. Park City hosted alpine skiing, bobsledding, freestyle skiing, luge, ski jumping, snowboarding, and tobogganing during the 2002 Winter Olympic Games, thereby solidifying the city's status as a winter sports mecca. Park City makes an amazing transformation after the snow melts, however, becoming a mecca for mountain biking. A National Off-Road Bicycle Association (NORBA) event has been held in the Park City area each year since the 1980s. Tour de France legend Lance Armstrong has raced here— on a mountain bike! Park City is friendly to road biking, too; USA Cycling has awarded the national road cycling championships to Park City on several occasions, the most recent being in 2005. Lance Armstrong won a national junior road race title in Park City long before turning professional.

The Heber and Kamas Valleys are located to the southeast of Park City. Although neither is as heavily populated as Utah Valley or Parleys Park, both picturesque valleys are home to several cities and towns. The Silver Creek Valley extends toward the northeast of Parleys Park. Interstate 80 follows this valley, ultimately turning northward for a stretch to follow the alignment of the Weber River. The freeway turns eastward at the mouth of Echo Canyon and heads toward Wyoming. Despite its accessibility, the Silver Creek Valley remains peaceful and quiet. Coalville, the seat of Summit County (which includes Park City), sits at the north end of the valley. Kamas Valley is the gateway to the Uinta Mountains. Only one road truly penetrates this mighty range: the Mirror Lake Scenic Byway. The highway climbs from the city of Kamas to Bald Mountain Pass (summit: 10,700 feet), then descends into Wyoming, arriving in Evanston some 80 miles later. The route is covered in a popular point-to-point road race each June (High Uintas Classic). *Road Biking Utah* features four rides in the Mountainland region. These are not the most "mountainous" rides in the book, despite the region's name. Expect some climbing, however.

31 Alpine Loop Challenge

The Alpine Loop Challenge is a mountainous 45.3-mile out-and-back ride through breathtaking scenery in the Uinta National Forest. The route covers portions of the Alpine Loop Scenic Byway—which is not really a loop—and the Provo Canyon Scenic Byway, starting and ending in Orem. The course features a variety of road types, including a bicycle path, the shoulder of a popular canyon highway, mountainous two-lane roads, and a narrow, twisting mountain road. The entire route can be completed only between late May and late October, when the Alpine Loop Scenic Byway is open. Elevations vary from 4,828 feet near the starting point in Orem to 7,980 feet at the junction with Cascade Springs Drive high in the Wasatch Mountains.

Start: Parking lot adjacent Provo Canyon Parkway, north of 800 North in Orem.
Length: 45.3 miles (out-and-back).
Terrain: Mountainous; two long, steep ascents and descents. Minimum and maximum elevations: 4,828 to 7,980 feet.

Traffic and hazards: US 189: 16,110 vehicles per day at the mouth of Provo Canyon in 2005; 9,330 vehicles per day at the SR 92 junction. SR 92: 385 vehicles per day north of US 189 (seasonally variable).

Getting there: From I-15, take exit 272 and head east on 800 North (SR 52). Just before the junction with US 189, turn left onto Provo Canyon Parkway. Turn right into the convenience mart parking lot—continue past the mart, into the back parking lot. This is the trailhead for the Provo Canyon Parkway (bike path). By bike, from Provo, access the Provo River Parkway and head north. The path uses wide city sidewalks along 2230 North and University Avenue before returning to a separate alignment at 4800 North. Continue northward to 800 North, in Orem, to the start of the course.

The Ride

The Alpine Loop is a route that twists through some outrageously scenic terrain in the mountains to the northeast of Provo. The "loop" is more of a horseshoe, accessible via American Fork Canyon in the north and from Provo Canyon in the southeast. Most of the loop is within the Uinta National Forest. Part of the forest unit is designated as the Mount Timpanogos Wilderness. Indeed, the centerpiece of the loop is Mount Timpanogos, which rises to 11,750 feet, complete with sheer cliff faces, jagged edges, and snowpacks that last well into July. The colors along the route are incredibly vivid: deep greens, brilliant golds, blazing scarlets, and pristine whites are just a few of those seen. The upper parts of the loop are closed during the winter (open from late May until late October). The lower parts of the loop enable access to Robert Redford's Sundance Resort (from Provo Canyon) and Timpanogos Cave National Monument (from American Fork Canyon) year-round.

Road Biking Utah's version of the Alpine Loop starts and finishes in the city of Orem. Orem is located directly to the north of Provo. Orem, self-proclaimed "Family

Climbing into the stratosphere of the Wasatch Range on the Alpine Loop.

City USA," was named in honor of Walter C. Orem, president of the Salt Lake and Utah Electric Interurban Railroad. Although Orem was first settled permanently in 1877, the community was not named until 1919. The city had an estimated population of 93,250 in 2008, making it Utah's sixth-largest city. The city's most famous residents are the members of the Osmond family. Computer software giants Wordperfect, Novell, and Caldera all got their start in Orem.

The Alpine Loop Challenge starts at the mouth of Provo Canyon, where the city limits of Provo and Orem seem to duel for the limited space. The steep mountains that line the canyon, part of the Wasatch Range, consist entirely of Paleozoic rocks, including lime, sandstone, and shale. In some places the wedges of rock are 25,000 feet thick. US 189—the Provo Canyon Scenic Byway—snakes up the canyon. There are several parks and trailheads along the highway; its proximity to the heavily populated Utah Valley makes the canyon a busy place. To separate themselves from motor vehicles, cyclists and runners are treated to a bicycle path that parallels US 189 for some distance. Nonetheless, SHARE THE ROAD signs are posted along US 189 to remind drivers of the presence of bicycles on the shoulders.

Start at the Provo Canyon Parkway (bike path) trailhead just north of 800 North near US 189 in Orem. The adjacent parking lot is literally in the back of a convenience mart that can be accessed from a road named Provo Canyon Parkway. The road is a dead-end street that is not to be confused with the Provo Canyon Parkway on which you will be riding. Enter the path from the lot and head into Provo Canyon. Enter Uinta National Forest just beyond the mouth of the canyon. The path passes several trailheads and parks along the way. The Provo River runs parallel to the path. The river originates at Washington Lake, high in the Uinta Mountains to the northeast. The river flows toward the southwest, eventually draining into Utah Lake. The path crosses under US 189 at mile 3.1, just prior to entering Nunn's Park. To the right is Bridal Veil Falls, a 607-foot waterfall spectacular that descends in two stages ("double cataract") from the towering cliffs above. During the winter, the waterfall freezes, becoming a magnet for hardy ice climbers. Continue past the falls to Vivian Park at mile 5.6. The bike path ends here; turn left onto South Fork Road to access the parallel US 189. There is a railroad crossing just after the turn. Railroad? Yes—the Heber Valley Railroad ("Heber Creeper") terminates here (see the Heber Valley Ramble). Turn right onto US 189 and head north. Stay to the right side of the shoulder to avoid the highway's rumble strips.

Enter a short tunnel at mile 6.5. The shoulder continues through the tunnel, so there is no need to panic in the darkness. Cautiously prepare for a left turn onto SR 92 (to Sundance) after exiting the short tunnel. Turn left at mile 6.9 to begin climbing the Alpine Loop. Note the SHARE THE ROAD sign on the right, reminding drivers of the presence of cyclists. The Sundance Hillclimb, a major bike race for the area's road cyclists, starts at this junction every year. The canyon's walls are lush; a creek rushes on the left. The climb gets noticeably steeper at mile 7.8. Sundance Resort is on the left at mile 9.2. The property is open year-round for skiing, mountain biking, and other activities. Downhill mountain bike races are held here every week during the warm season. Some of the Sundance Film Festival viewings are held at the resort every January; most of the other viewings are in Park City. The road narrows after passing the resort, as the steep climb continues. There are a few switchbacks. A pedestrian bridge on the horizon is a reference point for the Aspen Grove Family Center, a Brigham Young University complex, at mile 11.5. A Uinta National Forest fee-use-area booth is at mile 11.8; the booth is generally self-service and is intended for persons who plan to park or camp on forest grounds. There is no fee for through travelers. Densely wooded Mount Timpanogos Campground is on the right at mile 11.9. The road gets even narrower here and starts to wind. Be aware of the many blind corners, and keep right. The road passes through a lush garden of aspen trees. The whitish color of the bark is in fabulous contrast to the colors of the undergrowth and wildflowers (in season), as well as the deep greens in the background.

At mile 15.5, turn right onto Cascade Springs Drive (at the CASCADE SPRINGS sign). (Note that the Sundance Hillclimb does not turn here but continues on SR 92 to the summit.) All of that climbing you just did is rewarded with a long, fast descent. The rapid downhill ends abruptly at mile 18.1; a steep 1-mile climb follows. Beyond the crest of this climb is another fast, winding descent. The views from the road are stunning. The high mountains in the distance include Provo Peak (elevation 11,068 feet), Lightning Peak (10,056 feet), and Cascade Mountain (10,761 feet). Keep your eyes on the road; pull over and stop to get a longer look. The gradient of the descent eases at mile 21.5. There are restrooms on the right at mile 21.8, next to a parking lot for Cascade Springs. The road makes a hard right turn at mile 22.1. Enter Cascade Springs at mile 22.4—the end of pavement is just ahead. Take time to refresh here. The Cascade Springs are fast-flowing, producing some seven million gallons a day. Rocks set amidst ferns and flowers create a beautiful setting. Trout can be seen dashing through the water. After soaking in the blissful scene, turn around and start the return trip.

The return ride begins with a sharp turn to the left, to leave Cascade Springs, followed by rolling hills. Climbing begins in earnest at mile 23.5. The road winds up to mile 25.8, where there is a fast descent. The next climb begins at mile 26.9. The gradient eases (finally) at mile 29.0. The junction with SR 92 is at mile 29.4. Turn left here and begin to descend. The road winds through a grove of aspens—stay right along this narrow but lovely passage. Be especially alert through the blind corners. Mount Timpanogos Campground is on the left at mile 33.0. The road widens just beyond the gate and booth, at mile 33.2. Pass through the Aspen Grove complex at mile 33.4, continuing to descend. Sundance Resort is on the right at mile 36.0. Take your eyes off the road for one second (but no more) to see the ski lifts to the right. The road descends through a narrow canyon, with a creek rushing to your right. The highway ends at the US 189 junction, at mile 38.4.

Turn right here to start the descent of Provo Canyon. As with the ascent, stay to the far right to avoid the rumble strips on the shoulder. Enter a short tunnel at mile 38.7. The shoulder continues through the tunnel. After exiting the tunnel, cautiously move left for the left turn onto South Fork Road, to Vivian Park. Turn left here (mile 39.6), cross the "Heber Creeper" tracks, and turn right onto the Provo Canyon Parkway bike path. Follow the path as it passes by parks and negotiates a US 189 underpass (mile 42.2), while paralleling the Provo River. Reach the mouth of the canyon at mile 45.3. The ride ends here, adjacent the parking lot on the back side of the convenience mart.

Miles and Directions

0.0 Start at Provo Canyon Parkway trailhead north of 800 North in Orem. Head north on Provo Canyon Parkway bicycle path.

0.9 Canyon View Park.

1.2 Mount Timpanogos Park.

2.4 Canyon Glen Park; gradient of canyon increases.

3.1 Nunn's Park; path passes under US 189; now on northbound side of highway.

3.2 Bridal Veil Falls on the right (look up).

5.6 Vivian Park; end of path at park access road. Turn left here, onto South Fork Road. After 0.05 mile, come to a railroad crossing (one track).

5.7 At the stop sign at US 189, turn right (stay right on shoulder to avoid rumble strips).

6.5 Enter tunnel.

6.6 Exit tunnel.

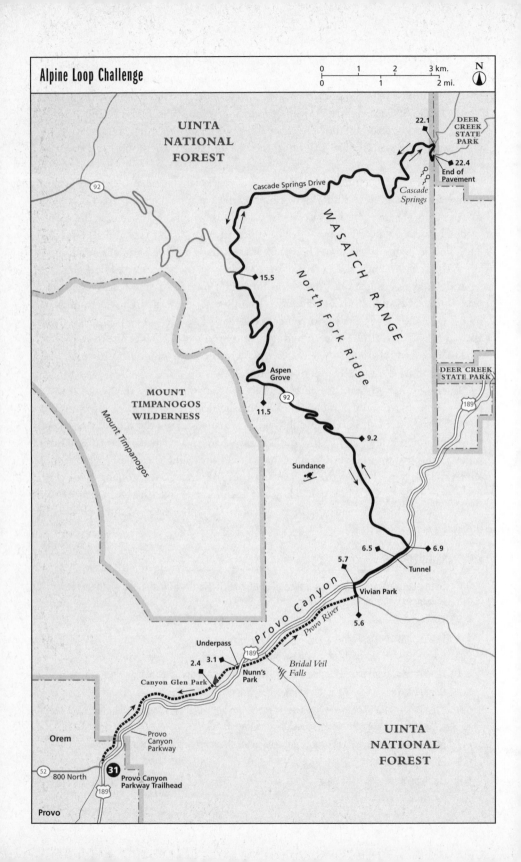

0   1   2   3 km.

0   1   2 mi.

N

UINTA
NATIONAL
FOREST

92

Cascade Springs Drive

22.1

DEER
CREEK
STATE
PARK

22.4
End of
Pavement

*Cascade
Springs*

WASATCH RANGE

North Fork Ridge

15.5

DEER CREEK
STATE PARK

189

Aspen
Grove

92

11.5

9.2

MOUNT
TIMPANOGOS
WILDERNESS

Mount Timpanogos

Sundance

6.5   6.9

5.7   Tunnel

Vivian Park

6.5

Provo Canyon

Provo River

5.6

Underpass

189

2.4   3.1

Nunn's
Park

*Bridal Veil
Falls*

Canyon Glen Park

UINTA

NATIONAL

FOREST

Orem

Provo
Canyon
Parkway

52

800 North

31

Provo Canyon
Parkway Trailhead

189

Provo

6.9 Turn left onto SR 92 (to SUNDANCE); begin climb.

9.2 Sundance Resort on the left.

11.5 Enter Aspen Grove area (Brigham Young University facility).

11.8 Uinta National Forest fee-use-area booth (self-service).

11.9 Gate (closed in winter); Mount Timpanogos Campground on the right. Road narrows and winds.

15.5 Turn right onto Cascade Springs Drive (to CASCADE SPRINGS); begin descent.

18.1 End of descent; begin steep climb.

19.1 Crest of climb; begin descent and curves.

20.5 Scenic view pullout on the right.

21.1 Winding descent gets steeper.

21.5 False end of descent; short uphill.

21.7 Descent continues.

21.8 Restrooms on right.

22.1 Gradient eases; sharp right-hand curve—begin false flat.

22.4 Enter Cascade Springs area; end of pavement—loop parking lot (information and restrooms).

22.5 Return to Cascade Springs Drive.

22.8 Sharp curve to left.

22.9 Begin steep climb.

23.1 Restrooms on the left.

23.3 Crest of climb; begin short descent.

23.5 Resume climbing.

23.9 Gradient eases.

24.1 Climb gets steeper.

24.5 Scenic view pullout on the left.

25.8 Crest of climb; begin descent.

26.6 Descent gets steeper.

26.9 End of descent; begin climb.

29.0 Grade eases; continue climbing.

29.4 At the stop sign at SR 92, turn left—begin winding descent.

33.0 Mount Timpanogos Campground on the left.

33.4 Aspen Grove Family Camp; end winding descent.

36.0 Sundance Resort on the right.

38.4 At the stop sign at US 189, turn right (stay right on shoulder to avoid rumble strips).

38.7 Enter tunnel.

38.8 Exit tunnel.

39.6 Turn left onto South Fork Road to enter Vivian Park. After 0.05 mile, come to a railroad crossing (one track).

39.7 Turn right onto Provo Canyon Parkway bike path.

42.1 Bridal Veil Falls on the left.

42.2 Nunn's Park; path passes under US 189.

42.9 Canyon Glen Park.

44.1 Mount Timpanogos Park.

44.4 Canyon View Park.

45.3 End of ride at trailhead north of 800 North, adjacent parking lot.

Local Information

American Fork Canyon and Alpine Loop Scenic Backway: www.fs.fed.us/r4/maps/brochures/amer_fork_alpine_loop.pdf. USDA Forest Service brochure with regional map.

City of Orem official Web site: www.orem.org.

Alpine Loop Scenic Byway information: www.utah.com/byways/alpine_loop.htm.

Provo River Parkway information: www.utah mountainbiking.com/trails/provorvr.htm.

Restaurants

The Shops at Riverwoods: Along the Provo River Parkway in Provo.

Gandolfo's New York Deli: 775 North State Street, Orem; (801) 734-1770; www.gandolfosdeli.com/photos.php?directory=Orem%20(N),%20UT&album=store.

Happy Sumo at Riverwoods: 4801 North University Avenue, The Shops at Riverwoods, Provo; (801) 225-9100; www.happysumosushi.com/promap.html.

Los Hermanos Mexican Restaurant: 395 North State Street, Lindon; (801) 785-1715; www.loshermanosrestaurants.com.

Tree Room: 8841 Alpine Loop Road, Sundance Resort, Provo; (801) 223-4200; www.sundanceresort.com/dine/tree_room.html. Dinner only; closed in November.

Tucanos Brazilian Grill: 4801 North University Avenue, The Shops at Riverwoods, Provo; (801) 224-4774; www.tucanos.com.

Accommodations

Best Western—Cotton Tree: 2230 North University Parkway, Provo; (801) 373-7044; www.bestwesternutah.com/hotels/best-western-cottontree-inn-provo/.

Days Inn: 1675 North Freedom Boulevard (200 West), Provo; (801) 375-8600.

Sundance Resort: 8841 Alpine Loop Road, Provo; (800) 892-1600 or (866) 259-7468; www.sundanceresort.com.

Bicycle Shops

Mad Dog Cycles: 360 East 800 South, Orem; (801) 222-9577; www.maddogcycles.com.

Park's Sportman: 644 North State Street, Orem; (801) 225-0227 or (800) 789-4447; www.parkssportsman.com.

Pedersen's Sports: University Mall E-98 (575 East University Parkway), Orem; (801) 225-3000; http://pedersensorem.com.

Urban Downfall Cycles: 327 East 1200 South, Orem; (801) 691-0250.

Maps

DeLorme: Utah Atlas & Gazetteer: Page 25 C8.

Rand McNally: Salt Lake City Street Guide: including Logan, Ogden, and Provo: Page 2821 C3.

Benchmark: Utah Road & Recreation Atlas: Page 43 D11.

32 Echo Canyon Ramble

The Echo Canyon Ramble is a 24.8-mile ride on gently rolling terrain, at altitudes ranging from 5,450 feet in Echo (town) to 5,761 feet in Hoytsville. The ride begins and ends in Coalville, remains within the confines of the Weber River valley and Echo Canyon, and traces portions of the California, Mormon Pioneer, and Pony Express National Historic Trails. The ride also parallels a portion of the Historic Union Pacific Rail Trail, although the route does not actually use the trail, which is mostly unpaved.

Start: Summit County Fairgrounds on Park Road in Coalville.
Length: 24.8 miles (one out-and-back section combined with one loop section).
Terrain: Gently rolling hills with several false flat sections. Minimum and maximum elevations: 5,450 to 5,761 feet.
Traffic and hazards: About 2,010 vehicles per day at the I-80 Echo Canyon Road underpass in 2005.

Getting there: Take I-80 eastbound to exit 162, Coalville; enter Coalville via 100 South to Main Street; turn left on Main Street, then right on Center Street, continuing to the Summit County Fairgrounds.

The Ride

Coalville, population 1,327 in 2008 (elevation 5,586 feet), is the Summit County seat. The city is situated at the confluence of Chalk Creek and the Weber River, the latter of which eventually drains into the Great Salt Lake. The city is also situated at the south end of Echo Reservoir, a privately owned body of water that features a camping and boating resort, at the north end of the Weber River valley. At the north end of Echo Reservoir, 6 miles to the north of Coalville, is the mouth of Echo Canyon. This narrow canyon, lined with steep walls on either side, was one of the most important passages to westward expansion. The California National Historic Trail, the Mormon Pioneer National Historic Trail, and the Old Lincoln Highway all came through Echo Canyon, headed for points west. The canyon was also used by the Pony Express during its eighteen-month run between 1860 and 1861. Today, the I-80 freeway, one of the nation's most important east–west interstates, travels through the canyon. The freeway splits into I-80 (to continue westward via Salt Lake City) and I-84 (to continue northward via Ogden) at the mouth of the canyon. Echo Canyon was so named because of the acoustics, which are nearly impossible to demonstrate today because of ever-present freeway noise. The railroad also passes through the canyon; in fact, the old Union Pacific Railroad grade, now a popular bicycle path, begins in Coalville. The Union Pacific Rail Trail—mostly unpaved, and an official Utah State Park—continues southward for 28 miles to Park City.

Today, Coalville's economy is based, in part, on county government activities, lumberjacking, and "satellite" tourism. (Although Coalville was named for the coal

Enjoying the lightly trafficked roads in Hoytsville, near Coalville.

mines in the area, there is not much mining activity today.) Coalville has a few budget alternatives to Park City's often pricey accommodations, while being accessible to the Wasatch Front's skiing and mountain biking. A popular road biking ride and annual race travels up Chalk Creek Canyon (via Chalk Creek Road) to the Wyoming state line, where the pavement ends, and back.

Start the ride at the Summit County Fairgrounds on Park Road in Coalville. Note that the fair is held for one week each August; access to the area may be restricted during this time. Head west on Park Avenue (poor pavement surface). The surface improves after crossing 100 East; you are now on Center Street. Turn right onto Main Street and head north. Take note of the Summit County Courthouse at 60 North Main Street. The building was completed in 1904 in the Romanesque Revival architectural style. There have been a couple of additions since then, but the original style has been retained. The building is on the National Register of Historic Places (NRHP). Also on the NRHP is the Thomas L. Allen House located at 98 North Main Street. Leave Coalville at mile 0.7; after a short climb, Echo Reservoir appears on the left. Echo Reservoir is privately owned, but there is a public beach and resort at mile 2.1 and a marina at mile 3.8. The reservoir is popular for boating, water sports, and fishing. The reservoir ends abruptly at Echo Dam at mile 5.0; from here, the road begins a short descent into Echo Canyon. After a sharp right-hand curve, the road passes under the Union Pacific Railroad. The road curves to the left shortly thereafter, passing under I-80. Turn left onto Echo Canyon Road on the other side of the underpass. The steep walls of the canyon will be on your right. The road curves to the right at mile 6.3 becoming Echo Road; veer right at mile 6.6 to get on the frontage road. Enter the small town of Echo. The town once "bustled," but the Great Depression dealt the town a major blow. Today, there are a few homes, a cafe, church, and small motel. The Echo Post Office, at 3455 South Echo Road, along with Echo School, at 3441 South Echo Road, are both on the NRHP. Continue through town; the frontage road curves to the left, stopping at the parallel main highway (SR 86). Stop here, then cross the highway and turn left to begin the return ride. Be cautious when crossing the highway; it is wide (four lanes) and divided.

Return via the same route to Coalville. The road bends to the left at mile 7.7. Turn right at mile 8.3 onto Echo Canyon Road, to pass under I-80. Curve to the right again at mile 8.5, passing under the Union Pacific Railroad at mile 8.8. After a short climb, Echo Reservoir comes into view on the right. The surface area of the lake averages about 1,000 acres. The lake is the scene of the Echo Triathlon, held here each July. The triathlon claimed to offer the largest cash purse of any triathlon in Utah in 2006. Echo Marina is on the right at mile 10.5, and the Echo Reservoir South Beach Resort is on the right at mile 12.2. Return to Coalville at mile 13.7. But don't stop! The ride is just a little more than half over.

Continue riding through town, heading south. Enter Hoytsville (now on South Hoytsville Road) at mile 15.2. Turn right on Hobson Lane at mile 15.4. Cross over I-80, then the Weber River, before making a sharp curve to the left. You are now on the west side of the valley on West Hoytsville Road, riding by a string of country residences along a narrow, rolling roadway. During the spring and fall (and the summer if there has been plenty of precipitation), the valley can be quite green and bucolic. Stop at Creamery Lane at mile 17.8; turn right here, then make a sharp curve to the left. At mile 19.3, turn left onto Judd Lane (no street sign). Cross over I-80 once again; stop and turn left onto South Hoytsville Road at mile 20.4. This is the final leg of the ramble. You are now on the east side of the valley, heading north along the typically gentle rolling terrain. Enter Coalville at mile 23.4 on Main Street. Turn right onto Center Street at mile 24.5 and head east. After the stop sign at 100 East, you will be on bumpy Park Road. End the ride at the Summit County Fairgrounds, just 0.1 mile beyond the stop sign.

Miles and Directions

0.0 Start at Summit County Fairgrounds on Park Road in Coalville; a 90-degree bend in the road marks the starting point. Head west (caution: bumpy road).

0.2 Go straight at the stop sign at 100 East; pavement now smoother.

0.3 At the stop sign at Main Street, turn right. Mini-mart on opposite corner.

0.7 Begin gradual climb; Union Pacific Rail Trail trailhead on the left.

0.9 Crest of climb; now on Echo Dam Road.

1.0 Echo Reservoir on the left.

2.1 South Beach Resort on the left (lavatory facilities).

3.8 Echo Marina on the left (lavatories).

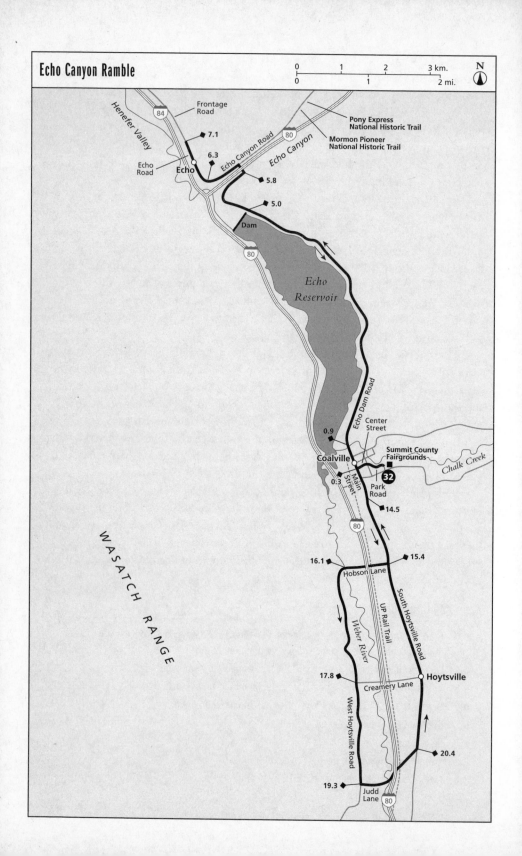

Echo Canyon Ramble

0   1   2   3 km.

0   1   2 mi.

N

Henefer Valley

84

Frontage Road

7.1

6.3

Echo Road

Echo

Echo Canyon Road

80

Echo Canyon

Pony Express National Historic Trail

Mormon Pioneer National Historic Trail

5.8

5.0

Dam

80

Echo Reservoir

Echo Dam Road

Center Street

0.9

Coalville

Summit County Fairgrounds

Chalk Creek

0.3

Main Street

32

Park Road

14.5

80

WASATCH RANGE

16.1

15.4

Hobson Lane

UP Rail Trail

Weber River

South Hoytsville Road

17.8

Creamery Lane

Hoytsville

West Hoytsville Road

20.4

19.3

Judd Lane

80

5.0 North end of reservoir; begin gradual descent.

5.4 Sharp curve to the right.

5.5 Pass under historic Union Pacific Railroad; I-80 freeway on the left.

5.8 Sharp bend to the left; now on Echo Canyon Road.

5.9 I-80 underpass.

6.0 Turn left (toward Echo), still on Echo Canyon Road.

6.3 Sharp curve to the right; now on Echo Road.

6.6 Veer right onto frontage road; enter Echo.

7.1 Bear left; turn left again at the stop sign to begin return ride on main highway (SR 86). Be careful crossing divided four-lane highway.

7.7 Sharp curve to the left.

8.3 At the stop sign at Echo Canyon Road, turn right.

8.4 I-80 underpass.

8.5 Sharp curve to the right; now on Echo Dam Road.

8.8 Pass under Union Pacific Railroad; sharp bend to the left.

9.0 Begin short climb.

9.3 Crest of climb at dam; Echo Reservoir now on the right.

10.5 Echo Marina on the right (lavatories).

12.2 South Beach Resort on the right (lavatories).

13.7 Enter Coalville.

14.5 Leave Coalville; now on South Hoytsville Road.

15.2 Enter Hoytsville.

15.4 Turn right onto Hobson Lane.

15.5 I-80 overpass.

16.0 Cross Weber River.

16.1 Sharp curve to the left. Now on West Hoytsville Road.

16.7 Begin gradual climb.

17.3 Begin gradual downhill with sharp curves.

17.8 At the stop sign at Creamery Lane, turn right, then make sharp bend left. Continue rolling terrain.

19.3 Turn left onto Judd Lane (no street sign).

19.8 I-80 overpass.

20.4 At the stop sign at South Hoytsville Road, turn left—continue rolling terrain.

23.4 Enter Coalville. Now on Main Street.

24.5 Turn right onto Center Street

24.7 Go straight at the stop sign at 100 East; now on Park Road (bumpy).

24.8 End of ride at Summit County Fairgrounds, where Park Road curves to right.

Local Information

Official Summit County Web site: www.co
.summit.ut.us.
Official city of Coalville Web site: www
.coalville.utah.gov.
Echo Reservoir information: www.waterquality
.utah.gov/watersheds/lakes/ECHO.pdf.

Restaurants

Denise's Home Plate: 49 North Main Street,
Coalville; (435) 336-2249.
Echo Café: 3595 South Echo Road, Echo;
(435) 336-5642.
Main Street Huddle: 38 South Main Street,
Coalville; (435) 336-4466.
Rodriguez Polar King: 128 North Main Street,
Coalville; (435) 336-2372.

Accommodations

Best Western Holiday Hills: 200 South 500
West, Coalville; (435) 336-4444 or (866)
922-7278; www.bwstay.com.
A Country Place: 99 South Main Street, Coal-
ville; (435) 336-2451 or (800) 371-2451;
www.acountryvacation.com.
Holiday Hills RV Park: Off I-80 at exit 162,
Coalville; (435) 336-4421; www.rvhills.com.
Moore's Motel: 90 South Main Street, Coal-
ville; (435) 336-5991.

Maps

DeLorme: Utah Atlas & Gazetteer: Page 18
C1.
Benchmark: Utah Road & Recreation Atlas:
Page 44 E2.

33 Heber Valley Ramble

The Heber Valley Ramble is a 20.5-mile ride that combines a 2-mile out-and-back
segment with a 16-mile loop through Heber Valley. The ride loops through Midway,
Heber City, Daniel, and Charleston in this "Switzerland of the West." The terrain is
never flat but features mostly gradual ascents and descents, and a few short climbs.
Elevations range from 5,425 feet in Charleston to 5,815 feet southeast of Heber City.
The ride takes place on state highways, city streets, and county roads, all having good
surfaces. A bike path adjacent one state highway segment is an alternative to riding
on that highway's shoulder.

Start: Harold P. Fabian Visitors Center, Wasatch
Mountain State Park, Homestead Drive at Warm
Springs Road at SR 222, Midway.
Length: 20.5 miles (loop, with a short out-and-
back segment at the start and finish).
Terrain: Gradual ascents and descents, with a
few false flats and rolling hills. Minimum and

maximum elevations: 5,425 to 5,815 feet.
Traffic and hazards: SR 113: 8,960 vehicles
per day through central Midway in 2005; 7,550
vehicles per day in Heber City; 2,725 vehicles
per day in Charleston. SR 222: 3,125 vehicles
per day near the SR 113 junction in Midway.

Getting there: From Salt Lake City: From I-80, exit at Silver Creek Junction and head south on
US 40. Turn right at the first signal onto River Road. Stay right at the first traffic circle and follow
the main road from there. Turn right onto Homestead Drive (SR 222). The Harold P. Fabian Visitor
Center is at the Homestead Drive/Warm Springs Road/SR 222 intersection. From Provo: From US
189, get onto SR 113. Once in Midway, follow SR 222, making several turns, to Homestead Drive.
The visitor center is located as described above.

The Ride

Heber Valley is nicknamed the "Switzerland of America" for good reasons: The lush, green agricultural valley is surrounded by ridges, rolling hills, and high mountains that are close enough to give the place a "snuggled" feel. Heber C. Kimball was a counselor to Brigham Young and is the source for the valley's name, as well as that of the main city. In my opinion, this is the most picturesque valley in Utah. Heber City, with a growing population of 9,830 in 2008, is the valley's central city. Midway, immediately to the west of Heber City, is a "suburb," having a population of 3,701 in 2008. The fringes of the valley are lined with small agricultural settlements and growing residential communities. In the southwest corner of the valley is Soldier Hollow, a cross-country skiing resort. The resort does not attract the large alpine skiing crowds, keeping the valley relaxed and peaceful (compared to Park City). Soldier Hollow was very busy, however, during the 2002 Winter Olympic Games, hosting all of the biathlon and cross-country skiing competitions. During the "off" season, Soldier Hollow hosts mountain biking and running events. Heber Valley was the site of a time trial stage in the 2006 Tour of Utah.

Heber Valley was investigated by Mormons in 1857. Initially, the men were fearful of harsh winters and year-round frost. Settlement eventually came in 1859; by 1862 a county incorporating Heber Valley, and stretching eastward to Colorado(!), had been established. Both Heber City and Midway were settled during the same period, both as pioneer towns, with families raising crops and tending livestock. A railroad connecting Heber City with Provo was completed in 1899. The train enhanced the economic potential of the valley. The railroad continues to operate, for fun, as the "Heber Creeper." The tracks, which no longer extend to Provo, terminate at Vivian Park (see the Alpine Loop Challenge). The Swiss look of the valley was perhaps an attraction to a number of Swiss immigrants, who settled in Midway in the late nineteenth century. "Swiss Days" are an annual event held during Labor Day in Midway. The buildings in modern-day "downtown" Midway emulate a Swiss architectural style. A geological oddity is a geothermal caldera located within Midway's corporate limits. The caldera is clearly visible on the grounds of the Homestead Resort on the west side of Midway.

The Heber Valley Ramble starts in Midway, passing through Heber City, Daniel, and Charleston. Charleston, located directly to the south of Midway, is incorporated, with a population of 457 in 2008. The northeastern fringe of Deer Creek State Park forms the western border of Charleston. From here, the Deer Creek Reservoir extends for about 7 miles toward the southeast. The lake features an abundance of trout, perch, walleye, and bass, making it a bonanza for anglers. Daniel is an unincorporated settlement. Although Daniel was an important biblical figure, the town of Daniel was named for Aaron Daniels, the community's first settler.

Start the ride at the Harold P. Fabian Visitor Center at Wasatch Mountain State Park, in the northeastern corner of Midway. The visitor center is located at the foot of

SR 222's descent from Guardsman Pass and Park City, both of which are to the north. Harold P. Fabian is recognized as the founder of the park. The park, covering 22,000 acres, was set aside in 1961 as a means of preserving the mountains adjacent Heber Valley. Begin by heading east on Homestead Drive (SR 222). The road promptly bends right to head south into Midway. Homestead Resort appears on the left at mile 0.6, including a geothermal caldera that is quite prominent. The natural dome, which resembles a miniature volcano, is partially filled with 90- to 95-degree F water that is used for diving, snorkeling, and other activities. The road heads downhill from here, bending left and then right to enter central Midway. Turn left onto Main Street at mile 2.0. Midway Town Hall is at 120 West Main Street. The building, featuring a Tudor Revival architecture, is on the National Register of Historic Places (NRHP). Pass the junction with SR 113 at mile 2.2. You are now on SR 113 and still on Main Street heading east. This is the starting point for the 16-mile, clockwise loop that makes up most of this ride. The Watkins–Coleman House, dating from the 1860s and on the NRHP, is at 5 East Main Street. Midway Social Hall, also used as an opera house and a Bishop's storehouse, is at 71 East Main Street. A series of houses owned by the Bonner clan, a family of Irish immigrants, is at 90, 103, and 110 East Main Street. All of these houses are on the NRHP. The Attewall Wooton Jr. House, dating from the nineteenth century and on the NRHP, is at 270 East Main Street.

A bend in the highway to the right at mile 3.1 signifies the limits of Midway. The highway bends left at mile 3.4, and the shoulder narrows. A parallel bike path, on the right, is an alternative to the highway. The path remains parallel to the highway until entering Heber City at mile 5.0. You are now on 100 South. The "highway" becomes decidedly residential, morphing into a tree-lined street through one of Heber City's central area neighborhoods. Continue across Main Street, past more of Heber City's homes. Turn left onto 500 East at mile 6.0 and then right onto Center Street at mile 6.1. Center Street begins a gradual climb into the foothills at mile 6.6. Turn right onto 2400 East at mile 7.6 and head south. The geology of the hills to your left consists of volcanic rock, while that of the hills on the horizon is built on the Oquirrh Formation, reaching a thickness of some 25,000 feet. Turn right onto 2400 South at mile 9.6 and head west. Note the antler arch at the adjacent private home. The road descends gradually. Turn left onto Mill Road (1200 East) at mile 10.7. Carefully cross US 40 at mile 10.9; continue southward to 3000 South. Make a right here and enter the small settlement of Daniel. Continue heading west. The variety in Utah's geology is quite evident in this ride; the side of the mountains toward which you are now heading is part of the Thaynes Formation, built up during the Triassic period. Turn left onto US 189 at mile 14.0. Wait for an opening before making the turn, since you will be making a right turn immediately after entering the highway, to continue heading westward on 3000 South.

Enter Charleston at mile 14.6. Charleston is actually "Charles' town," named for Charles Shelton, the original surveyor of the town site. Turn right onto SR 113 (3600 West) at mile 15.3 and head north. The highway has a narrow shoulder, but the daily traffic volume (2,725 vehicles per day in 2005) is low. The highway crosses over an inlet for the Deer Creek Reservoir at mile 15.8, passing through a wetlands area. A Heber Valley Railroad crossing is located at mile 16.9. The "Heber Creeper" typically makes five round-trips on Saturday and one or two round-trips on other days. The highway starts to climb gradually from here, as it enters Midway.

Turn left onto Main Street at mile 18.2, the starting point for SR 222. You have now completed the 16-mile loop and are returning to the starting point of the ride. Make a mental note of the marts and eateries as you ride through central Midway; it may be useful to return here for post-ride refreshment. Turn right onto 200 West at mile 18.4, then left onto 200 North at mile 18.7. Despite all of the turns, you are still on SR 222. The highway bends right at mile 19.3, becoming Homestead Drive. The road climbs gradually to mile 20.0, as you pass the Homestead Resort. Continue past the resort; the highway curves to the left at mile 20.4. Just beyond the turn is the intersection with Warm Springs Road (780 West). The Harold P. Fabian Visitor Center is on the right. The ride ends here, in the cradle of the Wasatch "Back."

Miles and Directions

0.0   Start at Harold P. Fabian Visitor Center, Wasatch Mountain State Park, Homestead Drive and Warm Springs Road and SR 222, Midway. Head east on Homestead Drive (SR 222). After 0.05 mile Homestead Drive bends right; now heading south.

0.6   Homestead Resort and geothermal caldera (dome) on the left.

1.2   Road bends left; now on 200 North (SR 222).

1.8   At the stop sign at 200 West, turn right (still on SR 222).

2.0   At the stop sign at Main Street, turn left (still on SR 222).

2.2   SR 113 junction; continue straight on Main Street—begin 16-mile loop.

3.1   Highway curves right; bike path on right. Leave Midway.

3.4   Highway curves left; shoulder narrows—use path on right as alternative.

5.0   Enter Heber City; now on 100 South.

5.5   Go straight at the traffic signal at Main Street—end SR 113.

5.7   Go straight at the yield sign at 200 East.

6.0   At the stop sign at 500 East, turn left.

6.1   At the stop sign at Center Street, turn right.

6.6   Begin gradual uphill.

7.6   Turn right onto 2400 East; now heading south.

8.6   Go straight at the stop sign at 1200 South.

9.6   At the stop sign at 2400 South, turn right. Begin gradual downhill.

10.7   Turn left onto Mill Road (1200 East).

10.9   Go straight at the stop sign at US 40.

11.2   At the stop sign at 3000 South, turn right (enter Daniel).

12.2   Go straight at the stop sign at Daniel Road.

13.2   Go straight at the stop sign at South Field Road (1200 East).

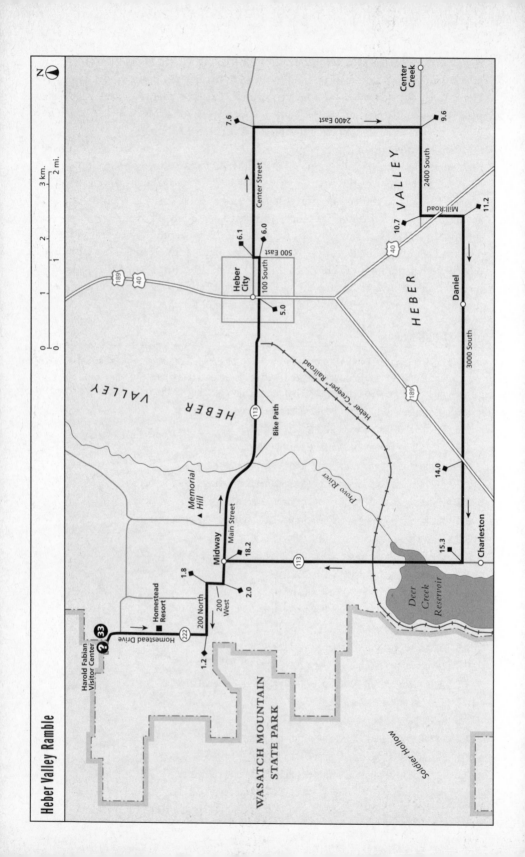

Heber Valley Ramble

14.0   At the stop sign at US 189, bear left (watch for traffic).

14.1   Bear right to continue on 3000 South.

14.6   Enter Charleston (no sign).

15.3   At the stop sign at SR 113 (3600 West), turn right.

15.8   Bridge across Deer Creek Reservoir inlet; leave Charleston.

16.9   Railroad crossing (one track).

17.1   Begin gradual uphill.

17.6   Enter Midway.

18.2   At the stop sign at Main Street (SR 222), turn left. End of 16-mile loop.

18.4   At the stop sign at 200 West, turn right (still on SR 222).

18.7   Road bends left; now on 200 North (still on SR 222).

19.1   Begin short climb.

19.3   Road bends right; now on Homestead Drive (SR 222).

19.7   Homestead Resort on the right.

20.0   Crest of climb.

20.4   Road bends left.

20.5   End of ride at Warm Springs Road and Harold P. Fabian Visitor Center.

Local Information

Town of Daniel Web site: http://danielutah.org.
City of Midway official Web site: http://midwaycityut.org.
Deer Creek State Park information: http://stateparks.utah.gov/parks/deer-creek.
Wasatch Mountain State Park information: http://stateparks.utah.gov/parks/wasatch/.
City of Heber City official Web site: www.ci.heber.ut.us.

Restaurants

Blue Boar Inn & Restaurant: 1235 Warm Springs Road, Midway; (435) 654-1400; www.theblueboarinn.com/dining/index.html.
Homestead Resort Restaurants (Fanny's Grill and Simon's Restaurant): 700 North Homestead Drive, Midway; (435) 654-1102; www.homesteadresort.com/dining.
Tarahumara: 380 East Main Street, Midway; (435) 654-3465; http://Tarahumara.biz.

Accommodations

The Blue Boar Inn: 1235 Warm Springs Road, Midway; (435) 654-1400 or (888) 650-1400; www.theblueboarinn.com.

Homestead Resort: 700 North Homestead Drive, Midway; (435) 654-1102 or (888) 327-7220; www.homesteadresort.com.
Inn on the Creek: 375 Rainbow Lane, Midway; (435) 654-0892; www.innonthecreek.com.
WorldMark by Wyndham: 868 West Lime Canyon Road, Midway; (435) 654-9234; http://trendwest.com/resorts/mw/ or www.worldmarktheclub.com/resorts/mw.
Zermatt Dolce (resort and spa): 784 West Resort Drive (800 North), Midway; (866) 643-2015; http://zermattresort.com.
There is camping in Wasatch Mountain State Park (five campgrounds): (435) 654-1791; http://stateparks.utah.gov/parks/wasatch.

Bicycle Shop

Brother's Bikes, 520 North Main Street, Heber City; (435) 657-9570; http://brothersbikes.com.

Maps

Rand McNally: Salt Lake City Street Guide: including Logan, Ogden, and Provo: Pages 194, 195, 206, and 207 GK99 on page 194.

34 Hobble Creek Canyon Cruise

The Hobble Creek Canyon Cruise is a 26.2-mile out-and-back ride up and down a canyon that features a gradual climb outbound and a gradual descent inbound. The ride starts and finishes at Kolob Park in Springville, a Provo suburb. The elevation ranges from 4,620 feet at Kolob Park to 6,070 feet at the turnaround, in Right Fork Hobble Creek Canyon. The route is on city streets and forest roads; the road surface is in good condition in and near the city of Springville; it is in fair condition deep within the Hobble Creek Wildlife Management Area.

Start: Kolob Park, 600 South 700 East, Springville.
Length: 26.2 miles (out-and-back).
Terrain: Steady ascent to the turnaround, followed by a descent. Minimum and maximum elevations: 4,620 to 6,070 feet.

Traffic and hazards: 400 South: 11,645 vehicles per day near Canyon Road in 2006. Canyon Road: 5,810 vehicles per day west of 1700 East; 2,460 vehicles per day east of 1700 East.

Getting there: From I-15, take exit 260 (Springville) and head east on 400 South (SR 77), into Springville. Turn right on 600 East and head south, past the church, to Kolob Park. Or take Utah Transit Authority route 820 or 822 from Brigham Young University in Provo to 400 South in Springville. Buses run every thirty minutes to two hours, depending on the time of day. Only route 822 runs on Saturday (hourly).

The Ride

The legend is that, on one night in 1849, Barney Ward and Oliver B. Huntington hobbled their horses (i.e., tied their legs together) in present-day Springville. Sometime during the night, the horses broke free and started moving up the adjacent canyon. Huntington eventually caught up to the horses, prompting the naming of the canyon as Hobble Creek. The creek drains from the mountains into Utah Lake, located to the west. The creek was an important water source for the Springville settlement, established in 1850. Today, Springville is one of Provo's growing "southern" suburbs, with a population of 28,520 in 2008. Springville is known as "Art City," in part because of the Springville Museum of Art (Utah's oldest museum) and a wonderful collection of outdoor sculptures. The city was also the birthplace of Cyrus Dallin, sculptor of the angel Moroni that rests atop the Salt Lake City Temple. Despite his contributions to the Utah arts community and Mormon church stateliness, Dallin was not Mormon and actually had another life as a world-class archer (bronze medal in the 1904 Olympic Games).

Hobble Creek Canyon is hugged by Powerhouse Mountain (elevation 7,990 feet) to the north and Ether Peak (elevation 7,533 feet) to the south. The canyon scenery is typical of that found in northern Utah: deep forestation mixed with open, often

Ready for the road (and the trails) in Hobble Creek Canyon.

pastoral areas, with a meandering creek or river flowing nearby. During certain times of the year—especially mid-fall—the plants and trees are awash in incredibly bright colors. It is also typical for the canyon geology to be "hidden" underneath the overgrowth, but with areas occasionally exposed to reveal eroded cliffs and dramatic rockfaces. All of these visual phenomena can be seen in Hobble Creek Canyon. Canyon flora and fauna are also typical of those found in northern Utah: pinyon pines and junipers giving way to evergreens as the altitude increases.

The ride starts at Kolob Park in Springville, at 600 South 700 East. The park is located immediately to the south of a church; the park's parking lot appears to blend in with that of the church. Kolob, according to Mormon doctrine, is the name of the star at the center of the universe. Head north on 700 East; the road jogs left and then right, becoming Averett Avenue. Turn right onto 400 South and head east. The road begins to climb, steeply then gradually, as you head toward the Springville "bench." Turn right onto 1300 East at mile 0.8. The road curves left, becoming Canyon Road at mile 1.4. A bike path begins on the right at mile 1.9. The path begins as little more than a sidewalk, but transforms into a separate path after leaving the residential areas of Springville. The path is an alternative to the roadway and may be a respite from seasonally heavy recreational traffic. Enter Hobble Creek Canyon at mile 2.5. Mountains rise high to the left and right as the canyon walls close in. The canyon walls are never "snug," however, leaving plenty of room for open space recreation (such as the Hobble Creek Canyon Golf Course just up the canyon, voted by *Deseret News* readers

Hobble Creek Canyon Cruise

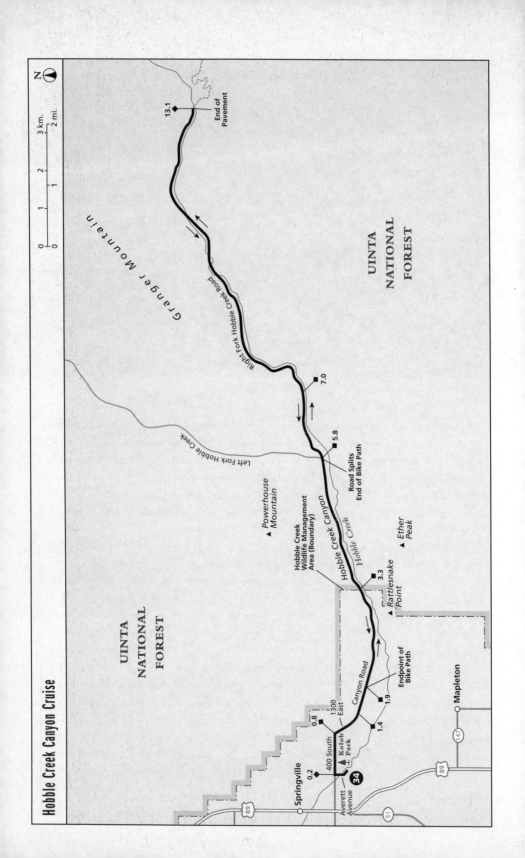

N

0 1 2 3 km.
0   1   2 mi.

Granger Mountain

UINTA
NATIONAL
FOREST

UINTA NATIONAL FOREST

End of Pavement

13.1

Right Fork Hobble Creek Road

Left Fork Hobble Creek

7.0

5.8

Road Splits
End of Bike Path

Powerhouse Mountain

Hobble Creek Wildlife Management Area (Boundary)

Hobble Creek Canyon

Hobble Creek

Ether Peak

3.3

Rattlesnake Point

Canyon Road

Endpoint of Bike Path

1.9

1.4

1300 East

0.8

400 South

Kolob Park

0.2

Springville

34

Averett Avenue

Mapleton

147

89

89

51

as the most beautiful in Utah). Enter the Hobble Creek Wildlife Management Area at mile 3.3. An information placard, with maps, is on the right at mile 4.3. You should not need a map if you stay on the main canyon road, however. The bike path crosses Canyon Road at mile 4.7 and continues on the left side of the road. The road splits at mile 5.8; to the left is Left Fork Hobble Creek Road, and to the right is Right Fork Hobble Creek Road. Bear right here. The bike path ends. Kelly's Grove is on the right, and Rotary Park is on the left.

As you head up the Right Fork road, the pavement surface condition deteriorates to "fair." Enter Uinta National Forest at mile 7.0. The road narrows at mile 9.8; stay right, and be cognizant of oncoming vehicles. The climb also gets steeper here. You will pass a number of campgrounds and recreational spots along the way, but you should find this portion of the ride to be, in general, quiet. Most of the campgrounds have lavatories. The pavement ends at a bridge over Right Fork Hobble Creek. The dirt road continues from here; pavement actually resumes after 8 miles, as the road enters Diamond Fork Canyon. The mountain in the foreground, to the right, is Pumphouse Hill (elevation 8,238 feet). Turn around here, at mile 13.1, to begin the canyon descent.

The canyon descent is initially fast, but the gradient eases at mile 16.7. The pavement surface improves at this point. From here, you will have to do more than coast to move at a decent speed. Exit Uinta National Forest at mile 19.1. The right and left forks of Hobble Creek merge at mile 20.5, adjacent Rotary Park and Kelly's Grove. Bear left here to return to Canyon Road. The parallel bike path is on the right. The bike path crosses the road at mile 21.5, and is on the left from here. Exit Hobble Creek Canyon at mile 22.9, to return to civilization. The bike path ends at mile 23.5, but a bike lane makes the road bike-friendly. Continue the gradual descent of Canyon Road, into Springville's residential areas. Turn left onto 400 South, at the stop sign, for the final descent of the ride. Look for Averett Avenue at mile 26.0; turn left here and head south. The street jogs left and then right, becoming 700 East, seemingly emptying into a parking area. Kolob Park is on the left, where the ride ends.

Miles and Directions

0.0 Start at Kolob Park, 600 South 700 East, in Springville. Head north on 700 East; the road jogs left, then right, becoming Averett Avenue.

0.2 At the stop sign at 400 South, turn right.

0.4 Begin short climb.

0.8 At the stop sign at 1300 East, turn right.

1.4 Now on Canyon Road; continue gradual climb.

1.9 Begin bike path (on the right).

2.5 Enter Hobble Creek Canyon.

3.3 Enter Hobble Creek Wildlife Management Area.

4.3 Information center, with maps, on the right.

4.7 Bike path crosses Canyon Road.

5.6 Kelly's Grove (restrooms) on the right.

5.8 Bear right at fork in road (Right Fork Hobble Creek Canyon); Rotary Park on the left. Bike path ends.

6.2 Road surface deteriorates to "fair."

6.9 Cattle guard.

7.0 Enter Uinta National Forest.

7.2 Cherry Campground on the right.

9.5 Climb gets steeper.

9.8 Road narrows.

11.5 Cattle guard.

12.4 Balsam Campground on the right (restrooms).

13.1 End of pavement at bridge; turn around here—begin descent.

13.6 Restrooms on the left (Balsam Campground).

14.6 Cattle guard.

19.1 Leave Uinta National Forest.

19.2 Cattle guard.

19.3 Cherry Campground on the left.

20.5 Merge with road from Left Fork Hobble Creek Canyon; now on Canyon Road.

20.8 Begin bike path on the right.

21.5 Bike path crosses road.

22.9 Exit Hobble Creek Canyon.

23.5 End bike path (on the left); cross road and return to right shoulder (if path was used).

24.8 Begin bike lane.

25.3 At the stop sign at 400 South, turn left—continue descent.

26.0 Turn left onto Averett Avenue.

26.2 End of ride at Kolob Park, on the left.

Local Information

Uinta National Forest information, USDA Forest Service: www.fs.fed.us/r4/uinta.

City of Springville official Web site: www.springville.org.

Hobble Creek Canyon bike path information: www.utahmountainbiking.com/trails/hobble creek.htm.

Restaurants

Art City Trolley: 256 North Main Street, Springville; (801) 489-8585.

Ginger's Garden Café: 188 South Main Street, Springville; (888) 372-4372; www.gingers gardencafe.com.

Joe Dandito's Mexican Fiestaurant: 1435 North Main Street, Springville; (801) 853-1500.

MKH Restaurants: 717 North Main Street, Springville; (801) 491-2946.

Steak & Everything Grill: 759 East 400 South, Springville; (801) 491-5098.

Timber Wolf Grill: 5496 East Hobble Creek Canyon Road (Hobble Creek Golf Course clubhouse), Springville; (801) 489-2783.

Accommodations

Best Western Mountain View Inn: 1455 North 1750 West, Springville; (801) 489-3641; http://bestwesternutah.com/hotels/best-western-mountain-view-inn/.

Days Inn: 520 South 2000 West, Springville; (801) 491-0300.

Springville Motel & Apartments: 282 North Main Street, Springville; (801) 489-9997 or (801) 491-6911.

There are campgrounds in Hobble Creek Canyon, as noted above: (801) 798-3571 or (801) 226-3564.

Bicycle Shop

Blayn's Cycling Service: 284 South Main Street, Springville; (801) 489-5106; www .blaynsperformancecycling.com.

Maps

DeLorme: Utah Atlas & Gazetteer: Pages 25–26 C8 on page 25.

Rand McNally: Salt Lake City Street Guide: including Logan, Ogden, and Provo: Pages 3143 and 3144 D3 on page 3143.

Benchmark: Utah Road & Recreation Atlas: Pages 51–52 E11 on page 51.

Panoramaland

Panoramaland—the name suggests that Utah is a giant theme park—covers west-central Utah, including Juab, Millard, Piute, Sanpete, Sevier, and Wayne Counties. Panoramaland is unique among Utah's regions in that the territory extends into the Colorado Plateau, gallops over the Wasatch Plateau, and stretches out onto the Great Basin. It is Utah's second-largest region, at 17,043 square miles. The region's population was about 71,592 in 2008, with about half of the population concentrated in nine cities, each having a population of over 2,000: Delta, Ephraim, Fillmore, Gunnison, Manti, Mt. Pleasant, Nephi, Richfield, and Salina. The largest city in Panoramaland is Richfield, which had a population of 7,217 in 2008. The other half of the population is scattered about countless small cities and towns, as well as unincorporated settlements. The economy is primarily agrarian, mining, and services-oriented, with the latter directed in part at the abundant recreational opportunities. Snow College, a two-year college located in Ephraim, serves as a starting point for a large number of Utah students who are bound for four-year colleges and universities elsewhere.

Panoramaland includes arguably the widest range of scenery of all of Utah's regions. Capitol Reef National Park is a highlight of the eastern "handle" of the region; Fishlake and Manti-La Sal National Forests blanket the mountains of the Wasatch Plateau in the center of the region, and the former lakebed of ancient Lake Bonneville dominates the western part of the region. The lakebed—now part of the Great Basin Desert—is not entirely flat and uninteresting, however. Several small mountain ranges are found here, including some with particularly intriguing names: Black Rock Hills, Confusion Range, and the Wah Wah Mountains are a few. Numerous valleys are positioned between the mountain ranges; some of the larger valleys are important population centers. These include Juab, which is home to Nephi; Pahvant, where Fillmore is located; Sanpete (Ephraim, Manti, Mount Pleasant); and Sevier (Richfield, Salina). Delta is one of the few large towns—in Utah and Nevada—in the Great Basin Desert (the desert continues beyond the state line, stretching westward across Nevada). Elevations in Panoramaland range from about 4,500 feet at Sevier Lake in Millard County to 12,139 feet in the Tushar Mountains, on the border between Piute and Beaver Counties. The six Panoramaland rides take in many of the region's major towns, along with the major attractions. Enjoy the panoramas.

35 Bicentennial Highway Classic

The Bicentennial Highway Classic is a 106.3-mile out-and-back ride over long false flats and rolling terrain that starts and finishes in Hanksville. Try not to be dissuaded by the length; the exciting scenery will help replenish some of your energy. The elevation ranges from 3,730 feet at the Hite Marina to 5,173 feet in the Poison Spring Benches. At the risk of sounding too mystical, there is a rejuvenating quality in riding in the clear air through this untamed, unabashed scenery. The ride is entirely on a state highway (SR 95) and a National Park Service road, so the pavement surface is generally smooth.

Start: Bureau of Land Management (BLM) office on 100 West, 0.5 mile south of SR 24 in Hanksville.
Length: 106.3 miles (out-and-back).
Terrain: Long, false flats and rolling terrain.

Minimum and maximum elevations: 3,730 to 5,173 feet.
Traffic and hazards: US 95: 685 vehicles per day south of Hanksville in 2005; 370 vehicles per day north of Hite.

Getting there: From I-70, take exit 149 and head south on SR 24 to Hanksville.

The Ride

The Bicentennial Highway, SR 95, was completed in 1976, the year of the U.S. bicentennial. The highway has otherwise little to do with U.S. independence or any bicentennial celebrations. The highway begins in Hanksville, at its junction with SR 24, and continues southeasterly to Blanding, 133 miles away. The countryside is remarkably scenic and can be thoroughly enjoyed with little interference from traffic: Fewer than 700 vehicles per day were using the highway in 2005. The highway is part of the Trail of the Ancients Scenic Byway. The largest town for miles around—actually the only town—is Hanksville. The town had a population of 204 in 2008. The town was named after Ebenezer Hanks, who moved here from Parowan (seat of Iron County) with several other families in 1882 after hearing about the valley's possibilities. Prior to its formal settlement, Hanksville was a focal point of Robbers Roost Country, which served as a hideout for Butch Cassidy and his Wild Bunch. Electricity arrived in 1960, and incorporation came in 1999. The town was a popular base during World War II when the search was on for uranium. There are a number of abandoned mines scattered about the hills surrounding the town. Today, Hanksville is a convenient base for exploration in the region: The San Rafael Swell and Goblin Valley are to the north, Capitol Reef National Park is to the west, and Lake Powell and Glen Canyon National Recreation Area are to the south. There is plenty in between, too, including the San Rafael Desert to the northeast and the imposing Henry Mountains to the south. The confluence of the Fremont River, Muddy Creek, and Dirty Devil

River is located just north of Hanksville and the SR 95/SR 24 junction. The Dirty Devil River flows south from here, eventually converging with the Colorado River at the northern tip of Lake Powell. The river's name originated from a vivid description provided by a member of John Wesley Powell's 1869 expedition party. Powell attempted to change the name to the Fremont River, since the two rivers merge near Hanksville, but the Dirty Devil moniker was more popular.

The ride begins in Hanksville (elevation 4,125 feet) at the Bureau of Land Management office. Park in the small visitor lot just south of 100 West and 360 South. Head north on 100 West; turn right onto SR 24 at mile 0.5. Head east through "central" Hanksville; there are several mini-marts here at which provisions can be obtained. The highway veers right at the edge of town, becoming SR 95 (continuing on SR 24 requires a left turn at the junction). The remoteness of Hanksville is quite evident after making this turn, because the horizon is unblemished as far as the eye can see! Begin climbing; notice the "goblin" and castle rock formations along the roadsides. This is a windswept landscape that changes with the shifting silt and sand. The "goblins" are generally small, dome-shaped sand dunes that are held in place by clusters of plants. The ominous range in the distance is the Henry Mountains. The highway crests at mile 4.0. From here, the highway begins a long series of false flats and long pitches through typical Utah desert scrub. The Henry Mountains "accompany" you on this journey, remaining on your right for a little over 20 miles. The peak is Mount Ellen, which tops out at 11,506 feet. Bull Mountain, at 9,178 feet, is in the foreground and may obscure the view of Mount Ellen. Enter Garfield County at mile 17.5. Note the rugged, reddish landscape, as the highway enters a formation of Jurassic rocks. The landscape becomes even more sculpted beyond mile 21.0 as the highway enters the Poison Spring Benches. There is an intrusion of white and coral-pink Navajo sandstone here. As in other parts of Utah, the erosion of this sandstone can present an astonishing appearance. Little Egypt is on the right, so named because it reminded explorers of the Egyptian sphinx. The Seeps Wash (usually dry) runs next to the highway. The junction with SR 276 is at mile 27.6; keep straight here, on SR 95. The shoulder narrows.

The highway begins to descend through North Wash Canyon. A second type of sandstone, Wingate, is now evident in layers below the Navajo sandstone. The sheer walls, erosion, and cavelike indentations make the length of this ride well worth the energy expense. There are restrooms at Hog Springs Rest Area (mile 34.9). As the highway descends, the stone formations seem to grow taller. Actually, they are: Now the bluish and purple mudstone of the Chinle Formation shows up underneath the Wingate sandstone. Dark red-brown marine siltstone of the Moenkopi Formation eventually appears below the Chinle. Enter Glen Canyon National Recreation Area at mile 38.1. You might swear that you have entered Capitol Reef National Park; the resemblance is remarkable. Rolling terrain begins at mile 41.7, followed by an 8 percent downgrade at mile 42.9. The highway descends through a spectacular cut that

Gateway to Hite Marina and Glen Canyon, at the far eastern end of Lake Powell.

clearly shows the layering of millions of years of uplifts and erosion. Enter a natural "gate" at mile 44.0; the terrain rolls from here. Petrified dunes—similar to those seen in Arches National Park—are abundant in this area. Cross the Dirty Devil River on a marvelous steel bridge at mile 47.2, followed by a Colorado River crossing at mile 49.3. With these two bridges behind you, you have rounded the northernmost "horn" of Lake Powell. The highway begins to climb through an otherworldly landscape of petrified dunes. Turn right at mile 50.6 toward Hite (unnamed road). A Glen Canyon National Recreation Area sign greets you after the turn. Enter Hite at mile 51.9 (elevation 3,900 feet). This is a small marina community that is a "relocated" version of the original Hite, which is now literally under Lake Powell. The original Hite was established by Cass Hite, a prospector and (male) member of the Quantrill Civil War guerillas. He was considered to be an outlaw. The community was located at an important ferry crossing of the Colorado River. The ferry was discontinued with the construction of the Glen Canyon Dam near Page, Arizona.

There is a small grocery store on the left at mile 52.2. Continue traveling toward the boat launch, straight ahead, at mile 53.0. There are restrooms here, and after making a left and traveling to the end of the pavement (mile 53.3), there are additional restrooms. Turn around here and begin the return ride. Notice the towering monuments on the horizon. Continue to SR 95 (mile 55.7); turn left and begin the long trip north. The highway descends to the Colorado River crossing (mile 56.8), then

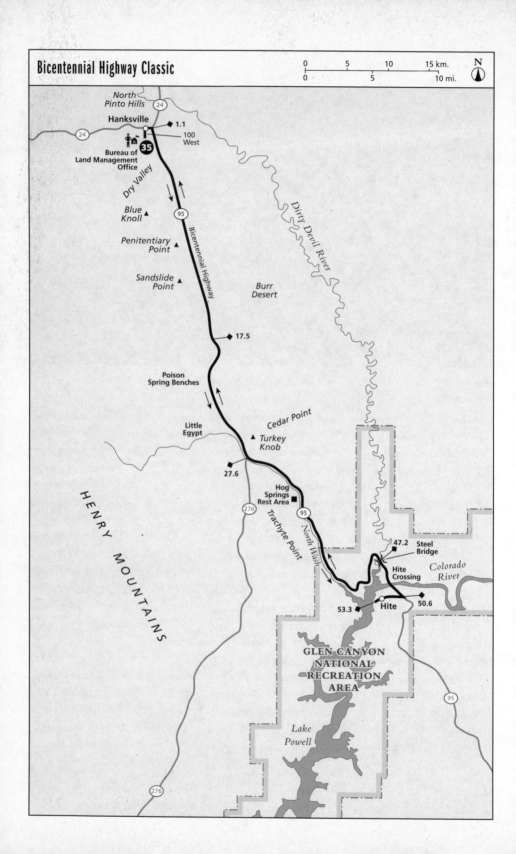

Bicentennial Highway Classic

0 — 5 — 10 — 15 km.
0 — 5 — 10 mi.

N

North
Pinto Hills
24

Hanksville
35
Bureau of
Land Management
Office

♦ 1.1
100
West

Dry Valley

Blue
Knoll ▲

95

Penitentiary
Point ▲

Sandslide
Point ▲

Bicentennial Highway

Burr
Desert

Dirty Devil River

♦ 17.5

Poison
Spring Benches

Little
Egypt

Cedar Point

▲ Turkey
Knob

♦ 27.6

276

Hog
Springs
Rest Area

95

North Wash

Tractyre Point

H E N R Y   M O U N T A I N S

♦ 47.2   Steel
Bridge

Hite
Crossing

Colorado
River

53.3 ♦   Hite   50.6 ♦

95

GLEN CANYON
NATIONAL
RECREATION
AREA

Lake
Powell

276

rolls to the Dirty Devil River crossing (mile 59.0). There are restrooms on the left at mile 60.5. Ascend through an awesome excavation that, although unnatural, reveals the ground's underlying striations in a functional way. Observe the changing colors all along the highway: Blue, purple, brown, red, pink, and white are all found through here before giving way to the beige and cream of the open desert. Pass through the "gate" at mile 62.1 and continue to climb. The highway crests at mile 63.3. An 8 percent downhill follows at mile 64.4. Leave the Glen Canyon National Recreation Area at mile 68.1. Low trees and sheer canyon walls dominate the scene for the next few miles. The Hog Springs Picnic Area (restrooms) is on the left at mile 71.3. Note the pockmarks in the rocks—spooked explorers thought that there were eyes inside the formations, staring back. The junction with SR 276 is at mile 78.5. Continue straight on SR 95 (although signs may say west, the prevailing direction of travel is north). The shoulder widens here. The Henry Mountains come into close view on the left at mile 80.2, as the highway returns to the Poison Spring Benches. The landscape soon changes to wide-open, expansive desert, with long pitches and false flats.

Enter Wayne County at mile 88.7. At various points, the highway appears to stretch into infinity. "What's out there?"—well, you know what is, but pretending that you don't know, and truthfully forgetting some of the details keeps you moving toward that horizon. Goblin formations—small, dome-shaped sand dunes—begin to appear at mile 103.8. The highway speed limit reduces as you approach Hanksville. The SR 24 junction is at mile 105.1; keep straight here to continue on SR 24 east. There are mini-marts adjacent the junction. Ride through town and turn left onto 100 West at mile 105.7. Head south on 100 West; pavement surface roughens at mile 106.0, but it is only another 0.3 mile to the BLM office and the end of the ride.

Miles and Directions

0.0 Start at the BLM office at 100 West and 360 South in Hanksville. Head north on 100 West.

0.5 At the stop sign, turn right onto SR 24.

1.1 Highway veers to the right; now on SR 95. Several mini-marts near this junction.

1.6 Cattle guard; begin upgrade.

4.0 Crest of climb; begin false flats.

12.4 Cattle guard.

17.5 Enter Garfield County; continue rolling terrain with long pitches.

19.8 Cattle guard.

23.5 Begin downgrade.

24.8 Cattle guard.

27.5 Cattle guard.

27.6 SR 276 junction; continue straight on SR 95.

27.8 Shoulder narrows.

29.4 Cattle guard.

34.9 Hog Springs Rest Area on the right (restrooms).

38.1 Enter Glen Canyon National Recreation Area.

41.4 Begin upgrade.

41.7 Crest; begin rolling terrain.

42.9 Begin 8 percent downhill.

44.2 End downhill; begin false flats and rolling terrain.

45.7 Restrooms on the right.

47.2 Cross the Dirty Devil River (steel bridge).

49.3 Cross the Colorado River (Hite Crossing Bridge); begin climb.

50.6 Turn right onto unnamed road toward Hite; Glen Canyon National Recreation Area sign near turn.

51.9 Small residential area on the left.

52.2 Grocery store on the left.

53.0 Restrooms on the right; boat launch ahead—curve left.

53.3 End of paved road; restrooms on the left. Turn around here and begin return trip.

54.0 Grocery store on the right.

55.7 At the stop sign at SR 95, turn left—begin downhill.

56.8 Colorado River crossing.

56.9 Begin climb.

57.9 Crest of climb; begin rolling terrain.

59.0 Dirty Devil River crossing (steel bridge).

60.5 Restrooms on the left.

62.1 Begin climb.

63.3 Crest of climb.

64.4 Begin 8 percent downgrade.

68.1 Leave Glen Canyon National Recreation Area.

71.3 Hog Springs Rest Area on the left (restrooms).

76.8 Cattle guard.

78.5 SR 276 junction; continue north on SR 95—shoulder widens.

78.7 Cattle guard.

81.4 Cattle guard.

86.4 Cattle guard; false flats and long pitches.

88.7 Enter Wayne County.

93.8 Cattle guard.

104.5 Cattle guard.

105.1 Continue straight as highway veers left; now on SR 24 (enter Hanksville).

105.7 Turn left onto 100 West.

106.0 Road surface gets rougher.

106.3 End of ride at 360 South, at BLM office.

Local Information

Town of Hanksville official Web site: www
.hanksville.com.

**Glen Canyon National Recreation Area,
National Park Service:** www.nps.gov/glca.

Restaurants

Blondie's Eatery & Gift: 300 North Highway
95, Hanksville; (435) 542-3255.

Duke's Slick Rock Grill: 68 East 100 North,
Hanksville; (435) 542-3441.

Red Rock Restaurant & Campground: 226
East 100 North, Hanksville; (435) 542-3235;
www.redrockcampground.net. Open March 15
through November 1.

Red Rock Steak House (at Hanksville Inn):
280 East 100 North, Hanksville; (435) 542-
3471; www.hanksvilleinn.com.

Accommodations

Hanksville Inn: 280 East 100 North, Hanksville; (435) 542-3471; www.hanksvilleinn.com.

Red Rock Restaurant & Campground: 226
East 100 North, Hanksville; (435) 542-3235;
www.redrockcampground.net. Open March 15
through November 1.

Whispering Sands Motel: 90 South Highway
95, Hanksville; (435) 542-3238; http://www
.whisperingsandsmotel.com.

Maps

DeLorme: Utah Atlas & Gazetteer: Pages 45,
53 E5 on page 45.

Benchmark: Utah Road & Recreation Atlas:
Page 77 A8.

36 Capitol Reef Country Cruise

The Capitol Reef Country Cruise is a 38.4–mile lollipop–shaped route 11 miles
outbound, followed by a 16–mile loop, then 11 miles inbound. The historic town of
Fruita serves as the base, as the ride visits Torrey, Teasdale, and the Capitol Reef environs (without entering the main park). Although this is a "cruise," the route is actually
quite hilly; the total length is shorter than that of a typical challenge, however. The
climbing starts immediately, leaving the second half of the course for "cruising."

Start: Fruita, historic pioneer town on Capitol
Reef Scenic Drive in Capitol Reef National Park.

Length: 38.4 miles (lollipop, with a 16-mile
loop serving as the turnaround).

Terrain: Rolling hills at high altitude (5,418
feet in Fruita; 7,125 feet in Teasdale).

Traffic and hazards: SR 24: 930 vehicles per
day between Capitol Reef and Torrey in 2005;
1,230 vehicles per day in Torrey. SR 12: 435
vehicles per day approaching Torrey from the
south.

Getting there: From I-70, take exit 149 to SR 24 west (actually south); travel to Hanksville,
then head west (on SR 24) to Fruita. Alternatively, take exit 48 from I-70 to SR 24 east (actually
south) near Richfield; continue through Loa, Bicknell, and Torrey to Fruita.

The Ride

Capitol Reef is an awe-inspiring national park located primarily in Wayne County, in south-central Utah. Unlike in Bryce Canyon, where the scenic drive looks down into the canyon, in Capitol Reef the alignment allows the traveler to look up at the monoliths. Capitol Reef's name reflects the combination of two perspectives on what is seen: Explorers thought that the rounded sandstone hills and buttes reminded them of the U.S. Capitol in Washington, D.C., while the uplifts and spires presented a barrier to travel that made explorers think of a coral reef in the ocean. The land was squeezed upward some seventy million years ago by gigantic seismic forces. Over time, erosion has carved the mammoth uplifts into arches, spires, and "thrones." If the land can be thought of as a large piece of paper, then Capitol Reef is a fold in the paper—in fact, the major geological feature of the Reef is Waterpocket Fold, which runs for about 100 miles from Thousand Lake Mountain in the north to Lake Powell in the south. The fold adds a vertical dimension to the "paper," although the surrounding landscape is certainly not flat!

Capitol Reef National Park was originally a state park called "Wayne Wonderland," established in the early 1900s. The state park became Capitol Reef National Monument in 1937, then a national park in 1971 following the growth in its stature after the development of Lake Powell, to the south. The park is not the most-visited in Utah—Arches, Bryce Canyon, Zion, and others all get more visitors. But this is a special place for the visitors who do come here, and there are probably a large number of returnees. The area—"Capitol Reef Country"—was relatively isolated until SR 24 was completed in 1962. The highway connects with I-70 toward the northeast, near Green River. The highway heads southwest from there, turns west at Hanksville, and runs from the east to the west side of the region before turning northward to meet up with I-70 once again, near Salina and Richfield. A scenic drive takes visitors through Capitol Reef, allowing one to get quite up-close-and-personal with the footings of the Reef's enormous "thrones." The drive, although paved, is not really suitable for road biking, as there are numerous wash crossings. Also, the road gets very narrow and twisty, making life a bit uncomfortable for the cyclist who happens to meet up with a motor vehicle.

The ride concentrates on Capitol Reef "country" and Fruita, which is a historic town located just inside the park. Fruita was a pioneer town established in 1878, eventually peaking during the 1920s and 1930s with the development of the local fruit industry. Once Fruita was absorbed by Capitol Reef, the town's population dwindled. Today, a number of old buildings, including a one-room schoolhouse, still exist as museum pieces. Long before the settlement of Fruita, the area was inhabited by Fremont and Paiute tribes. The Fremonts were nomads, so they left only traces of their inhabitance. Pioneer-era outlaws found the region particularly appealing for its numerous hideout possibilities.

Remarkable rock formation in Teasdale, near Capitol Reef.

Start in Fruita, at the parking lot (actually the overflow lot) just north of the Clifford Trail Visitor Center. Note that Fruita is located 1 mile south of the Capitol Reef National Park Visitor Center, so it is physically inside the park. There is no fee to enter Fruita. Deer are plentiful in this area. There are several rustic structures dating from Fruita's "heyday"—maybe "hay-day" is more appropriate—including a barn, blacksmith shop, and schoolhouse. The town is a popular tourist spot during the summer, so watch out for moving, turning, and parking vehicles. The entire town is on the National Register of Historic Places (NRHP) as the Fruita Rural Historic District. Head north on Scenic Drive. The road parallels Capitol Reef (i.e., Waterpocket Fold), with massive uplifts on your right. The visitor center is on the left at mile 0.9; you can get fluids and use the lavatories here. At mile 1.0, turn left onto SR 24 (Capitol Reef Country Scenic Byway).

. After crossing the Fremont River at mile 1.2, the climbing begins. The first climb is a steady 2 miles. The colors are vivid, as is the harshness of the landscape. The staggering scenery can make you forget about the exertion. The crest is reached at mile 3.4; the landscape changes to a typical Utah desert scene: scrub and low trees. Chimney Rock is on the right at mile 4.1; there are lavatory facilities. The terrain is rolling from this point. At mile 5.8, the landscape changes again, returning to the rugged, rocky scenes that are bountiful in this area. There are numerous interesting formations along here, including balanced rocks—large rocks that appear to be teetering on top of other rocks. The highway climbs again at mile 7.1, cresting at 7.6. Lodging

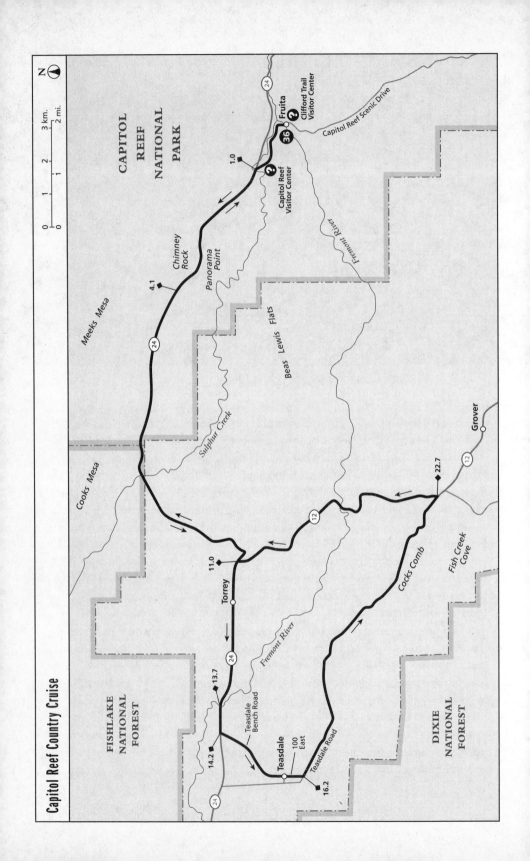

Capitol Reef Country Cruise

and dining facilities begin to appear at mile 8.7 as you approach the town of Torrey. The highway climbs again at mile 10.0, cresting at mile 10.8. The junction with SR 12 is at mile 11.0; keep straight here, although you will return to this junction after completing a 16-mile loop. Enter Torrey at mile 11.4

Torrey (population 191 in 2008; elevation 6,836 feet) serves as a gateway community to Capitol Reef. The town was established in the 1880s by Mormon pioneers and was named in honor of Colonel Torrey, one of Theodore Roosevelt's Rough Riders who fought in the Spanish-American War. The town's tree-lined Main Street is particularly attractive. Continue through town on that main street; the highway continues to climb, albeit gradually. Take note of the Torrey Log Church-Schoolhouse at 49 East Main Street, which is on the NRHP. Cross the Fremont River again at mile 13.7. Turn left at Teasdale Bench Road (800 North; mile 14.2) and head toward Teasdale. The climbing continues.

Notice the striking backdrop as you approach Teasdale. That is Cocks Comb (not to be confused with the larger, longer Cockscomb located southwest of here). The name refers to the jagged profile that resembles the comb of a rooster. Enter Teasdale at mile 15.6—you are now on 100 East. There are vending machines on the left at mile 15.7. Teasdale is unincorporated but had an estimated population of about 300. Teasdale was established in 1879 and was named for George Teasdale, one of the original twelve Mormon apostles. Teasdale's elevation is 7,125 feet, the high point of the course. Continue through Teasdale to Teasdale Road (mile 16.2); turn left here and begin heading southeast over rolling terrain. Notice the interesting house on the left at mile 16.6; the residence is in a unique rock setting, having the appearance of a live-in sculpture. Continue climbing and descending to mile 22.7, where the road Ts into SR 12. Turn left here (on the All-American Highway) and begin heading north toward Torrey. The highway descends to mile 24.7, at a Fremont River crossing, then starts to climb.

Enter Torrey at mile 27.4, at the junction with SR 24. There is a mini-mart on the corner. Turn right and begin the descent to Capitol Reef. The Reef is visible during the descent; the Henry Mountains are in the far distance. The first stage of the descent begins at mile 27.6, bottoming (actually a "false" bottom) at mile 28.4. There is a mini-mart at mile 29.3. The descent resumes at mile 30.8, reaching another false bottom at mile 31.3. Balanced rocks and other formations come into view at mile 32.6. Chimney Rock, with lavatories at the trailhead, is on the left at mile 34.3. The final, long descent begins at mile 35.0. Enjoy the layered colors as you drop down into the basin adjacent Capitol Reef. Cross Sulphur Creek at mile 37.2 and turn right onto Capitol Reef Scenic Drive at mile 37.4. The visitor center is on the right. Fruita is located 1 mile south of here. The ride ends in Fruita, at the overflow parking lot.

Miles and Directions

0.0 Start at the parking lot north of Clifford Trail Visitor Center in Fruita, on Capitol Reef Scenic Drive in Capitol Reef National Park. Head north on Scenic Drive.

0.9   Capitol Reef National Park Visitor Center on the left.

1.0   At the stop sign, turn left onto SR 24 westbound.

1.2   Begin 2-mile climb.

3.4   Crest of climb; begin descent.

4.1   Chimney Rock trailhead on the right—restrooms; begin rolling terrain.

5.8   Balanced rocks and other interesting formations on the right.

7.1   Begin climb.

7.6   Crest; begin rolling terrain.

8.7   Capitol Reef Resort and Restaurant on the right

9.1   Mini-mart.

10.0   Begin climb.

10.8   Crest of climb; mini-mart on the left.

11.0   Keep straight at SR 12 junction.

11.4   Enter Torrey; false flat through town.

13.7   Cross Fremont River; begin climb.

14.2   Turn left onto Teasdale Bench Road (800 North); continue upgrade.

15.6   Enter Teasdale; now on 100 East.

15.7   Vending machines on the left.

15.9   Go straight at the stop sign at 100 South; road narrows.

16.2   At the stop sign, turn left onto Teasdale Road (330 South).

16.6   Interesting house on the left.

17.5   Begin descent.

19.7   End of descent; begin climb.

20.6   Crest of climb; begin descent.

21.8   End of descent; begin climb.

22.1   Crest of climb; begin false flat.

22.7   At the stop sign, turn left onto SR 12; begin descent.

24.7   Cross Fremont River; begin climb.

26.7   False crest.

27.4   At the stop sign, turn right onto SR 24 (end of 16-mile loop).

27.6   Begin descent—expansive vista of Capitol Reef.

30.4   Base of descent; begin rolling terrain.

30.8   Begin descent.

31.3   Base of descent; begin rolling terrain

34.3   Chimney Rock trailhead (restrooms) on the left.

35.0   Begin long descent.

37.2   Base of descent; cross Fremont River.

37.4   Turn right onto Capitol Reef Scenic Drive; visitor center on the right.

38.4   End of ride in Fruita; return to parking area on the left.

Local Information

Capitol Reef National Park, National Park Service: www.nps.gov/care.
Official city of Torrey Web site: www.torrey utah.com.

Restaurants

Café Diablo: 599 West Main Street, Torrey; (435) 425-3070; www.cafediablo.net. Dinner only. Open April through mid-October.
Castle Rock Coffee and Candy: Junction of Highway 12 and 24 (685 East Highway 24), Torrey; (435) 425-2100; www.castlerockcoffee .com.
Red Cliff Restaurant (at Best Western Capitol Reef): 2600 East Highway 24, Torrey; (435) 425-3797. Breakfast and dinner.
Rim Rock Restaurant: 2523 East Highway 24, Torrey. Open March through December.
Slacker's (formerly Brink's Burgers Drive In): 165 East Main Street, Torrey; (435) 425-3710. Open March through October.

Accommodations

Austin's Chuck Wagon Lodge: 12 West Main Street, Torrey; (435) 425-3335 or (800) 863-3288; www.austinschuckwagonmotel.com.

Best Western Capitol Reef Resort: 2600 East Highway 24, Torrey; (435) 425-3761 or (800) 780-7234; www.bestwestern.com/ capitolreefresort.
Capitol Reef Inn & Café: 360 West Main Street, Torrey; (435) 425-3271; www.capitol reefinn.com.
Sandstone Inn & Restaurant (formerly Wonderland Inn): 875 East Highway 24 (junction Highways 12 and 24), Torrey; (435) 425-3775 or (800) 458-0216; www.capitolreefwonder-land.com.
Skyridge Bed & Breakfast: 950 East Highway 24, Torrey; (435) 425-3222 or (877) 824-1508; www.skyridgeinn.com.
Thousand Lakes RV Park: 1 mile west of Torrey on SR 24; (435) 425-3500 or (800) 355-8995; www.thousandlakesrvpark.com. Open March 25 through October 25.

Maps

DeLorme: Utah Atlas & Gazetteer: Page 52 A2.
Benchmark: Utah Road & Recreation Atlas: Page 76 B3.

37 Delta-Sevier River Ramble

The Delta-Sevier River Ramble is a 22.8-mile loop on nearly pancake-flat roads in the Sevier Desert. The ride visits Delta, Deseret, and Hinckley in this corner of the Great Basin. Canals extending from the Sevier River to the east enabled the introduction of agriculture to this otherwise dry area. The presence of water tames what would otherwise be a somewhat hostile environment. Elevations vary almost imperceptibly on the ride, from 4,586 feet in Deseret to 4,649 feet in Delta.

Start: Delta City Park, east side (100 North and 100 West) in Delta.
Length: 22.8 miles (loop).
Terrain: Flat, with one railroad overpass. Minimum and maximum elevations: 4,586 to 4,649 feet.

Traffic and hazards: US 6/US 50: 2,785 vehicles per day at the railroad overpass in Delta in 2005; 1,915 vehicles per day near Hinckley. SR 257: 1,230 vehicles per day through Deseret.

Getting there: From I-15, take exit 225 (Nephi) to SR 132 west. Get onto US 6 south in Lynndyl. Bear right at the US 50 junction and continue into Delta. Turn right at 100 West to access City Park.

The Ride

The Sevier River originates on the Paunsaugunt Plateau in northwestern Kane County, in southwest Utah. From there, the river flows in a horseshoe shape some 280 miles before emptying into Sevier Lake in west-central Utah. Sevier Lake is nearly always dry, however, because most of the waters of the Sevier River are diverted for irrigation. The lake reappears after heavy, continuous rainstorms, such as occurred during the mid-1980s. Sevier Lake was once part of ancient Lake Bonneville. When the lake does exist, it is endorheic, meaning that it has no outlet and is salty, similar to the Great Salt Lake. Despite the lake's nearly permanent dryness, the region surrounding the lake is referred to as the Sevier River Delta. The city of Delta was settled in 1907, somewhat late for a Utah town. Pioneer Mormon settlers sought out lands that were suitable for agriculture and grazing before venturing into the hostile Great Basin Desert in which Delta is located. A canal was built into the area, however, opening up possibilities for agriculture. The region soon became an important producer of alfalfa seeds and sugar beets.

Delta attracted new interest when, in 1942 during World War II, an interment camp for Japanese residents was opened at Topaz, about 7 miles northwest of Delta. During its peak residency, Topaz housed 8,255 Japanese, making it the fifth-largest settlement in Utah at the time. Remnants of Topaz, including the foundations of old buildings, still exist.

Today, Delta's economy is heavily dependent on the mineral and power resources in the area. The Intermountain Power Project, a coal-fired electricity-producing

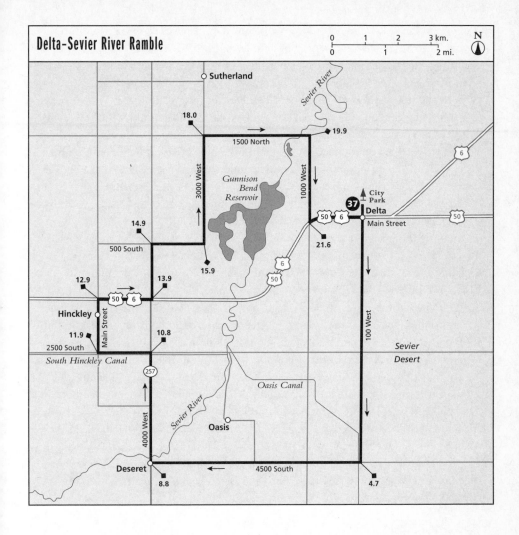

Delta–Sevier River Ramble

0   1   2   3 km.
0   1   2 mi.

N

Sutherland

18.0

19.9

1500 North

Sevier River

3000 West

Gunnison
Bend
Reservoir

1000 West

6

City
Park

37 Delta

50 6

Main Street

50

14.9

500 South

15.9

21.6

12.9

13.9

6

50 6

50

Hinckley

Main Street

100 West

Sevier
Desert

11.9

10.8

2500 South

South Hinckley Canal

257

Oasis Canal

4000 West

Sevier River

Oasis

Deseret

4500 South

8.8

4.7

plant, is located north of Delta. The plant supplies most of the power for Los Angeles, California. At the Brush Wellman plant, also north of the city, beryllium is mined and refined at one of the few concentrated sources of this lightweight metal. Delta is also a good base for geological prospectors (i.e., rock collectors), who are attracted to the abundance of specimens nearby. Finally, Delta is home to the Great Basin Heritage Museum, thereby serving as a gateway to the vast Great Basin Desert. Delta, with a population of 3,172 in 2008, is arguably the largest city in the 200,000-square-mile Great Basin. A number of towns and settlements grew up around Delta to facilitate the agricultural activities. These include Abraham, Deseret, Hinckley, Oasis, Sugarville, Sutherland, and Woodrow. None of the settlements are incorporated.

Start by heading south from Delta City Park on 100 West to Main Street. Cross Main Street (careful—the road is wider than you think) and continue south. Leave

Delta around mile 1.0, entering the agriculturally dominated open space that surrounds the city. The road passes a few farms and residences. Turn right at 4500 South and head west. Enter the community of Deseret at mile 8.0. Deseret was settled in 1860, some forty-six years before Delta. The community was split into Hinckley to the northwest, Oasis to the northeast, and Deseret in 1891. Deseret means "honeybee" in Mormon scripture and is a frequently recurring noun in Utah. Turn right onto 4000 West (SR 257) at mile 8.8 and head north. As you ride through Deseret, notice the Deseret Relief Society Hall at 4365 South 4000 West. The hall is on the National Register of Historic Places (NRHP). Turn left onto 2500 South at mile 10.8 and head west. Enter Hinckley at mile 11.6. Turn right onto Main Street at mile 11.9 and head north. Hinckley was settled in 1877. As you ride through town, notice the Hinckley High School Gymnasium and Millard Academy, both of which are on the NRHP.

Turn right onto US 6/US 50 at mile 12.9 and head east. There is a mini-mart on the corner. Turn left onto 4000 West at mile 13.9 and head north. After crossing the Highline Canal, turn right onto 500 South (mile 14.9). Turn left at mile 15.9 and head north on 3000 West. In the typically dry climate, the Gunnison Bend Reservoir is a welcome sight, coming up on the right at mile 16.3. There are a few park facilities and restrooms here. Just as the road enters the outskirts of Sutherland, turn right onto 1500 North (mile 18.0) and head east. The mountains in the distance are the Canyon Mountains. The road bends right, becoming 1000 West, at mile 19.9. Continue heading south, past some industrial development. Return to US 6/US 50 at mile 21.6; turn left here and begin the only climb on the route: a railroad overpass. The descent from the crest of the overpass takes you into Delta—the entry into the city is abrupt and somewhat dramatic. You are now on Main Street; notice Van's Hall at 321 West Main Street. The building, now used for commercial purposes, is on the NRHP. The only traffic signal for (tens of) miles around is at 200 West. Continue straight and turn left onto 100 West. City Park is adjacent; the ride ends at 100 North. Check out the Great Basin Heritage Museum while at the park.

Miles and Directions

0.0 Start at City Park in Delta, in parking area adjacent 100 West and 100 North. Head south on 100 West.

0.1 Go straight at the stop sign at Main Street (US 6/US 50); wide crossing.

1.0 Leave Delta.

4.7 At the stop sign at 4500 South, turn right.

7.7 Railroad crossing (one track).

8.0 Enter Deseret.

8.8 At the stop sign at 4000 West (SR 257), turn right.

8.9 Cross North Ditch channel.

10.8 Turn left onto 2500 South.

11.6 Enter Hinckley.

11.9 At the stop sign at Main Street, turn right.

12.9 At the stop sign at US 6/US 50, turn right. Sinclair (mini-mart) on the corner.

13.9 Turn left onto 4000 West.

14.7 Cross Highline Canal.

14.9 Turn right onto 500 South.

15.9 Turn left onto 3000 West.

16.3 Gunnison Bend Reservoir (park, restrooms) on the right.

16.5 Bridge over reservoir inlet.

18.0 At the stop sign at 1500 North, turn right.

19.9 Road curves right; now heading south on 1000 West.

21.6 At the stop sign at US 6/US 50, turn left.

21.8 Sinclair (mini-mart) on the left.

22.0 Begin railroad overpass.

22.4 Enter Delta.

22.5 Go straight at the traffic signal at 200 West.

22.7 Turn left onto 100 West.

22.8 End of ride at 100 North; turn left to enter parking area.

Local Information

City of Delta official Web site: www.deltautah
.com.

Restaurants

The Loft Steak House (Leo's): 411 East Main
Street, Delta; (435) 864-4790; www.theloft
steakhouse.com.

Mi Rancherito Mexican Restaurant: 540
Topaz Boulevard, Delta; (435) 864-4245.

Red Rock Cheese Shop: 1365 North US 6,
Delta; (435) 864-2430; www.redrockcheese
.com.

Top's City Café: 313 West Main Street, Delta;
(435) 864-2148.

Accommodations

Antelope Valley RV Park: 776 West Main
Street, Delta; (800) 430-0022; www.antelope
valleyrvpark.com.

Budget Motel: 75 South 350 East, Delta;
(435) 864-4533.

Days Inn Delta: 527 East Topaz Boulevard,
Delta; (435) 864-3882; www.daysinndelta
.com.

Deltan Inn Motel: 347 East Main Street,
Delta; (435) 864-5318.

Diamond D Motor Lodge: 234 West Main
Street, Delta; (435) 864-2041.

Van's Motel (or Willden Motel): 127 West
Main Street, Delta; (435) 864-2906.

Maps

DeLorme: Utah Atlas & Gazetteer: Page 34
D2.

Benchmark: Utah Road & Recreation Atlas:
Page 58 F3.

38 Eccles Energy Canyon Challenge

The Eccles Energy Canyon Challenge is a 56.0-mile, mountainous out-and-back ride that takes cyclists up Cottonwood Canyon to the crest of the Wasatch Plateau, down Eccles Canyon to Mud Creek Canyon, then up Mud Creek Canyon to Clear Creek. The return route retraces the outbound trip. The ride begins and ends in Fairview and covers a portion of The Energy Loop, a national scenic byway. Elevations range from 5,947 feet in Fairview to 8,910 feet atop the Wasatch Plateau. The route enters three counties: Sanpete, Emery, and Carbon.

Start: Iven R. Cox Lions Park on 100 South, east of State Street in Fairview.
Length: 56.0 miles (out-and-back).
Terrain: Mountainous, with steep climbs both outbound and inbound. Minimum and maximum elevations: 5,947 to 8,910 feet.

Traffic and hazards: SR 31: 1,115 vehicles per day east of Fairview in 2005; 870 vehicles per day in Manti-La Sal National Forest. SR 96: 355 vehicles per day between SR 264 and Clear Creek in 2005. SR 264: 555 vehicles per day between SR 31 and SR 96 in 2005. US 89: 5,765 vehicles per day in Fairview in 2005.

Getting there: From I-15, take exit 225 (Nephi) to SR 132 eastbound. The highway bends left in Moroni; continue straight onto SR 116. In Mount Pleasant, turn left onto US 89 north. The next city is Fairview. Turn right on 100 South; look for Iven R. Cox Lions Park on the left.

The Ride

The Huntington Canyon/Eccles Canyon Scenic Byways are among the most scenic in all of Utah. This is notwithstanding the extraordinary routes that penetrate southern Utah's "necklace" of national parks, monuments, and recreation areas. There are no national parks here—just a national forest—but the region arguably could be a national park. The byways comprise the so-called Energy Loop; one begins in Huntington, while the other begins near Scofield. The two highways converge on the crest of the Wasatch Plateau and then descend rather steeply into Fairview. This ride takes in the Eccles Canyon portion of the byways. The elevation ranges from 5,947 feet in Fairview, where the ride starts, cresting at 8,910 feet atop the Wasatch Plateau, then descending to the mouth of Eccles Canyon at 7,800 feet, and finally climbing again to 8,303 feet in Clear Creek; the profile is then retraced in the reverse direction for the return trip. The alpine environment of the Wasatch Plateau is extremely pristine and colorful. There are few trees up here, although there are isolated, dense groves of quaking aspens. But the flora offer a feast for the eyes: alpine sunflower, blue penstemon, bluebells, California corn lilies, charlock, columbine, delphinium, forget-me-nots, geraniums, green gentian, hyssop, purple lupine, scarlet gilia, sweet pea, and woodland star are abundant in late July and August. The season is short, so get up there! Snow cover can last into July at the higher elevations. Snow can return as early as mid-September.

The Energy Loop refers to the Huntington and Eccles Canyon Scenic Byways passage of Electric Lake—Eccles Canyon to the north, and Huntington Canyon to the south. Electric Lake is not really "electric"; you will not be electrocuted upon sticking a toe in the water. Your bicycle will not "glow" upon remounting. The lake functions as the storage reservoir for the steam turbines at the Huntington Power Plant, located about 40 miles down Huntington Canyon on SR 31. It is somewhat of a myth that a direct boost of energy can be received upon having a close encounter with the lake, but—what the heck? Sprinkle a few drops on your arms and legs and feel the surge.

The Eccles Energy Canyon Challenge is essentially an out-and-back ride between the city of Fairview (population 1,210 in 2008) in Sanpete County and the unincorporated town of Clear Creek in Carbon County. Fairview was settled in 1859, at the northern end of Sanpete Valley, as part of a "second wave" of Mormon immigration to the area. During the 1860s, a 10-foot-high wall was built around the center of town for protection during the Black Hawk War. The wall is long since gone, as are a large log meetinghouse and Poor House (infirmary). But several historic buildings remain from those early years, as well as quite a few very nice-looking houses. Today, Fairview is a quiet, agricultural, sheep-raising, and services-oriented community. It is the sixth-largest city in the Sanpete Valley. Given its location, the city is the unofficial "gateway" to the valley. Fairview was along the route of a 101-mile stage of the 2008 Tour of Utah. Clear Creek was established in the 1870s as a camp for the local coal mines. In 1898 a vein was discovered near the town, bringing about prosperity. The town flourished during the 1910s and 1920s, when the population reached about 600. The town was in decline by the 1950s. Clear Creek is listed on the Web site www.ghosttowns.com, but the current residents probably do not appreciate this. The town thrives briefly, each year, during deer hunting season (around September and October). Despite its functional history, Clear Creek's setting is quite appealing.

Park on-street adjacent Iven R. Cox Lions Park, located on 100 South just east of State Street in Fairview. Head west on 100 South to State Street, and then turn right and head north on State Street (US 89). Take note of Fairview City Hall at 85 South, and Fairview Amusement Hall at 75 South; both buildings are on the National Register of Historic Places. State Street bends to the left just north of 300 North. Stay to the right here; there are mini-marts on the left. There are no provisions on this route, so stock up here. Turn right at the stop sign (400 North, US 31) and head east. The road climbs as you leave the city and enter Cottonwood Canyon. You are now on The Energy Loop, although this is neither Huntington nor Eccles Canyon. The highway climbs at an average 6.5 percent gradient for the next 8 miles. The steep slopes of Oak Creek Ridge are on the left, and the narrow slopes of the Colton, Flagstaff, and North Horn Formations are on the right. Enter Manti-La Sal National Forest at mile 5.0. Notice the dense trees on the hillside on the right, although I observed that many of the trees were dead during my summer 2007 field visit. Continue climbing at an 8 percent grade through this section. You may recognize the changing colors, density, and height of the foliage as you enter an alpine environment. Turn left onto SR 264 at mile 9.2. The Skyline Trail crossing, representing the crest of the Wasatch Plateau, is shortly after the turn. The elevation is about 8,900 feet. Be prepared for cooler temperatures.

The highway now traverses the Wasatch Plateau in a glorious alpine setting. The wildflowers mentioned above should be in full bloom in late July and August. There are also isolated, dense groves of quaking aspens, such as the one at mile 9.6. Enter a huge, open meadow at mile 11.0—the temptation to frolic is strong. Keep pedaling; the small Beaver Dam Reservoir is on the right at mile 11.6, along with another grove of aspens. Begin to climb at mile 12.0; the climb crests at mile 13.6, adjacent the Flat Canyon Campground. Enter Emery County at mile 14.4; begin a short descent to the shore of Electric Lake. A lake access point is at mile 15.2; an information placard is posted at mile 15.8. The scenery through here is breathtaking, as the road meanders near the lake. This is an open sheep range, so you may see sheep grazing by the side of the road, adding to the idyllic appearance. The highway continues to wind upon leaving the lake area then starts to climb at mile 17.7 as the sharp curves continue. Enter Carbon County at mile 20.1; this is the crest of the climb. A steep descent through sharp, winding curves follows. The descent takes you down Eccles Canyon, one of the featured canyons of this route. Be particularly careful on the descent, as the speed can easily get quite high. The elevated tramway of the Skyline Mine appears on the left at mile 22.0. The mine produces 3.5 to 5 million tons of coal per year. The tramway runs alongside the highway for the next 2.4 miles.

At the base of the descent, at mile 24.8, turn right onto SR 96 and begin the climb toward Clear Creek. You are now in Mud Creek Canyon, climbing from 7,800 feet at the turn to 8,300 feet in Clear Creek. Clear Creek is discussed above. Mud Creek Canyon is a picturesque, alpine valley, with pine trees blanketing the slopes and crisp, clear air. A railroad track, constructed long ago to facilitate the movement of coal in and out of the area, parallels the highway. Enter Clear Creek at mile 27.7. This is no ghost town, although there are no services here. This is effectively the end of the highway; bear right onto one of the settlement's narrow streets. After the street bends left, make a sharp left to get on a returning, parallel street. It is a storybook setting, with the quaint cottages set amidst the imposing mountains and pine forest. After making the (very) short loop through town, return to SR 96 (mile 28.2) and begin the descent.

Turn left at the base of Mud Creek Canyon onto SR 264 (mile 31.3) and immediately begin climbing. Skyline Mine, along with the coal tramway, are now on your right. Notice the tumbling stream on the left. The conveyor ends at mile 34.1, but the climb continues. The crest is reached at mile 35.9; enter Emery County here and begin a steep, winding descent. There is a hairpin curve at mile 37.9; by now you will have caught glimpses of Electric Lake off to your left. Enter the meadow area and open sheep range at mile 38.4—another storybook setting. Electric Lake, along with an information placard, are on the left at mile 40.9. Begin to climb after leaving the lake environs, at mile 41.5. Enter Sanpete County shortly thereafter. Flat Canyon

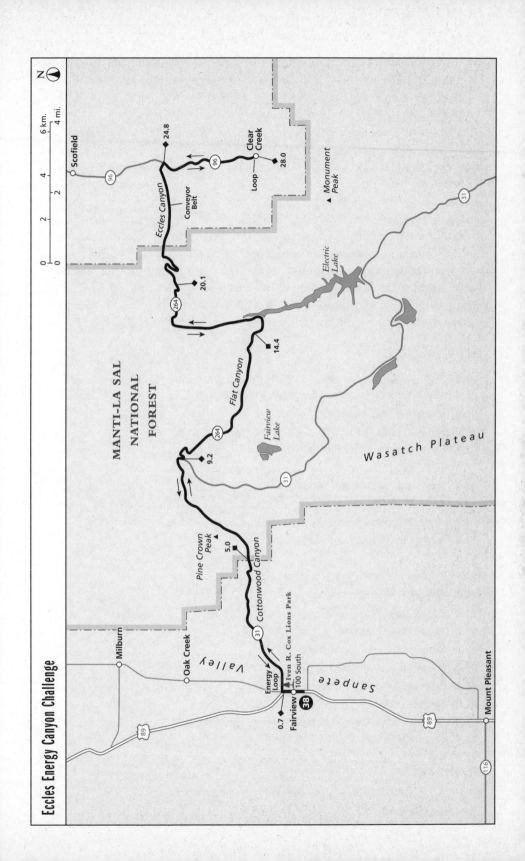

Eccles Energy Canyon Challenge

Campground is on the left at mile 42.5. The terrain is rolling and false flats. Begin to descend again at mile 44.1, with Beaver Dam Reservoir on your left. Enter a vast meadow area at mile 45.1. After traversing the meadow on false flats, the highway crosses the Skyline Trail. SR 264 bends sharply to the left here.

A stop sign is just beyond the curve; turn right here, onto SR 31, and begin the final descent of the course, through Cottonwood Canyon. The descent is generally at an 8 percent grade; be watchful of rocks in the road. Leave Manti-La Sal National Forest at mile 51.1, although you may barely notice if you are descending at a high speed. Be careful though; there is a sharp curve at mile 51.6. Avoid crossing the centerline here (or anywhere along the route). Sanpete Valley comes into view at mile 51.9. Notice how the trees get shorter as you descend. Exit Cottonwood Canyon at mile 53.8 and enter Fairview at mile 54.9. You are now on 400 North. Turn left onto State Street at the foot of the descent; convenience marts mark the intersection. After a short segment, turn left again, onto US 89 (and to stay on State Street). After a final, short pass through town, turn left onto 100 South and return to Iven R. Cox Lions Park to conclude the ride. Most of Fairview's eateries are on State Street.

Miles and Directions

0.0   Start at Iven R. Cox Lions Park on 100 South, east of State Street in Fairview. Head west on 100 South; turn right and head north on State Street (US 89).

0.6   Veer right at fork in highway.

0.7   At the stop sign at 400 North (SR 31), turn right and begin climbing.

2.3   Enter Cottonwood Canyon (also referred to as Fairview Canyon).

2.7   Gate (closed in winter).

5.0   Enter Manti-La Sal National Forest.

9.2   Turn left onto SR 264.

9.3   Skyline Trail crossing—crest of Wasatch Plateau; begin false flats.

11.6   Beaver Dam Reservoir on the right.

12.0   Begin climb.

13.6   Flat Canyon Campground on the right; begin false flats.

14.4   Enter Emery County.

14.6   Begin descent.

15.2   Electric Lake on the right.

17.7   Begin climb and sharp, winding curves.

20.1   Enter Carbon County; crest of climb.

20.2   Begin steep descent on sharp, winding curves.

22.0   Coal processing plant on the left (for next several miles).

24.8   Base of descent; turn right onto SR 96—begin gradual climb.

27.7   Enter Clear Creek.

27.8   Road splits; stay right—begin one-way loop.

28.0   Make a sharp left turn to return to town entrance.

28.2   End loop—return to SR 96; begin descent.

31.3   At the stop sign at SR 264, turn left and begin steep climb.

35.9   Crest of climb.

36.0   Enter Emery County; begin descent (steep, winding road).

37.9   Hairpin curve; continue descent.

38.4   Enter meadow area and open sheep range.

40.9   Electric Lake on the left.

41.5   Begin climb.

41.7   Enter Sanpete County.

42.5   Flat Canyon Campground on the left; grade eases—now on false flats.

44.1   Begin descent; Beaver Dam Reservoir on the left.

45.1   Enter huge, open meadow area.

45.7   End descent; now on false flats.

46.8   Skyline Trail crossing; highway bends left.

46.9   At the stop sign at SR 31, turn right and begin 8 percent downgrade through Cottonwood Canyon.

51.1   Leave Manti-La Sal National Forest.

51.6   Sharp downhill curve; exercise caution.

53.8   Exit Cottonwood Canyon.

54.9   Enter Fairview; now on 400 North (still SR 31).

55.4   Turn left onto State Street.

55.5   At the stop sign at US 89, turn left (still on State Street).

56.0   End of ride; turn left onto 100 South and return to Iven R. Cox Lions Park.

Local Information

Sanpete County Web site: http://sanpete county.org.

Energy Loop—Huntington/Eccles Canyon Scenic Byways information: www.byways.org/explore/byways/13831.

Manti-La Sal National Forest information, USDA Forest Service: www.fs.fed.us/r4/mantilasal.

Restaurants

Cruiser's Restaurant: 36 West Canyon Road, Fairview; (435) 427-9200.

Home Plate Café: 215 North State Street, Fairview; (435) 427-9300.

T-Cee's Dari Frez: 247 North State Street, Fairview; (435) 427-9550.

Accommodations

Skyline Motel: 35 East 200 North, Fairview; (435) 427-3312.

Maps

DeLorme: Utah Atlas & Gazetteer: Page 36 B1.

Benchmark: Utah Road & Recreation Atlas: Page 60 C1.

39 Fish Lake Challenge

The Fish Lake Challenge is a 53.7-mile clockwise loop in mountainous terrain at high altitude. Elevations range from 7,000 feet in Loa (Wayne County seat), where the ride starts and finishes, to 9,036 feet approaching Fish Lake from the southwest on SR 25. The high point of the route is also the high point of all *Road Biking Utah* rides. Your lungs will probably be measurably larger upon successfully completing the course; be sure to guard your pace, however, if you have not done any altitude training. The ride is entirely on state highways, so the pavement surface is generally smooth.

Start: Wayne County Community Center, Center and Main Streets, Loa.
Length: 53.7 miles (loop, with a short opening-ending out-and-back segment).
Terrain: Rolling hills and lengthy climbs at high altitude. Minimum and maximum elevations: 7,000 to 9,036 feet.

Traffic and hazards: SR 24: 2,080 vehicles per day in Loa in 2005; 1,185 vehicles per day at Wayne-Piute County line. SR 25: 60 vehicles per day adjacent Fish Lake (varies by season). SR 72: 280 vehicles per day in Fremont; 425 vehicles per day in Loa.

Getting there: From I-70, take exit 48 to SR 259 south. After a short distance, get onto SR 24 south. Continue on SR 24 to Loa, the Wayne County seat.

The Ride

Fish Lake is a 5-mile-long by 1.5-mile-wide lake located high in the mountains (elevation 8,843 feet) of the southern Wasatch Plateau. The lake occupies a graben and is sandwiched between the Mytoge Mountains, which shoot up to 10,095 feet on the southeast side, and the Fish Lake Hightop Plateau on the northwest side, which features peaks exceeding 11,000 feet. The lake is a well-known fishing spot; the Utah Division of Wildlife Resources stocks it with lake trout, rainbow trout, mackinaw, and splake. There can be up to 7,000 visitors at the lake on a peak summer weekend day. The lake is located in southern Sevier County, although either Piute or Wayne County must be accessed first, before entering this region of Sevier. The lake is the source of the Fremont River, which drains to the southeast, passing through Capitol Reef National Park before joining with the Dirty Devil River near Hanksville (see the Bicentennial Highway Classic). SR 25 on the northwest side of Fish Lake is a Utah scenic byway, although the segment between the lake and SR 72, on the north and east sides of the lake, is also quite scenic.

The closest town to Fish Lake, and the starting point for the Fish Lake Challenge, is Loa. Loa, population 516 in 2008, is the seat of Wayne County. The town was established in 1878 and was named by a town resident who had lived in Hawaii, one Franklin W. Young. Franklin was impressed by Mauna Loa and had returned to Utah with a rock taken from the slopes of the mighty volcano. Loa is the population and government services center of the predominantly agricultural Fremont River valley,

A small group of cyclists whizzes into Fish Lake National Forest (trees ahead).

although the town is not much larger than its neighbors. The valley is a high-desert area, although there is plenty of water flowing out of the mountains to sustain healthy crops. Fish Lake is high enough to be considered alpine, as is evident by the dense groves of aspen trees. One colony of aspens, named "Pando," has been determined to be a single male tree grouped with its clones, all connected by a massive underground root system. The entire clonal colony has been estimated to weigh about 6,600 tons, making it the heaviest living organism on earth.

Fishing is, of course, the number one sporting activity at Fish Lake. Hiking into the mountains, particularly those on the lake's northwest side, is also popular. Recently, a new sport—triathlon—has been proposed for Fish Lake, although environmental concerns had suspended the event as of this writing. The swim was planned to be mercifully short (just 400 yards), given the chilly lake temperatures.

Start the ride at the Wayne County Community Center, located on Center and Main Streets in Loa. The center was relatively new as of this writing, having opened its doors in August 2006. Turn left onto Main Street (SR 24) and head west (actually north first, and then west). Grab provisions at the mini-mart on your way out of town. Stay to the left at the Y intersection at mile 0.6 to remain on SR 24. The highway begins to climb here, cresting at mile 1.9. It then descends to mile 2.7, where the climbing resumes. The highway bends left at mile 4.3, followed by a blind curve to the right and the climb's crest at mile 4.6. Exercise caution here, as cyclists will be invisible to drivers around this turn. After 3 miles of false flats and rolling terrain, the highway descends, followed by a short climb. Rolling terrain resumes from here, although the prevailing direction is up. Enter Piute County at mile 11.4; the elevation at this summit is 8,385 feet.

Turn right onto SR 25 at mile 13.3; begin climbing. The highway reaches a false crest at mile 15.8, entering Sevier County at mile 16.2. Continue climbing at mile 16.5. The high point of the ride and *Road Biking Utah*, 9,036 feet, is reached at mile 17.4. Enter Fishlake National Forest at mile 17.5. You are met almost immediately by a grove of aspen trees, which are common around Fish Lake. As discussed above, Pando—only a well-trained eye could identify it—is actually a colony of clones from a single male tree. Fish Lake appears in the distance at mile 18.9; the highway descends to the lake. Lakeside Marina and Resort is at mile 20.7. From here, there is a series of resorts, marinas, campgrounds, and picnic areas, including Fish Lake, Twin Creek, Mackinaw, Bowery Creek, and Bowery Haven. Most lakeside facilities have lavatories. The highway begins to climb away from the lake at mile 26.4. By the time you reach Frying Pan Campground, at mile 27.9, you are no longer at Fish Lake, but are nearing Johnson Valley Reservoir.

The highway curves around the northwest horn of the reservoir at mile 29.5, adjacent Paiute Campground. An interesting black rock beach is on the right at mile 30.0. The Johnson Boat Ramp is on the right at mile 31.0. The highway begins to descend at mile 31.6, getting steeper at mile 32.2. The descent is short; after crossing the Fremont River at mile 32.5, the highway begins to climb. The climb crests at mile 33.1; after a false flat section, a lengthy descent begins at mile 33.7. The highway negotiates a series of sharp curves; watch your speed. Also, watch for rocks in the highway. The descent takes you past several canyons, including Splatter (mile 36.0), Ivie (mile 37.0), and Pole (mile 37.9). Lavatories are available at Pole Canyon, as well as at mile 39.7. The highway levels at mile 40.1, entering Wayne County at mile 40.7. Tiny Mill Meadow Reservoir is on the right; cross U M (Upper Mill) Creek, which feeds the reservoir, at mile 41.3 (through a hairpin turn). Exit Fishlake National Forest at mile 41.6; shortly thereafter, begin the final climb to the end of SR 25.

Turn right onto SR 72 at mile 43.4 and begin the steep descent into the Fremont River valley. The highway levels, transitioning into rolling terrain, at mile 47.1. Enter Fremont, an unincorporated settlement in the valley. The highway is surrounded by farmland, livestock, and horses. The highway bends right at mile 51.8, entering Loa at mile 52.7. Turn left onto SR 24 (Main Street) at mile 53.1. The ride ends at Center Street, adjacent the Wayne County Community Center, at mile 53.7.

Miles and Directions

0.0 Start at Wayne County Community Center, Center and Main Streets in Loa. Turn left onto Main Street (SR 24 west).

0.3 Mini-mart.

0.6 Stay left at Y intersection to remain on SR 24; begin gradual climb.

1.9 Crest of climb; begin descent.

2.7 End of descent; begin climb.

Fish Lake Challenge

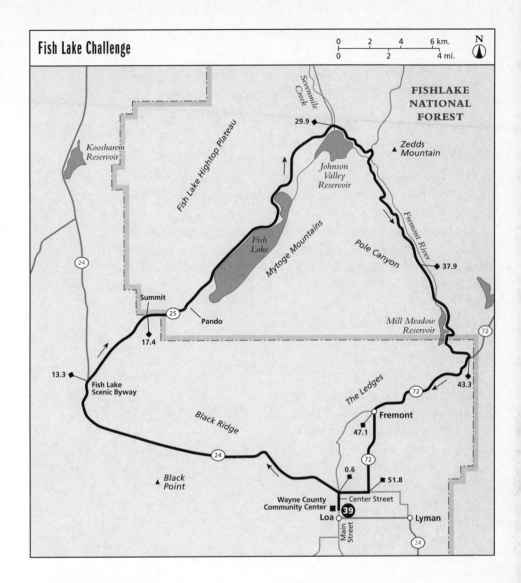

3.8 Gradient eases.

4.3 Highway bends left.

4.6 Crest of climb; highway bends right—blind curve (exercise caution!).

7.8 Begin short descent, followed by short climb.

8.8 Crest of climb; begin rolling terrain.

11.4 Summit (8,385 feet)—enter Piute County; begin descent.

13.3 Turn right onto SR 25 east; begin climb.

15.8 Crest of climb.

16.2 Enter Sevier County.

16.5 Begin climb.

17.4 Summit (9,036 feet)—begin rolling terrain.

17.5 Enter Fishlake National Forest.

18.0 Cattle guard.

18.9 Begin descent; Fish Lake on the horizon.

19.6 Highway levels.

20.0 Cattle guard.

20.7 Lakeside Marina and Lakeside Resort.

21.5 Restrooms on the right.

21.9 Fish Lake Lodge Resort on the right.

22.1 Twin Creek Amphitheater and picnic area on the right (restrooms).

22.3 Mackinaw Campground on the left.

23.0 Bowery Creek Campground on the left; restrooms on the right.

23.9 Vending machines on the right; Bowery Haven Resort on the left.

25.4 Highway bends sharply to the right.

25.9 Cattle guard.

26.4 Begin climb.

27.9 Frying Pan Campground on the left.

29.3 Highway levels.

29.5 Paiute Campground on the left.

29.9 Cross Sevenmile Creek.

30.0 Black rock beach on the right.

30.4 Cattle guard.

31.0 Johnson Boat Ramp on the right (restrooms).

31.6 Begin descent.

32.2 Descent gets steeper.

32.5 Cross Fremont River; begin steep climb.

33.1 Crest of climb; begin false flat.

33.5 Cattle guard.

33.7 Begin descent.

34.3 Descent gets steeper (8 percent grade); begin sharp curves.

36.3 Cattle guard; watch for rocks in highway.

37.0 Gradient decreases.

37.9 Pole Canyon; restrooms on the left.

39.7 Restrooms on the left.

40.1 Foot of descent; begin rolling terrain.

40.7 Enter Wayne County.

41.3 Cross U M (Upper Mill) Creek; hairpin turn.

41.6 Leave Fishlake National Forest.

41.7 Cattle guard; begin climb.

43.3 Cattle guard. After 0.05 mile, at the stop sign at SR 72, turn right and head south.

43.4 Cattle guard.

44.1 Begin 8 percent descent.

44.4 Cross Red Canyon Draw.

46.0 Gradient eases.

47.1 Enter Fremont.

51.8 Highway bends right.

52.7 Enter Loa.

53.1 At the stop sign at SR 24, turn left.

53.7 End of ride; turn right onto Center Street to return to Wayne County Community Center.

Local Information

Fish Lake National Forest, USDA Forest Service Web site: www.fs.fed.us/r4/fishlake.
Wayne County official Web site: www.waynecnty.com.

Restaurants

Country Café: 289 North Main Street, Loa; (435) 836-2047.
Maria's Grill: 193 East 200 South, Loa; (435) 836-2760.
Toscono's Pizza: 55 South Main Street, Loa; (435) 836-2500.

Accommodations

Road Creek Lodge: 300 South 600 West, Loa; (435) 836-2000 or (800) 388-7688; www.roadcreekranch.com.
Snuggle Inn: 55 South Main Street, Loa; (435) 836-2898 or (877) 505-1936; www.thesnuggleinn.com.

Maps

DeLorme: Utah Atlas & Gazetteer: Page 43 E8.
Benchmark: Utah Road & Recreation Atlas: Page 67 H11.

40 Fremont Indian Country Cruise

The Fremont Indian Country Cruise is a 45.4-mile out-and-back ride on flat segments and gently rolling hills. The route travels from Richfield, through Elsinore, Joseph, and Sevier, to Fremont Indian State Park and back. The elevation along the route ranges from 5,308 feet in Richfield to 5,542 feet in Sevier. The pavement surface ranges from generally smooth along state highways to rough along segments of the Sevier Highway (under reconstruction during my field visit in July 2008). The route generally parallels I-70 and the Sevier River.

Start: Richfield City Park, 100 East north of 300 North in central Richfield.
Length: 45.4 miles (out-and-back).
Terrain: Gently rolling hills and false flat segments. Minimum and maximum elevations: 5,308 to 5,542 feet.

Traffic and hazards: Main Street: 12,700 vehicles per day in "downtown" Richfield in 2005. SR 118: 6,500 vehicles per day at SR 120 in Richfield; 4,900 vehicles per day at SR 258 in Nibley. SR 258: 2,165 vehicles per day in Elsinore.

Getting there: Richfield is located adjacent I-70; exit 40 is at the north end of the city, and exit 37 is at the south end. In either case, take SR 120 into the center of the city. Look for Richfield City Park adjacent 300 North and Main Street.

The Ride

The Fremonts were a widely divergent and dispersed group of Native Americans who occupied Utah from about 2500 B.C. (although the culture did not develop distinguishing characteristics until A.D. 500) to about A.D. 1500. The Fremonts were primarily hunter-gatherers who did not necessarily share the same language or dialects. The most recent evidence of the Fremonts dates from about 1500, suggesting that they either died out or moved away around this time. The people tended to live in pit houses, made pottery, and created fabulous rock art. In 1983 highway construction workers discovered the largest known Fremont village near the I-70 freeway right-of-way. The freeway construction, unfortunately, eventually led to the destruction of the village. But the project was temporarily halted so that archaeologists could dig, collect, and document the discovery. Within just two years, artifacts, pictographs, petroglyphs, and other findings from the village had been preserved in Fremont Indian State Park, located about 20 miles southwest of Richfield in Sevier County. (Pictographs are paintings, while petroglyphs are carvings.) The Fremont Indian Country Cruise journeys from Richfield to the park and back, perhaps retracing a path traveled by the Fremonts.

Richfield was settled in 1864 when a group of ten men arrived from Sanpete County and spent the winter, planning and preparing for a larger settlement. Their efforts seemed to be for naught when, in 1867, the entire area was abandoned during the Black Hawk War. This series of about 150 battles and skirmishes, which started in 1865, pitted Ute, Paiute, and Navajo tribes against Mormon settlers, with little government intervention. The hostilities were inevitable given the rising tensions between the incoming "white folk" and the displaced, frequently disgraced, and often starving natives. The war finally ended in 1872 when federal troops were deployed to keep the Utes on the Uintah reservation (see the Dinosaur Country Cruise).

Resettlement began in 1871. Richfield eventually built up on agriculture and mining; penetration of the area by the Denver & Rio Grande Railroad in 1891 boosted the city's accessibility and potential. Today, Richfield is the most populous city in Panoramaland (population 7,217 in 2008) and is the commercial center of a large region. The city is the seat of Sevier County and is approximately halfway between Los Angeles, California, and Denver, Colorado. The latter fact makes Richfield a convenient rest stop for long-distance travelers on the I-70 freeway. Former U.S. Senator Jake Garn was born in Richfield, as was Walter Frederick Morrison, the inventor of the Frisbee.

Start at Richfield City Park on 100 East north of 300 North. Head south on 100 East to 300 North (SR 118). Turn right and head west to Main Street (signalized intersection). Turn left here; be patient and cautious in making this turn. Main

Street (SR 120) is Richfield's busiest street. Travel may be slow here, so take some time to observe some of the Richfield buildings that are on the National Register of Historic Places (NRHP). The Sevier County Courthouse, dating from the late nineteenth century, is located between 300 North and 200 North. The Richfield Main U.S. Post Office is at 93 North, and the Young Block (commerce and trade center) is located between 3 South and 17 South. As you continue south on Main Street, notice that most of Richfield's motels and eateries are concentrated here. After several traffic signals (Center Street, 640 South, 1100 South, and 1300 South), the road leaves the city. Continue straight onto SR 118 at the southern edge of the city (mile 3.5). Pastoral scenes of grazing horses and cattle are a common sight along the highway, as are snowcapped mountain peaks in the distance. Continue straight onto SR 258 at mile 6.4, as you ride along the northern limits of Nibley (not to be confused with the much larger city of Nibley, located in Cache County). The highway curves toward the west. Enter the town of Elsinore (population 741 in 2008). Perhaps Elsinore's greatest claim to fame is the story of ten-year-old Jason Hardman, who petitioned the town mayor to set up a library. Space was allocated in the town's public school, and Jason became the youngest librarian in the United States. Within five years, the library had collected 17,000 books, mostly from donations.

In heading west through Elsinore, it may appear as if you are heading directly for the I-70 freeway. Just before the interchange, however (mile 8.3), turn left onto the Sevier Highway. There is a mini-mart on the left. The highway begins to roll adjacent the valley; I-70 is on the right. The road surface is rough, as you are no longer on a state highway, but it was being rehabilitated during my July 2008 field visit. Enter the town of Joseph at mile 13.7. Although the immediate assumption is that the town's name refers to the biblical Joseph, or the Mormon visionary Joseph Smith, neither is correct; the town was named after Joseph Ford, a local miner. There is a country store on the left at mile 14.3. Begin a gradual climb upon leaving Joseph at mile 14.8. The highway crests at mile 15.7, followed by rolling terrain. Enter the small settlement of Sevier at mile 16.4. While Joseph's houses are stately and noble, Sevier's houses are decidedly run-down. One standout, however, is the Sevier Ward Church, on the highway; the building is on the NRHP. Cross US 89 at mile 17.8, followed by an I-70 overpass at mile 18.5. You are now on Clear Creek Canyon Road, having veered away from the Sevier River. The scenery here is quite dramatic. The construction of I-70 produced numerous impressive cuts in the rocky terrain; somehow the beauty of the canyon has been maintained and maybe even enhanced. Enter Fremont Indian State Park at mile 19.5. Steep cliffs are on both the right and left, although I-70 separates you from the left-side cliffs. There are numerous trailheads and information displays along the road. Many of the trails lead to Fremont Indian pictographs and petroglyphs. The park visitor center is at mile 22.6. This is the turnaround point. The center is open 9:00 a.m. to 5:00 p.m. daily; there are restrooms and vending machines, so this would be a logical place to relieve and replenish.

Entering the power and grandeur of Fremont Indian Country.

The return ride gives you a different perspective on the rugged sandstone cliffs that line Clear Creek Canyon. There are restrooms on the right at mile 23.2. Leave Fremont Indian State Park at mile 25.6. The I-70 overpass is at mile 26.6; cross US 89 at mile 27.3 and continue into Sevier. The road surface may be rough through here. Enter Joseph at mile 30.2; the country store that you passed on the way out is on your right at mile 30.8. Enter Elsinore at mile 36.4. Stop and turn right onto Main Street (SR 258) at mile 36.7. There is a mini-mart on the corner. The mountains of the Sevier Plateau are in the distance. SR 258 ends at mile 38.6; you are now on SR 118. After traveling several flat (actually slightly downhill) miles through agricultural lands, return to Richfield at mile 43.2. The return to civilization is signified by the WalMart on your right. Traffic volumes gradually increase as you encounter a series of traffic signals. Be cognizant of turning and parking vehicles along Main Street. Turn right onto 300 North (probably Richfield's busiest intersection). Move toward the center lane to prepare for the left turn onto 100 East, at mile 45.4. Return to Richfield City Park, on your left, to conclude the ride.

Miles and Directions

0.0   Start at 100 East and 300 North near Richfield City Park; turn right on 300 North (SR 118).

0.1   At the traffic signal, turn left onto Main Street (SR 120) and head south.

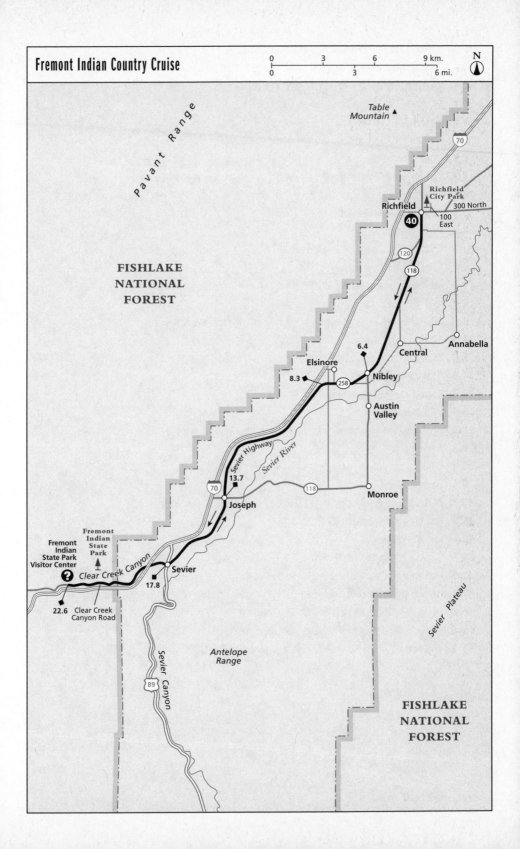

Fremont Indian Country Cruise

0   3   6   9 km.

0   3   6 mi.

N

Pavant Range

Table Mountain ▲

70

Richfield City Park

Richfield
300 North

40

100 East

120

118

FISHLAKE NATIONAL FOREST

Central   Annabella

6.4

Elsinore   Nibley

8.3   258

Austin Valley

Sevier Highway

Sevier River

70   13.7

118

Joseph   Monroe

Fremont Indian State Park Visitor Center   Fremont Indian State Park

?   Clear Creek Canyon

22.6   Clear Creek Canyon Road

Sevier   17.8

Sevier Plateau

Sevier Canyon

Antelope Range

89

FISHLAKE NATIONAL FOREST

0.3 Go straight at the traffic signal at Center Street.

1.0 Go straight at the traffic signal at 640 South/South Main Street/Cove View Road.

1.4 Go straight at the traffic signal at 1100 South.

1.7 Go straight at the traffic signal at 1300 South.

3.5 Now on SR 118 south.

6.4 Now on SR 258 south.

7.5 Enter Elsinore.

8.3 Turn left onto Sevier Highway; mini-mart on the left. Begin rolling terrain.

13.7 Enter Joseph.

14.3 Country store on the left.

14.8 Begin gradual climb.

15.7 Crest of climb; begin rolling terrain.

16.4 Enter Sevier.

17.8 Go straight at the stop at US 89; now on Clear Creek Canyon Road.

18.5 I-70 overpass.

19.5 Enter Fremont Indian State Park; information displays along the road.

21.9 Restrooms on the left.

22.6 Fremont Indian State Park Visitor Center; turn around here.

23.2 Restrooms on the right.

25.6 Leave Fremont Indian State Park.

26.6 I-70 overpass.

27.3 Go straight at the stop sign at US 89; now on Sevier Highway.

30.2 Enter Joseph.

30.8 Country store on the right.

36.4 Enter Elsinore.

36.7 At the stop sign at Main Street (SR 258), turn right—mini-mart on corner.

38.6 End of SR 258; now on SR 118.

43.2 Return to Richfield.

43.7 Go straight at the traffic signal at 1300 South.

44.0 Go straight at the traffic signal at 1100 South.

44.4 Go straight at the traffic signal at 640 South/South Main Street/Cove View Road.

45.1 Go straight at the traffic signal at Center Street.

45.3 At the traffic signal at 300 North, turn right.

45.4 End of ride; turn left onto 100 East and return to Richfield City Park.

Local Information

City of Richfield official Web site: www.rich fieldcity.com.

Sevier County official Web site: www.sevier utah.net.

Fremont Indian State Park information: www .utah.com/stateparks/fremont.htm.

Restaurants

Little Wonder Café: 101 North Main Street, Richfield; (435) 896-8960.

Pepperbelly's Mexican Restaurant: 680 South Cove View Road (680 South Main Street), Richfield; (435) 896-2097; www .pepperbellys.net.

Steve's Steakhouse: 647 South Main Street, Richfield; (435) 893-8880.

The Tomato Vine: 333 North Main Street (at Days Inn), Richfield (435) 893-9191.

Accommodations

Best Western Appletree Inn: 145 South Main Street, Richfield; (435) 896-5481 or (800) 528-1234.

Budget Host/Knights Inn: 69 South Main Street, Richfield; (435) 896-8228 or (800) 525-9024.

Romanico Inn: 1170 South Main Street, Richfield; (435) 896-8471 or (800) 948-0001.

Topsfield Lodge (& Steak House): 1200 South Main Street, Richfield; (435) 896-5437.

KOA Campground: 600 West 600 South, Richfield; (435) 896-6674 or (888) 562-4703; www.koa.com/where/UT/44109/.

Maps

DeLorme: Utah Atlas & Gazetteer: Pages 42–43 C5 on page 43.

Benchmark: Utah Road & Recreation Atlas: Pages 66–67 D7 on page 67.

Appendix A: Selected Bicycle and Transportation Organizations

Local, Regional, and State

Aggie Blue Bikes (bicycling advocacy in Cache County): www.usu.edu/ucc/bikes/.

Cache Valley Transit District (public transit service in Cache County): www.cvtdbus.org.

Mooseknuckler Alliance (Washington County): www.mooseknuckleralliance.org.

Salt Lake City Department of Transportation: www.slcgov.com/transportation/ BicycleTraffic/.

Salt Lake City Mayor's Bicycle Advisory Committee: www.slcgov.com/bike.

Salt Lake County Bicycle Advisory Committee: www.slcbac.org.

Salt Lake Critical Mass: www.slccriticalmass.org.

Utah Bicycle Coalition: www.utahbike.org.

Utah Department of Transportation: www.udot.utah.gov/index.php?m=c&tid=11.

Utah Transit Authority (public transportation provider for the Wasatch Front region): www.rideuta.com or www.utabus.com.

Utahns for Better Transportation: www.utahnsforbettertransportation.org.

Wasatch Front Regional Council (metropolitan planning organization for the Salt Lake City-Ogden-Layton urbanized areas): www.wfrc.org/programs/bikes.htm.

National

America Bikes: www.americabikes.org.

Bikes Belong: www.bikesbelong.org.

Critical Mass: www.critical-mass.org.

League of American Bicyclists: www.bikeleague.org.

National Center for Bicycling and Walking: www.bikefed.org.

Rails to Trails Conservancy: www.railtrailsorg.

Safe Routes to School: www.saferoutestoschool.org.

Thunderhead Alliance: www.thunderheadalliance.org.

Appendix B: References

Note: Additional references are in the "Local Information" listing for each ride.

Bennett, C. L. *Roadside History of Utah*. Mountain Press Publishing Co., Missoula, MT, 1999.

Benchmark: Utah Road and Recreation Atlas. 4th ed., Benchmark Maps, Medford, OR, 2008.

Bensen, J. *Scenic Driving Utah*. Globe Pequot Press, Guilford, CT, 1996.

Campbell, J., R. Rachowiecki, and J. R. Denniston. *Southwest: Arizona, New Mexico, Utah*. 3rd ed. Lonely Planet Publications, Victoria, Australia, 2002.

Chronic, H. *Roadside Geology of Utah*. Mountain Press Publishing Co., Missoula, MT, 1990.

County-Based Regions and Maps for Utah. Polidata Demographic and Political Guides, 2002.

Cycling Utah: Mountain West Cycling Journal. Newspaper published several times annually.

DeLorme: Utah Atlas and Gazetteer. DeLorme, Yarmouth, ME, 2008.

Destination: Salt Lake, Spring/Summer 2008. Wasatch Journal Media, www.visitsalt lake.com.

Fodor's Utah. 2nd ed. Fodor's Travel Publications, New York, 2006.

Insight Guides Utah. 1st ed. APA Publications, London, 2005.

Laine, D., and B. Laine. *Frommer's Utah*. 5th ed. Wiley Publishing, Inc., Hoboken, NJ, 2004.

McRae, W. C., and J. Jewell. *Moon Handbooks Utah*. 7th ed. Avalon Travel Publishing, Emeryville, CA, 2004.

Moab Menu Guide. Canyonlands Advertising, Moab, UT, 2006.

Pucher, J., and J. Renne. "Socioeconomics of Urban Travel: Evidence from the 2001 NHTS." *Transportation Quarterly*. Vol. 57, No. 3, Summer 2003, pp. 49–77.

Repanshek, K. *Hidden Utah*. 2nd ed. Ulysses Press, Berkeley, CA, 2003.

"Traffic on Utah Highways 2005." Utah Department of Transportation, Traffic Analysis Division, Salt Lake City, UT, 2006.

Utah Travel Guide: LIFE Elevated. Utah Office of Tourism, Salt Lake City, www.utah .travel.

Van Cott, J. W. *Utah Place Names*. The University of Utah Press, Salt Lake City, UT, 1990.

Web Sites

Wikipedia, online encyclopedia; information on a variety of topics: http://en.wikipedia.org.

Information on Utah's numbered (i.e., state) highways: http://members.aol.com/utahhwys.

Information on Utah's wildlife resources: http://wildlife.utah.gov.

National Park Service, public use statistics: http://www2.nature.nps.gov/stats/.

National Scenic Byways Program, Federal Highway Administration, Washington, D.C.: www.byways.org.

U.S. Census data and maps, Demographic and Economic Analysis, Governor's Office of Planning and Budget, State of Utah: www.governor.utah.gov/dea/census.

Online maps used to identify and confirm road names: www.maps.google.com.

National Register of Historic Places—database of historic buildings and districts, organized by state and county: www.nationalregisterofhistoricplaces.org.

Old Spanish Trail: www.oldspanishtrail.org.

About the Author

Wayne D. Cottrell lived in Utah from 1994 to 2005. During that 11.5-year period, he stayed active in Utah's road bike racing and duathlon scene, participating in criteriums, hillclimbs, road races, time trials, and run-bike-run events. While most of his racing was concentrated in the Wasatch Front region, occasional destination races led him to some of Utah's other urban concentrations and rural corners. Cottrell was a member of the Utah Cycling Association, and one of the highlights of this period was his participation in the Olympic torch relay in 1996. An article describing his 1996 Olympic torch relay experience appeared in *Cycling Utah*. He teaches and performs research studies in transportation engineering.